THE BALANCE OF PAYMENTS

THE BALANCE
OF PAYMENTS

HISTORY • METHODOLOGY • THEORY

by **MAX J. WASSERMAN**

Visiting Professor of International Economics
Patterson School of Diplomacy and International Commerce, University of Kentucky,

and

RAY M. WARE

Associate Professor of Economics
Transylvania College

SIMMONS-BOARDMAN PUBLISHING CORPORATION

New York

Library of Congress Catalog Card Number 65-19624
Manufactured in the United States of America

TO

ROSE AND SUE

Preface

Events since the end of World War II have served to under-line the growing importance of the balance of payments both as analytical tool and as a guide in the formulation of interna-tional economic policy. The foreign exchange operations em-ployed in defense of the rate of exchange; the use of exchange controls, tariffs, quotas and other barriers to trade; the elimina-tion of these controls and the return to convertibility; the man-agement of international reserves, among many others, are largely founded upon balance of payments considerations.

These conditions are typical of those which have led to the development of the balance of payments. Beginning in 1381, and continuing throughout the economic history of the trading coun-tries, the increasing complexity of international economic relations has emphasized the need for their measure and analysis. The bal-ance of payments was developed and has been steadily improved as a result of these demands. In view of the importance of the decisions and studies which are based upon it, this tabulation has become the focal point of the international economy.

While much has been written on the various aspects of this tabulation, there has been no comprehensive attempt to show the development of the balance of payments from its earliest beginning; to trace its growth, step by step; to show the dis-covery of procedures for gathering necessary data and to indicate its evolution toward a presentation useful in policy-making deci-sions. The object of the historical chapters of this book is to show the gradual development of the concepts, sources and methods of gathering and estimating data, and the organization of this material so as to form a useful statement. The historical chapters of this book indicate that the balance of payments grew because of specific needs and circumstances, that its form is evolutionary and will continue to change as these needs and cir-cumstances change.

It is clear that the nature and usefulness of the balance of payments can better be understood in the perspective of its historical development. For these reasons, the work of the United Kingdom, the United States, and the League of Nations was examined to prepare the historical chapters.

Since information on the sources of data used in preparing this compilation is not readily available, the succeeding chapter on methodology emphasizes this topic. This part of the book is followed by an analysis of a much neglected topic—the accuracy of balances of payments. The various means employed to measure balance of payments surpluses and deficits are then considered.

Given the importance of reserves in a world of fixed exchange rates, this subject is treated by including some of the new reserve substitutes and complements and by outlining the role of reserves in the defense of the rate of exchange. The principal theoretical aspect of the balance of payments, the automatic adjustment of imbalances, is described and extended by the inclusion of the changes instituted by the forward and Euro-Dollar markets and by feedback. The book ends with a consideration of the international payments system, including plans for its reform.

International rather than national in scope, this volume is directed toward an audience of academic, research, business, government and consulting economists; officials charged with the study and management of international economic relations; businessmen, military officers and others who consult or use the balance of payments in connection with their work and studies.

The authors are indebted to a large number of people for assistance in the preparation of the work. Russell F. Moore, the publisher, helped by his encouragement and wise counsel based on many years in the publishing business. Sue D. Ware had general editorial supervision of the project, and made many suggestions concerning the organization of the material. The excellent photography by W. E. Mitchell of the rare manuscripts was an important contribution to the historical chapters. The research assistance given by Juanita C. Jackson, Reference Librarian, University of Kentucky, was invaluable in the early stages of the historical chapters. Mrs. George Dodds assisted in the interpretation of several of the early English manuscripts.

Hal B. Lary, Associate Director, of the National Bureau of Economic Research; Douglass C. North, Director of the Institute for Economic Research, University of Washington; Matthew Simon, Assistant Professor of Economics at Queens College of the City University of New York; Herbert W. Hargreaves, Professor of Economics at the University of Kentucky; Mrs. Edward Fisk, Assistant Professor of English, Emeritus, Transylvania College; Poul Høst-Madsen, Assistant Director in the Research and Statistics Department of the International Monetary Fund; John Smith, Director, Balance of Payments Division of the Fund; Samuel Pizer, Assistant Chief, Balance of Payments Division, United States Department of Commerce; J. A. Rushbrook, Central Statistical Office of the United Kingdom; and Charles W. Hultman, Visiting Associate Professor of Economics, University of California (Riverside) read many of the chapters and gave valuable advice.

A number of authorities were helpful in advising the authors on various aspects of the work and in providing information not readily available elsewhere. Among this group were: Thomas J. Roche, Senior Exchange Officer, the Federal Reserve Bank of New York; Arthur H. De Palma, Assistant Treasurer, the J. Henry Schroder Banking Corporation of New York; Arie C. Bouter, Assistant Director, Balance of Payments Division of the International Monetary Fund; Edward M. Bernstein, Chairman, The Review Committee for Balance of Payments Statistics; Edward T. Crowder and John E. Reynolds of the Committee.

Ellen Minihan, Secretary of the William Andrew Patterson School of Diplomacy and International Commerce, assisted with the typing of the manuscript. Robert F. Benner and Philip G. Combs, graduate students of Patterson School, served as research assistants and helped prepare the index.

Thanks are due to A. D. Kirwin, Dean of the Graduate School of the University of Kentucky and other members of the Research Fund Committee for a research grant and a summer research fellowship which made much of the research involved in the preparation of this work possible.

The authors also thank the Transylvania Research Fund Committee members who contributed toward the expenses of conducting their research. The interest shown in the work and the encouragement given by Irvin E. Lunger, President, Leland A. Brown, Vice President and John R. Bryden, Academic Dean, all of Transylvania College was of substantial assistance to the authors. A. Vandenbosch, Director of the Patterson School and other University of Kentucky administrative officials cooperated by providing appropriate teaching schedules and an atmosphere conducive to objective research.

Although the authors are deeply grateful for all the help which they received, they alone assume full responsibility for the entire book.

Lexington, Kentucky
May 1965

MAX J. WASSERMAN
RAY M. WARE

Table of Contents

1

From Bullionism to the Balance of Payments

Three separate but related concepts are embodied in the phrase "from bullionism to the balance of payments." The first concept, bullionism, is concerned with the institutions prohibiting the free international flow of bullion. The second is the balance of trade doctrine which prescribes institutions to secure a favorable balance of trade to accomplish the same result. The third concept, that of the balance of payments, is the most comprehensive of the three because all of the economic transactions between the residents of one country and those of other countries are included.

The Bullionist Concept

Bullionism, an early form of Mercantilism, takes its name from the prohibition of the export of bullion. The series of laws prohibiting the export of bullion, known as the Bullion Ordinances, were enacted in England as early as 1303 during the reign of Edward I. The Bullionist policy was abandoned in 1663 when the export of bullion without a license was permitted.

Development of the Bullionist doctrine. Probably the earliest recorded comments concerning English international trade are those made in 1381 by Officers of the Mint, Richard Leicester, Lincoln (Goldsmith), and Richard Aylesbury. They reported to Parliament that the supply of gold and silver in England was being depleted because of the lack of an effective bullion ordinance. They suggested that this situation could be remedied by a Statute of Employment which would require foreign merchants to purchase English commodities equal to the amount of the commodities brought into England. If this were done, they said, no gold or silver would be needed to pay for the imports.[1]

A gradual development of terms by which the early writers expressed their desire for equality of exports and imports of merchandise (equilibrium in the balance of trade) occurred during the Bullionist period. In 1549 John Hales stated that there should be neither more nor less goods purchased than were "equivalent" to the goods received.[2] In the same year the unknown author of *Policies to Reduce this Realme of England unto a Prosperus Wealthe and Estate* used the term "overplus" to describe the excess of exports over imports, and asserted that bullion in the amount of the "overplus" would be brought into England.[3] This belief was shared by the unknown writer of *Memorandum prepared for the Royal Commission on the Exchanges* in 1564 when he said that an "overvallue" of English goods would bring money into England.[4]

John Stow stated that if commodities of greater value were carried abroad than were brought back, England would receive the "overplus" in money. However, if merchandise of greater value were brought back than that which was sent out could "countervaile," then England would pay for the "overplus" in money. Therefore, he concluded that "*Symmetria* and due proportion" of exports and imports should be maintained.[5] This is

---

[1] A. E. Bland, P. A. Brown, and R. H. Tawney (eds.) *English Economic History: Select Documents.* 2nd edition. London: G. Bell and Sons, Ltd., 1915, pp. 220-223.

[2] Frederic J. Furnivall (ed.). *William Stafford's Compendious or Briefe Examination of Certayne Ordinary Complaints.* London: N. Trubner & Co., 1876. Miss Lamond, in 1891 furnished evidence that John Hales was the writer of this tract and that William Stafford edited it. This evidence is recognized by the Dictionary of National Biography. Furnivall edited the above publication before there was proof to the contrary of Stafford's authorship. p. 56.

[3] R. H. Tawney and Eileen Powers (eds.). *Tudor Economic Documents.* London: Longmans, Green and Co., 1924, III, 324.

[4] *Ibid.,* p. 353.

[5] John Stow. *A Survey of London.* Reprinted from the text of 1603, with an introduction by Charles L. Kingsford. Oxford: Clarendon Press, 1908. II, 210.

perhaps the earliest statement concerning equilibrium in the balance of international accounts.

Earliest statements of trade. There were only two known statements of trade prepared and preserved in England for any period prior to the seventeenth century. Neither statement provided any indication of the countries with which trade was carried on, nor did they contain any items other than merchandise. The first was prepared for the twenty-eighth year of the reign of Edward III (1355). The person who prepared this statement is unknown. In 1623 Edward Misselden said that this document was located in the Record of the Exchequer.[6] He was apparently correct in this assertion because on March 25, 1964 the Secretary of the Public Record Office wrote:

> After a long and difficult search the balance of trade for 28 Edward III was finally traced in E. 122/175/4 folio 1, among the miscellaneous Customs Accounts of the King's Remembrancer's department of the Exchequer. You should note that subsidiary documents, showing how these totals were arrived at will be found in E. 122/248/1 and E. 122/158/20 fos. 1-3.

> The above three documents are all in a late sixteenth-century (or early seventeenth-century) hand, and the figures in them were extracted from the mid-fourteenth century enrolled customs accounts among the Pipe Office records of the Exchequer (series E.356), which are, of course, still extant.[7]

The summary of the balance of trade referred to above is shown in Table 1.1 and the subsidiary records are reproduced in Appendix A.1. Misselden copied the "Form" in the *Circle of Commerce* which was published in 1623. Gerald Malynes called it a "wormeaten" document of doubtful value which could as well be forgotten due to its lack of completeness.[8] The statement

---

[6] Edward Misselden. *The Circle of Commerce or the Ballance of Trade, in defense of Free Trade.* London: Printed for N. Bourne, 1623. p. 119.

[7] Letter from the Secretary, Public Record Office, March 25, 1964.

[8] Gerard Malynes. *The Center of the Circle of Commerce.* London: Printed by William Jones, 1623, p. 56.

TABLE 1.1
STATEMENT OF TRADE FOR THE TWENTY-EIGHTH YEAR OF EDWARD III

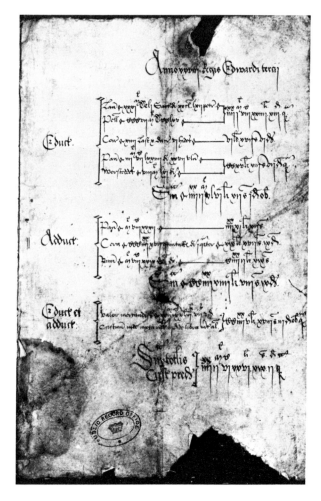

British Crown copyright; reproduced by permission of the Controller of H. M. Stationery Office.

Source: Great Britain, Public Record Office, *Customs Accounts of the King's Remembrancer's Department of the Exchequer.* E.122/175/4, folio 1.

was composed of a listing of the quantity and total value of each commodity traded, together with the customs collected on that commodity. The totals for exports and imports were determined from these listings and the difference between the two shown as the balance of trade.

The second statement of trade was prepared for the year 1570 and is illustrated in Table 1.2. As in the case of the first statement, neither the date of preparation nor the person who prepared the statement is known. Hubert Hall, a former employee of the Public Record Office, compiled a history of the custom's revenue of England exclusively from the original documents. One of his extracts, illustrative of the custom's revenue, was a reproduction of the tables of English exports and imports for 1570.[9] Exports and imports of each item were listed and a description of the commodities traded together with the quantity and value was given. Exports and imports were totaled and the smaller value of exports was subtracted from the value of imports. The difference was described as the "Balance in favour of Imports."

The Balance of Trade Concept: Origin and Application to England's Trade during the First Half of the Seventeenth Century

The early seventeenth century was marked by unsettled conditions in international relations. England, France, Holland and Spain were vying for world supremacy in industry and commerce. Wars were frequent and money was needed to pay foreign mercenaries and to support troops abroad. For these reasons, generalized purchasing power in the form of money was desired above all else. Attracting and holding gold and silver was the ideal of the advocates of both bullionist and balance of trade doctrines, but they differed in the means by which this goal was to be accomplished. Gerard Malynes proposed enforcement of the Bullion Ordinances and the Statutes of Employment for this purpose. Thomas Mun and Edward Misselden dis-

---

[9] Hubert Hall. *A History of the Custom-Revenue in England*. London: Elliot Stock, 1885, II, 243-244.

TABLE 1.2
STATEMENT OF ENGLAND'S TRADE, 1570

Source: British Museum, Cotton MSS, Titus B IV, folios 241-244.

TABLE 1.2 (Cont'd.)

puted the need for these laws. They proposed instead governmental policies to ensure an excess of exports over imports of merchandise.

As the Bullion Ordinances made the export of gold and silver a felony, it was necessary to use bills of exchange as the means of settling international trade accounts. Perhaps, at first, the rate of exchange between the coinage of various countries was at mint par; but if so, this rate was not long maintained. The price of foreign exchange was based upon supply and demand; and when the supply of bills of exchange of one country rose because of an excess of imports over exports, the money of that country became undervalued relative to that of other countries. Balance of trade doctrine replaced the older bullionist doctrine following the controversy over the prohibition of bullion exports and the regulation of exchange rates to correct this situation.

English balances of trade. One of the earliest applications of this doctrine occurred during the reign of James I when "Alderman Cockayne, an ambitious businessman, said he could provide employment by developing the dyeing and finishing industries so as to put an end to the export of 'white' cloth."[10] Parliament provided assistance to this plan in 1614 by prohibiting the export of this cloth. The Dutch retaliated with the development of white manufactures of their own, and the result was a general deterioration of English trade. Sir Lionell Cranfield, Surveyor-General of the Customs, and his assistant, John Wolstenholme were instructed to report on the state of foreign trade due to these events.

The report of Cranfield, completed in 1613, was in the form of a balance of trade (Table 1.3) for the seven years 1605 to 1611. His method of determining the balance of trade was to ascertain the customs collected upon the imports and exports in each of the years. He adjusted the customs collected upon the imports for merchandise recorded in the book of rates at less than their true value. He also adjusted customs collected upon

---

[10] Sir John Clapham. *A Concise Economic History of Britain from the Earliest Times to 1750.* Cambridge: University Press, 1949, p. 251.

TABLE 1.3
SIR LIONELL CRANFIELD'S BALANCE OF TRADE, 1605-1611

Reproduced by permission of the Trustees of the British Museum.
Source: British Museum, *Lansdowne MSS*, Vol. 152, folio 175 (renumbered).

TABLE 1.4
John Wolstenholme's Balance of Trade, 1613-1614

TABLE 1.4 (Cont'd.)

[Reproduction of a handwritten 17th-century manuscript ledger, "From Xpmas 1613 To Xpmas 1614 — Merchandizes importted," with columns £ s d.]

	£	s	d
Custome of Owte London is	004846	13	06
Custome of the owt Courts is	0015729	19	01
Custome of the silke is	0015562	—	—
Custome of browne goulds and silver is	0000700	—	—
frentч wins	0002000	—	—
Spanisk wins	0001200	—	—
Allowance of 5 p cent is	0004000	—	—
To be added ...	0012000	—	—
To be added ...	0004000	—	—
To be added ...	0006400	—	—
... the totall ...	0110056	12	07
... 20 ...	1201132	11	08
...	0413694	17	05
	2614777	09	01

	£	s	d
	0132948	02	9
	0116875	10	1
	0016072	12	8
	0321452	13	4

exports for merchants' profits. The difference between the adjusted figures for customs collected upon exports and imports was divided by seven to find the average per year. The result was multiplied by twenty (he assumed a five per cent customs duty) to find the average yearly value by which exports exceeded imports.

John Wolstenholme, Assistant Surveyor-General of the Customs, prepared two statements of trade, the first for the year ending Christmas 1613 and the second for the year ending Christmas 1614.[11] The latter is illustrated in Table 1.4. He submitted these reports on May 21, 1615. Wolstenholme began his report with the customs collected for each year. He adjusted the figure for customs collected on goods imported because of undervaluations in the book of rates and multiplied the adjusted amount by twenty to find the value of imports. The value of exports was calculated by adjusting the customs collected on exported merchandise for those articles free of customs duties. The adjusted figure was multiplied by twenty, and customs charges outward, merchants' profits, freight and miscellaneous charges were added to the product obtained. The amount by which exports exceeded imports was added to imports as the balancing figure.

Nature and usefulness of the balance of trade. A Deputy-Governor of the Merchant Adventures' Company, Edward Misselden, defended the company's practice of exporting bullion. He, along with Thomas Mun, developed the concept of the balance of trade. Both desired laws which hindered imports so that the excess of exports over imports would be paid in gold or silver. Misselden made the balance of trade the center of his arguments for the free export of bullion. He likened the statements of trade to scales in showing the results of commercial transactions with other countries. He said in this regard:

> For as a paire of Scales or Ballance, is an Invention
> to shew us the waight of things, whereby we may discerne
> the heavy from the light, and how one thing differeth

---

[11] British Museum. *Lansdown MSS.* Vol. 152, fols. 176-178.

from another in the Scale of waight; So is also this *Ballance of Trade,* an excellent and politique Invention, to shew us the difference of waight in the *Commerce* of one Kingdome with another; that is, whether the Native Commodities exported, and the forraine Commodities Imported, doe ballance or overballance one another in the *Scale of Commerce.*[12]

Misselden was familiar with two of the earlier statements concerning the balance of trade. He reproduced the statement of trade for the twenty-eighth year of Edward III, and Wolstenholme's balance of trade for 1612-13. He also prepared a statement of the balance of England's trade for the year ending Christmas 1622, which is illustrated in Table 1.5.

The statement which Misselden prepared is substantially the same in form and method as that prepared earlier by Wolstenholme. He recognized the need to include re-exports of foreign goods along with domestic goods in total exports. He added merchants' profits, freight, and other charges to the value of goods exported, so that they were valued on what is known as a c.i.f. basis (cost, insurance and freight). Misselden said the basis for valuation of imports should be their cost, including all charges in England.[13] This, too, was a c.i.f. basis of valuation, so that both exports and imports were valued on a comparable basis.

Misselden pointed out the relationship between the balance of trade and the capital of a nation.[14] The capital of a nation was reduced by importing more than was exported, because this excess could be paid only by increasing liabilities to foreigners or by reducing the claims on foreigners. Misselden believed that England had fallen "into a great *Under-ballance of Trade* with other Nations."[15] He said a nation should follow the example of the merchant who takes a *"Ballance* of his Estate: wherein he

---

[12] Misselden, *op. cit.,* pp. 116-117.

[13] Misselden, *op. cit.,* pp. 125-126.

[14] Capital is used here in its accounting sense, i.e., net worth, which is the excess of assets over liabilities.

[15] Misselden, *op. cit.,* p. 130.

TABLE 1.5
Edward Misselden's Balance of Trade, 1621-1622

Of Exchanges *in generall.*	127

vnto the *King & Kingdom*, in the courſe of trade.

And now we will come to the *Poſitiue Conſti-*
tution of our owne *Forme*, to bring to the *Ballance*,
the ſtate of the preſent time and trade : wherein
I will giue you a taſte of one yeeres collections of
the Kingdomes trade, in this forme following. viz.

§. 36.
The poſitiue
conſtitutió of
the forme of a
Ballance for
the preſent
time & trade.

The Ballance of the Trade of the Kingdome is Debitor, for
all the Exportations of the Merchandize thereof,
for one whole yeare, from Chriſtmas An. 1621.
to Chriſtmas An. 1622. as followeth.

	li.	ſh.	d.
Cuſtome of the Port of London —	50406.	06.	04
Cuſtome of the Out-ports —	26756.	18.	00
The Cuſtome of Wrappers of Clothes, Bayes, and Cottons, free of Cuſtume, being the tenth part of 50000. *pounds, which is the Cuſtome of them all* —	05000.	00.	00
The Cuſtome of the Fiſh of our owne fiſhing, and which is freed from Cuſtome by Statute, by computation —	07000.	00.	00
The Cuſtome of Goods ſhipt out by Certificate: viz. of forraine goods brought in, and for want of vent in the Kingdome, ſhipt out againe: which are freed of Cuſtome by his Maieſties gracious graunt of Priuy Seale —	08050.	00.	00
The Totall of all the Cuſtome is —	97213.	04.	04

E e 3

Which

Source: Edward Misselden, *The Circle of Commerce or the Ballance of
Trade, in defense of Free Trade.* London: Printed for N. Bourne,
1623, pp. 127-129.

TABLE 1.5 (Cont'd.)

128	Of Exchanges in generall.			
		li.	ſh.	d.
Which Totall being multiplied by twenty, becauſe the Cuſtome is valued by twelue pence in the pound, produceth the value of all the Goods Exported to amount vnto		1944264.	07.	01
The Net Cuſtome of which value, at twelue pence in the pound, the Wrappers, Fiſh, and Goods ſhipt out by certificate deducted, is the 2. ſummes firſt before mentioned, and is		0077163.	04.	04
The Impoſt of Bayes, Tinne, Lead, and Pewter, which onely are impoſed outwards, amounteth to		0007370.	01.	05
The Merchants gaine, fraight, and petty charges vpon 1944264.li. *being the whole value of the Exportations as aboue appeareth, at 15. per Cento, is*		0291639.	00.	00
The Totall Exportations with charges, Amount to		2320436.	12.	10

The

TABLE 1.5 (Cont'd.)

Of EXCHANGES *in generall.*	129

The Ballance of the Trade of the Kingdome is Creditor, for all the Importations of the merchandize thereof, for one whole yeare, from Christmas An. 1621. *to Christmas An.* 1622. *as followeth.*

	li.	*sh.*	*d.*
The Custome of the Port of London — 6 8 2 8 0 .		09 .	01
The Custome of the Out-Ports — 1 9 5 1 9 .		02 .	06
The Custome of Wines of all sortes, all other Merchandize being included in the former, is — 0 3 2 0 0 .		00 .	00
The Custome amounts to — 9 1 0 5 9 .		11 .	07
One third part thereof to be added, for the vnderrating of Goods in Custome, to that they are worth, or cost, is — 3 0 3 5 3 .		03 .	10
Also the allowance of 5. *per Cento vpon* L 9 1 0 5 9 . 11 . 7 .*is* — 0 4 5 5 2 .		19 .	07
The Totall Summe amounts to — 1 2 5 9 6 5 .		15 .	00
Which totall, being multiplied by 20 *produceth the value of all the Goods Imported, to amount vnto* — 2 5 1 9 3 1 5 .		00 .	00
Fine Goods secretly conueied inwards, more then outwards. — 0 1 0 0 0 0 0 .		00 .	00
The Totall Importations amount to — 2 6 1 9 3 1 5 .		00 .	00
The Totall Exportations — 2 3 2 0 4 3 6 .		12 .	10
The Remainder sheweth, that there is more imported this yeare then was Exported, by the summe of — 0 2 9 8 8 7 8 .		07 .	02

So

collecteth and considereth all his *Wares*, and *Moneys*, and
Debts (which merchants call) . . . a *Ballance* of Accompt, or a
Ballance of Trade."[16] The merchant did this to see if he lost or
gained by trade. If the owner of capital found that his expenses
exceeded his revenues, he could either decrease his expenses
or decrease his capital. Thus, by analogy, the King could enact
statutes to decrease imports or be prepared to see a decrease
in the "Estate of his *Kingdome*."[17] Misselden thought of treasure
as a means of financing the difference between exports and
imports. He said that when the commodities imported exceeded
the value of those exported it was a sign that trade was
"decayed" and that "the stocke of the Kingdome" was dwindling
because the "overplus" went out in "treasure."[18]

Limitations of the balance of trade. Misselden's chief
opponent, Gerard Malynes, was an economist, commissioner of
trade, and a member of Queen Elizabeth's commission for
establishing a par of exchange. Malynes said that gain acquired
by "*Commodities*, or by *Moneys*, or by *exchange of moneys*."
was the center of commerce, not the balance of trade.[19] He
considered the balance of trade peripheral in the circle of
commerce.

Malynes also denied Misselden's contention that the excess
of exports over imports would be brought back in bullion. He
said this occurrence was unlikely if it were more profitable to
accept bills of exchange or if there were interest owing to
foreigners. He also stated that the balance of trade for any
one year, or or any limited period, could be misleading because
of the continuing or long-term nature of many commercial
transactions.[20]

An early English concept of the balance of trade. The
third party in the controversy was Thomas Mun, a director of
the East India Company, who began writing in 1621 in defense

---

[16] Misselden, *op. cit.*, p. 130.
[17] Misselden, *op. cit.*, p. 131.
[18] Misselden, *op. cit.*, p. 117.
[19] Malynes, *op. cit.*, p. 6.
[20] Malynes, *op. cit.* p. 58.

of the company's exportation of bullion.[21] Concerning the proper valuation of exports and imports, Mun said:

First therefore, concerning our Exportations, when we have valued their first cost, we must add twenty-five *per cent.* thereunto for the charges here, for fraight of Ships, ensurance of the *Adventure,* and the *Merchants* Gains; and for our Fishing Trades, which pay no Custome to his Majesty. . . . Also we must add to our Exportations all the moneys which are carried out in Trade by license from his Majesty.

Secondly, for our Importations of Forraign Wares, the Custome-books serve onely to direct us concerning the quantity, for we must not value them as they are rated here, but as they cost us with all charges laden into our Ships beyond the Seas, in the respective places where they are bought: for the Merchants gain, the charges of Insurance, Fraight of Ships, Customes, Imposts, and other Duties here . . . are notwithstanding but Commutations amongst ourselves, for the Stranger hath no part thereof. . . . These and all other Wares, forraign or domestick, which are thus transported Outwards . . . [should be included in exportations].

Thirdly, . . . all Wares exported or imported by Strangers (in their shipping) be esteemed by themselves, for what they carry out, the Kingdom hath only the first cost and the custom: And what they bring in, we must rate it as it is worth here, the Custom, Impost, and petty charges only deducted.[22]

The comment above shows that Mun made a distinction between transactions with foreigners and with English residents. Only transactions with non-residents were to be included in the balances of trade. Customs duties and freight and insurance paid to English firms were excluded for this reason. Exports

[21] Thomas Mun, *A Discourse of Trade: From England unto the East-Indies.* (1621) Reprinted. New York: The Facsimile Text Society, 1930.

[22] Thomas Mun. *England's Treasure by Forraign Trade.* London: 1664. Reprinted. New York: Macmillan & Co., 1895, pp. 113-116.

were valued at cost including freight and insurance when the goods were transported in English ships, but at cost only when carried by foreign ships. Merchandise purchased abroad by English residents and carried in English ships was valued at its cost abroad, while goods brought into England by foreign owned ships included all charges in England except customs duties.

The present practice in the United Kingdom is to make no distinction as to whom the payment for freight and insurance is paid for the purposes of preparing the Trade and Navigation Accounts. In some cases, goods are imported on f.o.b. terms and the importer makes his own arrangements for freight and insurance. The importer then adds these costs to the f.o.b. value of the goods in making out his Customs and Excise Return from which the Trade and Navigation Accounts are compiled. However, imports are valued f.o.b. in the balance of payments accounts. The cost of freight and insurance is deducted from the Trade Accounts value of imports. Payments to foreign companies are included as debits in the invisibles account while those to domestic firms are omitted altogether from balance of payments accounts.[23]

Mun did not draw up a statement of trade, but discussed the types of transactions that should be considered in such a balance. In addition to merchandise imports and exports, Mun stated that the following transactions would have an influence on the balance of trade:

There must be good notice taken of all the great losses which we receive at Sea in our shipping either outward or homeward bound: for the value of the one is to be deducted from our Exportations, and the value of the other is to be added to our Importations: for to lose and to consume doth produce one and the same reckoning. Likewise if it happen that His majesty doth make over any great sums of mony by Exchange to maintain a forraign war, where we do not feed and clothe the Souldiers, and Provide the armies, we

---

[23] Letter from J. A. Rushbrook, Central Statistical Office, London, England, May 7, 1964.

must deduct all this charge out of our Exportations or add it to our Importations: for this expense doth either carry out or hinder the coming in of so much Treasure. And here we must remember the great collections of mony which are supposed to be made throughout the Realm yearly from our Recusants by Priests and Jesuits, who secretly convey the same unto their Colleges, Cloysters and Nunneries beyond the Seas . . . therefore . . . it must be esteemed and set down as a cleer loss to the Kingdome, except (to ballance this) we will imagine that as great a value may perhaps come in from forraign Princes to their Pensioners here for Favours or Intelligence. . . .

There are yet some other petty things which seem to have reference to this Ballance . . . to bring them into the accompt. As namely, the expences of travailers, the gifts to Ambassadors and Strangers, the fraud of some rich goods not entred into the Custom-house, the gain which is made here by Strangers by change and rechange, Interest of mony, ensurance upon English mens goods and their lives: which can be little when the charges of their living here is deducted; besides that the very like advantages are as amply ministered unto the English in forraign Countreys, which doth counterpoize all these things, and therefore they are not considerable in the drawing up of the said Ballance.[24]

It seems evident from this passage that Mun was familiar with many of the items that are common on today's balance of payments. From the number of transactions discussed by Mun as having an effect upon the balance of trade, it appears he understood the broader concept encompassed by the balance of payments. Yet, in spite of this apparent knowledge, he considered the balance of the merchandise transactions of all countries to be settled by gold and silver. He assumed exports were two million pounds in excess of imports and said this balance was "brought to us in treasure to ballance the accompt."[25]

---

[24] Thomas Mun. *England's Treasure* . . . *op. cit.*, pp. 116-117.
[25] *Ibid.*, p. 20.

A decade later, Henry Robinson, a London merchant, also recognized several items other than merchandise which would off-set the flow of gold and silver. He said that gold and silver would not necessarily be needed to pay for an excess of exports over imports provided foreigners used English ships because earnings from this source would help pay for the excess of foreign commodities. Robinson was aware that specie was used in pay-ment of the expenses of ambassadors and travelers abroad, and to remit earnings to foreigners who had investments in England. The necessity of making payments for rent and interest to these investors was an important source of foreigners' claims on sterling.[26]

The Balance of Trade Concept:
Application During the French Trade Controversy

The controversy over England's trade with France pro-vided the setting for the development of trade statistics and theoretical concepts of international transactions. The French and English trade rivalry during the latter part of the seventeenth century, as well as religious and political factors, was responsible for the turbulent relations between the two nations until 1713. The French trade aroused misgivings as early as the reign of Elizabeth, partly due to an alleged drain of money and partly due to the nature of the trade. British exports to France were mostly cloth and natural resources while the imports from France were chiefly wines and other luxuries. A commercial treaty which provided for the free movements of goods and services was con-cluded with France in 1606 and amended in 1610, 1629, and 1632. English merchants met with opposition in France in 1648, and trade was suspended when a French edict excluded English wool and silk manufactures. England retaliated with an embargo on French wines. The rivalry led to increasingly restrictive tariffs so that by 1667 the duty on English cloth amounted to fifty per cent of its value. Negotiations were conducted between the two countries for the redress of economic grievances, but

---

[26] Henry Robinson. *Englands Safety, in Trades Encrease*. London: Nicholas Bourne, 1641, pp. 49-52, 60.

Colbert's[27] influence was so strong in France that a reduction in these restrictions was impossible.[28]

A Catalogue of the French trade. The campaign for the prohibition of French imports was begun by Samuel Fortrey in 1663 when he produced data showing that trade with France was resulting in an annual loss of 1,600,000 pounds to England. Fortrey, a member of the King's Privy Council, produced a "Catalogue" of the French commodities imported annually into England. The "Catalogue" contained a listing of the principal items imported from France showing the value of each item and the value of all items in total.[29] In those times it was an easy matter to frighten a nation by drawing up an adverse balance of trade since such a balance was difficult to disprove.[30]

Demand for official statistics of trade. The desire for trade statistics led Parliament to set up a standing Council of Trade in 1650. The sixth article of its commission directed that it was to consider means of maintaining an exact account of goods exported and imported "to the end that a perfect Ballance of Trade . . ." could be taken.[31] The papers of this Council were dispersed and its work is known only by correspondence with other bodies. It does not appear to have carried the matter very far. Therefore, following Fortrey's presentation, the French trade was generally assumed to be a losing trade.

Early in 1673 the Council of Trade and Plantations took steps to put the account of the balance of trade into some satisfactory order.[32] The next year there were unsuccessful

---

[27] Jean Baptiste Colbert, the minister of finance under Louis IV, was the most noted and thorough of the French Mercantilists.

[28] Ephriam Lipson. *The Economic History of England.* 2nd ed. London: Adam and Charles Black, 1934, III, 99-103.

[29] Samuel Fortrey, "Englands Interest and Improvement" (1663). *A Reprint of Economic Tracts.* Edited by Jacob H. Hollander. Baltimore: John Hopkins Press, 1907, pp. 24-26.

[30] Max Beer. *Early British Economics from the XIIIth to the Middle of the XVIIIth Century.* London: George Allen and Unwin, Ltd., 1938, p. 194.

[31] G. N. Clark. *Guide to English Commercial Statistics 1696-1782.* London: Office of the Royal Historical Society, 1938, p. xii.

[32] *Ibid.,* p. xiv.

negotiations for a commercial treaty with France, and the English commissioners for this negotiation were provided with "A Scheme of Trade" with France for the year Michaelmas 1668 to Michaelmas 1669.[33] The statement, reproduced in Appendix A.2, was divided into two sections, one for exports and the other for imports. Each section was arranged in four columns showing the quantity, description, unit value and total value of each item.

A Committee of the Council again applied itself to the matter of trade statistics in 1679. The Committee requested the Commissioners of the Customs to furnish statistics on English imports and exports. Although the dispersal of the records of the Customs and the Committee makes it impossible to be sure of the entire results, a small book of tables remains. This book of tables, selections from which are presented in Appendix A.3, contained data concerning the imports and exports of the City of London with seventeen countries or areas for each of the two years ending Michaelmas 1663 and 1669. The tables were arranged to show the description, quantity, unit and total value of each item imported from or exported to each country or area. Exports and imports for each of the countries were summarized for each year.

Charles D'Avenant made the following comment on this book of tables in 1711, at the time it was forwarded to Parliament:

> This Accompt, as near as I can guess, was taken in the year 1679. It comprehends onley the Exports From and Imports To the Port of London, and takes no notice of Foreign goods Reexported. As to the goods Exported, in general they seem fairly valued. But, as to the goods Imported, they are in most instances over valued, Especially the Commodities brought from France. As to the Quantities of the respective Exportations and Importa-

---

[33] Michaelmas refers to the feast of St. Michael which occurs on September 29th and was often regarded as the end of a fiscal year on early statements of trade.

tions, I believe they might be truly Extracted from the Custom house books.[34]

The anonymous writer of *Britannia Languens* (1680) was familar with Fortrey's "Catalogue" and with the "Scheme of Trade" with France for the year ending Michaelmas 1669. He noted the seizures of English merchant ships by the French and said that the imbalance of trade between England and France would have been greater if account were taken of these losses. He commented on the greater expenses incurred by Englishmen traveling in France than the French incurred traveling in England. He said the French who came to England did so to accumulate estates by trading and when they did, they transferred these estates to France and by so doing diminished the wealth of England.[35]

Difficulty in finding the balance of trade. The belief that all foreign goods were purchased by the exchange of domestic goods and that any balance was liquidated by silver and gold was stated again in 1690 by Nicholas Barbon, in *A Discourse of Trade.*[36] Barbon was troubled by the difficulty of finding the balance of trade and the extent of the usefulness of this balance even if discovered. He said in this regard: "There is nothing so difficult, as to find out the *Balance of Trade* in any Nation; or to know whether there ever was, or can be such a thing as the making up the *Balance of Trade* betwixt one nation and another; or to prove, if it can be found out, that there is any thing got or lost by the *Balance.*"[37]

Inclusiveness of the balance of trade. Sir William Petty, one of the founders of the Royal Statistical Society and a political economist, recognized in 1690 that there were trans-

---

[34] British Museum, *Additional Manuscripts 36785,* fol. 1.

[35] "Britannia Languens, or a Discourse of Trade" (1680). Reprinted in *Early English Tracts on Commerce.* Edited by J. R. McCulloch. Cambridge: University Press, 1954, pp. 429-430.

[36] Nicholas Barbon. "A Discourse of Trade" (1690). *A Reprint of Economic Tracts.* Edited by Jacob H. Hollander. Baltimore: John Hopkins Press, 1903, pp. 35-37.

[37] Nicholas Barbon. *A Discourse Concerning Coining the New Money Lighter, In Answer to Mr. Locke's Considerations About Raising the Value of Money.* London: R. Chiswell, 1696, p. 36.

actions other than merchandise which affected the balance of trade. Among those mentioned were investments by foreigners in England, prizes of war and freight. He said the latter was "of the nature of an Exported Commodity, the overplus whereof, above what is Imported, brings home money. . . ."[38] He also stated that English lands sold to foreigners caused gold and silver to flow to England.[39]

Petty estimated the trade of England, Scotland and Ireland on the basis of listings of the principal articles traded, including gold and silver, with the value given for each article. He tested the accuracy of his estimates by comparison with the customs duties collected by the three kingdoms.[40]

In discussing the reasons for the disorder of England's coinage system, William Lowndes, the Secretary of the Treasury, stated that the market value of silver bullion would continue to be higher than its value in coins because of the necessity of exporting silver "to answer the Ballance of Trade. . . ."[41] However, realizing, as had several writers before him, that merchandise was only one of the transactions that caused an outflow of bullion, he included the foreign expense of war on the side of imports as an item to be considered in determining the balance of trade.[42]

After considering the coinage problem confronting Lowndes, Hugh Chamberlain, a physician and economist, argued against the prohibition of exporting gold and silver on the grounds that the flow of money was regulated by the balance of trade. He said that gold and silver were brought into England to pay for exports of commodities, services rendered to foreigners, and travel expenses of foreigners in England. An excess of imports over exports of merchandise, services, travel, expenses of English

---

[38] Sir William Petty. "Political Arithmetick" (1690). Reprinted in *The Economic Writings of Sir William Petty*. Charles H. Hull, ed., Cambridge: University Press, 1899, I, 260.

[39] *Ibid.*, p. 313.

[40] *Ibid.*, pp. 295-297.

[41] William Lowndes. *A Report Containing an Essay for the Amendment of the Silver Coins*. London: Printed by Charles Bill, 1695, p. 72.

[42] *Ibid.*, pp. 75-76.

residents living abroad, expenses of war, and diplomatic expenses were causes of the loss of gold and silver. Chamberlain concluded that merchandise exports must be sufficiently in excess of imports to pay for these charges if England was to keep its supply of gold and silver.[43]

Creation of the office of Inspector-General of Imports and Exports. There was a revival of the balance of trade doctrine and protectionist commercial policy among economists in 1688. Parliament began meeting annually in that year and gave special attention to trade. The members of Parliament desired information concerning the state of trade and were anxious to ascertain just how the desired balance of trade should be prepared so as to be accurate. At that time, the only available records were the books prepared by the customs house. The customs officials pointed out that any reports prepared from data contained in these books might not be within forty per cent of the real balance because of the disparity between the dutiable value and the market value of merchandise.[44]

On July 15, 1696, the Commissioners of the Customs wrote to Lowndes about the importance of having information concerning England's balance of trade and the difficulty they were encountering in complying with requests for such information. This was revealed in the following excerpt from their letter:

The Commissioners takeing into consideration the Great usefulness of keeping a Distinct accompt of the Importations and Exportations of all Commodities into and Out of this Kingdom; and to and from what places the same are Exported or Imported, In Order to make a Ballance of the Trade between this Kingdome; and any other part of the world, and finding the great Difficulty there is to come at such an Accompt, when at any time called upon for the same, For want of such a method, And Particularly being required by the House of Lords in the Last Session

---

[43] Hugh Chamberlain. *A Collection of some Papers writ upon Several Occasions, Concerning Clipt and Counterfeit Money, and Trade, so far as it relates to the Exportation of Bullion.* London: Printed for Benjamin Tooke, 1696, pp. 2-3.

[44] Clark, *op. cit.*, pp. 1-2.

of Parliament To lay before that House An Accompt of Three Years Exportations and Importations, They were forced to Returne answer from the officers of the Customs That they were not able during the Session To prepare such an Accompt. . . .[45]

The Commissioners requested that a new office be established for the purpose of accumulating the necessary data. They recommended William Culliford as being qualified to head such an office and requested that he be provided with clerks to assist in the performance of this work. Lowndes approved the Custom Commissioners' request and Culliford's appointment began a continuous history of English trade statistics. The appointment of Culliford to the office of Inspector-General turned out well. He had the qualities necessary to organize a statistical department and a thorough knowledge of the system of customs from which his data were to be obtained.[46]

Beginning in 1696, the customs authorities at various ports "required the recipient, sender or carrier of all dutiable commodities to complete certain forms" showing the type and quantity of the goods as well as the country of origin or destination. These documents became the basis of the statistics compiled by the Inspector-General's office.[47]

The new Inspector-General did not utilize the values for imports and exports provided by the customs officers because dutiable values had little relation to market values. He attempted to ascertain the prices as accurately as possible by consulting merchants engaged in foreign trade about the average current prices of the goods traded. These prices were altered from time to time by Culliford, but they later became fixed and were considered the official values by his successors until 1871.[48]

---

[45] Clark, *op. cit.,* pp. 3-4. Citing Great Britain, Public Record Office, Treasury, 1/38. fol. 302.

[46] Clark, *op. cit.,* pp. 4-6.

[47] Werner Schlote. *British Overseas Trade from 1700 to the 1930's,* translated by W. O. Henderson and W. H. Chalmer. Oxford: Basil Blackwell, 1952, p. 3.

[48] Clark, *op. cit.,* p. 10.

Culliford recognized that frequently the export accounts gave an erroneous view of the trade with particular countries because of the method of assigning exports. When ships were on trading voyages, often the first port of call was recorded as the destination of the merchandise exports. This tended to overstate the exports to a country whose ports were frequently the first stop for ships leaving England. On the other hand, exports to the country which actually received the merchandise were understated.[49]

Culliford maintained ledgers to accumulate the desired data on trade, the first of which began with Michaelmas 1696. Several copies of these ledgers were prepared: one copy went to the Board of Trade, a second to the Treasury, and the others remained in the Inspector-General's office. An annual abstract of the ledger, which was the balance of trade, was submitted to Parliament. All other documents prepared by his office were submitted upon request. These requests came from both Houses of Parliament, the Board of Trade and the Treasury. The documents varied in length from one to several pages, and the recipients often incorporated the information in reasoned reports.

The arrangement of the ledgers kept by the Inspector-General was similar to that of the Books of Rates used by the Customs officers to determine the duty to be paid on each article. These ledgers, selections of which are shown in Appendix A.4, were large folio volumes, one for each year, containing both imports and exports. The ledger tables showing the goods shipped through the port of London were followed by tables showing the goods shipped through the out-ports. Countries with which trade was conducted were in alphabetical order and the commodities were arranged alphabetically under each country with an estimate of the cost in the country of purchase. The exported goods of English manufacture were distinguished from foreign goods re-exported, and goods shipped by foreign vessels were distinguished from those carried in English ships.

----

[49] Great Britain, Parliament, House of Lords, *The Manuscript of the House of Lords, 1699-1702.* Series 17 (new series), IV, 436.

Abstracts of the data were given at the end of each ledger.[50]

Importance of the balance of trade. The East India Company was under almost constant criticism from its inception because of its exportation of bullion. Josiah Child, Chairman of the Board of Directors of the company, continued Mun's argument that the merchants' profits and freight earnings made the East India trade beneficial to England. He recognized the difficulty of obtaining accurate information from the customs-house books concerning the balance of trade as a consequence of unrecorded items such as freight, merchants' profits, smuggled goods, remittances for profits and interest, losses at sea, insurance and other earnings of English residents. Child also recognized discrepancies due to the difference between the recorded values and the market value of the merchandise.[51]

Child was emphatically in agreement with Misselden over the importance and usefulness of the balance of trade. He said the balance of trade was complex, but that "the right understanding whereof may be of singular use, and serve as a compass to steer by, in the contemplation and propagation of Trade for publick advantage."[52]

Child, as Mun had previously done, distinguished between the valuation of imports of merchandise in foreign and English shipping. Merchandise brought in by English ships was valued at its cost overseas whereas the value of imports brought to England in foreign ships included freight and other charges.

Financing the balance of account. One of the members of the Board of Trade, John Pollexfen, disputed Child's claim that the East India trade was beneficial to England. He said any excess of indebtedness to foreigners had to be paid by the export of goods. It did not matter whether this excess was due to the import of commodities, travel, military and diplomatic expenses abroad, or borrowing from foreigners. Any claim not

---

[50] Clark, *op. cit.*, pp. 7-8.
[51] Sir Josiah Child, *A New Discourse of Trade,* 4th ed. London: Printed for J. Hodges, 1698, pp. 165-169.
[52] *Ibid.*, p. 163.

paid by the export of goods had to be paid for in bullion or coin or be remitted by gift.[53]

Pollexfen considered trade advantageous when English ships were used to carry goods, when the goods were necessities, when manufactured goods were traded for unfinished goods, or when the balance of trade with a country was in favor of England.[54] Pollexfen believed that the results of carrying on a disadvantageous trade was increased foreign indebtedness and a decreased money supply because the "ballance of their Accompts" stood on the wrong side.[55] The remedy for disadvantageous trade could only be found by examining all transactions upon which the contracting of debt with foreigners depended and in regulations which would reduce the "Ballance of Accompts" with those nations.[56]

Relationships between accounts in the balance of trade. A statement of trade for the period Michaelmas 1696 to Michaelmas 1697 was prepared by Phillip Meadows who, along with Pollexfen, was a member of the Board of Trade.[57] The statement was a large table showing abstracts of the estimates of the original values (cost in the exporting country) of imports into the Port of London and the out-ports together with the estimates of the foreign goods exported from the Port of London and the out-ports. Total exports, including both English and foreign goods re-exported, were also shown.

The statement was arranged so that countries with which trade was carried on were listed in rows on the left side of the table with estimates of the values of imports and exports in columns. The balance of exports and imports and the totals of all the categories of imports and exports for each country and for all combined were given in the statement. This table con-

---

[53] John Pollexfen. *Of Trade, also of Coyn, Bullion. Of Improving our Woollen Manufacture. To Prevent Exporting Wooll. Of Ways and Means to Increase our Riches, etc.* London: John Baker, 1700, pp. 3-5.

[54] *Ibid.,* pp. 58-59.

[55] *Ibid.,* pp. 81-83.

[56] *Ibid.,* p. 40.

[57] Great Britain, Public Record Office, *Colonial Office Papers, 1700-1701.* Series 388, Vol. 8, D. 37.

tained the same information as the statements of the Inspector-General, but was arranged in a single table rather than a series of tables. This procedure tended to facilitate understanding of the information and the relationships involved.

Meadows considered the relationships between these accounts to be of equal importance to the actual figures themselves. He said the purpose of preparing such a statement was "to set forth in a Single View all these proportional Comparisons (which is indeed and it may be the only useful end of this great Labour) it seemed requisit to dispose the abstract into Columns, and to add thereto some others; such as in the present Scheme is done; From whence very many and almost infinite other proportions and deductions may easily be drawn."[58] He said that had there been space he would have also added salaries and "incidents" of management and allowance for damaged goods. This was the last significant work on the balance of trade before Charles D'Avenant.

Balance of trade statistics as a part of the national system of accounts. Culliford was succeded in 1703 by Charles D'Avenant in the office of Inspector-General. D'Avenant stated that any one who wished to determine a reliable balance of trade must consider "the wealth, stock, product, consumption, shipping, exportation and importation of his country; and . . . other places."[59] While there was great difficulty in obtaining the data needed, once it was found, he thought the conclusions drawn would be almost undeniable.

Part of the difficulty in obtaining an accurate statement of trade was due to the basis upon which merchandise imports and exports were valued. D'Avenant said "in stating the balance between two countries, the prime cost only in the respective countries should be calculated."[60] This would be

---

[58] *Ibid.*

[59] Charles D'Avenant, *The Political and Commercial Works of that Celebrated Writer Charles D'Avenant.* Edited by Sir Charles Whitworth. London: R. Horsfield, 1771, I, 147.

[60] *Ibid.,* V, 366.

an f.o.b. basis of valuation for both exports and imports and would put both on a comparable basis.

In addition to the problems relating to finding the balance of merchandise trade, there were other items which needed consideration. D'Avenant felt England did not always gain by trade simply by having an excess of exports over imports. He said there were other items such as the maintenance of troops abroad which could "interrupt all the profits to be expected from trade, . . . and leave us, at the foot of the account, losers in what is called the balance."[61] He also commented on the effect of the national debt of England, a large part of which was owed to foreigners and the habits of English monarchs and their court to travel abroad. Both, he said, were prejudicial to the balance of trade.[62]

D'Avenant held that transactions of this type caused England to lose gold and silver. He explained why there was a continuous flow of gold and silver to Holland although the balance of trade with Holland was always in favor of England. The Dutch had freight earnings from carrying English goods; remittances were made through Holland for the purpose of maintaining English troops on the continent; and the Dutch had large investments in England. He said of the Dutch:

> They are known to have considerable sums in the annuities, lotteries, East India bonds, stocks of the companies, and all the loans that are in the course of payment, and the produce of such effects lodged here must be returned to them either in bullion, bills of exchange, or commodities, which will be a constant drain to England, and a weight against us in the balance of trade in that country, so long as the funds continue.[63]

The conclusion of the French trade controversy. The half-century old argument, begun by Fortrey, over the desirability of trading with France came to a close in 1713 with a flurry of words between two opposing publications. England attempted

---

[61] *Ibid.,* V, 390.
[62] *Ibid.,* II, 295-296.
[63] *Ibid.,* V, 437.

to conclude a commercial treaty with France in that year as part of the Peace of Utrecht. The Whigs and Tories were opponents in the struggle over the proposed commercial treaty. The Whigs opposed the treaty and their views were expressed by the *British Merchant*. Henry Martin contributed to this publication. The Tories favored the treaty and were represented by the *Mercator* whose leading writer was Daniel Defoe.

The *British Merchant* republished the "Scheme of trade with France" for the year Michaelmas 1668 to Michaelmas 1669, showing Great Britain to have an unfavorable balance of trade with France.[64] The *Mercator* maintained that the trade with France was desirable and attempted to discredit the "Scheme of trade" presented by the *British Merchant*. This document, according to the *Mercator*, contained exports for 1668 and imports for 1674. Besides the obvious error of selecting different years for comparison of exports and imports, the *Mercator* said neither were representative years. The duties on English exports were doubled in 1667 and exports for 1668 would naturally be low, and imports from France were at an all time high in 1674. The *Mercator* stated that the scheme excluded re-exports of East India goods to France, overstated the quantity of linen and silk imported from France, and contained other errors as well.[65]

Finally, on October 22, 1713, the *Mercator* proclaimed: "It is now time to sum up the Articles on both sides, and begin to draw a Ballance of the Trade. . . ."[66] The statement, reproduced in Table 1.6, was arranged so that the left side of the sheet contained those items which made France a debtor to England; the right side contained those items which made France a creditor. This account of trade not only included exports sent directly to France, but also those routed through Holland and Flanders. Merchants' gains and freight were added to the value of the goods in England to bring their value up to their foreign

---

[64] *The British Merchant: A Collection of Papers Relating to the Trade and Commerce of Great Britain and Ireland*. London: Charles King, 1743, II, 296.

[65] *Mercator: or Commerce Retrieved*, May 28, 1713, No. 2.

[66] *Ibid.*, October 22, 1713, No. 65.

TABLE 1.6
ENGLAND'S BALANCE OF TRADE, 1685-1686

Numb. 65.

MERCATOR
O R,
Commerce Retrieved,
BEING
CONSIDERATIONS on the State of the *British* Trade, &c.

From **Tuesday**, October 20. to **Thursday**, October 22. 1713.

The Trade to France in English Goods, by way of Holland, asserted and demonstrated.
The like by way of Flanders.
The like by way of Genoa and Leghorn.
The whole Account brought to a Balance.
The Advantage of the French Trade undeniably plain.

BY all the Conduct of the Opposers of the French Trade, it appears they are perfectly thoughtless of what we are now speaking of, (viz.) The Quantity of English Manufactures, &c. sent into France, not directly from England, but thro' other Countries.

In order to prevent the Cavils and Deficiency of the Party, with which they support their deficient Arguments, the last MERCATOR directed them to the Maps of France, by which they will see, that some parts of the Dominions of the French King are so Situated, as that they can be no way supplied with English Goods, so as to have them at any reasonable Rates, but by way of Holland.

We told you, in order to remove the Cavils and Pretences of the Party, that the French have no Manufactures in those Countries; that they always deal in those Parts Consume great Quantities of our Goods; and that this Matter no way respected the War in the least.

It is necessary a little to name the Parts, and describe the Situation of them, to make the Reader of this Case appear more plain and undeniable.

These Countries therefore are the Provinces of *Champagne*; the three Bishopricks of *Metz, Toul, and Verdun*; the Country of *Dervin*, which may very well be said to be under French Dominion; part of the Provinces of *Burgundy* and *Franche Compte*, and all the upper and lower *Alsatia*; together with all that Country, which France possesses between the *Saar* and the *Mosele*, and between the *Saar* and the *Rhine*.

To Confirm what is alledged, it must first be proved, that these Countries cannot reasonably be supplied with our Goods from the Sea-Ports of France; and, secondly, that they are supplied from Holland.

That they cannot be supplied from the Sea-Coast of France, is evident to any one that considers their Situation: The City of *Metz*, which is the Mart of that part of the World for English Woollen Manufactures, may be the Standard for the rest, for it is the nearest of most of them; yet it is from *Metz* 156 English Miles to *Dunkirk*; 182 Miles to *Diep* or *St. Vallery*; 138 to *Paris*; 175 to *Roan*; it has no River-Navigation to any of these Places, nor within a Hundred Miles of it from any part of France: Which way then shall the English Goods be brought to *Metz? Strasburgh* is the Capital of *Alsace*; *Nancy* of *Lorrain*; the way to France by

these Parts is all by *Metz*: So that if *Metz* it self can not be supplied from France, much less can the other answers for also.

On the other side, The City of *Metz* stands upon the *Mosele*, by which, and the *Rhine*, it has an open and very great Navigation; and also by the *Maese* it stands upon the *Maese*, and has the like; it stands upon the *Rhine* it self.

All the upper part of *Champagne*, from the City of *Rheims*, is supplied by the *Maese*, even almost to *Liege*; all the three Bishopricks, the Duchies of *Bar* and *Lorrain*, and up to *Metz* and *Strasburgh* from *Metz*, aforesaid, and by the *Rhine*; and all this is fully furnished with English Goods from Holland by the *Rhine*; it can come no other way, unless some Hundreds of Miles by Land-Carriage.

If the Cavilling People object that these Parts are no part of France, that Cavil will not serve them, it may serve them, for what Knows the what it is that to the Year 1685? Then it was not all in the French King's Possession; and wants but little of being so now.

The next Question then is, Do these Countries Consume any of our Manufactures? Indeed we are talking to those, who by their own Confession do not understand, what they are talking about. This would be no Question; Since the City of *Metz* is Enrich'd, as above, the Mart of that Side of France for English Goods; and there are said to be more Wholesale Woollen-Drapers, as we call them, than in any City in France, except *Paris*.

If then so great a Trade is driven in these Countries for our Woollen Manufactures, as is known to be by all the Merchants, who Trade that way; and that all these Goods are brought from Holland, the difficulty from any other Navigation making it impracticable to bring them any other way; then so much of our Woollen Goods as the Dutch send into France by those ways, is, and ought to be esteemed a Branch of our Exportation to France: If any thing can be said to Contradict this, it would be much to the purpose, to hear it; the MERCATOR ventures to tell them, they cannot Contradict it by any thing but Clamour.

We have a great Noise made of our great Exports to Holland, and it is true we do Export great Quantities of Goods to Holland; But do the Dutch Consume

Source: *Mercator: or Commerce Retrieved*, October 22, 1713, No. 65.

TABLE 1.6 (Cont'd.)

it home, or send them forward to other Countries? our Manufactures are sent to France, what is it to the Question, who sends them? It is our Business to three them by all ways possible, and therefore it is our Interest to have the high Duties in France taken off, that all the Ways of Carrying our Goods unto France may be open; for if that is not done, the Dutch cannot Carry them in any more than we can. And this is the End of the Treaty of Commerce, which these Ignorant Men Oppose.

As Holland does this, so Flanders comes in for a share of this Trade; and though England, the Provinces of Artois and Hainault, the Lower Parts of Dauphine, and the Frontiers of France it self are supplied with English Manufactures from Flanders: It would be absurd and ridiculous to think these Countries should fetch the Woollen Manufactures by Land-Carriage from any Port of France to which of them which they have no Navigation; but they are all supplied by the Scheld and the Lys from Bruges and Ghent, except Lisle, which is supposed to have some Goods by Land-Carriage from Dunkirk, which is pretty very far off; yet all the City of Arras, the Country from Douay to Cambray and Amiens, and even into Picardy by Perronne, all is brought by the Scheld, as the part of Champaigne on that Side is by the Sambre quite and Guise and la Fere; and even to Paris it self: And the MERCATOR freely appeals to the Merchants, who deal this way for the Truth of this; and if they do not believe that an Hundred thousand Pounds

worth of English Manufactures and Merchandizes from England are sent that way into France, and yet we receive no French Goods back again by way of Flanders.

The Cities of Genoa and Leghorn will claim a Share in the like Trade, tho not with so evident a Necessity; and great Quantities of British Goods are every Year sent from those Ports to Marseilles, because our Ships bound to the Levant touch at Leghorn, and so on to Naples, the Rate of Messina, the Gulph of Venice, &c. and care not to go so deep into the Bay of Gulph of Lions as to Marseilles, which is out of their way: For this Reason there are great Trade from Leghorn to France for British Goods, and the Quantity, tho not easie to be guessed at, is very considerable.

However, as we can overlook great Sums in this Account, and have enough to spare them, the MERCATOR leaves it Unvalued, and only putting them in mind that it is so, passes it by as a Reserve.

It is time now to sum up the Articles on Both Sides, and begin to draw a Ballance of the Trade, that the Opposers of their Country's Good may see and blush at themselves, and that their Delusions may no more pass upon the poor abused People for Truth, or their Shams for Realities. And now it shall appear to all the World, who are Gainers by the French Trade, the French or We; and whether those, who are for the Trade, or those, who are for losing it, are Enemies to their Country.

Trade to France Debtor.	l.	p.	d.	Trade to France Creditor.	l.	s.	
To Profit and Loss for Value Exported directly, from Michaelmas 1685 to Michaelmas 1686, as per Account Mercator N. 63.	742,277	4	2½	By Profit and Loss for Goods Imported from Michaelmas 1685 to Michaelmas 1686, as per Mercator N. —.	889,904	1	
To Ditto for English Goods Exported to France via Holland in Ditto time	300,000	—	—	Trade Creditor by Gain to Ballance due to England	866,372	13	11½
To Ditto via Flanders	100,000	—	—		1,756,277	4	2½
To Ditto for the Corn Exported in their Years, amounting, one Year with another to a proportion of 50,000 Quarter, as is proved Mercator N. —	50,000	—	—				
To Ditto for the Advance upon the Sale of 742,277 l. being its Seventh Parts on English Account and Risque, at 10 per Cent.	64,220	—	—				
To Cash for the Freight of 50,000 Ton of Shipping at 20 l. per Ton for Goods Exported to France, which being paid by the French and being so much clear Money gain'd, is at 10 per Cent. Profit equal to the Export of Goods to the Value of	500,000	—	—	NOTE, The MERCATOR has Accounts sent him of above 60,000 Cheat in the Value of the Importations set down in the Opposers Scheme more than he has taken notice of, which he shall signify in its place, and which must be discounted out of the Sum above, and added to the Ballance of the Trade, which when brought in, will make the Trade to France appear to be fairly to our Advantage in the Exports and Imports above Nine hundred thousand Pounds a Year.			
	1,756,277	4	2½				

NOTE, If 10 per Cent. Profit be thought too much for the Trade, and they please to bring it to 5 l. per Cent. then the Gain of 50,000 l. by Freight, is equal to the Exportation of Ten hundred thousand Pounds in Goods, and either way it is equal in the Number of Poor employed.

NOTE ALSO, This is besides all the Ships employ-ed in the bringing Goods from France, for they carry but few Goods out, as has been shewn, which at a moderate reckoning will be above Five hundred Sail of Ships, which are the Occasion of the Subsistence of thousands of Poor, as has been sufficiently described by the MERCATOR.

NOTE ALSO, This is besides all our Exported Goods which go to France via Leghorn and Genoa, which is a very great Sum; and besides several other

Articles, which may be added hereafter, as, of di-vant Trade, Fish from Newfoundland, and the

ERRATA.

THE last MERCATOR being not revised, the following false Pointings have injur'd the Reason. Col. 1. l. 12. after say (;). Ib. after Leathersellers (, Ib. l. 14. after another (;). Ib. after Dinners (.) Ib. l. 22. after them (;). Ib. after Excusers (;) Ib. l. 25. after any (;). Ib. dele (,). Ib. read Spectator in Italick join'd to F Ib. desфиов, thus, Spectator Justidisque sit malignus. Col. 2. l. 1. after still (;).

LONDON: Printed for BENJ. TOOKE, at the Temple-Gate; and JOHN BARBER, on Lambeth-Hill.   (Price 3 Half-pence.)

selling price. Imports of merchandise from France were placed on the opposite side of the account. The difference between the two sides was entered as a balancing item so that both sides of the statement were of the same total value.

Balance of Trade: Development from 1714 to 1767

The many discussions arising from the proposed treaty with France laid the foundations of knowledge of international trade and finance for later economists and statisticians. Henry Martin, a participant in the conflict and later Inspector-General, was particularly benefited. The developmental work on the balance of payments during the interval 1714 to 1767 came chiefly from the Inspector-General's office and can be conveniently divided into three sections: accuracy of trade statistics, forms of presenting these statistics, and the methodology used in obtaining the data for statements of trade. A fourth section is added to indicate the important contributions made by compilers of trade statistics during this period.

Accuracy of the balance of trade. Henry Martin succeeded D'Avenant to the office of Inspector-General in 1714. Three years later he furnished the Commissioners of the Board of Trade a general account of the balance of trade with all parts of the world for a seventeen-year period beginning with the creation of the Inspector-General's office.[67] Martin observed that the balance of trade could not be assumed to be correct without certain adjustments. He recognized two items of income which were not included in the balance of trade as prepared by his office. The first of these items consisted of goods sent to England by Englishmen residing abroad, such as governors, planters, factors and agents. These people often invested in foreign goods and sent them to England for their own use or converted them into money or estates to remain in England. Since no payment was required, Martin suggested that imports be reduced by the estimated value of these imports.

---

[67] Clark. *Op. cit.*, pp. 62-69 citing Henry Martin Inspector-General of the Exports and Imports His Observations upon the Account of Exports and Imports for 17 Years ending at Christmas 1714 delivered in to the Board of Trade 1717/18. Public Record Office, *Colonial Office* 390/12, pp. 15-43.

The second adjustment was for the valuation of imports which were brought back by English ships on trading voyages. The goods imported were worth more than the goods exported because value was added through freight, insurance and merchants' profits. Since most of the increase in value accrued to English firms, Martin suggested that the value of imports be reduced to the value of the goods sent in exchange.

An addition to imports was needed to show the value of American ships sold in England at the completion of their voyage. As their purchase was not recorded in the custom-house books, they were not included in the balance of trade prepared by the Inspector-General's office. Martin also thought that exports should be reduced by the amount of any goods lost at sea while in transit to other countries. While the goods were recorded in the custom-house books, no payment would be made for them by foreigners. Martin concluded that it was impossible to know the proper amount of these adjustments; therefore, the sum of money paid for the difference between the values bought and sold could never be known.

Presentation of trade data. Martin's tenure in office was terminated in 1728, and John Oxenford was appointed Assistant Inspector-General. The Inspector-General's position had become a political sinecure, so the Assistant Inspector-General actually managed the office.[68] Oxenford, as his predecessor had done before him, recognized that the returns prepared by his office were not indicative of the amounts of payments required to settle international differences of account.

Oxenford prepared fifteen tables, accompanied by his observations on them, for the twenty-one year period beginning with the creation of the office of Inspector-General.[69] He did this to present the statistics of trade in better perspective. The tables were unique in that they began with data taken from the Inspector-General's ledgers but were adjusted for the estimated amounts which Oxenford believed necessary to state correctly

---

[68] Clark, *op. cit.*, p. 23.
[69] Clark, *op. cit.*, pp. 69-149, citing the Public Record Office, *Colonial Office 390/14.*

the balance of trade. Oxenford selected four areas: (1) East India and Turkey, (2) Africa and Madeira, (3) the Plantations, and (4) the remaining countries of the world, for the purpose of showing how the trade with the world was financed and how England paid for imports by exports of goods and services.

Oxenford ascertained from these tables that England had maintained a favorable balance of trade during the twenty-one year period. He said England was able to pay the foreign expenses of war, to re-acquire British securities held by foreigners, and to import foreign coin as a consequence of this favorable balance.

The situation appeared less favorable to other writers toward the middle of the eighteenth century. They were concerned about an alleged loss of gold and silver from England and the reasons for such a loss. Jacob Vanderlint, David Hume, and Joseph Harris recognized the importance of foreign transactions other than merchandise in determining the flow of gold and silver between countries. Vanderlint, in his tract *Money Answers All Things*, in 1734 spoke of the large national debt of England, part of which was owed to foreigners, as contributing to England's loss of specie due to "the Interest of which they are continually drawing from us. . . ."[70]

David Hume discussed several of the causes of the loss of specie from England. He felt that the main reason for this loss was the excess of merchandise imports over exports. However, Hume stated, there were other transactions, such as expenditures of the government in foreign countries for administrative and military purposes and interest on loans owed to foreigners, which were also responsible.[71]

Joseph Harris said of England's indebtedness "our debt to foreigners operates in the same manner as a ballance of trade against us, to the whole amount of the dividends owing to

---

[70] Jacob Vanderlint, "Money Answers All Things" (1734). *A Reprint of Economic Tracts*. Edited by Jacob H. Hollander. Baltimore: Lord Baltimore Press, 1914, p. 127.

[71] David Hume. *Political Discourses*. 2nd ed., Edinburgh: Printed by R. Fleming, 1752, p. 99.

them; and the same is true as to all foreign subsidies."[72]

Methodology used in obtaining data for the balance of trade. Oxenford's successor, John Tomkyns, served as Assistant Inspector-General from 1759 to 1785. His term was marked by changes in the office and in the methods of accumulating data to rectify the deficiencies in the statements being prepared at that time.

The statistics accumulated by the Inspector-General's office were more valuable as records of quantities of goods traded than as records of the monetary value of exports and imports. There were several reasons for this, one of which was the unsatisfactory relationship between the official and current prices of the goods traded. In addition, duty-free goods were probably over-valued; no estimates were made for smuggled goods; and fish sold by the British in foreign ports went unrecorded. Coin and bullion exports and imports were handled inconsistently. Imported coin and bullion were not recorded, while exports of foreign coin were included in total exports until 1765. There were other unrecorded items such as freight payments and the purchases of ships from foreigners. Last, the balance of trade presented a distorted view of trade relations with particular countries because exports were often assigned to the first port of call rather than to the actual country of destination.[73]

Tomkyns gave the following account of the Inspector-General's methods of obtaining data for his abstracts of trade:

Every Bill for an Import or an Export, at the Port of London, is brought to this Office, and the Quantity of every Article upon each of these Bills is entered in this Office, distinguishinig the Country from and to which each Article is brought or sent. Every Out Port sends to this Office a similar Quarterly Account of the Imports and Exports, of which Entries are made in this Office; and hence an Account may be obtained from this Office of the Quantity of every Article exported or imported, and to and from

[72] Joseph Harris, *An Essay upon Money and Coins*. London: Printed by G. Hawkins, 1757, p. 125.

[73] Clark, *op. cit.*, pp. 33-36.

what Country, at any Port of England, for any given time.[74]

The Inspector-General's ledgers for the year ending Christmas 1772 indicated the quantity, unit and total value of each commodity imported and exported. The articles of merchandise were listed in alphabetical order. Distinction was made between goods of English and foreign manufacture exported and goods carried in English and foreign ships. The ledgers indicated whether the goods passed through the port of London or the out-ports. In addition to the tables for merchandise, there were also tables showing the amount of foreign gold and silver coin and bullion exported each year.[75]

The imports and exports of all goods by country with which trade was carried on were followed by a summary (Table 1.7) comparing total exports with total imports. The table was arranged so that imports were on one side and exports on the other. The countries were listed alphabetically. There were columns to show whether England's trade with each country resulted in an excess of imports over exports. The amount of foreign coin and bullion was added to the amount by which merchandise exports exceeded imports. This was the balance of trade as given by the Inspector-General's office.

The Inspector-General of Exports and Imports began preparing a new type of statistical table, called *States of Navigation, Commerce and Revenue* in 1772. These new tables, more simple than the old, were described as follows:

First [there] are tables for shipping, then imports and exports by quantities and values, the same official values as those of the ledgers, under countries and species. At the end are general abstracts by species and 'grand divisions', that is continents, and then by countries without species. There is no distinction between London and the out-ports, and the tables of imports and exports do not distinguish

---

[74] Clark, *op. cit.*, p. 31. Citing J. Lane, *Reports of the Commissioners of Public Accounts*, 1787. III, 432.

[75] Great Britain, Public Record Office. *Customs* 3/72.

between those carried in English and those carried in foreign ships.[76]

Compilation of early trade statistics. In addition to the statistical work done by the Inspector-General's office, there were several other compilers of trade statistics worthy of note. Adam Anderson composed a history of commerce in the form of annals which contained statements of the balance of trade of Great Britain from 1701 to 1788.[77] He was aware that there were several transactions other than merchandise which combined to turn the rate of exchange against England. Anderson specifically mentioned dividends paid to foreigners, subsidies to foreign powers, ministers of state expenses in foreign courts, and drafts by English travelers in foreign countries.[78]

Two other compilers of English commercial statistics deserve mention. They are Sir Charles Whitworth and David Macpherson. Whitworth compiled trade tables for Great Britain from 1697 to 1773.[79] David Macpherson's four-volume work, *Annals of Commerce,* embodies the essence of Adam Anderson's *History of Commerce* and contains the commericial transactions of Great Britain from 1760 to 1800.[80]

The Balance of Payments

The development of the balance of payments actually began with the earliest comments concerning international transactions and the first statements of trade. As more and more items were included in statements of trade, they became less statements of the balances of trade and more nearly balances of payments.

---

[76] Clark, *op. cit.,* p. 29.

[77] Anderson closed his history with the year 1762, but contributors, one of whom was George Chalmers, Secretary of the Board of Trade, continued the work through the year 1788.

[78] Adam Anderson. *An Historical and Chronological Deduction of the Origin of Commerce from the Earliest Accounts.* London: J. Walter, 1787. I, xxxviii.

[79] Sir Charles Whitworth. *State of the Trade of Great Britain in its Imports and Exports, Progressively from the year 1697.* London: Printed for T. Cadell, 1776.

[80] David Macpherson. *Annals of Commerce.* London: Nichols and Son, 1805.

TABLE 1.7

ENGLAND'S BALANCE OF TRADE, 1771-1772,
ABSTRACTED FROM THE LEDGERS OF THE INSPECTOR-GENERAL
OF EXPORTS AND IMPORTS

Source: Great Britain, Public Record Office, *Customs*, 3/72, p. 273.

TABLE 1.7 (Cont'd.)

While the term "balance of trade" was often used to comprehend transactions other than merchandise, it was with the use of the new term "balance of payments" that there was a specific recognition of the distinction between a full international account of transactions and the balance of trade. The term did not immediately gain acceptance because it was ignored by the classical economists other than Ricardo. It might never have become a significant concept except for the later work of John Marshall, Thomas Tooke and other economists who had a greater interest in statistical records of international transactions than their contemporaries.

The last presentation of the Mercantilist doctrine was made in 1767 by Sir James Steuart in *An Inquiry into the Principles of Political Economy.* McCulloch said Steuart's book was the first English work which could be considered a systematic or complete view of the subject.[81] Bell considers Steuart one of the ablest of the eighteenth century writers before Adam Smith.[82] Steuart distinguished between the balance of trade and the balance of payments as follows:

> . . . there is a great difference between the wrong *balance of trade,* and the general *balance of payments.* The first marks the total loss of the nation when her imports exceed the value of her exports; the second comprehends three other articles, viz. 1. the expence of the natives in foreign countries; 2. the payment of all debts, principal and interest due to foreigners; 3. the lending to other nations.
>
> These three I call the general balance of foreign payments; and these added to the wrong balance of trade may be called the *grand balance* with the world.[83]

Steuart then discussed the relationship between the balance of trade, specie flows, and changes in international assets and liabilities. He said those who contended that the balance of

---

[81] J. R. McCulloch. *The Literature of Political Economy.* London: Longmans, Brown, Green and Longmans, 1845, p. 11.

[82] John Fred Bell. *A History of Economic Thought.* New York. Ronald Press, 1953, p. 90.

[83] James Steuart. *An Inquiry into the Principles of Political Economy.* London: Printed for T. Cadell, 1767, II, 162.

payments must be paid by specie were in error. According to Steuart, it was possible to finance the balance of payments by changes in international indebtedness or by changes in foreign investment without movement of specie. However, the result of an unfavorable balance of trade over an extended period of time would probably be the gradual transfer of ownership of property from the residents of that country to foreigners.[84]

Steuart's distinction between the balance of trade and the balance of payments made subsequent writers conscious of the necessity of considering the effects of all of a nation's international transactions upon the flow of money, credit and property between it and other nations. This concept began a new era in international commerce and financial statistics which has continued in importance to the present time.

---

[84] *Ibid.*, pp. 162-173.

2

The Development in the Balance of Payments in the United States and the United Kingdom from 1789 to 1873

The coining of the term "balance of payments" by Sir James Steuart was the beginning of a new way of thinking about international commercial and financial transactions. The political economists of several nations were no longer limited in their deliberations to merchandise trade and the flow of specie. They began to speculate about the balance of all current transactions and how this balance was to be financed.

The Beginning of American Trade Statistics

United States foreign trade statistics first appeared in 1791. The task of preparing statements of trade was assigned to the Treasury Department. The data needed for the preparation of the statements were obtained from the customs houses of the various ports. The trade accounts of the United States prepared from this data had many of the deficiencies previously evident in those of the United Kingdom. Even as late as 1867 the statistics of foreign trade were not considered accurate enough to be relied upon for policy-making decisions.

Early statements of trade in the United States. The first statement of trade of the United States was prepared for the year ending September 30, 1790. Alexander Hamilton, Secretary of the Treasury, presented it to Congress on February 15, 1791.[1] Goods were listed alphabetically in rows in the export tables and the countries to which the goods were shipped were listed horizontally in the columns or headings. Each country had two columns, one for quantity, the other for value. A summary showing the value and destination of the exports followed the general tables.

The import tables were arranged somewhat differently as countries were listed in rows while the goods imported were shown in columns. However, in subsequent reports, export tables were prepared similarly to those for imports. Imports were shown by quantity only for all goods except those subject to ad valorem duties. A report containing shipping information followed the tables of exports and imports.

Report of the Committee of Commerce and Manufactures. The Senate appointed a committee to investigate the methods and procedures of reporting trade statistics and to make recommendations for the improvement of these reports.[2] The statements prepared by the Treasury Department were based upon information furnished by the customs officials. It was the duty of the ships masters to report on their manifests the destination, kind, quantity, and value of the cargo. The reports often varied considerably in accuracy because of inadequate information.

The customs officials were aware of this situation and often substituted their own valuations whenever they thought necessary. There was considerable diversity among the various officers of different ports concerning the principles upon which they were to base their valuations and in what situations to apply them. In general, the practice was to use the current price of each article at the port of exportation. This price was an average of the prices current during the quarter of the year in which the goods were exported and was based upon whatever information the collector was able to obtain. The valuations

---

[1] U.S., *State Papers: Commerce and Navigation,* 1st Congress, 3rd sess., 1791, Doc. No. 6 and 2d Cong., 1st sess., 1791, Doc. No. 7.

[2] U.S., *State Papers: Commerce and Navigation,* 16th Cong., 1st sess., 1819, Sen. Doc. 225.

of the exports were, therefore, based partly on the values reported by the ships masters and partly on those determined by the customs officers. The Committee of Commerce and Manufactures believed this practice had a slight tendency to overstate the value of exports.

The valuation of imports was even less accurate. No report whatsoever was made of duty free articles, and only the quantities of articles subject to specific duties were reported. Therefore, the Treasury's published accounts of trade showed only the value of imported articles which were subject to ad valorem duties. Since it was believed that almost half of the imports were not reported, the accounts of imports were seriously understated. In addition, the imports which were reported were inadequately classified. All the articles which were subject to the same ad valorem duty were consolidated so that neither the value nor the quantity of individual articles was given.

Another serious source of error according to the Committee, stemmed from the different bases used in valuing exports and imports. Both were valued at American ports, which meant that exports were valued f.o.b. and imports c.i.f. This, the Committee said, reduced the utility of the accounts. Since imported goods included the costs of transportation and insurance, there was no basis for comparison with exported goods which excluded these charges.

The Committee also concluded that the statements of trade did not reveal accurately the destination of American exports. The customs officers treated the destination of the cargo as of little consequence, and accepted the ships masters' declarations without further investigation. These declarations were often the first port of call or any foreign place that the declarer desired to name.

The accounts of exports and imports were called "uncertain and delusive" by the Committee. While the Committee recognized the impossibility of ever achieving perfection in the statement of the accounts, it did feel that reasonably accurate statements were both necessary and attainable. To achieve this desirable goal, the Committee made several recommendations which it hoped would remedy the defects.

Reform of the United States merchandise accounts. Following the report of the Committee of Commerce and Manufactures, Congress promulgated "An Act to provide for obtaining accurate statements of the foreign commerce of the United States" on February 10, 1820. Beginning in 1821 the value of all imports, regardless of their tariff classifications, had to be determined by the customs officer. The valuation for imports was the sworn specie value at the foreign port from which they were shipped. The valuation for exports was the sworn currency value at the domestic port of exportation.

The merchandise accounts grew in volume, but they continued to be prepared in substantially the same manner in 1873 as they were in 1821. The chief classifications of domestic merchandise exports were: sea, forest, agriculture, and manufactures. Gold and silver continued to be carried in the merchandise account under separate classifications. Summary accounts indicated the shipping tonnage involved in the carrying of exports and imports, although no values were given for it. The method of collecting data for the annual reports remained substantially unchanged except to the extent that the law of 1820 was amended by that of July 28, 1866.

In 1867, the Director of the newly established Bureau of Statistics of the Treasury Department, Alexander Delmar, said that it was difficult to obtain accurate and comprehensive data needed to prepare reliable statements of trade since, with few exceptions, none were available. He enumerated various errors which decreased the usefulness of published reports of trade. To correct this situation, Delmar issued standardized forms to all customs houses along with detailed instructions for their use.[3]

---

[3] U.S., Treasury Department, *Annual Report of the Director of the Bureau of Statistics, on the Commerce and Navigation of the United States, for the Fiscal Year Ended June 30, 1867.* Washington: Government Printing Office, 1868, pp. X-XI.

Relationship Between Commercial and Financial Transactions in the International Accounts of the United States

The United States had an unfavorable balance of trade during most of the years from 1789 to 1873.[4] Interest was focused on the manner in which this unfavorable balance was financed both in the United States and abroad. Various service transactions were recognized to be important in determining the amount of the increasing foreign indebtedness of the United States. Most economists recognized that part of the deficit was financed by the sale of securities abroad and the remainder by gold. Banking panics occurred periodically in the United States as the result of gold flowing out in payment of claims which foreigners did not wish to hold on a continuing basis. Estimates were made of foreign indebtedness and the various service items so that more adequate knowledge of the actual financial condition would allow corrective policies to be pursued.

The balance of trade, services and capital. There were three noteworthy estimates made of the United States foreign indebtedness between 1790 and 1840. One of the earliest estimates was made by the Secretary of the Treasury on January 9, 1790. In this report, the principal of the foreign debt and the interest accrued as of December 31, 1789 was classified by lenders.[5] The second was made in 1838 when *Niles' National Register* published a list of American securities held abroad, principally in England.[6] The securities listed were principally state bonds and bonds of banks, rail, and insurance companies totaling $110,000,000. The third was made in 1840 by Adam Seybert, a member of the House of Representatives from Pennsylvania. He prepared a statement of the public debt of the United States for each of the years, 1791-1818, showing the

---

[4] Douglass C. North, "The United States Balance of Payments, 1790-1860," pp. 577, 581; and Matthew Simon, "The United States Balance of Payments, 1861-1900," pp. 699-700, National Bureau of Economic Research, *Studies in Income and Wealth.* Princeton: University Press, 1960, Vol. XXIV.

[5] Timothy Pitkin, *A Statistical View of the Commerce of the United States of America.* Hartford: Printed by Charles Hosmer, 1816, pp. 261-263.

[6] *Niles' National Register,* July 21, 1838, p. 322.

part held by foreigners. He also classified the debt for 1818 according to the type of security and security-holder for both the foreign and domestically held debt.[7]

Seybert saw the relationship between various service transactions, the balance of trade and foreign indebtedness. He estimated American freight earnings by applying an average per ton rate to the volume of goods carried in United States shipping. Seybert said that while the overall balance of trade with the world "produced an apparent unfavourable balance, amounting to 15,229,909 dollars per annum; but this sum . . . was more than counterbalanced by the profits for freight alone."[8] Besides the profits on freight, he stated that there were also considerable earnings from commissions. Seybert noted the unfavorable balance of trade with the United Kingdom during the early years of the nineteenth century, and stated that the United States would be unable to make payments on the British-held debts and accrued interest as long as this continued unfavorable.[9]

Condy Raguet, an attorney and president of the Chamber of Commerce of Philadelphia, was also interested in the effects of invisible transactions on the balance of payments. He said there were many debits and credits created by international transactions which did not appear in the custom house books.[10] Included in his list of these items were unreported specie imported and exported by emigrants and passengers, shipping earnings abroad, sale of ships abroad, remittances of revenues to non-residents, expenses of travelers in foreign countries, bankruptcy of persons to whom exported commodities were sold, and investments overseas. While the movements of tangible goods were generally recorded, those of an intangible nature were not.

United States foreign indebtedness. Ezra Seaman, attorney, writer and Treasury employee, examined the state of foreign

---

[7] Adam Seybert, *Statistical Annals.* Philadelphia: Thomas Dobson & Son, 1818, pp. 750-753, 757.

[8] *Ibid.*, p. 281.

[9] *Ibid.*, pp. 282-283.

[10] Condy Raguet, *A Treatise on Currency and Banking.* Philadelphia: Grigg and Elliott, 1840, p. 23.

commerce of the United States. He attempted to ascertain the effect of various tariff acts upon the amount of foreign indebtedness, the balance of trade and the flow of specie. For this purpose, Seaman selected eight periods ranging from one to six years running from October 1, 1820 to July 1, 1845.[11]

Seaman began with an estimate of the United States foreign indebtedness of $110,000,000 on October 1, 1820. He added to this amount imports and interest accrued during the period to find the total liabilities incurred. Exports, freight earnings and merchants' profits (estimated at fifteen per cent of exports) were deducted from this total as they offset the claims of foreigners. Seaman explained this procedure by saying that "all the money and products sent abroad to pay the interest on our foreign debt, and the dividends on our stocks held abroad, appear as part of our exports; and the proceeds of all loans, and monies and effects sent here to be invested in our stocks, appear in, and as a part of our imports."[12] Thus, the balance of indebtedness was determined at the end of each period by summarizing the total claims of foreigners on the United States and vice versa. This balance was the new starting point for each succeeding period.

Seaman excluded from the balance of indebtedness the accounts receivable which were lost because of the bankruptcy of foreign merchants, importers and corporations and the loss of the market value of stock held by foreigners. He included indebtedness incurred for the purchase of Florida in 1822. Seaman concluded from this calculation that the balance of indebtedness was lower during periods when higher tariffs were in effect. He said that American credit was nearly exhausted during the last three years of free trade from 1840 to 1842. With higher rates under the tariff act of 1842, the foreign debt diminished and the quantity of specie increased.

Seaman viewed the balance of payments as an international account which would always be in balance when all current

---

[11] Ezra C. Seaman, *Essays on the Progress of Nations*. New York: Baker and Scribner, 1846, pp. 266-272.

[12] *Ibid.*, p. 266.

and capital transactions were considered. He summed up this concept as follows:

> It must be evident to any one who will take the trouble to reflect on the subject, that whenever our imports as a nation, at our custom house valuations, exceed our exports, the freight earned by American vessels, and the profits of that part of our exports and imports made by American merchants, that the excess or balance must exist as a debt against us; that whenever the balance of trade is against us, our foreign debt is accumulating to the precise amount of such balance, and of the interest on our former debt added to it; that our exports, freights, profits, and foreign debt, must be precisely equal to our imports, and the interest on our foreign debt, and that the two must balance each other, like a banker's account.[13]

Possibly one reason for Seaman's failure to emphasize specie flows as a balancing item was due to the practice of custom officers to include specie as part of exports and imports; to regard it as a commodity rather than a monetary transaction. However, he was quite as concerned with specie flows and the quantity of specie in the country as he was with the balance of foreign indebtedness. He examined the imports and exports of specie to see the effects of changes in the tariff acts upon the amount of specie in the country. Seaman began in 1820 with an estimated quantity of specie of $25 million. He added imports of specie to this quantity as shown on the custom house books, together with an estimate of the amount of specie brought in by emigrants which had not been recorded. He deducted from this amount exports of specie and estimates of the domestic use of specie in excess of domestic gold and silver production.[14] This adjustment was an original contributions of Seaman's. It was not made in the United States balance of payments until 1927. However, in calculating the balance of indebtedness, he used the custom house figures for exports and imports rather than his own adjusted figures of specie flow.

---

[13] *Ibid.*, p. 270.
[14] *Ibid.*, pp. 244-247.

Seaman made several contributions to the development of the balance of payments. He estimated emigrants' transfers of specie, made adjustments for the domestic use and production of specie, and clearly showed the relationships among merchandise exports and imports, invisible items, liabilities to foreigners and specie flows. In addition, he indicated the effect of the liability for dividends, profits and interest on foreign investment in the United States upon the balance of indebtedness. Adjustment for the reduction of foreign indebtedness resulting from repudiated state debts and the bankruptcy of American debtors was another of his contributions.

Secretary of the Treasury's report on securities. In compliance with a request of the Senate, James Guthie, Secretary of the Treasury, furnished information concerning foreign investments in American securities as of June 30, 1853.[15] The information was submitted in ten documents.

1. A letter from the Register of the Treasury giving the amount of federal securities outstanding with an estimate of the amount held by non-residents of the United States.

2. A statement of the outstanding bonds of the individual states as compiled from returns received by the Treasury from the chief officials of those states distinguished as to foreign and domestic holders.

3. A statement of the outstanding bonds of the individual states with estimates of those held by foreigners as estimated by Winslow, Lanier & Co. This estimate was approximately $38,-000,000 higher than that reported by state officials.

4. A statement of the bonds of cities, towns, and counties as far as could be ascertained from returns made to the Treasury and reports made by brokers, indicating the amounts held by foreigners.

5. A statement of bank stock held by foreigners as reported by the banks.

6. A statement of the foreign ownership of stock of insurance companies as reported by these companies to the Treasury.

---

[15] U.S., 33d Cong., 1st sess., *Sen. Ex. Doc.* 42, 1853-1854.

7. A statement of the foreign ownership of stocks and bonds of railroad companies as determined from reports of the railroads, data from the *American Railroad Journal* and reports from brokers.

8. A statement of the foreign ownership of stocks and bonds of canal and navigation companies as reported by these companies.

9. A statement of the foreign ownership of miscellaneous stocks and bonds as reported by the companies concerned.

10. A general summary of foreign indebtedness (shown in Table 2.1).

TABLE 2.1

SUMMARY OF UNITED STATES FOREIGN INDEBTEDNESS, JUNE 30, 1853.

	Total.	held by foreigners.
United States stocks	$ 58,205,517	$ 27,000,000
State stocks	190,718,221	72,931,507
113 cities and towns (bonds)	79,352,149	16,462,322
347 counties (bonds)	13,928,369	5,000,000
985 banks (stocks)	266,724,955	6,688,996
75 insurance companies (stocks)	12,829,730	378,172
224 railroad companies (stocks)	309,893,967	8,244,025
Do_____do_____(bonds)	170,111,552	43,888,752
16 canal and navigation companies (stocks)	35,888,918	554,900
Do_____do_____(bonds)	22,130,569	1,967,547
15 miscellaneous companies (stocks)	16,425,612	802,720
Do_____do_____(bonds)	2,358,323	265,773
Total	$1,178,567,882	$184,184,714

If the estimate of Winslow, Lanier & Co. be preferred, as to the amount of state stocks held by foreigners, $110,972,108 must be substituted in the second line of the second column, and the total will then be—

Aggregate of stocks and bonds	$1,178,567,882
Aggregate held by foreigners	222,225,315

Source: United States, 33d Congress, 1st Session, *Senate Executive Documents* No. 42, p. 53.

The international role of specie and bills of exchange. Francis Bowen, a professor of philosophy at Harvard, stated in his *Principles of Political Economy* that the exports of a country paid for its imports, with money playing no part other than to facilitate the exchange of goods. He said: "When, in the course of international trade, one country becomes indebted to another, the question whether the deficiency shall be made up by remittances of money or of goods, is one that determines itself. . . . The merchant will send the one which he thinks is less valuable at home, and more valuable abroad, than any other commodity."[16] Bowen also stated that a country could "buy no more foreign products than it has domestic products with which to pay for them. Money and bills of exchange cannot help us pay our debts; they only facilitate and represent the operations out of which those debts have grown."[17]

United States balance of payments, 1868-1869. David A. Wells, Special Commissioner of the Revenue, submitted his fourth annual report to Congress on industry, commerce and revenue in December of 1869. He said that foreigners were so uncertain of the future of the United States during the War between the States, that American securities of all types had been returned for sale at almost any price. By 1863 the United States had virtually no foreign indebtedness. However, by the time of Wells' report in 1869, foreign indebtedness was estimated at approximately $1,400,000,000.[18]

Wells said, "Enormous as is this sum, the process of incurring indebtedness still continues as actively as ever."[19] The reason for this was the adverse balance of payments of the United States. Wells prepared an account of such payments for the fiscal year ending June 30, 1869. This account, shown in Table 2.2, indicated that the United States was annually becoming more indebted to foreigners because of the excess of merchandise imports over exports, interest paid on the outstanding indebtedness, freight and American tourist expenses aboard.

---

[16] Francis Bowen, *The Principles of Political Economy.* Boston: Little, Brown and Company, 1865, pp. 327-328.

[17] *Ibid.*, p. 323.

[18] David A. Wells, *Revenue of the United States.* A reprint of the official report of Wells, U.S. Special Commisioner of the Revenue. London: Macmillan and Co., 1870, p. 28.

[19] *Ibid.*, p. 31.

TABLE 2.2

DAVID A. WELLS' BALANCE OF PAYMENTS OF THE UNITED STATES WITH
FOREIGN COUNTRIES FOR THE FISCAL YEAR ENDING JUNE 30, 1869

Imports of merchandise, gold value		$417,371,765
Exports (gold values)	$275,611,591	
Re-exports, &c.	10,907,753	
		286,519,344
		$130,852,421
Less excess of foreign goods, in bond, 1869 over 1868		14,702,079
Adverse balance 1868-69 merchandise account		$116,150,342

Movement of Specie and Bullion.

Exports	$42,915,966
Re-exports	14,222,414
Total	$57,138,380
Imports	19,654,776
Loss of specie and bullion	$37,483,604

If we suppose the excess of specie and bullion exports to
have been devoted exclusively to the liquidation of balances incurred on the merchandise account, the remaining balance on
this account to be settled for in some other manner would be
$78,666,738.

To this sum must be added the following other items:—

Obligations for interest (paid), estimated	$80,000,000
Excess of freights carried in foreign bottoms	24,000,000
Expenditures of Americans in foreign countries	$25,000,000

Assuming that the sums chargeable to smuggling and undervaluation of imports are counterbalanced by the undervaluation
of exports, the sum total of the adverse balance of indebtedness
of the United States to foreign countries will, at the present time,
probably average about $210,000,000 per annum.

Source: David A. Wells, *Revenue of the United States*. London: Macmillan
and Co., 1870, pp. 31-33.

Wells was quite concerned over the means of financing such an adverse balance of payments, particularly should it continue over an extended period of time. He said:

To meet and settle this constantly increasing and adverse balance there would seem to be, under the present condition of prices and cost of production in the United States, but one resource, viz., to remit certificates of indebtedness—national, State or corporate. And this process is undoubtedly adopted and goes on, month after month and year after year, without occasioning thus far any marked disturbance in the trade and commerce of the country.

Now, whether so great an exchange of evidences of indebtedness for foreign commodities or foreign services is advantageous to the country at large, or how long such a method of liquidating balances can continue, are questions which it is not necessary to immediately consider, inasmuch as we would rather direct attention at this point to the fact that, while before the war we were able to wholly pay for our foreign imports and services with the products of our own industry, including, after the discovery of California and up to the beginning of the war, such a proportion only of our product of gold as it would have been practically useless and even mischievous for us to retain, we are not now so doing, and this latter circumstance would seem to prove beyond question that the aggregate of national production does not maintain the same proportion as formerly to the aggregate of national consumption.[20]

Wells also cautioned the Congress of the United States that sale of securities to foreigners was only deferring payment. He said that, in the long-run, exports of goods and services had to pay for imports as this was an absolute condition upon which commerce was based.

The methodology used by Wells in estimating the accounts appearing in his balance of payments was advanced for his time.[21] He classified the securities composing the foreign indebtedness

[20] *Ibid.*, pp. 33-34.
[21] *Ibid.*, pp. 28-33.

of the United States thus: federal, state, and municipal bonds; railway bonds and shares; canal bonds; mining bonds and shares; real estate mortgages; bank deposits, bills of exchange, and commercial credit. Jay Cook & Co. prepared for Wells an estimate of federal securities outstanding. Estimates of outstanding obligations of the various states and municipal governments which were originally sold abroad were obtained directly from those agencies. Estimates of corporate securities held abroad were based upon reports of the companies and information obtained from bankers. Interest payments were computed by applying a rate of six per cent to the estimated amount of foreign indebtedness.

Net freight payments to foreigners were calculated by subtracting the value of imports and exports carried in American ships from the value carried in foreign ships and applying an average freight charge of eight per cent to the excess. This average eight per cent rate was used after determining the average freight charges as a percentage of the value of the principal articles traded.

The amount estimated for American tourist expenditures abroad was based upon a four-year average of American visitors to foreign countries and foreign visitors to the United States. An estimated $1,000 expenditure per person was applied to the numerical difference in tourism between the two.

This was the stage of development of the balance of payments concept in the United States in 1873. Similar advances were being made in the United Kingdom and they are the subject of the following section.

Bullion Controversy in the United Kingdom, 1797 to 1821

The Bank of England was forced to cease the redemption of paper money in specie because of the scarcity of gold following a run on the Bank on February 25, 1797. This non-convertibility was confirmed by Act of Parliament in May of 1797 and renewed until 1821. The immediate cause of the panic was the threat of a French invasion. However, the gold stock of the Bank had been dwindling for years prior to this occurrence. Beginning in 1793, the specie and bullion supply of the Bank was reduced far below its usual amount. The Committee of Secrecy was appointed to determine the reason.

Witnesses before the Committee of Secrecy. The Committee of Secrecy examined records of imports and exports to see if an unfavorable balance of trade for the preceding years was the cause of the outflow of bullion. Records of trade indicated an excess of exports over imports for each of the years 1793 through 1796. This was contrary to the balance of trade theory which assumed that there would be an inward flow of specie equal to the favorable balance of trade. As this was not the case, other reasons were sought to explain the outflow of gold.

Various witnesses were called before the Committee in an effort to find the explanation. One of these witnesses was Thomas Irving, who succeeded John Tomkyns as Assistant Inspector-General in 1786 and became the Inspector-General the following year when the incumbent of that office died.[22] There had been continuous criticism of the official rates by which exports and imports were valued for almost one hundred years. The validity of these criticisms was recognized by Irving when he warned the Committee that very little reliance could be placed on the value of British manufactures exported in any respect other than in comparisons between different periods. This was due to the lack of care with which entries for non-dutiable goods were made as to type, quantity and quality and the official values placed on merchandise which differed materially from its current value. He said the same problem of valuation existed for imports and re-exports of foreign goods.

In addition to the problems of current values, Irving felt that freight earnings were excluded from the balance of trade. He said the official value for imports was supposed to be their value in the country of origin and the official value of exports their cost in British ports. This method of valuation, he said, appeared to be incorrect in principle because freight added value

---

[22] Great Britain, Parliament, House of Commons, *Reports 1796-1797,* No. 134, XIX, pp. 108-111.

to the commodity. When goods were exported in British ships, freight should be added to the value of exports; and when foreign ships carried goods into Great Britain, freight should be added to their value. Thus, he preferred a c.i.f. to an f.o.b. basis of valuation.

Irving also called attention to the omission from the balance of trade publications of one side of several transactions. He noted especially goods sent to England by persons residing abroad whom he considered English residents, goods in payment of interest on foreign loans, and goods from the East Indies which were payments for territorial revenues accrued by the Crown. In each of these cases, the imports were recorded and helped make it appear that England had an unfavorable balance of trade. However, the offsetting entries were omitted for income from services rendered foreigners, interest, and government revenues. Irving said that instead of regarding these imports as unfavorable they should be regarded as additions to England's wealth.

Two other balance of payments accounts, government capital transactions and unilateral transfers were brought to light by John Pudget in his testimony before the Committee of Secrecy. The Committee established the fact that approximately 300,000 pounds in specie was annually sent to Ireland. They attempted to find the reasons for this movement from John Pudget, an agent for the Bank of Ireland. He stated that most of the flow was due to government loans to Ireland, but that part was due to the private transfer of funds from England to Ireland.[23]

Benjamin Winthrop, a director of the Bank of England, was also called before the Committee. When asked the cause of the decrease in the Bank's holdings of bullion, he answered:

I should impute it, in a great Measure, to the Imperial Loan; to the subsidy to the King of Prussia; to the Amount of Bills drawn for the Expenses of War on the Continent; to the Bills drawn from the West Indies; to the Amount of Neutral Cargoes; and, in general, to such causes as appears

---

[23] *Ibid.*, pp. 38-40.

to me to have no connection with trade or with any Balance of Trade.[24]

Winthrop was then asked, "Do you conceive, that the Drains, which you have mentioned, have been so large as to counteract the Operation of the Balance of Trade in bringing the Specie into the Kingdom?"[25] He replied in the affirmative.

Winthrop, it appears, conceived the balance of payments as encompassing the balance of merchandise trade; current items such as military expenses abroad and subsidies to foreign governments; capital items, such as government loans to foreign governments; and monetary movements, such as bills of exchange. He believed the balance of all these items was paid in specie.

The Chancellor of the Exchequer, William Pitt, was also called before the Committee to give his explanation of the loss of gold. In doing so, he distinguished between the balance of trade and the balance of payments. He said that it was difficult to determine how far "the Balance of Foreign Commerce . . . may have been likely to affect the Balance of actual Payments . . ." between England and foreign countries because neither the quantity nor value of imports and exports could be ascertained with accuracy.[26] However, he concluded that the "Balance of actual Payments" would have been in favor of England so far as commercial transactions were concerned. He believed that if no other circumstances had interfered, the quantity of cash or bullion would have increased. The transactions which the Chancellor said would counteract the effects of a favorable balance of trade were "the great Amount of Sums expanded Abroad, either on account of Subsidies or Loans to Foreign Powers, or on account of Naval or Military Services, in different Parts of the World, defrayed by this Country."[27]

Pitt recognized the differing effects on England's balance of payments of changes of foreign capital in England. He said the transfer of property from England to foreign countries would

[24] *Ibid.*, pp. 42-43.
[25] *Ibid.*, p. 43.
[26] *Ibid.*, p. 100.
[27] *Ibid.*, p. 101.

be a cause for the loss of gold. On the other hand, no remittance of specie was required when property of foreigners was brought into England for the purpose of investment. Pitt stated that the net effect of all the transactions previously mentioned would increase or decrease the coin or bullion of the country "or, as far as this has not actually taken place, there must have been a corresponding Alteration in the State of Debts and Credits between this Country and other Countries."[28]

Terminology. Two of the more active participants in the bullion controversy were John Wheatley and John Foster. Wheatley used the term balance of trade to include invisible and capital transactions as well as merchandise. He identified a favorable balance of trade with a favorable exchange rate. Wheatley stated that in spite of an excess of merchandise exports over imports, the exchange rate had often been unfavorable because of the necessity of making payments to foreigners for things other than merchandise. He specifically mentioned such transactions as expenditures of British residents abroad and dividends paid to foreign owners of British securities. Wheatley said that foreign claims would be paid by bills of exchange when the exchange rate was favorable, and by bullion when it was unfavorable.[29]

Foster presided at the Parliamentary hearings of 1804 on the Irish currency situation. He believed that the nature and effects of the balance of trade had to be clearly determined before the unfavorable exchange rate and the resulting loss of specie in Ireland could be explained. He indicated that confusion over terms was a partial cause of the controversy:

> In the following inquiry, to avoid confusion, two distinct terms shall be used as expressive of two distinct ideas. By the *balance of trade,* the difference between commercial exports and imports shall always be understood; by the *balance of debt,* the difference between money to be paid,

---

[28] *Ibid.,* pp. 101-102.
[29] John Wheatley, *Remarks on Currency and Commerce.* London: Cadell and Davies, 1803, pp. 73-74, 88-91.

and money to be received. The balance of trade necessarily forms a part of the balance of debt.[30]

Foster said the balance of debt would tend toward equilibrium because gold would flow into that country which had excessive debt claims upon other countries. Gold movements would then lessen the pressure on the exchange rates.

The Bullion Report of 1810. The Bullion Committee consisted of twenty-one members including Francis Horner, who was chairman. The Committee was appointed to investigate the cause of the high price of gold, the money in circulation and the state of the exchange rate.[31] This committee received reports from William Irving, the Inspector-General, concerning the British trade for the years 1805 through 1809 to discover whether or not the financial problems were due to an unfavorable balance of trade.

The Committee recognized the deficiency of the data included in the report. It specifically noted the absence of the freight, interest, monetary transactions between the governments of England and Ireland, smuggled goods, bullion and government bills of exchange drawn for the purpose of supporting foreign military forces.

Since the Committee was already convinced that it was the balance of payments rather than the balance of trade which determined the flow of specie, it would seem that the next logical step would have been to make some attempt to quantify the items mentioned above to determine the claims for payment and receipt, or, in other words, to have prepared a balance of payments. Instead, it made some adjustments to Irving's report, included cash and bullion as part of the exports and imports, and arrived at an adjusted balance of trade. The adjusted statements showed an excess of exports over imports. On the basis

---

[30] John Leslie Foster, *An Essay on the Principle of Commercial Exchanges.* London: Printed for J. Hatchard, 1804, p. 4.

[31] Great Britain, Parliament, House of Commons, *Report from the Select Committee on the High Price of Gold Bullion.* Reprinted in the *Paper Pound of 1797-1821,* with an introduction by Edwin Cannan. London: King and Son, Ltd., 1919, pp. 26-29, 69.

of these and other findings, the Committee felt that the difficulty was due to an excess issue of inconvertible paper currency. It recommended that specie payments by the Bank of England should not be resumed in less than two years from the date of the report.

Reforms in the merchandise accounts. Despite the criticism of the trade accounts aroused by the bullion controversy, few changes were made until 1853. At that time the responsibility for preparing the statements of trade was transferred from the Customs Department to the Statistical Department of the Board of Trade. However, the Statistical Office of the Customs Department again assumed the task in 1871.

A. W. Funblanque, the head of the Statistical Department, recognized the inaccuracy of the statement of trade because of the continued use of the official values for imports and exports of foreign goods.[32] Declared values had been used for the exports of domestic goods since 1798, although the official values were also given. Beginning in 1854, values for imports and re-exports were based principally upon the average market prices in London and Liverpool. These values included charges for freight and landing, but excluded customs duties.[33]

In a memorandum by the Inspector-General of Imports and Exports, concerning the method of determining the values of imports, John A. Messenger stated that declared values were used for those articles of imports in which the tariff prescribed their value to be stated. In other cases, the value was computed using average prices of the articles in London, Liverpool and Hull. These average prices were supplied by leading merchants and brokers and by three employees who were retained for the purpose of obtaining these prices. The average of the prices was determined monthly. In those cases where the prices of articles varied according to the country of origin, separate prices for

---

[32] Great Britain, Parliament, House of Commons, *Accounts and Papers.* 1854-1855, LI, p. iv.
[33] *Ibid.,* p. 337.

each country were used.[34] This practice was continued until 1871 when declared values were used exclusively in all the accounts.[35]

A United Kingdom Balance of Payments, 1814-1832

John Marshall, a statistical writer, presented an account showing the value of imports and exports with each part of the world for 1814-1832. He arranged the countries into three groups so that he could show the relationships among commercial transactions, loans, services and short-term monetary movements. The three groups were: Europe (Table 2.3); Africa, America and the Foreign West Indies; and the East Indies and China, British West Indies and the whale fisheries. By this means, Marshall attempted to show how the United Kingdom's excess of exports over imports was paid by other countries.

This is the first time anyone in England had made a formal attempt to show, by means of a single statement, the relationship between commercial and financial transactions. The figures for each years' trade did not balance, but they were arranged in such a way as to place together all the transactions which created claims for payment on the United Kingdom. The transactions which created claims for payment on the United Kingdom were imports of merchandise, English tourist expenditures, freight paid to foreigners, loans and investments in other countries made by residents, and the withdrawal of foreign investments from the United Kingdom. Marshall termed the total of the foreign claims on the United Kingdom the "total equivalents" of the United Kingdom's exports of merchandise and bullion and of the interest earned on foreign loans.

According to Marshall, when the excess of bullion exports over imports was added to the merchandise export surplus, it would approximate an "Amount to the Sum for which Annuities

---

[34] *Annual Report on the Commerce and Navigation of the United States, 1867, op. cit.,* pp. LXXIV-LXXVII. This report contains a reprint of the memorandum issued by the Statistical Department of the Board of Trade in April 1864.

[35] Great Britain, Parliament, House of Commons, *Accounts and Papers,* 1871, LXIII, p. 2.

TABLE 2.3

UNITED KINGDOM BALANCE OF PAYMENTS FOR 1819

European Countries from whence Imported	£
1 Russia	2,589,922
2 Sweden	164,799
3 Norway	101,899
4 Denmark	170,786
5 Prussia	624,125
6 Germany	576,067
7 Holland	635,279
8 Flanders	203,856
9 France	642,012
10 Portugal, Azores and Madeira	509,572
11 Spain and the Canaries	875,392
12 Gibraltar	14,572
13 Malta, and Ionian Isles	132,888
14 Italy	972,647
15 Turkey and the Morea	266,548
16 Guernsey, Jersey, and Man	151,680
From all Europe into Ireland	—
a Total Imports, UNITED KINGDOM	8,632,047
b By Government Bills	1,500,000
c By Loan and Investment Bills	5,000,000
d By Absentee Bills	6,000,000
e By Foreign Stock withdrawn	2,000,000
f By Foreign Freights	750,000
g Excessive advance in price	—
h Total Equivalents for *j–l.*	23,882,047
i To EXPORTS.	25,572,643
j To do. direct from Nos 23-5.	3,000,000
k To Interest on c.	1,500,000
l To excess of Bullion Exported.	—

Source: Adapted from John Marshall, *A Digest of all the Accounts Relating to the Population, Productions, Revenues, Financial Operations, Manufactures, Shipping, Colonies, Commerce, etc. of the United Kingdom of Great Britain and Ireland.* (London: Printed by J. Haddon, 1833), p. 120. f.

were created during the same period—the way in which the excess of Value Exported was Equalized, or Balanced in Commercial Account, having been by the *Bills* drawn in different parts of the World by the Agents of the Government on Account of Subsidies, Secret Services, and for Supplies for the Fleet and Armies every where distributed; which Bills, or an amount equivalent thereto, were Annually converted into Stock, for which Annuities were granted."[36]

Equilibrium in the Balance of Payments

There were many efforts during the latter part of the nineteenth century to understand the relationships between the balance of payments and the rates of exchange. The distinction between the balance of trade and the balance of payments was involved in these attempts. There was much interest and concern over the means of financing an adverse balance of payments and how equilibrium was to be restored, both in the long and short-run.

Defense of the principles embodied in the Bullion Report of 1810. Three outstanding economists, David Ricardo, Henry Thornton and Thomas Tooke, explained their concept of achieving balance of payments equilibrium while speaking in defense of the Bullion Report. David Ricardo, one of the founders of the classical school of political economy, was also a successful trader on the London Stock Exchange. He influenced the Bullion Committee Report of 1810 by his theory explaining the high price of bullion. In answer to criticism of the conclusions of the Committee report, Ricardo said there had to be a favorable balance of trade or else no explanation could be given for the payment of Great Britain's foreign expenditures. He said: "On a view of the whole trade of the country, we have discharged a debt to Europe by the exportation of goods to some other part of the world, and the balance of payments, however large it may

---

[36] John Marshall, *A Digest of all the Accounts Relating to the Population, Productions, Revenues, Financial Operations, Manufactures, Shipping, Colonies, Commerce, etc. of the United Kingdom of Great Britain and Ireland.* London: Printed by J. Haddon, 1833, p. 120a.

be, must ultimately be paid by the produce of the labour of the people of this country."[37] Apparently he meant that the foreign receipts of a country from the foreign sale of goods and services must in the long-run equal its payments.

Henry Thornton, a successful banker, was considered one of the foremost authorities on finance by his colleagues in Parliament. He achieved this recognition as a result of the bullion controversy as he was one of the members of the Bullion Committee of 1810 that investigated the high price of gold. In discussing the reasons for having renewed the law suspending cash payments by the Bank of England, he contributed to the development of the balance of payments concepts.[38]

Thornton did not distinguish between the balance of trade and balance of payments until 1811 in a speech before Parliament. Earlier, he used the term balance of trade in the sense of balance of payments. He spoke of the types of transactions which would make the balance of trade favorable or unfavorable. Among these transactions were subsides to foreign countries, loans to other countries, dividends paid to foreign owners of British stocks, property sent to the West Indies for the purpose of investment, capital transfers to Great Britain from the East Indies, bills of exchange and gold bullion.

Thornton was also concerned with the equilibrium of commercial transactions. He believed that the balance of trade could not continue for any great length of time to be either highly favorable or highly unfavorable, because the balance had to be paid in bullion or else constitute a debt. He could not imagine that bullion could flow out of a country indefinitely or that other countries would wish to extend unlimited credit. In the long-run, England's capacity to buy abroad, then, was restricted to the ability of English residents to finance their purchases from foreigners by receipts from the foreign sales of goods and serv-

---

[37] David Ricardo, "Reply to Mr. Bosanquet's Practical Observations on the Report of the Bullion Committee," Reprinted in *Economic Essays*, ed. E. C. K. Gonner. London: C. Bell and Sons, 1926, p. 105.

[38] Henry Thornton, *An Enquiry into the Nature and Effects of the Paper Credit of Great Britain*, edited by F. A. von Hayek. New York: Farrar and Rinehard, Inc., 1939, pp. 141-145, 332.

ices. In the short-run this was not necessarily the case, and an unfavorable balance of payments could be financed by bullion or short-term debt.

In 1840 Thomas Tooke sought the answer to the continued pressure upon the exchanges and the resulting loss of bullion from the United Kingdom.[39] He said that in the last two decades of the eighteenth century, the causes were the support of troops abroad and subsidies paid to foreign powers. In 1818, according to Tooke, the explanation was found in unusually large merchandise imports and foreign loans negotiated with investors in the United States. The causes in the late 1830's were again due to heavy merchandise imports, substantial credits to the United States and the purchase of Dutch and American securities. The pressure on the foreign exchange rate and the resulting flow of gold was not only due to the merchandise account, but to various invisible transactions as well. Thus, the balance of payments was influenced by merchandise, subsidies, military expenses abroad, foreign loans and investments, and short-term credits.

Inclusiveness of the balance of payments. In 1852 an economist, J. R. McCulloch, distinguished between the balance of trade and the balance of payments by limiting the balance of trade to merchandise transactions. He regarded the balance of trade theory as erroneous because it ignored the effect of other international transactions upon the balance of payments.[40]

A decade later, George Joachim Goschen, a director of the Bank of England who subsequently (1886) became Chancellor of the Exchequer, studied the circumstances under which the foreign exchanges were influenced by the balance of trade. Goschen used the term "balance of trade" synonymously with international indebtedness. He said it was an error to imagine international indebtedness to be incurred simply by the importa-

---

[39] Thomas Tooke, *A History of Prices and of the State of Circulation in 1838 and 1839.* London: Longman, Orme, Brown, Green and Longmans, 1840, pp. 71-73.

[40] J. R. McCulloch, *A Dictionary, Practical, Theoretical, and Historical, of Commerce and Commercial Navigation,* edited by Henry Vethake. Philadelphia: A. Hart, 1852, I, pp. 61-63.

tion of foreign commodities, and to look upon the balance of trade as consisting only of imports and exports of merchandise. Instead, it was necessary to examine all the transactions with other countries before the mutual indebtedness could be determined. He stated that payments for any purpose had "the same effect as payments for direct importations."[41]

According to Goschen, a foreign loan was a favorable item in the balance of indebtedness of the recipient country rather than that of the lender. At the time the loan was contracted, it had the same effect upon the balance of indebtedness of the lending country as an import and as an export to the borrowing nation. Interest on debts were included in the balance of indebtedness because they constituted an immediate liability. Profits, commissions, and freights earned were all considered as having the same effect as commodity exports. Interest and commissions paid to English investors were part of the receipts by which England paid its foreign liabilities.[42]

When the indebtedness of a country became excessive and the liabilities could no longer be settled by shipments of bullion, equilibrium was restored by exporting securities. Goschen said that long-term debts did not enter into consideration until the time for payment because "the balance of trade depends upon the transactions which have to be settled, not upon those which by common consent, are held in abeyance for a long term of years."[43] Since long-term securities involved no immediate claim they were not regarded as offsetting current debts.

Payment of foreign liabilities. John Elliott Cairnes, a professor of political economy, used the United Kingdom and the United States to illustrate the relationship between the balance of trade, invisible items and indebtedness.[44] For the years 1856 to 1870 inclusively, imports into the United Kingdom exceeded ex-

[41] George Joachim Goschen, *The Theory of the Foreign Exchanges.* London: Effingham Wilson, 1861, p. 12.

[42] *Ibid.,* pp. 13-19.

[43] *Ibid.,* p. 16.

[44] John Elliott Cairnes, *Some Leading Principles of Political Economy Newly Expounded.* New York: Harper and Brothers, 1874, pp. 355-358. Cf. Adam Seybert, 1818.

ports by 57,000,000 pounds sterling. He thought that this annual amount was partly paid in services, mostly freight, but that mainly it was paid by profits, interest and dividends on Britain's foreign investments. The normal state of trade in the United Kingdom should be an excess of imports over exports to offset extensive foreign investment if equilibrium was to be achieved in the balance of payments.

Cairnes said the United States offered an illustration of the opposite type. Americans traveled extensively abroad and borrowed heavily in Europe which tended to create money obligations. Therefore, the normal state of trade for the United States was an excess of exports over imports, for this was the only way that the liabilities to foreigners could be discharged.[45]

---

[45] *Ibid.,* pp. 359-372.

3

Current Transactions and Capital Investment in the Balance of Payments, 1874-1914

The protectionist versus the free trade controversy was resumed in the United Kingdom as a result of the depressed conditions of foreign trade in the 1870's. A decade later a similar discussion arose in the United States over the continued loss of gold reserves despite a favorable balance of trade. During both of these discussions estimates were made of services and foreign investments and indebtedness. The search for bases for these estimates increased the knowledge of the interrelationships among the items in the balance of payments. Perception of these relationships was essential to the development of a concept which was inclusive of all the international economic transactions of a nation.

The United Kingdom's Trade Deficit and Foreign Investment

Extensive use was made of trade statistics by the protectionists to show that the United Kingdom was suffering from its one-sided free trade policy. Interest grew in finding a method of measuring the balance of trade and determining the means by which it was financed. Those who desired greater tariff protection for British goods insisted that the United Kingdom's unfavorable balance of trade was being financed by a reduction in foreign investment. The free traders refuted this argument by pointing to the invisible transactions which were largely in favor of the United Kingdom and which prevented the loss of gold and the reduction of foreign investment.

Adjustments to the merchandise account. Stephen Bourne, Chief of the Statistical Department of H.M. Customs, made several adjustments to the balance of trade of the United Kingdom to show more accurately the excess of merchandise imports over exports for the period 1854 to 1876.[1] He said that while the change to computed values for imports in 1854 was desirable, the reported values of imports and exports still did not provide a suitable basis for comparison because of the method of valuation. Both exports and imports were valued in British ports, thus imports included charges for freight while exports did not.

Bourne estimated the freight charges attributable to imports to correct this deficiency. Freight charges were calculated by selecting the principal articles imported and obtaining quotations of freight charges for each commodity from the exporting country. The percentage of average freight charges to the value of each principal article imported was computed, and then applied to total imports. The freight charges were then deducted from imports, which were valued c.i.f., to adjust them to an f.o.b. basis.

Two adjustments were made to the reported values of exports. They were increased by the value of ships sold to foreigners and by the sales of fuel and ships stores to foreign ships in British ports. The estimate for the sale value of ships was based upon inquiry as to the average price per ton of shipping sold.

Bourne explained that the trade deficit was financed by the annual income on foreign investments, government revenues from India, profits on foreign trading, and shipping earnings. These earnings were sufficient to offset the charges for the excess of merchandise imports over exports and to enable the United Kingdom to increase its foreign investment.

Financing a trade deficit. William Rathbone, a Liverpool merchant, stated in a letter to the editor of *The Economist* in

---

[1] Stephen Bourne, "The Growing Preponderance of Imports over Exports in the Foreign and Colonial Trade of the United Kingdom," *Journal of the Royal Statistical Society,* March, 1877, pp. 24-29.

1877 that trade statistics as published by the Board of Trade required adjustments to determine the proper excess of merchandise imports over exports. One adjustment was needed to eliminate payments made to British shipping companies for freight and insurance charges on merchandise imports which were reported at a c.i.f. value. The second was to add the freight and insurance earnings of British companies to the reported value of exports, which were reported on an f.o.b. basis. These adjustments eliminated the transactions involving only residents of the United Kingdom and placed both exports and imports on a comparable c.i.f. basis. Rathbone said that a more reliable balance of merchandise trade could be determined from the adjusted values.

He was concerned that the United Kingdom had been living beyond its means internationally and, as a result, was faced with the danger of decreasing its net foreign investment. He said there were five ways in which imports could be financed: by exports of merchandise and freight earnings; profits of trade abroad other than in the export trade; earnings on foreign investment; sale of securities to foreigners; and exports of specie. Rathbone considered the first three ways of financing the most desirable, because purchases from foreigners were paid by current earnings from foreigners. The last two means of financing purchases abroad were by the reduction of capital, that is, net foreign investment.[2]

Effect of a change in residence on foreign investment. Edward Wagg wrote to the editor of *The Economist* commenting upon Rathbone's letter of the previous month. He added an item which he thought Rathbone should have considered in "settling the balance of trade."[3] Wagg said: "Vast fortunes are realised in the new country, and large numbers of colonists return home, bringing with them their wealth to add to the capital already accumulated at home. Such new capital must surely be reckoned on the credit side of our national account."[4]

[2] *The Economist*, November 24, 1877, pp. 1394-1396.
[3] *The Economist*, December 8, 1877, p. 1458.
[4] *Ibid.*

Wagg stated that if this adjustment were considered, then Rathbone would be incorrect in his belief that England was financing imports through reduction of investments abroad.

Increasing foreign investment. A. D. McKay, a Liverpool businessman, wrote to the editor of the *Economist* explaining how the United Kingdom was increasing its foreign investments by means of services rendered foreigners.[5] He showed this by adjusting the Board of Trade returns for the years 1858 to 1876. McKay used a nineteen-year period because the figures for any particular year were unimportant, and data on international transactions only became meaningful when examined for a series of years.

The returns published by the Board of Trade concerned only merchandise; and even then, exports and imports were valued on different bases. McKay made adjustments to put both on a comparable basis and estimated several service transactions, such as insurance and commissions, which were not included in the published statistics. The estimates were crude and were based primarily upon percentages of the value of exports and imports.

McKay summarized these adjustments in tabular form. Receipts exceeded payments in this presentation and McKay assumed the balance financed additional foreign investment.

Total claims and demands on foreign countries. William Newmarch, in an address to the Royal Statistical Society, presented his interpretation of the effect of England's policy of free trade, in view of high tariffs used by other countries and the growing competition from other rising manufacturing nations.[6] He concluded that tariffs merely reduced trade and hurt everyone, but did not alter England's trading position in the world, and that the existing free trade policy was best for England at that time.

---

[5] *Ibid.*, pp. 1458-1459.

[6] William Newmarch, "On the Progress of the Foreign Trade of the United Kingdom since 1856, with Especial Reference to the Effects Produced upon it by the Protectionist Tariffs of other Countries," *Journal of the Royal Statistical Society*, June 1878, pp. 197-202.

In his capacity as editor of the *Journal of the Royal Statistical Society*, Newmarch proposed a plan for the regular and systematic presentation of the official returns of the Board of Trade "into a concise and tabular form." The form and arrangement of these abstracts were intended to present a uniform record so that, when continued through a series of years, the character and changes in trade would be evident. He believed that such a presentation of Britain's trade beginning in 1856 would either substantiate or refute the controversy over the doctrine of free trade.

Newmarch analyzed the United Kingdom's trade statistics for the years 1856 to 1877 and found that imports had grown relatively faster than exports. This, alone, was inconclusive for if "the total claims or demands of the United Kingdom on foreign countries" were desired, Newmarch said it would be necessary to make the following estimates:

1. For merchandise, freight, and profits, etc. thereon, exported; and also for freight and charges on merchandise imported.

2. For interest and dividends on capital belonging to natives or others resident in United Kingdom, and invested or employed abroad.

3. For fortunes accumulated by British and foreign subjects abroad, and yearly transferred to the United Kingdom.

4. For the principal or capital amounts sent abroad from the United Kingdom, to be invested or employed in foreign and colonial loans; in bonds, etc., of foreign and colonial undertakings; and in advances in foreign and colonial territories.[7]

Invisible transactions. Sir Robert Giffen, assistant editor of the *Economist* until his appointment as Chief of the Statistical Department of the Board of Trade in 1876, emphasized several points concerning the accuracy of trade statistics.[8] Absolute ac-

---

[7] *Ibid.*, pp. 202-203.

[8] Robert Giffen, "The Use of Import and Export Statistics," *Journal of the Royal Statistical Society*, June 1882, pp. 181-194.

curacy could not be attained because of smuggling and lack of knowledge on the part of the shippers and importers concerning values. Giffen estimated the range of error on this account to be as high as six per cent in many cases.

There were also problems involving comparison of data for a series of years. Official values were used for imports up to 1854, computed values to 1871 and declared values subsequently. There were serious discrepancies introduced by these changes in the bases for valuation. There was also a change in the method of assigning imports and exports to particular countries. In former years, the country of shipment basis was used whereas the new basis in use was the ultimate origin or destination of the goods. Comparability of trade statistics over a series of years was also impaired by fluctuations in prices, disturbances in trade patterns due to wars and to new gold discoveries. In view of all these considerations, published statistics of trade had to be used with care or erroneous conclusions could be drawn from them.

Giffen said that merchandise trade was only a part of the international accounts of a country which also included services. He estimated the annual revenue from freight, insurance and bankers' commissions which he said was really "an invisible export."[9] Giffen believed if these items were so considered that it would "revolutionise the conception of the international balance between this country and other nations."[10]

Giffen contended that the capital of the United Kingdom was not impaired by the excess of merchandise imports over exports. As a matter of fact, he said the United Kingdom was steadily increasing overseas investments because of the many invisible items which increased the United Kingdom's foreign receipts over payments. This current balance was used to purchase foreign securities. Giffen thought it should be evident to anyone who watched the London Stock Exchange that Britain's foreign investments were increasing because there was a constant increase in the number of foreign securities being sold in the United Kingdom.

---

[9] *Ibid.*, p. 219.
[10] *Ibid.*, pp. 219-223.

Sources of foreign investments. Stephen Bourne agreed with Giffen that it was erroneous to claim that the United Kingdom was reducing its foreign investments because its merchandise imports exceeded its exports. There were service transactions such as freight, insurance, bank charges and commissions, ships sold to foreigners, interest on overseas investments and profits on commercial operations abroad to be considered. He said of these earnings: "They doubtless largely exceed any quantity of goods we may import above those for which our exports pay, and furnish the source from whence we extend our investments, contract for loans, and purchase property abroad.[11] Bourne included bullion and coin in his calculation of the balance of trade, but looked upon it as "a floating balance available by the lenders of money in exchange for bills of exchange, loans and investments, with which it is constantly interchangeable. . . ."[12]

Study of the balance of trade of the United Kingdom from 1865 to 1902. George J. Shaw-Lefevre was unimpressed by arguments that the wealth of the United Kingdom was being drained by the excess of imports over exports. He said it was evidence of accumulating wealth, not poverty. He also stated that if it were true that more had been purchased abroad than could be paid during the preceding forty years, the process of ruin would have long since been complete. Actually, he said, the reverse was true. During the period 1865 to 1902 there had been a net increase in England's stock of gold and silver and an increase in foreign investment.[13]

Shaw-Lefevre said the reason that England's trade returns showed an excess of imports over exports was due partly to the basis of valuation (imports, c.i.f.; exports, f.o.b.) and partly to the omission from the returns of the many sources of British overseas receipts. Or, as Thomas Irving had pointed out a century

---

[11] Stephen Bourne, "Progress on the External Trade of the United Kingdom in Recent Years," *Journal of the Royal Statistical Society,* June 1893, p. 191.

[12] *Ibid.,* p. 190.

[13] George J. Shaw-Lefevre (Baron Eversley), *The Balance of Trade.* London: Cassell and Co., Ltd., 1903, p. 5.

earlier, the trade returns showed the results of only half of the entry for these transactions. The imports were recorded but not the receipts from overseas sources by which the imports were paid.[14]

To correct the deficiencies in the published accounts of England's international accounts, Shaw-Lefevre adjusted the merchandise account and added the other transactions which had not previously been taken into account. The results of his study of England's international accounts from 1865 to 1902 were summarized in a revised statement of accounts which is shown in Table 3.1. Included in the statement were sources of British receipts, such as interest, governmental income from India, pensions paid to British residents by other countries, personal service earnings of British residents temporarily overseas, and transfers of property by persons changing their residency from other countries to England.[15]

The statement showed an excess of receipts over payments for goods and services. According to Shaw-Lefevre this excess was used to increase England's foreign investments. He attempted to substantiate the accuracy of this estimate by calculating the increase in England's foreign investments during this period. He made these estimates by capitalizing the interest income from overseas investments as shown by the records of the Excise and Revenue Departments. It was noted that the amounts shown in the statement were not to be taken as exact, because many were only approximations. However, he felt that they were sufficiently in agreement with the actual situation to warrant general conclusions.[16]

The detrimental effects of the free trade policy. John Holt Schooling, a consulting actuary for insurance companies, contended that England was suffering from a "one-way" concept of free trade. While England allowed imports to enter freely, the other nations of the world were imposing duties which decreased England's exports. He analyzed the trade statistics of eighteen

[14] *Ibid.*, p. 7.
[15] *Ibid.*, pp. 9-10.
[16] *Ibid.*, pp. 12-15.

TABLE 3.1

GEORGE JOHN SHAW-LEFEVRE'S BALANCE OF TRADE

000,000 omitted.

Years.	1. Value of Imports, after deducting Re-exports, and 5 per cent. for freight on British ships, insurance, and commissions.	2. Value of Exports, adding 10 per cent. on Exports and Re-exports for freight on British ships, insurance, &c., and for exporters' profit.	3. Difference between 1 and 2, the net excess of Imports over Exports.	4. Estimated interest on British capital invested in Foreign and Colonial securities bearing Income Tax.	5. Estimated annual remittances to England from Indian Government, and other remittances of Englishmen abroad and in colonies, not paying Income Tax.	6. Total of 4 and 5.	7. Difference between 6 and 3, representing probable annual investments abroad of British capital.
1865	206	187	19	28	25	53	34
1866 to 1870 yearly average.	232	209	23	35	27	62	39
1871 to 1875	284	270	14	45	29	74	60
1876 to 1880	308	225	83	55	31	86	3
1881 to 1885	316	261	55	57	33	90	35
1886 to 1890	308	265	43	67	35	102	59
1891 to 1895	339	255	84	80	37	117	33
1896 to 1900	389	281	108	88	39	127	19
1901, 1902 2 years' average.	432*	306*	126	92	40	132	6

The estimated capital sum on which interest was due in 1865 ... ... £ 560,000,000

The aggregate of investments between 1865 and 1902 1,290,000,000

The present estimated capital sum 1,850,000,000

* Deduction has been made from the amount of exports for the years 1901 and 1902 of the values of new ships exported, which were included for the first time in the Trade Returns of the Board of Trade, and were not included in those of previous years. For these years the amounts were 8 millions and 7 millions. There are no means of ascertaining how much should have been added to the values of exports for previous years. It is probable that the values of new ships exported gradually rose in the 35 years from 1865 to 1900 from 2 or 3 millions to 7 millions, and averaged about 5 millions. On the other hand, the values of the excess of Imports over exports of gold and silver coin and bullion are not included in the yearly values of imports. These have averaged about 5 millions a year. It has been thought therefore, that the two items may fairly be considered as balancing one another on the opposite sides of the international account.

Source: George John Shaw-Lefevre (Baron Eversley), *The Balance of Trade*. London: Cassell and Co., Ltd., 1903, p. 23.

of England's largest trading partners and found that in all but three of them, England's share of their imports had declined.[17]

Schooling hoped to prove the superiority of investigation of economic fact over doctrine as a guide to the formulation of trade policy. He sought to establish the practice of investigating trade tendencies over a long period of years. He said a period of twenty-five years was necessary to obtain a broad view of the course of trade. By watching changes in the proportion of each class of imports to total imports over a period of years, changes in the course of trade could be ascertained.[18]

Schooling criticized the Board of Trade for publishing what he called "a mass of crude statistics" with which it was impossible for anyone to see vitally important trends in trading relationships with other nations.[19] He thought isolated statistics of trade were of no value, and only when they were grouped and summarized could soundly based conclusions be drawn from them.

Schooling was aware that the import surplus was partially financed by the invisible items in the balance of international payments. However, he believed the remainder was financed by transferring United States securities to American ownership and increasing the foreign ownership of British securities.[20]

Estimates of the United Kingdom's foreign investment. Sir George Paish presented two papers before the Royal Statistical Society, the first in 1909 and the second in 1911, concerning the estimation of the United Kingdom's foreign investments.[21] There was a great deal of interest in these estimates because of the controversy over England's trade policy and claims that these investments were being liquidated. As such a comprehensive study had not previously been made, there was little factual basis

---

[17] John Holt Schooling, *The British Trade Book*, 3rd. ed., London: John Murray, 1908, pp. 153-191.

[18] *Ibid.,* pp. XXXIII, 14-15.

[19] *Ibid.,* p. 286.

[20] *Ibid.,* pp. 90-93.

[21] Sir George Paish, "Great Britain's Capital Investments in Other Lands," *Journal of the Royal Statistical Society*, September 1909, pp. 465-480, and "Great Britain's Capital Investments in Individual Colonial and Foreign Countries," *Journal of the Royal Statistical Society*, January 1911, pp. 167-187.

for proving or disproving these contentions. Once a benchmark was established, similar studies could determine changes that occurred. This was the purpose of Paish's second study completed in 1911.

Paish reported that the Commissioners of Inland Revenue set out in detail the amount of income derived from some but not all foreign investments. Although the Commissioners included income from capital loaned to various foreign governments, a large amount of income from various industrial, commercial, and financial institutions was not detailed. Therefore, he supplemented the Commissioner's data by surveying the companies operating abroad which had raised capital in the United Kingdom and ascertained the amount of their overseas investments and annual profits.

Paish excluded all conversions from new subscriptions so that there would be no duplications of capital raised. He also omitted from his total any loans in default. New securities were taken at the price of issue less commissions so as to arrive, as nearly as possible, at the exact amount of aggregate subscriptions. He included only those portions of international loans that had been subscribed in Great Britain.

The relation of foreign investment to the balance of trade. Edgar Crammond, Assistant Secretary of the Liverpool Stock Exchange, attended the meeting of the Royal Statistical Society at which Paish's first paper was presented. He agreed with Paish's estimate of income on foreign investment, but said he wanted to stress "the important part investments of capital abroad played in the adjustment of the trade balance. . . ."[22]

Crammond noted the excess of imports over exports (both including specie), but said in considering the balance of trade, one would have to consider invisible imports and exports. Therefore, the amount of capital invested abroad should be added to the debit balance obtained from the excess of imports of commodities and specie over the exports of commodities and specie. Two other debit items were also included: earning of foreign

[22] Edgar Crammond, "Discussion on Mr. George Paish's Paper," *Journal of the Royal Statistical Society*, September 1909, p. 481.

banks in the United Kingdom and the interest paid foreigners on British securities. These debits were offset by income on foreign investments, freight, earnings of exporters, insurance companies, banks and commission houses carrying on business aboard. Crammond said this was a "rough attempt at a balance sheet."[23]

The export of capital from the United Kingdom. Charles K. Hobson, an employee of the Board of Trade, made a study of the relationship between the balance of trade and the movement of capital. He said the statements of trade prepared by the Board of Trade included transactions which should be excluded, and at the same time omitted transactions which should be taken into consideration in "a national balance-sheet of commercial transactions."[24]

The merchandise account was the first to draw the attention of Hobson. He suggested that imports, valued on a c.i.f. basis should be reduced by the amount of payments made to British firms for freight and insurance. Since exports were valued on an f.o.b. basis, the account should include the earnings of British firms for freight and insurance. The merchandise account also excluded transactions in ships and diamonds which were relatively important foreign transactions. Hobson then noted the absence from the Board of Trade returns of banking commissions; government receipts; foreign communication services; tourist expenditures; emigrants' remittances; diplomatic, consular and military expenses of the government.[25]

Although Hobson could find little basis for estimating some of these transactions, he attempted to calculate those of the greatest importance. He estimated freight by three different methods. The first method involved the use of average receipts per ton of shipping. In the second, world exports, assumed on an f.o.b. basis, were subtracted from imports, assumed to be on a c.i.f. basis. Freight was then allocated to countries on the basis of their shipping tonnage. The third method of estimating freight

---

[23] *Ibid.*, p. 482.

[24] Charles K. Hobson, *The Export of Capital.* London: Constable and Co., Ltd., 1914, p. 164.

[25] *Ibid.*, pp. 166-168.

was based upon the total expenditures of the shipping lines. These expenditures included an imputed rate of return on invested capital. Total revenues from freight were assumed equal to total expenditures. Hobson reduced shipping earnings by the amount of British shipping expenditures in foreign ports for fuel, stores, repairs, and other items. This deduction was estimated by an account of expenses of two tramp steamers on seven voyages. Their expenses averaged approximately thirty per cent of their total receipts.[26]

Government services were estimated by scheduling the commissions payable to the Bank of England and Ireland for the management of debt, charges on account of departments in India, military stores and charges. The figures for remittances were based upon money orders issued in the United Kingdom and abroad as given in the annual report of the Postmaster-General. The amounts used for ship sales were obtained from the register of shipping.[27]

Hobson summarized the results of his study of the United Kingdom's foreign investment in two tables. In the first, he subtracted the merchandise import surplus, which included gold and silver, from the estimates of the various invisible transactions. This left a balance which he considered a combination of capital and interest. These two accounts were separated in the second table by subtracting the interest income as reported to the Inland Revenue Department from total capital and interest. Hobson considered the balance remaining to be the net addition to the United Kingdom's investment, or as he termed it, the export of capital.[28]

Balance of Trade, Foreign Indebtedness and Gold Movements: The United States, 1874 to 1914.

The United States began to have a favorable balance of trade in 1874, and continued to have such a balance with few exceptions through 1895. In spite of this, the United States ex-

---

26 *Ibid.*, pp. 171-187.
27 *Ibid.*, pp. 188-196.
28 *Ibid.*, pp. 197-204.

ported gold in all but eight of these years (1878-1883, 1887-1888). Only three of the years that gold was exported (1875, 1889 and 1893) showed an unfavorable trade balance.[29] The cause, as explained by several writers of the period, was attributed to current transactions other than merchandise in which United States expenditures usually exceeded receipts. In discussing this question, the relationships among the balance of trade, services, transfers, investment and specie were shown by these writers. They were clearly and concisely summarized by George Paish preparatory to presenting a balance of payments for the United States in 1909.

Loss of gold from the United States 1874 to 1895. One of the earliest articles concerning the loss of gold from the United States appeared in *The Commerical and Financial Chronicle* in 1882. Summary schedules were given of the merchandise trade and the United States stock of gold during 1881 and 1882. The relationship between them was explained in the following statement:

It appears from the foregoing statements as to the condition of our trade, taken in connection with the other well-known items against us, of interest, freights, . . . that it is sufficiently evident that we are now in debt to Europe, and that if gold is not sent in considerable amounts, it is because of balances left here, securities purchased and loans made. Some seek to offset against this adverse showing, the gold brought by immigrants, on the basis of an estimate by a European authority on an average of $200 for each head of a family.[30]

A decade later, J. C. Cross explained the reason for this continued depletion of the gold reserve of the United States by saying: "The excess of exports over imports, by which the United States habitually discharges its indebtedness to this and other

---

[29] Matthew Simon, "The United States Balance of Payments 1861-1900," National Bureau of Economic Research, *Studies in Income and Wealth,* Princeton: University Press, 1960, XXIV, pp. 700-705.

[30] *The Commercial and Financial Chronicle,* May 6, 1882, p. 500.

European countries, is not now sufficiently large for the purpose, and gold is being exported to make up the deficiency."[31] He asserted that despite policies to curtail imports and increase exports to "restore the equilibrium between her receipts and payments"[32] the gold drain continued because of new liabilities arising from the purchase of American securities in the London market. Apparently the loss of gold was at least partly caused by a change in liabilities from a long to a short-term status. As insufficient bills of exchange were available to pay these new liabilities, they were paid in specie.

Alfred S. Heidelbach, investment banker, said gold was needed to pay this indebtedness because of the unwillingness of foreigners to hold, or to continue to increase their holdings of, United States securities. Therefore, gold, the only international medium of exchange, was required to meet these obligations. Despite a favorable balance of trade the United States increased its short-term indebtedness to foreigners because of American residents' travel abroad, freight, dividends and interest and profits of foreign companies operating in the United States. These invisible items were estimated at $350,000,000 per year.[33]

The editor of *The Commercial and Financial Chronicle*, William B. Dana, agreed with Heidelbach's reasoning but felt that his estimates of the invisible items were too high.[34] He presented a table for the five year period, 1890 to 1894, showing the net balance of merchandise and silver and the net gold exports for each of the five years. The balance of trade was in excess of $800,000,000 or an average of $160,000,000 per year during this period. Dana said this annual sum was sufficient to pay all charges for interest, dividends, freight and travel abroad and for the retirement of some of the United States foreign indebtedness. He claimed that the outflow of gold was in payment

---

[31] *The London Times*, May 22, 1894, p. 9.

[32] *Ibid.*

[33] Alfred S. Heidelbach, "Why Gold is Exported," *Forum*, February 1895, pp. 647-651.

[34] William B. Dana, "Why Do We Export Gold," *The Commercial and Financial Chronicle*, March 30, 1895, pp. 542-544.

of American securities returning to the United States and could be verified by bankers and security dealers.[35]

The estimates of Heidelbach and the resulting controversy with Dana brought out clearly the relationships which existed among the balance of trade, invisible transactions, specie and capital flows. Understanding of these concepts was necessary to their later presentation in statements of the balance of payments.

An international balance sheet, 1895. In 1895, *The Journal of Commerce and Commercial Bulletin* presented an international balance sheet for the United States. The statement was prepared in the belief that it was as important for a nation to know the state of its foreign transactions as for a merchant to know the financial condition of his business. In spite of this need, the "balancing of the international account has hitherto been a process so vague and incomplete as to be virtually valueless for purposes of practical guidance."[36]

The statement prepared by the *Journal* is presented in Table 3.2. The greatest difficulty in preparing this statement was that of finding proper bases for making the estimates; only merchandise, silver and gold bullion and specie were recorded in custom house records. Exactness was not claimed, but the estimates were felt to be as complete and reliable as was possible from the available information.[37]

The method used to estimate the various current transactions was to obtain information from leading firms in international commerce and from available government reports. The figure for interest payments to foreigners was based upon an estimated outstanding investment total of $2,000,000 at an average rate of return of four and one-half per cent. Information on travel expenses abroad was obtained from the banks, chiefly those in New York, which issued letters of credit. The estimate of money brought to the United States by immigrants was based upon information provided by the Commissioner of Immigration at New

---

[35] *Ibid.*, April 13, 1895, pp. 630-633.

[36] "Our International Balance Sheet," *The Commercial Year Book.* New York: *The Journal of Commerce and Commercial Bulletin,* 1896, I, p. 225.

[37] *Ibid.*, pp. 226-231.

TABLE 3.2

UNITED STATES BALANCE OF PAYMENTS, 1887-1893

Debtor Items—

On investments account	$90,000,000
Traveling credits	47,000,000
Inward freight charges per foreign vessels	24,777,000
Outward passenger fares per foreign steamships	8,698,000
Undervaluations of imports	5,000,000
Total debtor items	$175,475,000

Creditor Items—

Money brought by immigrants	$14,000,000
Outlays of foreign ships in port	8,250,000
Port outlays of passenger steamships	6,600,000
Outward earnings American vessels	1,900,000
Total of credit items	$29,750,000
Total debtor items	$175,475,000
Total creditor items	29,750,000
Debtor balance	$145,725,000

It thus appears that the various items of the international account, outside imports and exports of goods and specie and of the movement in securities, yield a net debtor balance of $145,000,000.

This result affords an indication of the course of the foreign exchanges during recent years. Selecting the seven fiscal years 1887 to 1893, both inclusive, we find items for the combined years to have been as follows:

Imports merchandise	$5,489,500,000	
Imports specie	332,700,000	
Total		$5,822,200,000
Exports merchandise	$5,774,700,000	
Exports specie	571,500,000	
Total		$6,346,200,000
Excess of exports		$524,000,000
Debtor balance on other items as above—seven years at $145,000,000		1,015,000,000
Debtor balance		$491,000,000

This calculation shows an adverse balance for the seven years of $491,-000,000 or an average of $70,000,000 per year; which it is to be presumed has been settled by the transmission of securities. This may not be a welcome rate of increase in our foreign borrowing; but we do not think intelligent observers will consider the showing improbable.

Source: "Our International Balance Sheet," *The Commercial Year Book.* New York: *The Journal of Commerce and Commercial Bulletin,* 1896, Vol. I, p. 226.

York concerning the number of immigrants and the average sum each carried.

Freight payments to foreign shipping firms was calculated by applying an average ratio of freight charges to the value of each type of goods. This ratio was obtained by examining the principal articles imported and the country of importation, showing the value of the goods and freight charges. On the basis of this sample, which included two-thirds of the total imports by value, the average ratio to the value of goods was determined.

The estimate for the expenditures of foreign ships in American ports, obtained from shipping agents, was judged to be approximately one-third of their freight receipts. Passenger fares paid foreign shipping companies were calculated from a survey of four shipping lines which estimated their average receipts from each of three classes of passengers to foreign destinations from the port of New York.

Effect of change of residence upon international indebtedness. Worthy P. Sterns, Professor of Economics at the University of Chicago, explained how international indebtedness was affected by a change of residence from one nation to another. He used as an example the fortunes of the Astor and Vanderbilt families. Sterns said that when William W. Astor became a resident of England "the international indebtedness of the United States was increased by the value of his real estate in New York."[38] He also stated: "When Miss Vanderbilt married the Duke of Marlborough she added the market price of her railroad stocks to that indebtedness."[39]

American international indebtedness in 1899. Nathaniel T. Bacon, a railroad executive, made the first comprehensive survey of American securities held abroad.[40] He obtained his information from bankers, brokers, companies whose securities were known to be held overseas and from income and estate tax re-

[38] Worthy P. Sterns, "The International Indebtedness of the United States in 1789," *Journal of Political Economy*, December 1897, p. 28.

[39] *Ibid.*

[40] Nathaniel T. Bacon, "American International Indebtedness," *Yale Review*, November 1900, pp. 265-285.

turns as well as records of the various foreign stock exchanges. Bacon analyzed the indebtedness under eleven classifications: U. S. bonds, state bonds, county and municipal bonds, railroad stocks, railroad bonds, industrial securities, bank securities, mining securities, real estate, real estate mortgages, and life insurance.

Bacon began his survey in London with a study of Burdette's *Official Intelligence,* a London Stock Exchange publication which gave statistics of all securities traded. He found few state, county or municipal bonds listed; and, except for a few British corporations operating in the United States, there were almost no British holdings of American industrial securities; the largest of these holdings were railroad securities. Further information on British portfolios of American securities was obtained from the Inland Revenue Office and from income and estate tax reports. The holdings of other countries were estimated by similar methods. Even with the information available, Bacon set a margin of error of twenty-five per cent on his estimate. Bacon said to offset these debts, Americans had few holdings of European securities, but did have large investments in Canada and Latin America. These investments centered primarily upon rails in Canada and mines in Canada and Mexico. He summarized the net foreign indebtedness of the United States as of January 1, 1899. United States items of foreign indebtedness were shown as credits and its foreign investments as debits in the summary.

The mechanism of international payments. Charles J. Bullock, Professor of Economics at Harvard University, discussed the nature of the international payments systems.[41] He said that drafts and bills of exchange were generally used to pay most international debts, while specie was used only to settle the remaining balances. Bullock listed five ways in which international indebtedness was created: an excess of merchandise imports over exports, investment of capital in foreign countries, interest accruals and commissions, freight charges on imported merchandise, and expenditures of travelers abroad.

Bullock contrasted the commercial situation of the United

---

[41] Charles J. Bullock, *Introduction to the Study of Economics,* 2nd ed., rev., New York: Silver, Burdett and Company, 1900, pp. 339-342.

States and the United Kingdom. While the United States current transactions, other than merchandise, resulted in increased indebtedness to foreigners, those of the United Kingdom made that country an international creditor. For this reason, Bullock said the United States had to maintain a favorable balance of trade to pay for its other expenditures abroad. On the other hand, the United Kingdom could have an unfavorable balance of trade indefinitely without the necessity of shipping gold in payment.

Estimate of immigrant remittances for 1907. Charles F. Speare estimated that out of the savings of the foreign-born in America, $250,000,000 annually went abroad.[42] He gave the distribution of this sum by countries. Speare surveyed representative banks in Detroit, Cleveland, and other cities where large amounts of drafts payable to foreign payees were sold. He found that money orders were the most popular form of immigrant transfers, making up approximately one-third of the total. In addition, immigrants also took sums of money with them when they visited their home country.

Balance of payments of the United States, 1908-1909. George Paish, editor of the *Statist*, examined the relationships existing between capital investment and the balance of trade; specie movements and the balance of trade; and service transactions and the balance of trade. He also made estimates of the balance of United States indebtedness and the principal service items and drew up a balance of payments for 1908-1909 from this data.[43]

Paish divided the countries of the world into two classes for the purpose of illustrating the relationship between the balance of trade and foreign investment—those whose imports exceeded exports and those whose exports exceeded imports. Countries which had an unfavorable balance of trade were generally lending nations while those whose exports exceeded imports were

---

[42] Charles F. Speare, "What America Pays Europe for Immigrant Labor," *North American Review,* January 1908, pp. 106-116.

[43] U. S. National Monetary Commission, George Paish, *The Trade Balance of the United States,* Washington: Government Printing Office, 1910, XXXII, 155-197.

usually debtors. The reason for this, Paish said, was that debtors had to pay interest by means of a favorable balance of trade. Paish recognized the different stages of maturity of creditor nations from those which were beginning to invest abroad to those having new investments which were exceeded by interest received. The balance of trade varied from case to case. His illustrations were based upon the simplifying assumptions that there were no transactions other than for merchandise, interest, and capital movements.

After the development of national and international banking, the use of credit instruments became the primary medium of exchange rather than specie, and the chief means of settling international balances of payments. This left specie to be used mainly as banking reserves which served as the basis for credit. Under these circumstances, movements of gold and silver were less related to trade balances than to the needs of the banking system. Paish found that there was no necessary relationship between foreign investment and the movement of gold. Borrowing countries generally used the proceeds of their loans to buy goods, not gold and silver.

Paish said that the balance of payments was affected not only by the balance of trade, capital and specie movements, but also by services. These services consisted of freight, tourist expenditures, earnings of non-residents in temporary or seasonal employment, emigrants' funds at the time of migration and their later remittances, educational expenses in foreign institutions, insurance, commissions and professional fees. Countries which had large service exports such as freight and interest receipts generally had a merchandise import surplus.

After setting forth the basic principles upon which the balance of payments was based, Paish explained the methods used in estimating the various invisible exports and imports contained in the statement. He estimated the foreign indebtedness of the United States at approximately $6,500,000,000 with an annual interest charge of $300,000,000. Partially offsetting these investments of foreigners in the United States were American investments of about $1,500,000,000 in other countries, primarily in Canada and Latin America. These investments earned about $75,000,000 annually. The net amount for interest was then entered in the balance of payments.

The number of residents of the United States visiting other countries was estimated to be approximately 200,000 a year, and Paish assumed that each traveler spent an average of $1,000 during his stay. This amount included fares and expenses in other countries for food and transportation; but excluded expenditures for clothing and jewelry which were declared at the customs offices and, thereby included in imports. Tourist expenditures of foreigners in the United States were estimated at $30,000,000 leaving a balance of $170,000,000 for tourist expenditures.

He believed the number of emigrants leaving the United States annually approximated 300,000 and that each carried $200 on the average. Approximately offsetting this amount was the sum carried by immigrants coming into the United States. They averaged 1,000,000 or more annually and it was believed that they carried $50 or more with them. Since the two sums just about balanced out, transfers were omitted from the balance of payments.

Paish could not find a satisfactory basis for an estimate of immigrant remittances. He relied largely upon Charles F. Speare's sources, but felt that Speare's estimates were excessive since all the remittances were not gratuitous and therefore the actual transfers probably did not exceed $150,000,000.

Tables were compiled to show the value of imports and exports carried in foreign vessels from 1890 to 1908. The data in these tables indicated that foreign shipping was used for about 85 per cent of goods imported, and about 92 per cent of goods exported from the United States. In general Americans paid only the freight charges on the goods coming into the country. Credit was given to the United States for the portion of exports carried in American shipping and the expenses of foreign shipping in American ports. The net expenditure of the United States for shipping was set at $25,000,000 annually.

Insurance was the last service item discussed. It was recognized that American insurance companies had premium income from foreigners which was offset by claims, and that foreign insurance companies had similar premiums and claims. Accordingly, payments and receipts from insurance balanced and could be excluded.

Paish then prepared a balance of payments for 1908-1909 which is reproduced in Table 3.3. He said that the balance on the current account (which included specie) was financed by permanent or temporary investments. This investment came from changes in the reserves of the companies in which foreigners held securities as well as from new obligations.

TABLE 3.3
FOREIGN TRADE OF THE UNITED STATES, 1908-9

Merchandise:
  Exports—
    Domestic   \$1,638,000,000
    Foreign   25,000,000
      Total   \$1,663,000,000
  Imports   1,312,000,000

    Excess of merchandise exports over imports..\$351,000,000
Gold:
  Exports   \$92,000,000
  Imports   44,000,000

    Excess of gold exports over imports   48,000,000
Silver:
  Exports   \$56,000,000
  Imports   44,000,000

    Excess of silver exports over imports   12,000,000

    Total excess of merchandise, gold,
      and silver exports over imports   \$411,000,000
Remittances for interest, etc.:
  Interest   \$250,000,000
  Tourist expenditures   170,000,000
  Remittances to friends   150,000,000
  Freight   25,000,000

    Total remittances   595,000,000
    Excess of sum remitted for interest, tourists, to friends, and
      for freights over trade balance   184,000,000

This balance of \$184,000,000 has been liquidated by permanent or temporary investments of capital by other countries in the United States.
Source: U.S. National Monetary Commission, George Paish, *The Trade Balance of the United States.* Washington: Government Printing Office, 1910, Vol. XXXII, p. 197.

4

Development of the United States Balance of International Payments, 1915-1947

The most important developments in the United States balance of payments occurred after World War I. This is probably due to the assumption of leadership in world economic affairs by the United States. The United States shed the role of an international debtor and became one of the financial centers of the world. This change, together with the subsequent world-wide depression, stimulated interest in the financing of foreign transactions. The development began with J. Laurence Laughlin's "International Balance Sheet" for 1915-1917, continued with the work of Bullock, Williams, Tucker, and Vanderlip and culminated in the outstanding work of the Department of Commerce.

International Balance Sheet, 1915-1917

Laughlin, a professor at the University of Chicago, analyzed the means by which the international accounts of the United States were settled during the first three years of World War I. He concluded his analysis with a summary of international receipts and payments of the United States for these years.[1]

Laughlin was concerned with the inter-relationships among exports and imports of goods and services, capital movements and the flow of gold. He stated that the United States was a debtor nation in 1914 to the estimated amount of four to six

---

[1] J. Laurence Laughlin, *Credit of the Nations*. New York: Charles Scribner's Sons, 1919, pp. 281-341.

billion dollars. Should creditors of the United States wish to sell the securities they held, then payment would have to be made by additional exports of merchandise and services or gold. This actually occurred during World War I. Europe began to call home capital by flooding the United States markets with securities. The exchanges were unable to absorb the securities, and there was a resulting decline in security prices.

Although the German fleet disrupted trade during the early months of the war, the United States merchandise export surplus for the three years 1915-1917 amounted to almost seven billion dollars. Laughlin prepared an international balance sheet, presented in Table 4.1, to show how this balance was financed. Although his statement did not balance, he attempted to show that the credit on the merchandise account was financed by the repatriation of United States securities, loans from private and governmental sources, services, gifts and gold.

TABLE 4.1

INTERNATIONAL BALANCE SHEET OF THE
UNITED STATES FOR 1915-1917

Cr.		Dr.	
Merchandise balance	$6,865	Securities returned	$2,200
Relief funds	90	Loans by non-government institutions	1,570
		Loans by the United States	2,149
		Dividend account (3 years)	600
		Freights and insurance (3 years)	75
		Imports of gold	1,111
		Remittances to friends (3 years)	450
	$6,955		$8,155

Source: J. Laurence Laughlin, *Credit of the Nations*. New York: Charles Scribner's Sons, 1919, p. 341.

Unofficial Estimates of the Balance of Payments, 1914-1921

Two economics professors, a government economist, and a business executive were responsible for beginning a series of balance of payments which led directly to the official balance of payments prepared by the Department of Commerce. Their greatest contribution, perhaps, was in the development of sources of data and techniques of estimating international transactions for which little information was available.

United States balance of payments, 1914-1918. Two professors of economics, Charles J. Bullock and John H. Williams of Harvard and Rufus S. Tucker, Assistant Chief of the Division of Finance and Investment of the Department of Commerce, prepared a balance of payments for 1914-1918.[2] The statement, presented in Table 4.2, was prepared as a summary of the various types of international transactions in which the United States was engaged. The more important accounts in this tabulation, based on a criteria of value, were merchandise and gold, capital movements and freight. Information on merchandise and gold were obtained from the reports of *Foreign Commerce and Navigation* prepared by the Department of Commerce.

The large value of United States exports was to a great extent due to the increased demand in Europe for manufactured goods and foodstuffs and to their consequent rise in price. It was also attributable to the shifting of Asian and South American purchases of manufactured goods from Europe to the United States. The excess balance of exports over imports totaled $11,808,000,000 during the period, 1914-1918.

This large balance of foreign indebtedness on the merchandise account had to be financed. Part of this indebtedness was paid by the United States import of slightly over one billion dollars in gold. The gold inflow was caused by the shortage of dollar exchange and its resulting higher price. However, the export of capital by the United States was more important than the flow of gold in settling the international balance. During

---

[2] Charles J. Bullock, John H. Williams, and Rufus S. Tucker, "The Balance of Trade of the United States," *The Review of Economic Statistics,* July 1919, pp. 215-254.

TABLE 4.2

BALANCE OF INTERNATIONAL PAYMENTS OF
THE UNITED STATES, JULY 1, 1914
TO DECEMBER 31, 1918
(UNITS OF $1,000,000)

	Credit	Debit
1. Exports of merchandise and silver	$22,974	
2. Exports of gold	739	
3. Interest on American capital abroad	1,010	
4. Freight payments receivable on exports carried in American vessels	919	
1. Imports of merchandise and silver		$11,166
2. Imports of gold		1,768
3. American securities returned from Europe		2,000
4. Public and private loans to foreign countries		8,840
5. Interest on foreign capital in the United States		360
6. Freight payments payable on imports carried in foreign vessels		1,084
7. Payments for the chartering of foreign vessels		261
8. Immigrants' remittances		600
Totals	$25,642	$26,079*
Net balance†		437

* The marine and other insurance payments which we have computed constitute so small a sum ($9,000,000), and the element of error in computation is so uncertain, that this item is omitted from the balance.
† Probably covered by cash balances of foreign banks in the United States, credits extended and not used, and such other items as merchandise exports paid for but not sent forward within the period.

Source: Charles J. Bullock, John H. Williams, and Rufus S. Tucker, "The Balance of Trade of the United States," *The Review of Economic Statistics*, July, 1919, p. 251.

World War I, there were three types of capital flows of great importance. Approximately two billion dollars of American securities held by foreigners were repatriated during the war years, and more than eight billion dollars of public and private loans were made to foreign countries.

The estimates for the return of American securities were based primarily upon a survey made in 1917 by L. F. Loree of 144 American railroads having mileage of one hundred miles or more. He assumed that railroad securities composed about four-fifths of the total securities returned.

Private loans floated in the United States were estimated to be approximately $1,520,100,000 based upon a statement prepared by the Guaranty Trust Company of New York. The statement was prepared from an itemized list showing the date and the original amount of issue of foreign loans placed in the United States from August 1, 1914 to January 1, 1919. Public lending was in the form of loans and credits to foreign governments beginning in 1917. This information was taken from the *Federal Reserve Bulletins* for November 1, 1918 and January 1, 1919.

Shipping earnings of American vessels increased during the war, but were still less than American freight payments to foreign shipping companies. The development of procedures for making these estimates was a necessary step in the development of the balance of payments. The objective was to find the freight charges on imports and exports as a proportion of the value of total goods carried, and then to allocate this figure as to United States and foreign earnings. To this end the average monthly and quarterly quotations for designated commodities were obtained from thirty shipping companies in New York. These companies carried goods between the United States and thirteen neutral countries during the six-month period January to June 1918. Actual rates paid were taken from the records of a New York brokerage firm, and representative rates on the principal exports and imports between the Far East and Pacific ports were obtained from the Shipping Board at San Francisco. A representative rate on the goods carried to and from each of these countries was chosen from the data obtained. This rate, when multiplied by the volume of goods carried, gave the total freight charges paid on imports and exports during the sample period.

This charge was then allocated between American and foreign ships on the basis of data contained in the records of the United States Shipping Board and the Bureau of Foreign and Domestic Commerce. These records showed the control and distribution of ships engaged in foreign trade and the value of goods carried by nationality during the six month period. The proportion of freight charges to the value of goods carried and the proportion of the goods carried by American and foreign ships were calculated from this compilation. Shipping receipts and payments were obtained for the balance of payments by applying these rates to the exports and imports of the 1914-1918 period.

Accounts of lesser importance were insurance, tourist expenses, immigrants' remittances and interest. Estimates of the first two accounts were not included in the balance of payments for this period. Marine insurance was not included because of its small net value and the uncertainty of the data upon which it was calculated, but was instead carried as a memorandum entry on the statement. The item was small because the premiums paid to foreign firms were netted against claims paid by these firms to American residents and the operating expenses incurred by them in the United States. Only the profits were remitted. American companies also conducted similar transactions with foreigners. Therefore, according to an investigation conducted by the *Spectator*, the net remittances for this service from the United States were less than nine million dollars. Tourist expenditures were omitted because they were virtually nonexistent during the war. Immigrants' remittances were based upon a prewar estimate of twenty-five dollars per person. Estimated interest payments and receipts were based upon annual average investments at assumed rates of return.

United States balance of payments for 1919. Frank A. Vanderlip and John H. Williams completed a study of the United States international transactions for 1919.[3] The purpose of this study was to attain greater understanding of the future of the

---

[3] Frank A. Vanderlip and John H. Williams, "The Future of Our Foreign Trade," *The Review of Economics Statistics Supplement*, April 1920, pp. 1-28.

United States' foreign trade by analysis of its balance of payments for 1919. This was a continuation of the previous study by Bullock, Williams, and Tucker. The sources of data and methodology were substantially unchanged.

Distinction was made between visible transactions, merchandise and specie, and invisible items, which were not recorded in official trade statistics. The source of information for the visible transactions came from official records. The data for the invisible ones came from a variety of sources, both private and governmental. The sources included J. P. Morgan and Company, the Guaranty Trust Company of New York, the United States Treasury and the Shipping Board.

The study attempted to determine how the relatively large export surplus of the United States was financed, and the form of the balance of payments was designed to reveal the answer. It showed that eighty per cent of the balance of the visible transactions were financed by the export of capital, chiefly in the form of direct government credit.

United States balance of payments for 1920. John H. Williams continued the unofficial study of the balance of payments of the United States.[4] The manner of presentation and much of the methodology remained substantially unchanged from the previous year. However, new sources of data which are of significance to balance of payments methodology were developed. These new sources improved the accuracy and completeness of estimates for governmental transactions, capital movements and transportation.

Williams prepared supplemental schedules for the relatively large group of government transactions. The sources for these data were the Assistant Secretary of the Treasury who was in charge of foreign loans, the War Department Claims Board for funds received from Germany toward the cost of the army of occupation, the reports of the Secretary of the Treasury for data on export credits granted, the Controller of the American Red

---

[4] John H. Williams, "The Balance of International Payments of the United States for the year 1920," *The Review of Economic Statistics Supplement,* June 1921, pp. 169-212.

Cross for foreign remittances, and the report of the United States Liquidation Commission of 1920 for the sale of War Department property in Europe.

After World War I relatively large purchases of speculative foreign governmental securities were made by United States residents. The source of information for the purchases of foreign government, provincial and municipal bonds was J. P. Morgan and Company. For data concerning other forms of American capital sent abroad, Williams conducted an inquiry with twenty banks and investment houses handling most of these securities. Each house was asked to give the amount of securities it had handled individually and to estimate the total which passed through the market. A summary of all loans placed in the United States and outstanding on January 1, 1921 was provided by the Guaranty Trust Company of New York. This summary together with a similar compilation by J. P. Morgan and Company for the previous year provided information on capital flows. Data on United States citizens' earnings from interest and dividends on foreign investments were obtained from the *Statistics of Income* (Commissioner of Internal Revenue).

Williams estimated freight earnings and payments according to methods used in the preparation of the 1914-1918 balance of payments. However, he improved the account by deducting from shipping earnings the expenses of American ships in foreign ports and adding estimates of the expenditures of foreign ships in American ports. Williams noted that C. K. Hobson's detailed account of receipts and expenditures of ships on seven voyages in 1907 had showed the expenses in foreign ports to be thirty per cent of total receipts from freight. He also referred to the study "American Shipping Earnings and the Balance of Trade" in the *Federal Reserve Bulletin* of April 1921 which estimated port charges to average about one-quarter to one-third of gross freights. Nevertheless, Williams felt that one-fifth was more appropriate.

United States balance of payments for 1921. John H. Williams carried forward the study of the United States balance of payments to 1921.[5] The methodology of previous studies was continued with further refinement and better sources of data, particularly for the movement of short-term capital. The nature of the balance of short-term indebtedness, which had previously been neglected, received closer attention. Two studies, one by the Federal Reserve Board, the other by a leading New York bank, helped clarify the situation. The results of the first study were published in the *Federal Reserve Bulletin*. It revealed the net cash balances of foreign residents in American banks. In the second study, a New York bank sent questionnaires "to the principal domestic banks, private bankers, and foreign banks of New York, two large banks of Boston, and the more representative members of the American Manufacturers Export Association and the Exporters and Importers Association"[6] requesting information concerning their bank balances abroad, their holdings of exchange and short-term foreign securities, and their trade accounts and bills receivable and payable. On the basis of these reports, Williams assumed that the balance consisted mainly of changes in bank balances and merchandise credits. However, he did not assume that the balance of the remaining accounts was exactly offset by changes in short-term capital for two reasons. First, the data were incomplete. Second, all the items in the balance of payments were subject to varying degrees of inaccuracies in reporting or in estimating. Therefore, the balance also included a statistical discrepancy which is presently known as the errors and omissions account.

Official Balance of Payments of the United States 1922-1946

The changed position of the United States from a debtor nation to an international financial center in a relatively short span of years provided the impetus for the rapid development of a statement of international economic transactions which was sufficiently accurate to provide a guide to the proper monetary

---

[6] *Ibid.*, p. 208.

[5] John H. Williams, "The Balance of International Payments of the United States for the year 1921, with an Estimate of the Unfunded Foreign Balance on January 1, 1922," *The Review of Economic Statistics*, July 1922, pp. 201-214.

and fiscal policies and to serve as a means of evaluating the effect of past transactions. That the United States Department of Commerce made the effort to provide such a tabulation can be seen from this study, which is divided into three parts for analytical purposes: form of presentation, basic concepts, and sources and methodology.

Form of presentation. The first balance of payments *officially* prepared for the United States was for 1922.[7] It was substantially a continuation of the series begun by Bullock, Williams and Tucker in 1919. The statement was prepared under the direction of Grosvenor M. Jones, Chief of the Division of Finance and Investment in cooperation with Williams. Williams and Tucker analyzed and prepared the data for publication. The first statement was a departure from the form used earlier by Williams. Its arrangement was rather clumsy, and possibly for this reason the presentation for the following year (shown in Table 4.3) was changed.

The balance of payments for 1923 was composed of three divisions: current transactions, capital movements, and gold and silver. Current transactions were defined as those which were complete within a period of one year and which were not expected to lead to payments or receipts in subsequent years.[8] These transactions consisted of both visible and invisible items. Capital transactions were defined as those which were expected to give rise to profits and interest in later periods.[9] Only long-term debts were included in this section as very little was known of short-term capital at that time. The net amount of changes in short-term capital was reflected in the net debit or credit balance, as well as errors and omissions from other transactions. The only exception to this was the United States currency which at that time was considered a long-term liability. Gold and silver

---

[7] Department of Commerce, Bureau of Foreign and Domestic Commerce, "The Balance of International Payments of the United States in 1922," *Trade Information Bulletin, No. 144,* Washington: Government Printing Office, 1923.

[8] *Trade Information Bulletin, No. 340,* p. 1.

[9] *Ibid.*

TABLE 4.3

ESTIMATED BALANCE OF INTERNATIONAL PAYMENTS OF
UNITED STATES, 1923
(Millions of dollars)

Items	Credit	Debit	Balance
CURRENT ITEMS			
Merchandise	4,208	3,819	+389
Current invisible items:			
Interest and dividends	567	150	+417
Ocean freights	65	73	−8
Governmental payments	—	19	−19
Services to tourists	100	500	−400
Charitable and missionary expenditures	—	70	−70
Immigrants' remittances	60	350	−290
Total, current invisible items	792	1,162	−370
Total, current items	5,000	4,981	+19
MOVEMENT OF CAPITAL			
New foreign loans, exclusive of refunding loans	32	377	−345
Sale and purchase of outstanding securities	339	33	+306
Foreign bonds paid off	23	—	+23
Principal of interallied debt	91	—	+91
United States currency	50	—	+50
Total, capital items	535	410	+125
GOLD AND SILVER			
Gold	29	323	−294
Silver	72	74	−2
Total, gold and silver	101	397	−296
Total balance, all items	—	—	−152

Source: U. S. Department of Commerce, Bureau of Foreign and Domestic
Commerce, "The Balance of International Payments of the United
States in 1923," *Trade Information Bulletin No. 215.* Washington:
Government Printing Office, 1924, p. iii.

TABLE 4.4

UNITED STATES BALANCE OF INTERNATIONAL PAYMENTS IN 1932

Item	Credits (exports)	Debits (imports)	Balance
Merchandise	1,612	1,323	+289
Merchandise adjustments[1]	105	147	—42
Freight and shipping	73	118	—45
Tourist expenditures	71	446	—375
Immigrant remittances	6	138	—132
Charitable, educational and other contributions	—	31	—31
Interest, dividends, commissions, etc.	461	68	+393
War-debt receipts	99	—	+99
Government transactions, excluding war-debt receipts	31	101	—70
Miscellaneous invisible items	78	33	+45
Total current items[2]	2,536	2,405	+131
Gold movements (including earmarking)	860	871	—11
Currency movements (net)	—	80	—80
Total gold and currency movements	860	951	—91
Short-term capital movements[3]	—	—	—371
Long-term capital movements[4]	862	645	+217
Total capital movements	—	—	—154
Unestimated items, errors, omissions, etc.[5]	—	—	+114

[1] This term consists roughly of 3 parts: (1) exports and imports of goods for which data are available but not recorded in the official trade figures (e.g., ships, bunker fuel sold in the United States, silver, etc); (2) goods whose export or import is wholly or partly omitted from official trade data (e.g., unrecorded parcel-post shipments, goods smuggled into the country, etc.); (3) corrections of certain recorded trade figures to allow for possible overvaluation (in case of goods sent on consignment) or undervaluation (in case of imports subject to ad valorem duties), uncollectible accounts, etc.

[2] These figures include several small items which are, strictly speaking, of a capital, rather than current, nature; for example, receipts of principal on

accounts were considered of sufficient importance for separate classification.

There was little actual change in the manner of presenting the summary of international transactions as late as 1932. However, Table 4.4 shows that there was a rearrangement of the groupings, some additional transactions, and some reclassifications.

The current accounts remained largely unchanged except for merchandise which was no longer distinguished from the other current transactions. The distinction between visible and invisible items was dropped from the summary of international transactions in 1924 and except for 1926 did not appear again.

There was considerable reshuffling of the monetary accounts. Gold, formerly in the third group, was moved up to a position between the current and capital groups in 1932. Silver was reclassified as merchandise, and shipments of United States currency

---

war debt account, and unestimated portions of several items in Government transactions such as payments by the Alien Property Custodian. On the other hand, gold exports and imports, which ordinarily may be considered as current outgo or income, are classified separately because of the "noncurrent" nature of a great part of the gold exports during 1932.

[3] This figure represents the net change in the country's short-term position during the year. Data on gross movements are not available and would serve no particular purpose. The net change in 1932 is determined by deducting the year's decline in United States balances held abroad from the decline in foreign balances held here.

[4] This item takes account of all security movements between the United States and foreign countries and includes international sales and purchases of long-term issues, new underwriting, sales and purchases of properties not represented by security issues, and security transfers resulting from redemption and sinking fund operations.

[5] An unestimated part of this item is accounted for by the year's net change in outstanding commercial accounts abroad—presumably a net collection in 1932—of American exporters. The remainder, it must be assumed, is the net result of errors and possible omissions or duplications.

Source: United States Department of Commerce, Bureau of Foreign and Domestic Commerce, "The Balance of International Payments of the United States in 1932," *Trade Information Bulletin No. 814.* Washington: Government Printing Office 1933, p. viii.

were reclassified as monetary rather than capital transactions in 1926.[10]

The capital section no longer consisted of long-term transactions alone. Short-term items began to appear in the balance of payments of 1924 for changes in foreigners' bank deposits in United States financial institutions.[11] By 1926, information was shown for bank deposits in foreign banks, accounts receivable and payable with foreign firms, commercial bills and United States short-term securities.[12] However, the change in commercial accounts (accounts receivable and payable) which was shown in 1931 was not shown in 1932.[13] Instead this change was reflected in the *unestimated items, errors, omissions, etc.* account of the 1932 statement.

Only minor changes were made in the presentation of the United States balance of payments between 1932 and 1940. Silver was removed from the merchandise category in 1934 and placed as a separate item in the monetary section which consisted of gold, silver and currency movements. The reason for this change was the increased silver movement due to the Silver Purchase Act of 1934.[14] From this time forward, the United States imported short-term capital on a large scale due in part to the political and financial situation of Europe, and also to the growing importance of the United States as a financial center. In 1937 currency was again classified as a capital item because foreigners were in effect holding short-term non-interest bearing notes.[15] Emphasis shifted from the debit-credit column headings to receipts from foreigners and payments to foreigners, although debits and credits were shown in parentheses.[16] This change was

---

[10] *Trade Information Bulletin, No. 503,* p. v; and *No. 814,* p. viii.

[11] *Trade Information Bulletin, No. 340,* p. iii.

[12] *Trade Information Bulletin, No. 503,* pp. v and 45-46.

[13] *Trade Information Bulletin, No. 803,* p. viii; and *No. 814,* p. viii.

[14] *Trade Information Bulletin, No. 833,* p. 44.

[15] Department of Commerce, Bureau of Foreign and Domestic Commerce, *Economic Series No. 3,* Washington: Government Printing Office, pp. 2, 91.

[16] *Trade Information Bulletin, No. 819,* p. xi.

made for purposes of clarity so that readers of the statements could more easily interpret them.

In 1943 Hal B. Lary, then Assistant Chief of the Statistics Unit of the Bureau of Foreign and Domestic Commerce, completed a comprehensive analysis of the United States international transactions which covered the years 1919 to 1939. A table entitled "World Supply and Use of Dollars, 1919-1939" supplemented the balance of payments summary for these years. This presentation is illustrated in Table 4.5. The form is important because it was the forerunner of the type of balance of payments statistics to be published after World War II.

The first statements published pertaining to the war years appeared in the *Foreign Commerce Weekly* in 1945.[17] Quarterly reports began to be published in the *Survey of Current Business* in 1946.[18] The form of the presentation for both remained substantially unchanged in the statement for the years 1940-1945 which was published in 1948. Table 4.6 shows the form of that presentation.

The form of presentation of these statements was quite different from that of the statement for 1932. No longer were the three column headings of receipts, payments, and balance used. Instead, payments and receipts appeared in rows as major classifications of transactions, which included all items previously classified as either current or capital. The difference between receipts and payments from this grouping of accounts was emphasized. Theoretically, this difference was exactly offset by the net inflow of gold and short-term capital, but actually the two differed due to errors and omissions. The source of errors and omissions was not known, but was thought to be in varying degrees, in all the accounts.

---

[17] Department of Commerce, International Economics and Statistics Unit of the Bureau of Foreign and Domestic Commerce, "International Payments of the U. S. During the War," *Foreign Commerce Weekly,* March 10, 1945, pp. 6-7, 31.

[18] Department of Commerce, International Economics Division of the Bureau of Foreign and Domestic Commerce, "International Transactions of the United States During First Quarter 1946," *Survey of Current Business,* July 1946, p. 17.

TABLE 4.5

WORLD SUPPLY AND USE OF DOLLARS, 1919 TO 1923

(In millions of dollars)

Type of transactions	1919	1920	1921	1922	1923
I. Factors supplying dollars (payments to foreign countries):					
A. United States merchandise imports	3,904	5,278	2,509	3,113	3,792
B. Other current payments:					
Shipping and freight	818	848	334	341	332
Travel expenditures	123	190	200	243	360
Personal remittances	732	579	393	269	309
Institutional contributions	140	118	106	93	84
Interest and dividends	130	120	105	105	130
Government aid and settlements	2,844	286	86	48	21
Other government items	772	140	82	69	66
Silver	89	88	63	71	74
Miscellaneous adjustments and services, net	79	68	98	30	14
Total other current payments	5,727	2,437	1,467	1,269	1,290
Total current payments	9,631	7,715	3,976	4,382	5,082
C. Outflow of long-term capital:					
New loans to foreign countries	371	500	567	666	317
New direct investments abroad [1]	94	154	111	153	148
Amortization payments to foreigners	20	20	20	20	20
Net purchases by United States of outstanding securities	234	739	179	110	......
Total long-term capital outflow	719	1,413	877	949	485
Total dollars supplied through current and long-term capital transactions	10,350	9,128	4,853	5,331	5,567
II. Factors using dollars (receipts from foreign countries):					
A. United States merchandise exports	7,920	8,228	4,485	3,832	4,167
B. Other current receipts:					
Shipping and freight	1,109	1,119	394	286	302
Travel expenditures	56	67	76	61	71
Personal remittances	40	63	49	48	65
Interest and dividends	544	588	405	544	676
Government aid and settlements	1,212	214	98	175	255
Other government items	9	9	11	15	22
Silver	239	114	52	63	72
Miscellaneous adjustments and services, net					
Total other current receipts	3,209	2,174	1,085	1,192	1,463
Total current receipts	11,129	10,402	5,570	5,024	5,630
C. Inflow of long-term capital:					
Amortization payments to United States [1]	335	581	285	134	82
Net sales by United States of outstanding securities					358
Total long-term capital inflow	335	581	285	134	440
Total dollars used through current and long-term capital transactions	11,464	10,983	5,855	5,158	6,070
Excess of dollars used (+) over dollars supplied (−)	+1,114	+1,855	+1,002	−173	+503
III. Factors supplying or using dollars ("balancing items"):					
A. Short-term capital movements, net:					
Outflow (−) or inflow (+) of United States funds	(1)	(1)	(1)	(1)	−82
Outflow (−) or inflow (+) of foreign funds	(1)	(1)	(1)	(1)	+49
Net short-term capital movement	(1)	(1)	(1)	(1)	−33
B. Net gold movement	+164	+50	−686	−235	−295
C. Unexplained items	−1,278	−1,905	−316	+408	−175
Net movement of all "balancing items"	−1,114	−1,855	−1,002	+173	−503

Note: The years 1924 to 1939 have been omitted.
Source: United States Department of Commerce, Bureau of Foreign and Domestic Commerce, *Economic Series, No. 23*, "The United States in the World Economy", prepared by Hal B. Lary and Associates. Washington: Government Printing Office, 1943, Facing p. 216, No. 2.

TABLE 4.6

INTERNATIONAL TRANSACTIONS OF THE UNITED STATES, 1940 TO 1945

Item	1940	1941	1942	1943	1944	1945				
						Total	First quarter	Second quarter	Third quarter	Fourth quarter
I. Receipts, total	5,780	7,210	13,077	21,716	24,485	19,249	5,517	6,235	4,030	3,467
A. Goods and services, total	5,355	6,896	11,769	19,134	21,438	16,073	4,382	4,997	3,450	3,244
1. Goods	4,124	5,343	9,187	15,115	16,969	12,222	3,455	3,906	2,543	2,318
2. Income on investments	564	544	514	508	572	555	129	147	129	150
3. Other services	667	1,009	2,068	3,511	3,897	3,296	798	944	778	776
B. Unilateral transfers	59	43	1,002	2,137	2,407	2,991	1,039	1,395	493	64
C. Long-term capital, total	366	271	306	445	640	185	96	−157	87	159
1. Movements of United States capital invested abroad	209	193	219	402	406	155	96	−187	87	159
2. Movements of foreign capital invested in United States	157	78	87	43	234	30	—	30	—	—
II. Payments, total	4,344	6,578	13,159	23,732	26,154	21,009	6,110	6,813	4,539	3,547
A. Goods and services, total	3,636	4,486	5,356	8,096	8,966	9,424	2,689	2,925	2,082	1,728
1. Goods	2,713	3,486	3,965	5,427	5,589	5,829	1,519	1,681	1,414	1,215
2. Income on investments	210	187	159	155	161	168	35	39	39	55
3. Other services	713	813	1,232	2,514	3,216	3,427	1,135	1,205	629	458
B. Unilateral transfers	269	1,179	7,338	15,044	16,549	10,028	3,137	4,017	1,746	1,128
C. Long-term capital, total	439	913	465	592	619	1,557	284	−129	711	691
1. Movements of United States capital invested abroad	192	508	294	486	560	1,467	190	−71	679	669
2. Movements of foreign capital invested in United States	247	405	171	106	59	90	94	−58	32	22
III. Excess of receipts (+) or payments (−), total	+1,436	+632	−82	−2,016	−1,669	−1,760	−593	−578	−509	−80
A. Goods and services	+1,719	+2,410	+6,413	+11,038	+12,452	+6,649	+1,693	+2,072	+1,368	+1,516
B. Unilateral transfers	−210	−1,136	−6,336	−12,907	−14,142	−7,037	−2,098	−2,622	−1,253	−1,064
C. Long-term capital	−73	−642	−159	−147	+21	−1,372	−188	−28	−624	−532
V. Net inflow (+) or outflow (−) of funds on gold and short-term capital account, total	−2,713	−1,108	+90	+1,982	+1,706	+1,888	+620	+631	+582	+55
A. Net increase (−) or decrease (+) in United States gold stock	−4,243	−719	+23	+757	+1,350	+548	+180	+157	+201	+10
B. Net movement of United States short-term capital abroad	+177	+11	−115	+43	−183	−13	−9	+130	+21	+205
C. Net movement of foreign short-term capital in United States	+1,333	−400	+182	+1,222	+509	+1,653	+449	+594	+360	−205
V. Errors and omissions	+1,277	+476	−8	+34	−37	−128	−27	−53	−73	+25

Source: U. S. Department of Commerce, International Economics Division of the Office of Business Economics, "International Transactions of the United States During the War, 1940-45," *Economic Series No. 65,* Washington: Government Printing Office, 1948, p. viii.

Basic concepts of the balance of payments. The United States Department of Commerce (hereafter referred to simply as Commerce) first defined its concept of the balance of payments in 1925, as "a statement of all the valuable things received from other countries balanced against all the valuable things transferred to other countries during a given period of time."[19] Subsequently, the concept was more precisely stated in the introductory statement to the 1937 balance of payments.[20]

The balance of international payments of a country consists of the payments made, within a stated period of time, between residents of that country and residents of foreign countries. It may be defined in a statistical sense as an itemized account of transactions involving receipts from foreigners on the one hand and payments to foreigners on the other. Since the former relate to the international income of a country, they are called "credits," and, since the latter relate to international outgo, they are labeled "debits."

In the compilation of the items which enter into a balance-of-payments statement, the fact of residence, rather than nationality, is ruling. Thus, for example, the expenditures of alien residents of the United States visiting in foreign countries are considered as payments by "Americans" to foreigners, and income derived from investments in this country by United States citizens permanently residing abroad is similarly classified. Again, the United States branches and affiliates of foreign corporations are treated, from a balance-of-payments point of view, as domestic entities and the foreign subsidiaries of American corporations as foreign entities—in either case upon the basis of domicile. This procedure relates directly to one of the basic purposes of the balance-of-payments schedules, which are designed to show the sources of the supply of foreign currencies, or of foreign exchange, arising out of claims against foreigners and the nature of the demand for foreign currencies

---

[19] *Trade Information Bulletin, No. 399,* p. 1.
[20] *Economic Series No. 3,* p. 1.

from persons with payments to make abroad. Conversely, the balance of payments of the United States indicates the sources of the supply of dollars, or of dollar exchange, arising out of claims against this country by foreigners and the nature of the demand for dollar exchange from foreigners with commitments to meet in the United States.

In general, the balance of payments of 1937 was comprised of only cash transactions and transactions involving foreign exchange. However, there were several notable exceptions, such as the shipment of goods abroad by charitable organizations for which no payment was expected and exports and imports financed by acceptance credit.

Commerce made it clear that it did not consider any of the individual items on the balance of payments as "functional or causal."[21] The interrelationships among the items could only be demonstrated theoretically upon the basis of other information or by quantitative comparison. The reason for this lack of causality was due to "the fact that any particular credit transaction gives rise to a claim upon a foreign country which, through the operation of the foreign exchange market, becomes a part of the mass of claims available, without distinction as to origin, for purchase by persons with commitments to meet in foreign countries."[22]

The new arrangement of the United States balance of payments for 1919-1939 and for 1945, illustrated in Tables 4.5 and 4.6, differed from previous statements because the concepts upon which they were prepared were different.

In the past the balance of international payments was ordinarily considered as a statistical tool for analyzing the international financial position of a country. From this point of view only transactions that involved present or future payments in a more or less literal monetary sense needed to be included. Unless a particular export of goods, for instance, involved an immediate payment or created a monetary claim on (or extinguished a monetary debt to) a for-

---

[21] *Ibid.*, p. 6.
[22] *Ibid.*, p. 7.

eign country, it was not included in the statement of foreign transactions. The effects on the domestic economy of international trade were of interest primarily in explaining the working of the adjustment mechanism under which an excess of exports or imports would set in motion certain economic changes (primarily in interest rates and prices) that would tend to reverse the flow of payments and restore equilibrium in the international accounts.

In recent years the development of national accounting—national income and product data—has led to a more thorough consideration of the place of foreign transactions in the domestic economy. In particular, it has seemed advisable to show in the balance-of-payments statement the extent to which domestically produced goods and services have been transferred to foreign countries and vice versa, and how the difference (the export or imports surplus) was financed.

If a country exports more than it imports, the excess can be financed in one of three ways.

1. By international gifts or contributions, such as lend-lease, reparations, or personal gifts such as so-called immigrant remittances. It should be noted that this result may be accomplished either by giving the foreign countries the goods and services (e.g., through lend-lease) or giving them the money with which to buy goods and services (e.g., personal or immigrant remittances).

2. By long-term capital movements. The export-surplus country may be making long-term loans and other investments abroad, or the foreign countries may be liquidating their investments in the exporting country.

3. By the use of liquid foreign-exchange reserves, normally gold and short-term foreign-exchange holdings. The exporting country may accept gold, increase its holdings of foreign currency or other short-term claims on foreign countries, or the foreign countries may reduce their short-term claims on the exporting country.[23]

_____
[23] *Economic Series, No. 65,* p. 164.

Under this new concept, unilateral transfers and capital transactions were grouped with current transactions because they were considered autonomous, thus a part of the dollars supplied or used. According to the Commerce concept, the combination of these three types of transactions produced a balance of payments which most nearly conformed to the definition of that term by those who were oriented toward classical economic thought.[24] The net balance of these three types of transactions was offset by changes in gold and short-term capital balances. Changes in gold and short-term capital were considered passive and to result from temporary differences between the receipts and payments of all other transactions. However, factors external to the balance of payments, such as interest rates and crises, could cause them to change independently of other transactions.[25] It was observed by Commerce that the balance of payments reflected *all* the country's international transactions and at the same time showed "the net effect of these transactions on the nation's international financial position."[26]

Methodology and sources of data. The sources of data available to balance of payments statisticians were meager at the time Commerce began its series in 1922. Accordingly sources of data had to be developed and statistical bases established for estimating those transactions for which little or no information was available. The development of procedures and sources of data for each of the major transactions is analyzed in general terms to show how the balance of payments was prepared. These transactions include merchandise, transportation, travel, unilateral transfers, income on investments, government transactions, long- and short-term capital (each distinguished as to foreign and domestic), gold and errors and omissions.

The *merchandise* account was the largest item in the United States balance of payments during this period; and despite the fact that exports and imports had long been recorded in custom-

---

[24] *Ibid.,* p. 165. Cf. William Rathbone, Chapter III.

[25] *Economic Series, No. 23,* "The United States in the World Economy," prepared by Hal B. Lary and Associates. Washington: Government Printing Office, 1943, pp. 33-35.

[26] *Economic Series No. 65,* p. 165.

house records, it continued to be a source of trouble for the balance of payments statisticians. Since the officially recorded exports and imports statistics of the United States did not precisely measure the cash claims of a country's foreign trade transactions, certain adjustments were required.

The only adjustment to the merchandise account in 1922 was to include the estimated value of parcel post packages. The estimate was based upon a value-weight ratio obtained from a sample count in the New York post office.[27] The balance of payments for 1924 was the first to contain an estimate for merchandise smuggled into the United States.[28]

Adjustments began in 1926 for bunker coal and oil sales to foreign vessels and American ships' purchases abroad, ships stores and repairs, sales and purchases of ships, since these items were not entered in the custom house records. The source of data for these adjustments was the United States Shipping Board for ship repairs, the Bureau of Navigation for ship sales and purchases, the Department of Commerce for bunker sales, and the Merchant Fleet Corporation for expenses in foreign ports. An adjustment was also made in 1926 for a special class of imports—goods produced by American capital abroad—proceeds of which remained in the home office.[29]

In 1927 adjustments were made to the merchandise account for bad debts and uninsured pilferage and destruction of goods in transit, because cash claims were extinguished.[30] Adjustments were made in 1928 for year-end lags in invoice terms because "a balance of payments should record only cash claims matured and actually honored during the year," and more than half of United States foreign trade was financed by sixty- to ninety-day dollar acceptances.[31]

A correction was made in 1929 to reduce the cost of imports because dollar exchange was purchased at a premium.[32] Several

[27] *Trade Information Bulletin No. 144*, pp. 15-16.
[28] *Trade Information Bulletin No. 503*, p. 4.
[29] *Ibid.*, pp. 1-4.
[30] *Trade Information Bulletin No. 552*, p. 5.
[31] *Trade Information Bulletin No. 625*, p. 6.
[32] *Trade Information Bulletin No. 698*, p. 8.

deductions were made from the merchandise account in 1931 for exports of machinery sent to subsidiaries abroad because no remittances were forthcoming, possible losses on consignment shipments, goods shipped under cash-discount terms, payments by United States exporters for fees on consular invoices, and the value of household goods brought into and taken out of the country by aliens.[33]

These merchandise adjustments began appearing as a separate item in the balance of payments in 1932 (see Table 4.4). This practice was continued through 1940, but disappeared from subsequent summary statements (see Table 4.6). By 1945, the merchandise account included goods, title to which changed hands internationally, whether or not they physically crossed frontiers. It also included goods given away as well as goods sent to foreign branches and subsidiaries. The valuation of both exports and imports was assigned at the frontier of the exporting country as declared at their actual wholesale price or at the cost to the exporters.[34]

Several adjustments were made in 1945 to the merchandise account so that the account included silver; net domestic gold production and consumption; foreign coins; and some unrecorded items, such as parcel post packages. It excluded noncommercial imports and exports such as household goods. Information from government agencies concerned was substituted for known entries in customs reports for governmental merchandise transactions.[35]

The *transportation* account included "all international payments and receipts arising out of the international movements of goods and persons, specifically: (1) freight and passenger revenues paid by Americans to foreign air and ocean carriers and similar revenues received by American carriers from foreigners, (2) expenditures of American carriers in foreign ports and foreign carriers in American ports, (3) revenues and expenditures in Canada of American railroads operating in that country, and

---

[33] *Trade Information Bulletin, No. 803*, pp. 13-14.
[34] *Economic Series No. 65*, p. 168.
[35] *Ibid.*, pp. 172-174.

(4) revenues received by American railroads for hauling foreign goods (but not passengers) in transit through the United States."[36]

The method of estimating such charges in 1922 was substantially that followed by Williams in 1921.[37] The account was broadened to include estimates of railroad freight in 1926. The data concerning payments to Canadian lines for freight were obtained from statistics supplied by the Dominion Bureau of Statistics. An average ton-mile earnings ratio was applied to the volume carried by the Canadian line to calculate the estimated payment. Improvement was also made in estimating ocean freight.[38] The source of data continued to be the Shipping Board until the estimates of freight and domestic ships were taken over by the United States Maritime Commission in 1937.[39]

According to Commerce "estimates of earnings of United States and foreign vessels in the carriage of United States foreign trade during the war were based upon tonnage and rate data supplied by the United States Maritime Commission and the War Shipping Administration, and value data from the Bureau of the Census."[40] Earnings from air freight were calculated from "Census Bureau data on exports to and imports from individual countries, and freight rates filed at the Civil Aeronautics Board and published in Air Transportation."[41] Passenger fares were calculated by multiplying the average passenger fares, obtained from questionnaires, by the number of passengers in each travel area. Port expenditures were estimated as a fixed percentage of gross revenue from the carriage of freight and passengers.[42]

The *travel* account included all expenditures of American residents (except United States government personnel) in foreign countries. Estimates of these expenditures were based upon

---

[36] *Ibid.*, p. 168.
[37] *Trade Information Bulletin, No. 144*, p. 11.
[38] *Trade Information Bulletin, No. 503*, pp. 6-8.
[39] *Economic Series No. 3*, p. 29.
[40] *Economic Series No. 65*, p. 174.
[41] *Ibid.*, p. 175.
[42] *Ibid.*, pp. 175-176.

questionnaires mailed to passport applicants selected at random. Average per capita expenditures were computed by class of steamship accommodation and by geographic area visited. Information concerning non-residents' travel in the United States was obtained from consular, customs and immigration officials.[43]

The data available concerning overseas travel greatly improved during this period as did techniques of making the estimates. Expenditures of American travelers in Canada were taken into account in 1923 as were those in Mexico in 1926. Questionnaires directed to travelers were introduced in 1927 and by 1930 "detailed records of oversea travel by citizens, showing destination, class of accommodation, and flag of carrier, became available, thus making possible more accurate calculations of gross expenditures and of the necessary deductions for fare payments to United States vessels."[44] The travel account in 1931 included expenditures of passengers on special cruises and aircraft for the first time. In 1934 questionnaires were first used on alien residents making temporary visits abroad.[45] However, the outstanding study of travel during this period was made in 1939 by August Maffry. It was the first detailed analysis of the nature and volume of overseas travel made in the United States.[46]

According to the Department of Commerce "all transfers of value, in the form of goods and services or money and other capital assets, not accompanied by a *quid pro quo* in one of these forms" were included in the *unilateral transfers* account.[47] In the earlier part of this period immigrant remittances were the chief items in this account, although charitable and missionary expenditures were significant. From 1940 onward, the account included lend lease and other government payments which dwarfed personal and institutional remittances. The sources of

[43] *Ibid.*, pp. 168, 177-181.

[44] *Economic Series No. 4*, "Oversea Travel and Travel Expenditures in the Balance of International Payments of the United States 1919-1938," prepared by August Maffry. Washington: Government Printing Office, 1939, p. 57.

[45] *Ibid.*

[46] *Ibid.*, pp. 1-95.

[47] *Economic Series No. 65*, p. 169.

information for these transfers were varied, but they included banks on which drafts were drawn in favor of foreign payees; the Annual Report of the Postmaster General for postal money order data; religious, scientific and philanthropic organizations for reports on institutional remittances; the Lend Lease Administration and other government agencies for governmental remittances and receipts.[48]

In 1945 the *income on investments* account included all interest, dividends and profits paid or credited during the period. Earnings of subsidiaries were included only to the extent of dividend distributions, while branch profits were included at the time they were credited to the home office account. This account included government as well as private payments and receipts.[49]

The basic method for computing estimated payments and receipts was from known outstanding securities and average yields. However, income tax records and questionnaires were extensively relied upon also. A more complete discussion of the sources of data concerning this account is given in the sections on long- and short-term capital.

Government transactions included "all expenditures and receipts of federal agencies and their personnel abroad for the purchase of services."[50] In general, the source of information was from the governmental unit engaged in the transaction, either directly or through the Clearing Office for Foreign Transactions.[51]

The *long-term capital* section of the balance of payments consisted of two main classes: American investments in foreign countries and foreign countries' investments in the United States. In 1929 the Department of Commerce attempted to measure approximately thirty different items of capital movements into and out of the United States.[52]

The growth of the United States as a creditor nation made

[48] *Ibid.*, pp. 186-188.
[49] *Ibid.*, pp. 181-183.
[50] *Ibid.*, p. 169.
[51] *Ibid.*, p. 184.
[52] *Trade Information Bulletin No. 698*, pp. 46-60.

the need for accurate estimates essential for two reasons. First, the *change in* foreign investment was needed to complete the capital section of the balance of payments. Second, balance of payments statisticians needed to know the amount of outstanding foreign investments to estimate interest and dividend income from these sources. At the beginning of the Commerce series, reliance was placed mainly on the 1921 compilations of foreign securities outstanding in the United States made by J. P. Morgan and Company and the Guaranty Trust Company of New York plus the net increase in investments shown by the annual balance of payment reports.

The Bureau of Foreign and Domestic Commerce began its current record of foreign capital issues publicly offered in the United States in the summer of 1922. Sources of information were varied; they included financial journals, files of bank circulars, economic services and investment manuals. Those sources were supplemented by inquiries to issuers and underwriters. The tabulations were checked against privately compiled data and discrepancies were reconciled by direct inquiries.

The Bureau of Foreign and Domestic Commerce attempted to improve the accuracy of these compilations by rechecking the annual schedules of foreign securities publicly offered and by collecting data on direct investments. The results of this study, made by Ralph A. Young, were published in "Handbook of American Underwriting of Foreign Securities."[53]

As the position of the United States as an international creditor grew, available data on the subject became increasingly inadequate. It was this situation which prompted the first comprehensive study of American direct investments abroad made by Paul D. Dickens in 1929.[54] Direct investments, as defined by Dickens, included "commercial and industrial properties situ-

---

[53]Department of Commerce, Bureau of Foreign and Domestic Commerce, *Trade Promotion Series No. 104*, "Handbook on American Underwriting of Foreign Securities," prepared by Ralph A. Young. Washington: Government Printing Office, 1930.

[54] *Trade Information Bulletin No. 731*, "American Direct Investments in Foreign Countries," prepared by Paul D. Dickens. Washington: Government Printing Office, 1930.

ated abroad and belonging to residents of the United States and its Territories, from which a return is normally expected."[55]

The study was based on information received from approximately 1750 businessmen. The list of companies having foreign investments was compiled from the *Petroleum Register,* the *Mines Handbook, Moody's Manual* and reports by consular offices of the State Department. The names of 2500 corporations were obtained in this way. A questionnaire was mailed to the president of each of these corporations requesting book value or fair market value of their foreign investments.[56]

Dickens devoted several months to eliminating duplications from the two surveys and to adding "foreign securities taken in the United States before 1914 and those privately taken since then; to ascertaining carefully the amount of each issue outstanding at the end of 1930 after refunding, sinking-fund, and redemption operations; to allowing for 'foreign securities transferred to and from the United States through stock markets;' and to arranging the statistics by countries."[57] This study covered all types of long-term investments abroad as of the end of 1930. At that time there were three classifications of foreign investment: direct, portfolio, and foreign securities internationally transferred. Dickens made a second comprehensive study of American direct investments abroad in 1936 using substantially the same sources of data, methods of compilation and presentation.[58]

The earliest official sources of information on foreign investment in the United States became available as a result of the American Dollar Securities Committee and the reports of the Alien Property Custodian. The American Dollar Securities Committee was "appointed by the British Government to mobilize

---

[55] *Ibid.*, p. 1.

[56] *Ibid.*, pp. 3-4.

[57] *Trade Information Bulletin, No. 767,* "A New Estimate of American Investments Abroad," prepared by Paul D. Dickens. Washington: Government Printing Office, 1931, pp. 1-2.

[58] *Economic Series No. 1.,* "American Direct Investments in Foreign Countries—1936," prepared by Paul D. Dickens. Washington: Government Printing Office, 1938.

securities held by British subjects for use in supporting sterling exchange."[59] The report of the United States Alien Property Custodian gave information on the account of enemy property seized.[60]

Estimates of foreign investments in the United States made in 1927, 1929, 1931 and annually to 1936 were obtained from questionnaires addressed to foreign representatives of the Departments of Commerce and State. These estimates were based upon the opinions of informed individuals and were often no more than guesses.[61]

In 1926 the Bureau of Foreign and Domestic Commerce had approximately fifty district and cooperative offices located throughout the country and sixteen commodity divisions in Washington. One of their duties was to report the capital composition of foreign firms applying for Bureau services. The estimate of new direct investments in the United States in 1926 was ascertained by questionnaires to the Bureau's affiliates.[62] Estimated changes in old securities were derived from questionnaires sent to international bankers, investment trusts and stock and bond brokerage firms.[63]

The first comprehensive study of foreign investment in the United States was made by the Finance Division of the Bureau of Foreign and Domestic Commerce in 1935. Data on foreign investments were compiled and analyzed in five categories: direct investments, common stock, preferred stock, bonds and other investments.[64] Data on these holdings were obtained from the State and Commerce Departments, trade associations, business periodicals and manuals both foreign and domestic, newspapers and corporate stockholders' lists. The valuation for direct investment was based upon the stated or par value of

[59] Department of Commerce, Bureau of Foreign and Domestic Commerce, *Foreign Investments in the United States*. Washington: Government Printing Office, 1937, p. 25.

[60] *Ibid.*

[61] *Trade Information Bulletin No. 552*, pp. 8-9; *No. 698*, pp. 11-12; and *Foreign Investment in the United States*, p. 6.

[62] *Trade Information Bulletin No. 503*, p. 41.

[63] *Trade Information Bulletin, No. 625*, p. 45.

[64] *Foreign Investment in the United States, op. cit.*, p. 9.

the stock, interest on surplus or deficit, principal amount of bonds and notes, and net advances and intercompany accounts. Market values were used for common stock and par values for preferred stock.[65]

When the balance of payments for 1940-1945 was prepared the information for private direct long-term investment abroad came from questionnaires requesting corporations to reveal advances to and from their foreign subsidiaries; changes in their equities in foreign branches; and (beginning with the last half of 1945) data concerning purchase and sale of subsidiaries' securities. Supplemental information was obtained from forms filed with the Securities and Exchange Commission and the Bureau of Internal Revenue. Little information was available as to foreign investments in the United States in 1945.[66]

Information concerning new issues of foreign securities in the United States was obtained from underwriters and financial services. Discounts and commissions were deducted from the face value of the new issues. For the first time refunding issues were included as new issues.

The source of information concerning transactions in outstanding foreign and domestic securities was obtained from the Federal Reserve Banks based upon reports of banks, brokers and dealers. Governmental long-term loans, such as those made by the Export-Import Bank, and the Reconstruction Finance Corporation, either came directly from the International Economics Division of the Department of Commerce, published statements of the agency concerned, or the Clearing Office for Foreign Transactions.[67]

Movements of *short-term capital* proved to be a very difficult item for the balance of payments statistician to estimate. So little was known of these transactions in 1922 that they were included in an account entitled "the unfunded credit balance" which was a combination of errors and unrecorded transactions.[68]

---

[65] *Ibid.*, pp. 88-90.
[66] *Economic Series No. 65*, pp. 188-190.
[67] *Ibid.*
[68] *Trade Information Bulletin No. 144*, pp. 19-20.

The only information concerning short-term transactions was obtained from questionnaires sent to fifteen hundred international banking and commercial firms. The questionnaires continued to be sent to international bankers and investment firms, but no information was available concerning exporters' and importers' accounts receivable and payable until 1933 when blocked accounts due to exchange controls again provided information on the changes in these accounts.[69]

The balance of payments showed only changes in bank deposits from 1923 to 1925, but in 1926 the questionnaires were broadened so as to provide information concerning bank deposits, loans and advances and commercial and Treasury bills.[70] The results of the questionnaires were so doubtful in 1927 that no amounts were shown in the statement for that year. The questionnaire was revised in 1928 and directed to 188 of the leading financial institutions in the United States, including the twelve Federal Reserve Banks and the largest investment trust companies.[71]

The *net* change in international banking short-term assets and liabilities was shown as a separate item in the capital section of the 1927 balance of payments. By 1933, the detail schedule of short-term capital showed a miscellaneous section for exporters' and importers' accounts receivable and payable, which was separated in 1934 from changes in bank funds.[72] In 1937 short-term capital was shown in three separate classifications – bank funds, miscellaneous, and United States currency.[73]

The international movements of United States currrency were contained in the balance of payments from 1923 to 1926. Although estimates of this item were not made from 1927 to 1929, they were begun again in 1930. The source of information on currency movements was primarily from reports of the Fed-

[69] *Trade Information Bulletin No. 819*, pp. 41-43.
[70] *Trade Information Bulletin No. 503*, pp. 45-46.
[71] *Trade Information Bulletin No. 625*, pp. 47-48.
[72] *Trade Information Bulletin No. 826*, p. 4.
[73] *Economic Series No. 3*, p. 2.

eral Reserve Bank of New York prepared from monthly questionnaires to fifteen banks in New York City.[74]

In the balance of payments for 1940-1945, short-term capital transactions were shifted from the capital section into a "balancing" section where United States and foreign transactions were distinguished. According to the Department of Commerce:[75]

The short-term capital account includes all international claims payable within 1 year. Private short-term claims comprise bank deposits, bills, acceptances, commercial paper, short-term State and municipal obligations, brokerage balances, commercial deposits abroad for the direct account of United States firms, advance payments for merchandise, and United States currency and coins held abroad. Foreign short-term claims on the United States Government include holdings of United States Government short-term obligations, deposits with the Treasury, and various claims arising out of the provision of currency for expenditures by our armed forces. United States Government short-term claims on foreigners include holdings of foreign currencies, deposits abroad, and various advances and settlements.

The sources of information for this account were the Federal Reserve's monthly compilation for the Treasury Department which appeared in both the *Federal Reserve Bulletin* and the *Treasury Bulletin*. Data on commercial balances not reported by the banks were collected by the Federal Reserve Banks from exporters and importers.[76]

The *gold* account has appeared on the United States balance of payments in a separate category since 1922.[77] The reasons for this were discussed in the concepts section of this study, and its place on the balance of payments was shown in the presentation section. There are only two changes in this account that need further clarification.

---

[74] *Trade Information Bulletin No. 698*, p. 64.
[75] *Economic Series No. 65.*, p. 170.
[76] *Ibid.*, pp. 189-190.
[77] *Trade Information Bulletin No. 144*, p. 3.

First, the practice of earmaking gold began with post-World War I currency reconstruction when central bankers were able to count gold abroad as gold in vault. The earmarking of gold was simply the separation of gold in vaults to designate changes in ownership rather than physical shipment. This adjustment appeared first in the 1927 balance of payments. The Federal Reserve Bank of New York provided data for this adjustment.[78]

Second, the net domestic production or consumption of gold was shown in the balance of payments as adjustments to the merchandise and gold accounts. This procedure first began in the 1940-1945 balance of payments. The Bureau of the Census provided the information for this adjustment.[79]

The *errors and omissions* account was recognized as the difference between the total debits and credits in the 1923 balance of payments. At that time the difference was thought to be due almost entirely to short-term capital transactions for which there was little available information.[80] However, the basis for estimating some accounts had such varying degrees of accuracy that many of the accounts could be in error as much as $150,000,000 in *either* direction.[81] Commerce pointed out in 1928 that the errors and omissions account would be larger except that errors tended to offset one another.[82] While the accuracy of the balance of payments improved as the sources of data and methods of making estimates improved, absolute accuracy was not, of course, claimed by the Department of Commerce.

---

[78] *Trade Information Bulletin No. 552*, pp. 49-50.
[79] *Economic Series No. 65*, pp. 191-192.
[80] *Trade Information Bulletin No. 215*, p. 2.
[81] *Trade Information Bulletin No. 144*, p. 2.
[82] *Trade Information Bulletin No. 625*, p. v.

5

Balance of Payments Concepts, 1915-1947: The United Kingdom and the League of Nations

The period 1915 to 1947 is important in the study of the balance of payments as many advances were made in the form of presentation, methodology and underlying theoretical concepts. The United States made its greatest progress in reporting international economic statistics during these years. Similar achievements were made in the United Kingdom and by the League of Nations.

The Balance of Payments in the United Kingdom

The trading history of the United Kingdom between 1915 and 1947 was distinguished by two closely related events. First, there was a reversal of the nineteenth century economic policy which regarded the control of the trade balance as a matter of no concern to the government. Second, there was difficulty in financing goods and services purchased from other countries.

In general, the United Kingdom had three chief means of paying for imports: exports of merchandise, primarily manufactured goods; earnings from foreign investments; and earnings from shipping. An examination of each of these items reveals the cause of the financial difficulty.

The United Kingdom failed to meet competition from the United States and other industrial countries in foreign markets, and its exports of manufactured goods suffered a relative decline. Earnings from foreign investments were reduced because a large portion of British foreign investments was liquidated during both world wars to finance needed imports. Shipping earnings were reduced because of shipping tonnage lost during these wars. This combination of events was sufficient to motivate the United Kingdom to a greater understanding of foreign economic transactions. It is somewhat surprising, therefore, that the United Kingdom lagged behind both the United States and the League of Nations in developing sources, methodological procedures and forms used in presenting balance of payment data.

Balance of payments presentation in the United Kingdom. The *Board of Trade Journal* began publishing annual articles on the balance of trade for 1919.[1] The summary of the transactions for each year was shown in a one-column table in which each of the estimates for net invisible exports was listed and their sum deducted from the adverse balance of trade.

The form of presentation of the United Kingdom balance of payments for 1922 is illustrated in Table 5.1. The excess of imports over exports of merchandise and bullion was shown in the first row of the statement. This excess was deducted from net invisible exports and the remaining balance was considered available for foreign investment.

There were only a few changes in the form of the balance of payments in the following years although the number of items presented grew in number. Government payments and receipts were included for the first time in 1925.[2] Other transactions, such as sale of old ships, tourist receipts in the United Kingdom and personal remittances, were also included in the miscellaneous grouping of receipts from other sources.

The information concerning new issues of securities was discontinued in 1926. Thus, the estimated debit or credit balance on the current account became the final figure on the statement.[3] Gold bullion and specie were removed from the merchandise account and not shown elsewhere on the balance of payments

---

[1] "The Balance of Trade. An Estimate of Invisible Exports," *Board of Trade Journal,* January 15, 1920, pp. 71-73.

[2] *Board of Trade Journal,* January 21, 1926, p. 69.

[3] *Board of Trade Journal,* January 27, 1927, p. 93.

TABLE 5.1

United Kingdom Balance of Trade in 1922

	1907	1910	1913	1920	1922
			In million £		
Excess of Imports of Merchandise and Bullion	142	159	158	343	170
Net Income (from Overseas Investments)	160	187	210	200	175
Net National Shipping Income	85	90	94	340	110
Commissions	25	25	25	40	30
Other Services	10	10	10	15	10
Total "Invisible Exports" on Balance	280	312	339	595	325
Available for Investment Overseas	138	153	181	252	155
New Overseas Issues on London Market in year*	91	207	198	53	135
New Overseas Issues on London Market in following year*	142	166	159	116	—

*For 1913 and subsequent years the figures are taken from the tables given in the Monthly Review of the London Joint City and Midland Bank. For earlier years the figures are taken from the "Economist."

Source: "The Balance of Trade in 1922. Investments abroad and Shipping Earnings," *The Board of Trade Journal*, March 29, 1923, p. 386.

from 1931 forward.[4] Although the name of the statement was changed in 1933 from the balance of trade to the balance of payments, this did not result in the inclusion of any capital transaction or gold movements.[5]

Ernest C. Snow, a government official, presented a paper on the balance of trade to the Royal Statistical Society in 1932. He suggested that the balance of trade as presented by the Board of Trade might be better arranged so as to show how the United Kingdom paid for its overseas purchases. To overcome this weakness he designed a statement to show how the United Kingdom paid for imports of foodstuffs and raw materials with the exports

---

[4] *Board of Trade Journal*, February 18, 1932, p. 216.
[5] *Board of Trade Journal*, February 22, 1934, pp. 277-281.

TABLE 5.2

UNITED KINGDOM BALANCE OF TRADE, 1929-1931

	1929	1930	1931[1]
		£ Millions	
What we received.			
Excess Imports of Food Stuffs and Raw Materials	660	551	468 (462)
Our Means of Payment.			
Excess Exports of Manufactured Goods (including parcel post)	278	164	52 (53)
Shipping Earnings	130	105	?
Overseas Investments[2]	270	235	?
Interest and Commissions	65	55	?
Other Sources	55	31	?
Total	798	590	

Notes: [1] Data was incomplete at the time of the preparation of the table.
[2] This is actually earnings on overseas investments.

Source: Ernest C. Snow, "The Balance of Trade," *Journal of the Royal Statistical Society*, Part I, 1932, p. 80.

of manufactured goods and various services. This statement is illustrated in Table 5.2. The effects it may have had on the official balance of payments can be estimated by comparison with the current account of the official statement of 1946 shown in Table 5.3.

The series of articles on the balance of payments published in the *Board of Trade Journal* was discontinued in 1939. The official balances of payments re-appeared after World War II as part of the national income accounts prepared by the Central Statistical Office in collaboration with other departments.[6] The form of presentation changed considerably from the pre-war Board of Trade tabulations as shown in Table 5.3. The statement was divided into two main sections, one for current and the other for capital transactions. The current account was arranged

―――――――

[6] Great Britain, Treasury, *National Income and Expenditure of the United Kingdom, 1938 to 1946*, Cmd. 7099. London: His Majesty's Stationery Office, 1947, p. 7.

TABLE 5.3

UNITED KINGDOM BALANCE OF PAYMENTS, 1946

I. CURRENT ACCOUNT

£ Millions

	Payments	1946		Receipts	1946
1.	Imports (f.o.b.)—		10.	Exports and re-exports	890
	(a) Food and drink	555	11.	Shipping	150
	(b) Tobacco	70	12.	Interest, profits and dividends	150
	(c) Materials	360	13.	Other (net)	72
	(d) Petroleum	60			
	(e) Other	65			
	Total	1,110			
2.	Government expenditure—				
	(a) Military (net)	225			
	(b) Relief and rehabilitation	97			
	(c) Cost of Germany (net)	38			
	(d) Other (net)	−60			
	Total	300			
3.	Shipping	140			
4.	Interest, profits and dividends	70			
5.	Film remittances (net)	17			
6.	Tourist payments	25			
7.	Total payments	1,662			
8.	Balance on current account	−400			
9.	Total payments less deficit	1,262	14.	Total receipts	1,262

TABLE 5.3 (Continued)

II. Capital Account

		£ Millions
15.	Gold and U.S. dollar reserves	61
16.	United States and Canadian lines of credit	−279
17.	Other loans to H.M. Government	38
18.	Net sterling, etc., liabilities	−148
19.	External capital assets	− 70
20.	Subscriptions under Bretton Woods Agreement Act, 1945	33
21.	Other	− 35
22.	Total external investment (equal to balance on current account)	−400

Source: Great Britain, Treasury, *National Income and Expenditure of the United Kingdom, 1938 to 1946*, Cmd. 7099. London: His Majesty's Stationery Office, 1947, p. 7.

so that payments were on the left side and receipts on the right side. Payments, less the deficit on the current account, equaled total receipts.

The capital account showed the *net* change for foreign and domestic as well as long- and short-term capital. It also included gold and United States dollar reserves. The net change in capital was shown as being exactly equal to the deficit on the current account. One of the capital accounts (Subscriptions under Bretton Woods Agreement Act, 1945) included an allowance for errors and omissions which made this exact balance possible.

The first presentation of the balance of payments of the United Kingdom as a separate publication was for 1947 as shown in Table 5.4. Although the division between the current and capital accounts remained, there were changes in form from the previous year.

The current account was rearranged and the difference between payments and receipts was designated the surplus or deficit on the current account. The capital account was given in much greater detail (not shown in Table 5.4) than in previous years. Its three main classifications were for gold and dollar

TABLE 5.4

UNITED KINGDOM BALANCE OF PAYMENTS, 1947

CURRENT ACCOUNT

	£ millions	1947
Payments		Provisional
1.	Imports (f.o.b.)	1,574
2.	Government expenditure	211
3.	Shipping	163
4.	Interest, profits, and dividends	94
5.	Film remittances (net)	13
6.	Tourist payments	50
7.	Total payments	2,105
	Receipts	
8.	Exports and re-exports (f.o.b.)	1,125
9.	Shipping	180
10.	Interest, profits, and dividends	145
11.	Other (net)	− 20
12.	Total receipts	1,430
	Surplus (+) or Deficit (−) on Current Account.	
13.	With the Sterling Area	+ 80
14.	With Western Hemisphere	− 680
15.	With Rest of World	− 75
16.	Total	− 675

CAPITAL ACCOUNT

	Summary	
17.	Net drain on United Kingdom gold and dollar reserves	1,023
18.	Net decrease in United Kingdom external capital assets	− 206
19.	Net increase in sterling balances	− 142
20.	Total Overseas Disinvestment	675

Source: Adapted from Great Britain, Treasury, *United Kingdom Balance of Payments,* Cmd. 7324. London: His Majesty's Stationery Office, 1948, pp. 3-4.

reserves, British residents' investments abroad, and foreigners investments in the United Kingdom. The last two classifications included both short- and long-term capital transactions. The fourth section was the balance of the first three, and showed the net overseas disinvestment. This disinvestment was exactly offset by the surplus or deficit on the current account.

Concepts upon which the United Kingdom balances of payments were prepared. The basic belief among balance of payments statisticians during the early part of this period was that the current section of the balance of payments contained transactions of a revenue nature. The current accounts were viewed as somewhat analogous to the revenue and expense accounts of commerical enterprises. The difference between receipts and expenditures in the current account was assumed to be a surplus or deficit which affected *net* overseas investment. Net foreign investment was increased by a surplus and decreased by a deficit. This change in overseas investment could be of a long- or short-term nature and could be a change in foreign liabilities as well as in foreign assets. These generalizations are detailed in the following paragraphs.

In 1921 C. K. Hobson was concerned with the measurement of the balance of trade.[7] He was interested in estimating those transactions which would tend to give residents of the United Kingdom claims on foreigners, and vice versa. Hobson excluded from this measurement all movements of capital or gold and included only what was then termed current transactions. The difference between the two types of offsetting claims was considered by Hobson to represent an export of capital.[8]

Besides Hobson's concept of the measurement of the balance of trade, the principles upon which the balance of payments was prepared during this period were not specifically stated and must largely be ascertained from the statements themselves. However, there were three instances in which comments help in the clarification of these concepts.

---

[7] C. K. Hobson, "The Measurement of the Balance of Trade," *Economica*, May 1921, pp. 132-146.

[8] *Ibid.*, p. 146.

In 1936 the purpose of the annual articles in the *Board of Trade Journal* on the balance of payments, with the summary of transactions that each contained, was stated to be as follows: "To estimate the net balance on all transactions of a revenue character between the United Kingdom and other countries, including those transactions originated by Governments as well as those which arise from dealings between individuals."[9] The next occasion when the British concepts of the balance of payments were revealed occurred in the supplementary comments on the 1925 statement. The excess of current receipts over current expenditures abroad was considered available for overseas investment. To show that this was actually the case, the lower portion of the statements provided information on new securities issues in British security markets in each of the selected years and for the following year. The latter was presumably because there could be some lag in converting a surplus into foreign investment. However, by 1925, it was believed that there was no *necessary* relationship between the balance on the current account and new long-term investment.[10] The reason for this was the recognition of the changes in short-term capital which were not reported. The third statement of basic concepts was in 1932. Prior to that year gold bullion and specie were included in the merchandise account. It was then recognized that "the recorded movements of gold were in large part not connected intimately with trade transactions."[11] Instead, gold movements were thought to be more closely related to capital than merchandise and were removed from the current accounts.

Although the balance of payments statisticians distinguished between current and capital transactions, certain transactions classified as current could be reclassified as capital under different circumstances. Gold and receipts and repayments of the principal of foreign loans and debts of the government are examples of this reclassification.

Sources and methodology of the United Kingdom balance

---

[9] *Board of Trade Journal*, February 20, 1936, p. 259.
[10] *Board of Trade Journal*, January 21, 1926, p. 70.
[11] *Board of Trade Journal*, February 18, 1932, p. 216.

of payments. Estimates were made before World War II for only current transactions. Those transactions were grouped into six general classifications: merchandise, government, shipping, investment income, commissions and miscellaneous. It was only after World War II that various long- and short-term capital items were also estimated.

The statistics for the *merchandise* account were obtained from general trade accounts which were kept in accordance with the *Import and Export List* issued jointly by the Treasury and the Commissioner of Customs and Excise. As late as 1938, the balance of payments in the United Kingdom was published with imports valued on a c.i.f. and exports on an f.o.b. basis.[12] It was not until 1946 that both exports and imports were both on a comparable f.o.b. basis of valuation.[13] Adjustments to the merchandise accounts were made so that the figures covered "actual payments for imports, and not arrivals as recorded in the Trade and Navigation accounts."[14]

The second of the six general classes of transactions included on the United Kingdom balance of payments was the *government* account. Government transactions, first mentioned in 1926, included payments of principal and interest on loans from the United States and Canada; receipts of principal and interest on loans to other governments; interest received from Suez Canal shares; and reparations recoveries. Prior to 1926, governmental receipts of income were included in the income from overseas investment account.[15] Official government records were the chief source of information.

The third important class of international transaction in the United Kingdom was the *shipping* account. This account included the gross earnings of British shipping companies from the carriage of both freight and passengers and payments made

[12] *Board of Trade Journal*, February 23, 1939, p. 285.
[13] *National Income and Expenditure of the United Kingdom, 1938 to 1946, op. cit.*, p. 57.
[14] Great Britain, Treasury, *United Kingdom Balance of Payments, 1946 and 1947*, Cmd. 7324. London: His Majesty's Stationery Office, 1948, p. 5.
[15] *Board of Trade Journal*, January 21, 1926, p. 69.

by foreign ships in British ports for bunkers, stores and other expenses. Expenditures made by residents of the United Kingdom for freight and passenger fares on foreign ships and all expenses of British ships in foreign ports were deducted from the receipts from foreigners for similar transactions in the United Kingdom.[16]

The value of imports and exports carried in British vessels first became available January 1, 1936. Prior to that time the only measure available concerning the proportion of goods carried in British ships was the net tonnage of shipping entered and cleared with cargo under the British flag. In order to test the accuracy of the estimates of shipping earnings, the Chamber of Shipping and the Liverpool Steam Ship Owners' Association conducted an inquiry in 1936 among their members to ascertain freight receipts, expenditures abroad and amounts received for the carriage of passengers both resident and non-resident of the United Kingdom.[17]

Before 1946, merchandise imports were valued c.i.f. and included charges for freight. Surveys showed that approximately two-thirds of the imports were carried by British ships and therefore, did not constitute an international transaction. Approximately three-fourths of British exports, all of which were valued on an f.o.b. basis, were carried in British vessels. To the extent that the goods were carried in foreign ships, payment claims were underestimated.[18]

Another source of British receipts was *income on overseas investments*. The estimates of income from overseas investment were based upon gross receipts of British companies operating abroad less income paid to foreigners for their investments in the United Kingdom. The account included dividends received, head office expenses in the United Kingdom for British companies operating abroad, and net additions to reserves and undistributed profits.[19]

[16] *National Income and Expenditure of the United Kingdom, 1938 to 1946, op. cit.,* p. 57; and *Board of Trade Journal,* February 22, 1934, p. 277.
[17] *Board of Trade Journal,* February 17, 1938, p. 231.
[18] *Board of Trade Journal,* February 23, 1939, p. 285.
[19] *Board of Trade Journal,* February 20, 1936, pp. 260-261.

The early sources of information on investments abroad were the surveys completed by Paish in 1909 and 1911. Subsequently, a study was made by Robert Kindersley, the senior representative on the Dawes Committee of 1924, and director of the Bank of England from 1914 to 1946.[20] Kindersley made an examination of new issues of securities, sinking fund payments and principal repayments on securities of foreign governments and commercial enterprises listed on United Kingdom stock exchanges, and those British companies known to have foreign operations. He obtained his information from investment and commercial banks, from stock exchanges and from annual reports of companies operating abroad. These investments were classified by country, industry and class of security.

Kindersley said the amount of income shown by the survey should not be used in a balance of payments as the net earnings on overseas investments for several reasons. First, there should be a deduction for the income accruing to foreigners from investments in the United Kingdom. Then, account had to be taken of changes in reserves and head office expenses in the United Kingdom of companies operating abroad. Furthermore, there were substantial defaults of government and commercial bonds to be taken into consideration in the balance of payments.

The transactions under the general heading, *commissions*, included charges associated with acceptance credit; discount on foreign bills, bank interest, commissions and other charges on new issues paid by overseas borrowers; merchanting commissions on overseas produce; brokers' commissions; insurance remittances from abroad; and earnings on exchange transactions. Deductions from the total of these earnings were made for similar charges paid to foreigners.[21]

The last classification on the balance of payments was the *miscellaneous* account which included tourist expenditures, film royalties, second-hand ships, diplomatic expenses, emigrant remittances and transfers of assets of emigrants. Estimates for

---

[20] Robert Kindersley, "British Overseas Investments in 1931," *The Economic Journal*, June 1933, pp. 187-204.

[21] *Board of Trade Journal*, February 20, 1936, p. 261.

tourist expenditures were based upon sampling of certain groups of tourists and estimates by officials on expenditures of other groups. The product of the number of tourists and the average expenditure per person constituted the estimated tourist expense. Emigrants' remittances were similarly estimated.[22]

The preceding sources of information were used before World War II for the various current accounts. The primary sources of data for the accounts appearing in the balance of payments of the United Kingdom for 1946 and 1947 were exchange control records.[23]

League of Nations

Up to this point, the historical study of the balance of international payments has been concerned exclusively with its development in individual countries, the United States and the United Kingdom. This procedure has been followed for two reasons. First, these two countries have been leaders in the development of sources of data, methodology and presentation of the balance of payments. Second, it would be an almost insurmountable task to accumulate historical data from all the countries of the world. However, examination of the work of the League of Nations permits the introduction of data from other countries, particularly for 1922 when the member countries' balance of payments were published in the same form as they were submitted to the League. The contribution of the League of Nations to the balance of payments was in the standardization of the form of presentation so that the member countries' statements were prepared on a comparable basis. The study of the League's work conforms to the previous outline for the United States and the United Kingdom concerning form of presentation and basic concepts. However, the sources of data and methodology are omitted because they would appear redundant after having described those of two major countries.

Form of presentation. The League of Nations began its work

---

[22] *Ibid.,* pp. 261-262.

[23] Great Britain, Treasury, *United Kingdom Balance of Payments, 1946 to 1949,* Cmd. 7928. London: His Majesty's Stationery Office, 1950, p. 11.

on the balance of payments to shed light on problems of currency stabilization and persistent payments difficulties. Thirteen countries submitted balance of payment data to the League for the first time in 1924. No effort was made by the League to induce conformity to any standardized procedures, and the statements for the calendar year 1922 were published in 1924 in the form given by each country.

It is interesting to note that no official balance of payments was at that time being prepared for the Netherlands, Italy, Denmark, Switzerland or Norway, and that neither France nor Germany reported any data to the League. France's first balance of payments appeared in the League's annual publication for 1931. This was not an official estimate but one prepared by Pierre Meynial and published in the *Revue d'économie politique* for each of the years 1927-1929.[24]

Three of the member countries' statements submitted to the League are illustrated to show the stage of development of the balance of payments in those countries. The three statements selected were relatively more developed than those of most other countries.

Sweden's balance of payments for 1922, shown in Table 5.5, contained both capital and current international transactions. On the receipt, or credit, side the transactions were classified so that capital transactions were separated from those of a current nature. A distinction was made between visible and invisible exports, and exports of gold and silver were separated from other merchandise exports. While payments, or debits, were unclassified, each debit transaction corresponded closely to similar credit transactions.

Argentina's balance of payments for 1922, illustrated in Table 5.6, was prepared by M. C. A. Tornquist and published in the *Revista de Economica Argentina* and in the *Review of the River Plate*.[25] This statement was of simpler construction than Sweden's balance of payments. Its capital, current and monetary transactions were rather indiscriminately mixed under

---

[24] League of Nations, *Memorandum on International Trade and Balance of Payments 1927-1929*, Geneva, 1931, II, p. 88.

[25] League of Nations, *Memorandum on Balance of Payments and Foreign Trade Balances 1910-1923*, Geneva, 1924, I, p. 36.

the general debit and credit classes. However, it was relatively well developed from the standpoint of the inclusion of many types of capital transactions.

Italy's balance of payments for 1922, presented in Table 5.7, was prepared by Professor Mortara and published in the *Rivista Bancaria* on February 20, 1924. This statement made a clear distinction between current visible and invisible transactions. Gold was shown separately from merchandise, but was included in

TABLE 5.5

APPROXIMATE BALANCE OF PAYMENTS MADE BY SWEDEN IN 1922
(Kr., 000,000's omitted)

CREDIT			DEBIT		
Movements of capital:					
1. Swedish securities sold	20		1. Foreign securities purchased	50	
2. Other capital imports	20	40	2. Swedish securities repurchased	50	100
Interest and other invisible items:			3. Service of foreign debt	17	
3. Interest and dividends from capital abroad	15		4. Interest on foreign capital in Sweden	10	
4. Remittances from Swedes in America	15		5. Excess losses	10	
5. Freight receipts, less cost of bunker coal, oil, etc., purchased abroad, port charges, etc.	130	160	6. Net tourists' expenditure	30	
Merchandise:			7. Foreign relief, foreign lottery-tickets purchased (net)	13	80
6. Exports of merchandise		1,151	8. Imports of merchandise		1,118
Gold and silver coin and bullion:			9. Imports of gold and silver coin		299
7. Exports of gold and silver coin		331	TOTAL		1,597
TOTAL		1,682	BALANCE		85

Source: League of Nations, *Memorandum on Balance of Payments and Foreign Trade Balances 1910-1923*, Geneva, 1924, Vol. I, p. 34.

TABLE 5.6

ARGENTINE BALANCE OF PAYMENTS, 1920-21, 1921-22
(Peso oro, 000's omitted)

CREDIT.

	1920-21 1921-22
Exports of merchandise	1,389,460
Issues of existing companies	17,500
Investment of new capital in Argentine	38,000
Amortization on British and French Debt	83,680
Interest on British and French Debt	5,610
Interest on foreign bonds	5,000
Correspondents abroad	1,470
Loan in U.S.A.	66,000
Credits obtained by State Railways	22,200
Export of foreign bonds	} 6,500
" Argentine bonds	22,050
Sale of ships	4,300
Money spent by foreign travellers	9,500
Decrease in gold stock	18,700
TOTAL	1,689,970

DEBIT.

Imports of merchandise	1,504,760
Service of foreign debt	87,100
" Cedulas Hipotecarias	13,950
Railway company dividends and interest	100,300
Earnings of other foreign capital	66,400
Remittances of foreign residents	68,000
Expenditure by Argentine travellers abroad	43,000
Argentine bonds repatriated	63,130
Foreign mortgage capital repaid	2,000
Other capital repaid, etc.	3,400
Interest payments to U. K.	3,940
Municipal short-term loans	1,650
Subscriptions to foreign loans	—
Increase in stock of gold	—
Sums remitted to ex-belligerent countries	2,250
TOTAL	1,959,880
BALANCE	−269,910

Source: League of Nations, *Memorandum on Balance of Payments and Foreign Trade Balances, 1910-1923*, Geneva, 1924, Vol. I, p. 36.

the same classification. The most complete section of this statement was that for invisible exports and imports which was quite detailed. A clear distinction was made between the current and the capital accounts. The capital section provided less information and was perhaps weaker than the other two sections of the statement.

TABLE 5.7

ITALY'S BALANCE OF PAYMENTS, 1922
(Lire, 000,000's omitted)

I.—*Visible items.*

	Debit	Credit
1. Merchandise shown in Trade Returns	6,462.4	
2. Gold	37.7	
3. Reparation deliveries, etc.		440.5

II.—*Current invisible items.*

	Debit	Credit
4. Expenditure of Italian vessels abroad and foreign vessels in Italy	203.1	
5. Sea freight on goods, net		527.0
6. Land freight on goods, etc., net	132.3	
7. Sea freight.—Passengers, net		115.6
8. Expenditure of visitors, net		2,500.0
9. Remittances of emigrants, net		3,400.0
10. Money-orders received		274.7
11. Interest on Italian public debt (payable)	115.6	
12. Interest on bank debts (net balance)	140.0	
13. Dividends of industrial undertakings		30.0

III.—*Capital Movements.*

	Debit	Credit
14. Public debt certificates sold		460.0
15. Public debt, amortisation of	412.8	
16. Investments in foreign securities	12.0	
Total	7,515.9	7,747.8
		−231.9
		7,515.9

Source: League of Nations, *Memorandum on Balance of Payments and Foreign Trade Balances, 1910-1923*, Geneva, 1924, Vol. I, pp. 23-24.

None of the three statements provided any information concerning short-term capital movements. All three totaled debits and credits and found a balance. This balance in each statement was an errors or omissions account which was thought to be chiefly explained by changes in short-term capital.

The following year (1925) the League of Nations sent a blank form, along with explanatory notes, to each member nation. It was expected that this would result in a greater degree of comparability and more precision in the statements. The League did not publish in full detail the form of presentation of every country. British India was one of those in which all classifications were shown.

The League's form of presentation, as shown for India in Table 5.8, emphasizes two main classifications: inward or credit

TABLE 5.8

Balance of Payments for India, 1924
Inward or Credit Movements (Exports)

	Amounts	Sub-Totals and Total
I. *Capital items.*	Lakhs of rupees	
1. Receipt of payments on account of foreign loans matured and paid		
2. Foreign securities re-sold abroad		
3. Government securities sold abroad	26,23	
3a. Securities of Municipalities and Local Boards sold abroad	2,78	
4. Funds brought in by immigrants and returned emigrants		
5. Other foreign capital invested in India	6,85	35,86
II. *Merchandise.*		
6. Merchandise exported (as per trade returns)	3,77,40	
7. Adjustment for under- or over-valuation of (6) in order to arrive at the commercial value f.o.b.		3,77,40
III. *Bullion, specie and currency notes.*		
8. Gold bullion and specie exported (as per trade returns)	7	

TABLE 5.8 (continued)

INWARD OR CREDIT MOVEMENTS (Exports)

		Lakhs of rupees	
		Amounts	Sub-Totals and Total
	III. *Bullion, specie and currency notes*		(continued)
9.	Silver bullion and specie exported (as per trade returns)	3,94	
10.	Currency notes	20	
11.	Adjustment for under- or over- valuation of (8), (9) and (10) in order to arrive at the commercial value f.o.b.		4,21
	IV. *Interest and dividends on capital invested abroad.*		
12.	Interest and dividends on capital invested abroad	2,63	2,63
	V. *Other items.*		
13.	Shipping freights, charter money, passage money and similar earnings received by national ships on account of all foreign trade		
14.	Port receipts from foreign shipping in national ports	2,00	
15.	Transport and other charges received for foreign goods transhipped or in transit		
16.	Commissions, insurance, brokerage and similar receipts		
17.	Post and telegraph earnings	28	
18.	Emigrants' remittances and money gifts from abroad		
19.	Receipts from foreign tourists and travellers		
20.	Diplomatic, consular and similar expenditure in India		
21.	Receipts for services rendered in India for "persons" domiciled abroad		
22.	Government receipts from abroad (not elsewhere included)	14,65	
23.	Other current items		16,93
	Total		4,37,03

TABLE 5.8 (continued)

OUTWARD OR DEBIT MOVEMENTS (Imports)

Lakhs of rupees

I. *Capital items.*	Amounts	Sub-Totals and Total
24. Repurchase of national securities formerly held abroad	99	
25. Purchase of foreign securities issued abroad	12,77	
26. New foreign capital issues subscribed in India		
27. Funds taken out by emigrants and by returning immigrants		
28. Other investments abroad of India's capital		13,76
II. *Merchandise*		
29. Merchandise imported (as per trade returns)	2,34,82	
30. Adjustment for under- or over-valuation of (29) in order to arrive at the commercial value c.i.f.	11,74	2,46,56
III. *Bullion, specie and currency notes.*		
31. Gold bullion and specie imported (as per trade returns)	29,28	
32. Silver bullion and specie imported (as per trade returns)	24,25	
33. Currency notes	1,25	
24. Adjustment for under- or over-valuation of (31), (32) and (33) in order to arrive at the commercial value c.i.f.		54,78
IV. *Interest and dividends on foreign capital invested in the country.*		
35. Interest and dividends on foreign capital invested in India	35,00	35,00
V. *Other items.*		
36. Shipping freights, charter money, passage money and similar earnings paid to foreign ships on account of all home and foreign trade other than imports into India		

TABLE 5.8 (continued)

OUTWARD OR DEBIT MOVEMENTS (Imports)

Lakhs of rupees

V. *Other items* (continued)	Amounts	Sub-Totals and Total
37. Port expenses incurred by national shipping in foreign ports		
38. Transport payments to foreign carriers		
39. Commission, insurance, brokerage and similar payments	1,00	
40. Post and telegraph payments	45	
41. Immigrants' remittances and money gifts sent abroad		
42. Expenditure abroad by national tourists and travellers		
43. Diplomatic, consular and similar expenditure abroad	5,00	
44. Payments for services rendered abroad for "persons" domiciled in India		
45. Government expenditure abroad (not elsewhere included)	53,78	
46. Other current items		60,23
Total		4,10,33
BALANCE (decrease in floating indebtedness)		+26,70

Source: League of Nations, *Memorandum on Balance of Payments and Foreign Trade Balances, 1910-1924*, Geneva, 1925, Vol. I, pp. 30-32.

movements (exports) and outward or debit movements (imports). Within each of these classifications the transactions were divided as to capital, merchandise, bullion, specie and currency notes, interest and dividends on capital, and miscellaneous grouping of accounts simply designated as other items.

The statements of member nations published by the League of Nations were presented differently in 1927. The new form, shown in Table 5.9, changed the emphasis from debits and credits to the distinction between the current and capital accounts. This was done by placing each in separate sections. The current accounts included monetary movements of bullion, specie and currency notes, and exports and imports of merchandise and services. The difference between the debits and credits in the current account measured the surplus or deficit from these transactions.

TABLE 5.9

OUTLINE FORM OF THE BALANCE OF PAYMENTS
AS RECOMMENDED BY THE LEAGUE OF NATIONS IN 1927

Current Items

Inward or Credit Movements (Exports)
    I. Merchandise
    II. Bullion, specie and currency notes
    III. Interest and dividends
    IV. Other items
        Total

Outward or Debit Movements (Imports)
    I. Merchandise
    II. Bullion, specie and currency notes
    III. Interest and dividends
    IV. Other items
        Total

Surplus (+) or deficit (−) on account of current items

Capital Items

Inward or Credit Capital Movements
    I. Long-term operations
    II. Short-term operations
        Total

Outward or Debit Capital Movement
    I. Long-term operations
    II. Short-term operations
        Total

Net inward (+) or outward (−) movement of capital

Source: League of Nations, *Memorandum on International Trade and Balances of Payments 1913-1927*, Geneva, 1928, Vol. I, pp. 154-157.

The second major classification of the 1927 balance of payments was the capital section. This section was subclassified as to long- and short-term transactions. However, the reclassification of short-term capital, or floating indebtedness, did not change the nature of the transactions included in the account or in any way make the statement more accurate. It simply became a balancing figure rather than a remainder as it had been in the past. The net change in the capital account was considered the net inward or outward movement of capital, which exactly offset the surplus or deficit in the current account.

The form of the balance of payments presented by the League changed again in 1928. Debits and credits for each account were placed in juxtaposition rather than in sequence.[26] Otherwise, the form of presentation remained basically unchanged until after World War II.

The League of Nations published annual statements of member nations from 1924 to 1939. The series was then discontinued because of the outbreak of World War II. A special volume was prepared in 1945, presenting information which became available after 1938. A large part of the data pertained to the pre-war period, and the figures for the war years were preliminary. This special volume, although prepared by the League of Nations, was published by the United Nations because of the transfer to that agency of certain economic and statistical activities before the completion of the project.[27]

The importance of the work of the League of Nations toward standardization of the balance of payments is indicated by the following comment:

It may be mentioned in this connection that, in 1938, the League's Committee of Statistical Experts began studying the classification of internation business transactions with a view to the framing of a new model scheme. This study was interrupted by the war, but was resumed in 1945 to reach the stage of a draft classification. This classifica-

---

[26] League of Nations, *Memorandum on International Trade and Balances of Payments,* Geneva, 1930, Vol. II.

[27] United Nations, *Balances of Payments 1939-1945,* Geneva, 1948, p. 5.

tion, together with certain explanatory information, was set out in a *Note on Balance of Payments Statistics* and communicated to governments for observations and comments in the early part of 1946. In conformity with a subsequent recommendation by the United Nation's Statistical Commission, the note in question is being published as part (Issue No. 7) of the League of Nations series *Studies and Reports on Statistical Methods.* Several of the suggestions made in this note have been adopted in the *Balance of Payments Manual* prepared by the staff of the International Monetary Fund in collaboration with members of the United Nations Secretariat, as well as national economists and specialists.[28]

The model presentation recommended by the League for reporting purpose was a starting point for the balance of payments work of the International Monetary Fund. This model was comprised of a summary statement supported by detailed schedules of each of the major sectors contained in the summary (Table 5.10).

The distinction between current and capital transactions was continued by the League in the summary of international economic transactions. However, some accounts were reclassified as capital rather than as current accounts as had been the case in previous years. A new section was established for all transfers of a financial nature which lacked a quid pro quo, such as emigrants' remittances and emigrants' funds. These types of transactions had formerly been included in the current section of the statement. Another important change was the lack of any surplus or deficit designation for the balance on the current account. Instead, the debits and credits for each account were juxtapositioned with comparison made simpler by the addition of a third column for the balance on each account.

The League of Nations basic concepts of the balance of payments. The League's concept of the balance of payments in 1924 can be shown by two comments made by the League's compiler, A. Loveday, in his general review of the statements. The first

---

[28] *Ibid.,* pp. 5-6.

TABLE 5.10

MODEL FORM FOR RECORDING INTERNATIONAL TRANSACTIONS
PREPARED BY THE LEAGUE OF NATIONS IN 1947.

Groups	Credit	Debit	Balance
A. Current business transactions:			
I. Goods			
II. Yields on investments			
III. Services			
Total A			
B. Unilateral transfers			
C. Capital and gold:			
I. Long-term capital			
II. Short-term capital			
III. Gold holdings			
Total C			
Total, all groups			

Source: United Nations, *Studies and Reports on Statistical Methods,* "Note
on Balance of Payments Statistics." Report drawn up by the Subcommittee on Balance of Payments Statistics of the League of
Nations Committee of Statisical Experts, Geneva: United Nations,
1947, p. 13.

comment concerned the nature and measurement of the surplus
or deficit of the balance of payments.

Very different interpretations are frequently given to
the terms 'negative' or 'positive' balance of payments—or
the equivalent more popular and misleading expressions
'unfavourable' or 'favourable' balance. An uncovered balance cannot exist. To every debtor there is a corresponding
creditor and for every payment effected a corresponding
receipt of payment. Balances result, therefore, simply from
the systems of accounting, and systems vary. In the majority of the statements given above, where a surplus or deficit is shown, that surplus or deficit represents changes in
the floating commercial loans and advances of a country.[29]

[29] *Memorandum on Balance of Payments and Foreign Trade Balances,
1910-1923, op. cit.,* I, p. 37.

According to Loveday, a surplus or deficit in the balance of payments depended upon the accounting system used. When all international transactions were included, the statement balanced because for every payment there was a receipt. However, a majority of the nations grouped payments and receipts in such a way as to include gold and to exclude short-term capital. The surplus or deficit (balance) was therefore, measured in terms of changes of short-term capital.

This balance also included *net* errors and omissions, which was relatively large in countries having depreciated currencies or whose merchandise accounts were based upon official values in a period of rapidly changing prices. The balance of payments accounts also varied considerably in accuracy. While some were recorded or could be estimated within reasonable limits of accuracy, estimates were based upon very sketchy information. Tourist payments and receipts, for example, were considered quite unreliable.

The concept of the surplus or deficit changed the following year (1925) as Table 5.8 indicates. The difference between the debits and credits on the *current* account (which included gold) was considered the measure of the surplus or deficit. This surplus or deficit was offset by capital movements. The concept changed again after World War II as Table 5.10 shows—gold was moved out of the current section into the capital section and there was no designation of a surplus or a deficit.

The second comment concerned the type of international transactions which were included or excluded from the balance of payments, depending upon how the term international transactions was defined. Loveday referred to Professor Mortara's distinction between four different types of statements. They were:

(a′) Balance of international payments effected during a given period.

(a″) Balance of international payments corresponding to exchanges effected in a given period.

(b′) Complete balance of international economic exchanges including payments effected during a given period.

(b") Complete balance of international economic exchanges including payments corresponding to exchanges effected in a given period.[30]

Professor Mortara said that, in practice, balance of payments compilers had not adhered strictly to any one of the above types. Loveday said the majority of the statements belonged to the first two types. He stated further that it was "not possible to ascertain exactly for what proportion of visible imports of any given year payment was actually effected within that year" although sometimes adjustments were made to correct this situation.[31]

The concepts underlying the new form of presentation of the balance of payments in 1927 changed somewhat from previous years, particularly in regard to the measurement of the surplus or deficit. Although admittedly arbitrary, a distinction was made between the current and capital accounts. The current accounts included exchanges of goods and services with foreign countries while the capital accounts included all long-term transactions in securities, purchases and sales of real estate and changes in all short-term claims and debts. Gold was considered as current rather than a capital account because it was merchandise to a gold producing country, and was often used for nonmonetary purposes in importing countries. This new arrangement was considered preferable for the following reason:

The balance of each of the accounts (current and capital) will then express the change which has taken place in the foreign indebtedness or in the net assets of the country abroad, apart from changes which are not due to foreign transactions and accordingly have no equivalent in the balance of payments account, e.g., changes in the book value of foreign investments.[32]

---

[30] *Ibid.*, I, pp. 37-38, citing *Revista Bancaria*, February 20, 1924, p. 74. Professor Mortara unofficially prepared Italy's 1922 balance of payments which was accepted by the League.

[31] *Ibid.*, I, p. 38.

[32] *Memorandum on International Trade and Balance of Payments 1913-1927*, Geneva, 1928, I, pp. 58-59.

This concept was further elaborated in 1928 and 1929 by the explanation of the timing at which transactions were recorded in the accounts. It was intended that they be recorded at the time obligations were incurred, rather than when payments were made or received.[33] Therefore, the difference between the debits and credits on the current account were theoretically offset by changes in international indebtedness. Any balance remaining was assumed due to errors and omissions. These principles were said to be accepted by most independent compilers.[34]

For this reason there was some doubt as to whether such statements could be called balance of payments. However, the term was used because there was no other generally accepted term that expressed the "true nature of the accounts."[35] Later, the term recommended by the Sub-Committee on Balance of Payments Statistics in 1947 was "International Transactions Account."[36]

---

[33] *Memorandum on International Trade and Balances of Payments 1926-1928,* Geneva, 1929, I, p. 6.

[34] *Memorandum on International Trade and Balances of Payments 1927-1929,* Geneva, 1931, II, p. 6.

[35] *Ibid.*

[36] United Nations, *Studies and Reports on Statistical Methods,* "Note on Balance of Payments Statistics." Report drawn up by the Sub-Committee on Balance of Payments Statistics of the League of Nations Committee of Statistical Experts, Geneva, 1947, p. 8.

6

Nature of the Balance of Payments

Balance of payments basic concepts and methodology were well established when the International Monetary Fund (IMF) published the first edition of its *Balance of Payments Manual* in 1948. This attainment was largely the result of the pioneering work done by early British writers on economics, students in the United States and other countries and the League of Nations.

Since that date, the progress made by the IMF can be noted by consulting the subsequent editions of its *Manual* which appeared in 1950 and 1961 and by the balances of payments presented in the fifteen editions of its *Balance of Payments Yearbook* which have appeared through 1963. The advances made by the United States are indicated in the presentations of the balances of payments of this country which appear regularly in the Department of Commerce's (Commerce) monthly periodical, *Survey of Current Business* and in the *Balance of Payments* Statistical Supplements to the *Survey*, which appeared in 1958 and 1963. Developments in the United Kingdom have been evidenced by the semi-annual *White Papers* published by the Financial Secretary to the Treasury and more recently by the quarterly articles in *Economic Trends*, published by the Central Statistical Office.

This recent progress has been characterized by improvements in existing concepts and methodology rather than by revolutionary change. Underlying concepts have been sharpened and made more exclusive. Balances of payments have been drawn up in greater detail with the inclusion of a larger number and more detailed breakdown of the accounts. The sources for the entries to this tabulation have been substantially enlarged and improved as exchange controls were refined, government statistical services developed and the contributions to data gathering and processing were more fully utilized. Although balance of payments methodology has not taken any great leaps forward since 1948, the number of small steps in advance have constituted a substantial improvement in the art. Given the large and growing interest in these tabulations, there will no doubt be continued improvement in them and their underlying methodology.

Although the term balance of payments is sanctioned by tradition, it is not an accurate title for a tabulation showing a nation's international transactions. It would perhaps be more exact to use the expression, balance of international transactions, or statement of international transactions to characterize this compilation, where international transactions are held to be those between residents and non-residents of a country. The balance of payments includes receipts as well as payments and carries transactions other than commercial receipts and payments.

The use of the word balance, also based on historical precedent, implies that the emphasis of the tabulation is upon the equality of receipts and payments or upon a selection of accounts held to constitute the "balance." Although surplus and deficit measurement is one of the more important uses of a balance of payments, it is not the only use to which the tabulation is put.

At the outset of its work on this compilation, the IMF considered the title, international transactions account, which had been recommended by the Subcommittee on Balance of Payments Statistics of the League of Nations in 1947, in preference to balance of payments. However, the IMF decided that tradition had long sanctioned the latter term and, therefore, continued to use it.[1]

The balance of payments, like certain other tabulations, does

---

[1] See: *Note on Balance of Payments Statistics.* Report of the Subcommittee on Balance of Payments Statistics of the League of Nations Committee of Statistical Experts. Studies and Reports on Statistical Methods, No. 9, Geneva, 1947.

not show cumulative totals, but only the changes of the accounts during the period stated, usually a year, although some countries publish these statements for each quarter and month as well. However, cumulative totals for a defined and limited period can, of course, be computed. As noted in Chapter 7, Commerce also prepares tabulations showing long-term international investment totals.

Definition of the Balance of Payments

The balance of payments may be defined as a statistical presentation of economic transactions during a given period between the residents of one country and those of the rest of the world, another country, group of countries or specified international organizations. Two terms in this definition call for clarification: economic transactions and residents.

Economic transactions. The term economic transactions is defined by the IMF as the provision of an economic value by one economic unit to another. Five types of economic transactions may be distinguished:

a. Purchases and sales of goods and services against financial items, i.e., the interchange of goods and services against claims and monetary gold;

b. Barter, i.e., the interchange of goods and services against other goods and services;

c. The interchange of financial items against other financial items, e.g., sales of securities against money, or the repayment in money of commercial debts;

d. The provision or acquisition of goods and services without a quid pro quo, e.g., under grants in kind;

e. The provision or acquisition of financial items without a quid pro quo, e.g., in payment of taxes or as a gift.[2]

Resident. In law, the term resident, as distinct from domiciliary or citizen, has a more or less exact meaning. As used in balance of payments methodology, its meaning is less precise; some variation in the definition of the term prevails among the

---

[2] International Monetary Fund (IMF). *Balance of Payments Manual.* Washington: International Monetary Fund, 3rd ed., 1961, p. 1.

several nations and exceptions are made where they appear warranted.

The IMF definition of resident turns around the concept of permanent place of living and general center of interest.[3] Commerce, in its definition, states that: "In general, individuals are considered residents of the country in which they ordinarily live."[4] Members of the diplomatic and consular staffs, official missions and military personnel stationed abroad together with students, tourists and persons undergoing medical treatment abroad are generally considered to be residents of their home country. Other persons travelling, fulfilling engagements, working or living abroad temporarily are usually classified as residents of their home country.

Agencies of business firms are ordinarily regarded as residents of the country in which they are incorporated or operate. Some nations apply the rule of incorporation for subsidiaries; for branches, the rule of operation. The IMF stresses operations in its classification of both. In some cases, a firm is treated by Commerce as a resident of the country where it operates, regardless of the one in which it is incorporated, particularly if it has no assets in the latter country. Thus, a few United States incorporated companies whose assets are entirely owned abroad and having no American operations are not considered as United States residents. Similarly, the United States does not regard a company organized in a given country as a resident of that country if it operates entirely elsewhere. The IMF recognizes similar exceptions to its rules of residence.

Intergovernmental organizations such as the United Nations, the IMF, and the International Bank for Reconstruction and Development, are not regarded as residents of any particular country regardless of where they are located and operate, but are placed in a separate "geographic" classification as international organizations. Transactions with such institutions are held

---

[3] IMF. *op. cit.*, p. 3.

[4] United States Department of Commerce (Commerce). *Balance of Payments of the United States: 1949-1951: A Supplement to the Survey of Current Business.* Washington: U.S. Government Printing Office, 1952, p. 16.

to be with non-residents for balance of payments purposes.

Official government agencies located abroad, such as embassies, consulates and missions, are viewed as residents of their home country by both Commerce and IMF, and transactions between these agencies and their governments are held to be domestic rather than international. Both agencies look upon the overseas missions or establishments of religious, charitable, scientific, educational, health and welfare institutions as residents of the country in which they carry out their operations.[5]

Uses of the Balance of Payments

Preceding chapters have indicated that the balance of payments was originally developed by the Mercantilists and their opponents to sustain their points of view. The early uses of the balance of payments were thus something less than objective.

It is still possible to use this compilation in a non-objective manner to sustain one point of view or another. Some nations, by using specialized definitions of surpluses and deficits, employ the balance of payments in part for "window dressing" to exaggerate or minimize these magnitudes. In general, however, the balance of payments has broken its subjective shackles and has become a leading tool for the analysis of international economic relationships.

The balance of payments as a mirror of the international economy. Perhaps the most important use of the balance of payments is to shed further light on the operations of an economy by showing the nature and magnitude of its overseas transactions, thereby extending the frontiers of knowledge. More specifically, the balance of payments shows what was received from abroad in goods, services, unilateral transfers and capital and what was given in payment. It thus provides objective information which assists a nation in judging whether or not the game was worth the candle.

The balance of payments reveals the pattern of the external economic relationships of a nation and, over time, indicates the

---

[5] For further details concerning definitions of residence see: IMF, *op. cit.,* pp. 3-6, and Commerce *op. cit.,* p. 16.

changes which have taken place in them. Compared with the magnitudes on the other national accounts, it shows the proportion of output which was sent to, and received from abroad as well as those elements of income which were paid to, and originated in, foreign sources. It assists in discovering the extent to which a nation is dependent upon other countries and vice versa.

The economic theorist finds the balance of payments a basic tool of analysis. In conjunction with other quantitative and factual data, it enables him to rectify, abandon or modify hypotheses; to study the automatic establishment of international economic equilibria; or to construct new theories and models.

The balance of payments illustrates the degree to which a nation's creditor or debtor, investor or disinvestor position changes during a stated period. The unilateral transfers, donations, or the transfers account reveals the extent to which a country is either aiding or receiving aid from others (exclusive of loans). By comparing this account with that of other nations, the share of this aspect of the world's economic burden, either given or received by any country, can be ascertained. Similar analyses can be made for any of the other individual accounts or groups of accounts carried on the tabulation. Analyses of the balances of payments of the less developed nations, recipients of foreign aid, can be used to show whether or not these countries are becoming internationally self-sustaining, thus permitting inferences to be drawn concerning one phase of the effectiveness of aid programs.

The balance of payments, like other national accounts, reflects certain aspects of the performance of an economy. When analyzed, it may point out that the operation of the economy leaves something to be desired and aids in discovering the seat of the problems. It likewise indicates the impact of domestic policies and programs on the external economic relationships of a country and presents magnitudes for assessing the possible effects of the external upon the domestic economy. It is an essential tool in the kit of the modern statesman charged with the task of policy formulation in modern directed or partially directed economies.

Significance of balance of payments surpluses and deficits. Many students of the international economy regard the magnitude, character and movement of balance of payments surpluses and deficits as one of the more important features of this compilation. The existence of a deficit indicates that a nation may have been living beyond its means internationally; that it has paid more to foreign residents than it has received. A non-reserve center cannot run a deficit indefinitely. Sooner or later its holdings, its capacity to procure additional reserves by borrowing, drawing on the IMF or by obtaining grants from other governments is likely to disappear. Deficits in the case of such countries are a distinct danger signal. Although the balance of payments may indicate the immediate source of the deficit in the several accounts which it carries, it seldom points a finger definitely at the cause.

Deficits and surpluses are commonly classified as either temporary or fundamental, although other classifications are possible such as seasonal, sustainable or non-sustainable, cyclical, structural and others. Any nation may experience temporary deficits or surpluses; it is the fundamental ones which give cause for concern. A single or related group of causes which generally are not revealed by the balance of payments alone, may be responsible for a deficit or surplus. These causes are often inflation, deflation, a non-equilibrium par or rate of exchange, changes in national income, prices, rates of interest or unbalanced economic development. In other cases the reasons may be more complex and involve a number of factors. Surpluses and deficits are more in the nature of a symptom than a diagnostic tool.

Balance of Payments and the National or Social Accounts

Efforts to measure the performance of an economy during a stated period have long occupied the attention of economists and a variety of statistical compilations have been prepared to aid in attaining this goal. These efforts culminated in the establishment of the national or social accounts which include the income and product accounts, input-output tables, flow of funds accounts as well as the balance of payments. Great improvements in social accounting technology have been made recently and, since the advent of the Keynesian economics, these tabulations have occupied an increasingly important place in economic analysis.

The National Income and Product Accounts. The national income and product accounts measure certain aspects of the performance of an economy. This performance is conceptually measured from three points of view: (1) value added by industry, (2) distributive shares, (3) expenditures on final products. In practice Commerce merges the first two. In either case, they are merely different aspects of the same thing. The first two are often referred to as the income account and the latter the output or product account.

The national income and product accounts shed light on the performance of an economy but they do not, of course, tell the whole story. They enable an analyst to chart the movements of an economy during the different phases of the business cycle; its rate of growth or decline; to ascertain the division of the national product among the several factors which produced it and to determine whether or not the share of any given factor is increasing relative to the whole; to compare a country's material standard of living with that of other nations.

These accounts show the national income of an economy generally by factor shares as indicated in Table 6.1, and gross national product by categories, Table 6.2, and by sectors, Table 6.3. The totals presented on these tables are not equal because of the exclusion in some, and the inclusion in others, of indirect taxes, transfer payments and other items. The national income and product accounts are commonly presented in greater detail than indicated on these summary tables and include other classifications and breakdowns of special interest to students of the various aspects of an economy. Foreign transactions as compiled on the balance of payments, its supporting tables and worksheets, enter into the composition of several items on the national income and product accounts.

TABLE 6.1

SUMMARY U.S. NATIONAL INCOME ACCOUNT BY FACTOR SHARES, 1963
(in billions of dollars)

Compensation of employees	340.3
Proprietor's income	50.6
Rental income of persons	12.3
Corporate profits and inventory valuation adjustment	50.8
Net interest	24.4
Total	478.4

Source: *Survey of Current Business,* Vol. 44, No. 7, July 1964, p. 8.

TABLE 6.2

SUMMARY U.S. NATIONAL PRODUCT ACCOUNT BY CATEGORIES, 1963
(in billions of dollars)

Personal consumption expenditures		375.0
Gross private domestic expenditures		82.0
Net exports over imports of good and services		4.4
Exports	30.7	
Imports	26.3	
Government purchases of goods and services		122.6
Total		583.0

Source: *Survey of Current Business,* Vol. 44, No. 7, July 1964, p. 8.

TABLE 6.3

SUMMARY U.S. GROSS NATIONAL PRODUCT BY SECTORS, 1963
(in billions of dollars)

Business	433.0
General government	38.1
Households and institutions	18.2
Rest of the world	3.3
Total	492.6

Source: *Survey of Current Business*, Vol. 44, No. 7, July 1964, p. 14.

The item, net exports or imports of goods and services on the income and product accounts is derived from the balance of payments. Net transfer payments by government and net foreign investment (not shown on Tables 6.1, 6.2, 6.3, but carried on more detailed breakdowns) are computed in part from data shown on, or used in, the preparation of these statements. The item, rest of the world (Table 6.3) used in certain national product breakdowns, is in effect, the net balance of payments or certain of its component items.

In the income and product accounts, the emphasis is on transactions among residents although they must cover those of residents with foreigners as well. In the rest of the world sector carried on these presentations, the signs are the reverse of those used on the balance of payments. The balance of payments shows transactions of residents with foreigners while the rest of the world account covers transactions of foreigners with residents. The rest of the world account follows the traditional usage of the positive and negative signs as in standard accounting practice.

The national income accounts are customarily divided into sectors; business or enterprise, government, households and institutions, and the rest of the world as shown on Table 6.3. They are called functional sectors because they represent decision-making units. Some income and product account tabulations divide the economy into institutional sectors and others into industry groups.

TABLE 6.4

HYPOTHETICAL INPUT AND OUTPUT TABLE BY SECTORS

(in billions of dollars)

			Inputs			
Outputs	Busi-ness	Govern-ment	House-holds	Capital	Rest of World	Total
Business	280	10	130	20	5	445
Government	25	5	5	5	5	45
Households	120	15	5	—	5	145
Savings (capital)	15	5	10	—	20	50
Rest of world	5	—	5	5	5	20
Total	445	35	155	30	40	705

In both balance of payments and national income practice, a given transaction calls for at least two entries, a debit and a credit. Thus, in the income accounts, the payment of dividends is usually recorded as a debit to the business or enterprise and a credit to the households or institutions account.[6]

The sector presentation requires an account for the rest of the world to record the non-resident side of international transactions. Without a rest of the world account, an import of goods for the business sector would be entered in but one sector of the tabulation and two are required under the double entry system.

---

[6] Balance of payments practice follows the custom of entering the debits on the right side of an account and the credits on the left. This is the reverse of the commercial accounting practice of entering debits on the left and credits on the right. As far as is known, no reason underlies the balance of payments practice other than tradition and custom. The invention of the double entry system of debits and credits is generally ascribed to the Italian Franciscan Monk, Luca Pacioli, in his work, *Summa Arithmetica,* published in Venice in 1494. The French accounting historian, G. Reymondin, is of the opinion that this system was already in use before Pacioli described it. See: G. Reymondin, *Bibliographie Méthodique des Ouvrages en Langue Française Parus de 1543 à 1908 sur la Science des Comptes.* Paris: V. Giard et F. Brière, 1909, p. 11.

In the case of this transaction, the enterprise sector is debited with the value of the import and the rest of the world sector is credited.

The balance of payments forms an integral part of the income and product records. Its emphasis is, of course, on the performance of the economy in the field of international economic relations, rather than in its domestic aspects. As the previous chapters have indicated, the balance of payments is by far the oldest member of the national accounting family and it has had considerable influence upon the methods employed by the others.[7]

---

[7] For the basic methodology underlying the preparation of United States income and product accounts see: U. S. Department of Commerce, *National Income*, 1954 edition, a Supplement to the *Survey of Current Business*, Washington, U. S. Government Printing Office, 1954. This basic methodology was revised in: U. S. Department of Commerce, *U. S. Income and Output*, A Supplement to the *Survey of Current Business*. Washington: U. S. Government Printing Office, 1958. A succinct account of the role of the balance of payments in the national accounts according to the procedures of the International Monetary Fund is presented in: International Monetary Fund, *Balance of Payments Manual*. Washington: International Monetary Fund, 3rd ed., July 1961. See also: S. Kuznets, *National Income and Its Composition, 1919-1938*. New York: National Bureau of Economic Research, Inc., 1941, Vol. 1 and II. Tables showing the national income and product of the United States are given in the *Survey of Current Business*, published by the U. S. Department of Commerce, usually in the national income (July) issue of each year.

In spite of the fact that the balance of payments and the national income and product accounts are both parts of the national or social accounts, there are important differences in concepts, definitions and statistical treatment between them. The principal differences are found in the balance of payments and the income accounts treatment of the components of net foreign investment (national income accounts) and the balance on the current account (balance of payments); government non-military grants in kind; net personal remittances; net payments of public debt interest. These items are reconciled statistically in tabulations which accompany the national income presentations usually carried in the July issue of the *Survey of Current Business* ("National Income Number."). See, specifically, "National Income and Product," *Survey of Current Business*, Vol. 44, No. 7 (July 1964), p. 24. In the *Report of the Review Committee for Balance of Payments Statistics* to the Bureau of the Budget, Appendix A, this Committee recommended that the concepts, definitions and statistical treatment employed in the national income accounts be brought to conform to those employed in the balance of payments (see Chapter 8).

Input-output tables. In 1758 the French physician, Dr. François Quesnay, published his important *Tableau Economique* and with it laid the cornerstone of the Physiocratic School of economic thought.[8] Quesnay intended to show that agriculture was the basis of the economy and his *Tableau* was designed to support this contention graphically. It was not until almost two centuries later that economists saw in the *Tableau* an early, if not the first, effort to illustrate the interrelationships between the several sectors of an economy which are today known as the input-output tables.

Another French economist, Léon Walras, writing in 1874, further developed the principles announced by Quesnay in discussing the conditions essential for economic equilibrium.[9] It remained, however, for American economist Wassily Leontief, to give a definitive statement of the input-output principles.[10] Leontief's original formulation of modern input-output analysis has been further developed by the author himself and others.[11]

The development of the input-output concept was important because the income and product accounts, with their division into the customary multi-sector presentation, is broadly classified and does not show some of the interrelationships required for an adequate picture of the operations of the economy. Even if the

---

[8] Quesnay's original *Tableau Economique* was published in a very limited edition, principally for the edification of the King and his advisors, and copies of the original are apparently lost. The text of a later edition of the *Tableau Economique* is reproduced in the standard edition of Quesnay's works: Auguste Oncken, (ed.) *Oeuvres Economiques et Philosophiques de F. Quesnay Fondateur du Système Physiocratique*. Paris: Jules Peelman et Cie., 1888, pp. 305-328. See especially Oncken's footnote to the text of the *Tableau, op. cit.*, p. 307. Two years after its appearance, the *Tableau* was presented in a more highly developed form by the Physiocrat, the Marquis V. Riquetti de Mirabeau, writing under the pseudonym, l'Ami des Hommes. See: l'Ami des Hommes, *Tableau Economique avec ses Explications*. (No place indicated), 1760.

[9] Leon Walras, *Eléments d'Economie Politique Pure*. Paris: F. Pichon, 4th ed., 1900.

[10] Wassily Leontief, *The Structure of the American Economy, 1919-1929*. Cambridge, Mass.: Harvard University Press, 1941.

[11] An excellent and succinct account of the input-output tables and their methodology is given in: John P. Powelson, *Economic Accounting*. New York: McGraw-Hill Book Co., Inc., 1955, pp. 425-451.

sectors were further divided into sub-sectors, the consolidation and summarization of the data required to elaborate them, would hide many important details. The input-output tables, by revealing certain structural features of the economy and showing the manner in which some industries (output) depend upon others (input) for their supplies and components, provide additional information needed for more profound analyses.

Modern input-output tables are another integral part of the national accounts and represent an extension of the concepts of the national product accounts. Table 6.4 (on page 167) illustrates this fact by showing the supply of goods and services utilized by the national product sectors in their operations, and the product created by these sectors through the use of these supplies.

In addition, the input-output tables present the business sector in greater detail than the product accounts, which show this sector as a consolidated statement where relations among its component units have been eliminated. The input-output tables divide the business sector among the several industries which compose it and indicate the interrelationships among them.

Table 6.5 shows the input and output of three industrial groups, termed the business sector. This table indicates what each group acquired from and furnished to others as well as the resulting product values created. In the *columns* under the sales or final demand sector and in the *rows* of the purchases or payments sector, additional data are provided to bring the totals of the table into conformity with those of the national product.

Input-output technicians commonly divide the sectors into two groups: the *autonomous* and the *industry* sectors. The autonomous sectors are those which are capable of consuming or storing products. They include the government, households, capital, rest of the world and the inventory sectors. The function of the industry sectors is to provide the autonomous sectors with products (see Table 6.5).

Thus the input-output tables indicate both the economic interdependence of the sectors and the results of the decisions

TABLE 6.5

Hypothetical Input-Output Table by Industries and Other Sectors

(in billions of dollars)

Outputs / Industry or Processing Sector	Processing or Industry Sector			Inputs Inventory (+)	Sales or Final Demand Sector		Capital	Rest of World (+)	Total
	Industry A	Industry B	Industry C	Inventory (+)	Government	Households	Capital	Rest of World (+)	
Industry A	10	15	5	2	3	10	3	5	53
Industry B	5	15	10	3	2	10	2	3	50
Industry C	7	13	10	4	1	3	5	3	46
Purchases or Payments Sector									
Inventory (−)	4	6	10	2	3	1	2	2	30
Government	2	3	1	2	1	3	1	2	15
Households	10	15	5	1	4	1	0	2	38
Depreciation	0	1	2	0	0	0	0	0	3
Rest of World (−)	3	2	1	0	0	0	0	2	8
Totals:	41	70	44	14	14	28	13	19	243

Source: Adapted from an unpublished Ms. by Professor Glenn Buriss formerly of the University of Kentucky.

of the industry sectors. They portray some aspects of the structure of the economy and show the interdependent participation of all sectors in product creation and use.[12] These tables follow the usual rules of accounting debiting and crediting, i.e., inputs are debits and outputs credits. The inputs of the business sector are the outputs of the others and vice versa.

A rest of the world sector, based upon balance of payments data, is included in these tables just as in the income and product account (see Tables 6.4 and 6.5). This sector represents a consolidation of the goods, services and unilateral transfer items carried on the balance of payments, but debited and credited from the point of view of foreigners. This point of view requires that the signs $(+)$ and $(-)$ be the reverse of those used on the balance of payments. The excess of inputs over outputs represents an increase in resident asset claims on foreigners and is termed net foreign investment. An excess of outputs over inputs implies an increase in foreigner's claims on assets of the reporting country and is an increase in foreigner's investments in that country.[13]

The balance of payments is not only a member of the same family to which the input-output tables belong, it forms an integral part of these tables. The imports of goods and services, taken from the balance of payments, are a part of the inputs of the industries or sectors represented. Exports to foreign residents constitute a part of the market for the outputs of these sectors.

Prior to Wassily Leontief's contribution, economic theorists used hypothetical curves to represent the co-ordinates of demand and supply. The input-output technique permits the use of curves based upon actual magnitudes to represent these and other economic functions. The underlying technology of these tables falls within the field of matrix algebra and may involve the use of complex mathematical procedures.

These tables may enable the economist to project the results of changes in the economy such as the impact of shifts in outputs upon inputs; to indicate the industries which are gaining in

---

[12] Cf. Powelson, *op. cit.*, pp. 426-427.
[13] Cf. Powelson, *op. cit.*, p. 440.

strength and those which are declining; to discover the results of changes in technology upon the structure of the economy; to determine the effects of foreign aid programs on the several national product sectors.[14] Walter Salant and Beatrice Vaccara projected the effects in import liberalization upon employment in the United States through the use of input-output tables.[15]

These tables are not only of use to the economist who deals in quantitative relations, they are also of value to statesmen charged with the task of economic planning in partially or totally state-directed economies. In spite of their utility in planning under complete socialism, communism or state capitalism, as far as is known, only a few such countries employ them. Hungary publishes comprehensive input-output tables, although the extent to which they are actually used in planning is not apparent.[16]

Flow of Funds Accounts. The flow of funds system of national accounts is of recent development and was originated and carried forward in the United States. The pioneer work in this area was performed by Professor Morris A. Copeland of Cornell University in cooperation with the Board of Governors of the Federal Reserve System.[17] When Copeland's exploratory work showed the feasibility of such a system, the Division of Research and Statistics of the Federal Reserve System undertook to maintain the accounts on an annual basis.[18]

---

[14] Cf. Powelson, *op. cit.*, pp. 425 and 449.

[15] Walter S. Salant and Beatrice N. Vaccara. *Import Liberalization and Employment: Effects of Unilateral Reductions in U. S. Import Barriers.* Washington: The Brookings Institution, 1960.

[16] Cf. Kozponti Statisztikae Hivatal, *Statisztikae Evkonyi 1958.* Budapest:Kozponti Statisztikae Hivatal, 1958, pp. 376-387.

[17] Morris A. Copeland, *A Study of Money Flows in the United States.* New York: National Bureau of Economic Research, Inc., 1952.

[18] Board of Governors of the Federal Reserve System, "A Flow-of-Funds System of National Accounts," *Federal Reserve Bulletin,* October 1955, pp. 1085-1124. This was an advance publication of the first chapter of the Federal Reserve Board's *Flow of Funds in the United States 1939-1953.* Washington: Government Printing Office, 1955.

The accounts have been published on a quarterly basis since August 1959.[19]

The flow of funds accounts, which are regarded as a part of the United States social accounts, are designed to reveal the movement of funds through the major sectors of the economy. They include transactions in existing assets as well as transactions for those newly created. Savings and investment totals are given for each sector of the economy and in aggregate for the entire economy. These accounts were developed to show the relationships between output and prices on the one hand and money, credit and investment on the other. Thus, interaction of saving and investment, borrowing and lending, receipts and expenditures are shown in a combined flow for each sector and for the economy as a whole.

The summary of the flow of funds accounts provides the framework for the system and gives an overall view of the pattern of financial flows among sectors as shown on Table 6.6. It is arranged in the form of a matrix in which the sectors of the economy are shown in columns and the transactions which occur in those sectors in rows.

The economy is divided into eleven sectors which are classified into five major groupings. Each sector is composed of economic units which are similar in function and institutional structure. The first group contains only one sector, *consumer and non-profit organizations*. The second group is that *of non-financial business* which consists of three sectors: (1) farm, (2) non-corporate, and (3) corporate. The third general group-

---

[19] United States, Board of Governors of the Federal Reserve System, "A Quarterly Presentation of Flow of Funds, Savings and Investment," *Federal Reserve Bulletin*, August 1959, pp. 828-859, 1046-1062. In 1962 the first publication of the flow of funds accounts on a seasonally adjusted basis appeared in "Flow of Funds Seasonally Adjusted," *Federal Reserve Bulletin*, November 1962, pp. 1393-1407. The Board of Governors of the Federal Reserve System has published a series of supplements the last of which was *Flow of Funds Accounts, 1945-1962*. Washington, 1963. The quarterly data of the accounts has also been compiled by the Board of Governors, *Flow of Funds Accounts, Unadjusted Quarterly 1952-1962*. Washington: 1963.

ing of sectors is *government*, composed of two sectors: (1) the U. S. government and (2) state and local government.

The fourth group presents the financial sectors and constitutes a unique feature of the flow of funds accounts as they are not treated separately in the national income accounts of the United States. The group includes four sectors: (1) banking system, made up of the commercial banks, the Federal Reserve System, the Exchange Stabilization Fund and the Treasury's gold and silver accounts; (2) savings institutions consisting of mutual savings banks, savings and loan associations, and credit unions; (3) insurance composed of all the domestic insurance companies and private pension and retirement plans; (4) financial not elsewhere classified (n.e.c.) presenting sales, industrial and personal finance companies, mortgage firms, security and commodity dealers and brokers, and other financial institutions not elsewhere classified. The last group, rest of the world, has only one sector, summarizing the transactions of the residents of the United States with nonresidents.

These eleven sectors, in their various group arrangements, are shown in the columns of the flow of funds summary. Each sector has two columns, one for the uses of funds and another for the sources of funds of that sector. The transactions which take place in each of these sectors are shown in the rows of the summary of the flow of funds. Transactions are divided into current nonfinancial flows, capital nonfinancial flows and financial flows.

The current nonfinancial flows are shown only in the sector statements of sources and uses of funds and do not appear in the summary table except as gross savings in the first row of that table. The derivation of gross savings is shown in detail in the individual sector statements. In general, gross saving for each sector is the excess of current receipts over current expenditures for goods, services and transfers.

Nonfinancial capital transactions are divided into purchases of consumer durables, residential construction, plant and equipment expenditures, and the net change in inventories. These appear individually in the flow of funds summary.

TABLE 6.6
Summary of Flow of Funds Accounts for 1962
(in billions of dollars)

Transaction Category	Consumer and non-profit organization U	S	Non-financial business sector U	S	Government sector U	S	Financial sector U	S	Rest of the World U	S
A. Gross savings		86.6		49.8		−8.5		2.3		−2.2
B. Gross investment (C+D)	91.2		47.2		−9.5		4.2		−.9	
C. Private capital expenditures, net	69.5		56.2				.7			
Consumer durables	48.2									
Residential construction	17.7		5.6							
Plant and equipment	3.6		45.7				.7			
Inventory change			5.0							
D. Net Financial investment (E−F)	21.7		−9.1		−9.5		3.5		−.9	
E. Financial uses, net	43.6		10.1		8.8		52.2		3.2	
F. Financial sources		21.9		19.3		18.3		4.1		
Gold and official U.S. foreign exchange							−.9		−.9	
Treasury currency	5.1				.1	3.5	.9	3.5		
Demand deposits and currency	24.7		−2.1	2.6	1.0	1.0	.1	28.6	.1	.3
Time and savings accounts	4.2							4.1		
Life insurance reserves	8.5							5.0		
Pension fund reserves	3.4									
Credit market instruments		22.0	2.5	20.6	6.5	13.3	50.6	5.7	1.1	2.3
Security credit	−.1	.1			.2	.4	.8	.9		
Trade credit			5.1	1.1			.3			
Equity in noncorporate business	−2.6		−2.6	.1						
Miscellaneous financial transactions	.2		2.0		.1	1.0	.5	1.0	.8	1.3
G. Sector discrepancies (A−B)	−4.7		2.6		1.0		1.9		.1	

Note: Details may not add to totals because of rounding.
The table has been simplified for illustrative purposes.
U=uses S=source of funds.

Source: Adapted from *Federal Reserve Bulletin*, August 1963, p. 1153.

There are eleven categories of financial transactions, some of which are further sub-classified. These categories are: (1) gold and official U.S. foreign exchange, (2) treasury currency, (3) demand deposits and currency, (4) time and savings accounts, (5) life insurance reserves, (6) pension fund reserves, (7) credit market instruments, (8) security credit, (9) trade credit, (10) equity in noncorporate business and (11) miscellaneous financial transactions.

The financial uses and sources of funds for each sector are recorded on a net transaction basis. Estimates of the amounts of financial assets and liabilities are made at the end of each quarter for each sector of the economy. Changes in assets represent funds used and changes in liabilities outstanding provide the source of funds. The net financial investment for each sector is the difference between the net acquisitions of financial assets and the net change in liabilities.

The net financial investment of each sector measures the funds advanced by that sector to other sectors of the economy. The net financial investment plus private capital expenditures equals gross investment for each sector as shown on Table 6.6. Gross saving is then equal to gross investment except for the statistical discrepancy.

The sources of data for flow of funds accounts were given in "A Quarterly Presentation of Flow of Funds, Savings and Investment" in the *Federal Reserve Bulletin* for August 1959.

Estimates in this presentation are based on data collected, compiled, and processed by a large number of sources, both governmental and private. The principal Governmental sources are the Securities and Exchange Commission, the Office of Business Economics and the Census Bureau of the Department of Commerce, the Treasury Department, the Federal Deposit Insurance Corporation, and the Federal Reserve System. The principal nongovernmental sources are insurance publications, the Institute of Life Insurance, National Association of Investment Companies, National Association of Mutual Savings

Banks, United States Savings and Loan League, and various private research organizations.[20]

There is a certain similarity between the flow of funds accounts and the balance of payments. The Board of Governors of the Federal Reserve System stated:

> The flow-of-funds sector accounts can be visualized as a set of interlocking balance-of-payments, each of which, in major respects, is similar in format to balance-of-payments statements that have been developed to record the flow of international payments. Each flow-of-funds sector account records the sector's purchases and sales of commodities and services, its credit and capital outflows and inflows, and the changes in its monetary balances.[21]

The balance of payments summarizes the transactions of residents of the United States with non-residents. On the other hand, the rest of the world sector of the flow of funds account shows a summary of the transactions of non-residents with residents of the United States.

The balance of payments and the rest of the world sector on the flow of funds accounts both pertain to a similar economic category. They differ only in coverage and classification of some transactions. One of these differences relates to transfers in kind which are excluded from the flow of funds accounts but included as exports and unilateral transfers on the balance of payments. Another consists of imputed transactions, such as changes in the monetary gold stock due to an excess of domestic gold production over consumption, which are recorded in the balance of payments and excluded from the flow of funds accounts. The sector account, rest of the world, is essentially based upon balance of payments data adjusted for differences in the coverage and classification of transactions.

For example, the net savings in the rest of the world sector (which was —$2.2 billion in 1962) resulted from an excess of imports over exports of goods and services and unilateral transfers. This dissaving was conceptually matched by a decrease

---

[20] Ibid., pp. 845-846.
[21] *Flow of Funds in the United States, 1939-1953*, p. 2.

in net financial investment. The balance of payments of the United States for 1962, after adjustment, shows an export surplus larger than transfers to foreigners by $2.2 billion with a resulting foreign investment of this amount.

Balance of Payments Presentation

The balance of payments is sometimes presented in two major forms; the basic or standard and the analytical statements.[22] These tabulations usually consist of gobal, or balances of payments of one country with the rest of the world; bilateral, or those between two nations; regional, or those between one nation and a group of countries.

Types of balances of payments. The standard table usually presents all of the balance of payments figures which are available in any single tabulation and summarizes the data found in its supporting tables. These supporting tables give further details as well as breakdowns of the individual balance of payments accounts. Analytical balances of payments are rearrangements of the data shown on the standard tabulations presented in a form designed to aid in the solution of some particular problem. The most important analytical tables are those prepared to measure the surplus or deficit resulting from a nation's international transactions.

Publication of balances of payments. The IMF publishes annually in its *Balance of Payments Yearbooks,* the standard (basic) global compilations of some seventy-five member and other nations which compile these statements. These tabulations are usually accompanied by supporting tables as well as analytical balances of payments and by explanatory notes. Some countries include bilateral and regional balances of payments as well.

Commerce publishes the standard balances of payments of

---

[22] The IMF prefers the term basic balance of payments. Unfortunately, basic balance is also used in conjunction with surplus and deficit determination in contradistinction to overall balance. To avoid confusion, the term standard, in preference to basic, balance of payments is used throughout this work.

the United States in its *Survey of Current Business,* on a global, bilateral and regional basis together with analytical balance of payments, supporting tables, notes, and text analysis. Commerce issues Supplements to the *Survey of Current Business* which carry these tabulations for a period of years and include a large number of supporting tables. These Supplements usually present revised data and embody the latest improvements in Commerce balance of payments methodology. The last of these Supplements was published in 1963 under the title: *Balance of Payments Statistical Supplement, Revised Edition.*[23]

The central banks, government statistical offices and minis-

---

[23] At present, Commerce publishes preliminary balance of payments tables in releases to the press six weeks after the quarter to which they refer. These preliminary data are also published in the *Survey of Current Business* some ten weeks after the close of the quarter to which they apply. The *Economic Indicators,* published monthly by the Joint Economic Committee of Congress, also carries these preliminary figures. Revised statistics for each quarter are published in the *Survey* about three months after the close of the quarter to which they refer. Summary balance of payments figures are also published in the *Federal Reserve Bulletin.* Special balance of payments figures are carried in the *Economic Report of the President* and in other government publications. The June issue of the *Survey* publishes statistics for the preceding calendar year and comparable data for earlier years. In addition, the *Survey* publishes special annual articles giving supplementary data on merchandise trade, transportation, travel as well as special articles on long-term capital. The Department of Commerce publishes comprehensive data on government grants and capital in a quarterly bulletin, *Foreign Grants and Credits of the United States Government.* The Treasury and the Federal Reserve System publish detailed statistics on United States banking claims and liabilities, securities transactions, reserve assets and liabilities in their monthly *Bulletins.* The Bureau of the Census furnishes a large number of press releases and reports relating to merchandise trade. Some of these appear monthly, others quarterly or on an irregular basis. The Review Committee for Balance of Payments Statistics, established by the Bureau of the Budget (see chapter 8), recommended that Commerce publish a *Balance of Payments Yearbook* annually as a Supplement to the *Survey of Current Business.* This proposed *Yearbook* should carry all of the balance of payments tables prepared by Commerce and contain annual and quarterly statistics for five years or more and longer series when revisions have been made. A list of the tables proposed by the Review Committee is given in Appendix E of its *Report.* See: *Report of the Review Committee for Balance of Payments Statistics* to the Bureau of the Budget. Washington: U. S. Government Printing Office, 1965, Chapter 10.

tries of several countries also publish their balances of payments in more or less detail. As is the case with Commerce's *Survey of Current Business*, these tabulations may be accompanied by analytical articles discussing and analyzing the developments shown on the compilations.

Source work on methodology. The basic description of the IMF's balance of payments methodology is presented in its *Balance of Payments Manual*, third edition, July 1961. The methodology employed by Commerce is given in its *Balance of Payments of the United States, 1949-1951* (A Supplement to the *Survey of Current Business*, 1952). Commerce methodology has undergone change since the issue of this Supplement, which is no longer up-to-date. The basis upon which the United Kingdom prepares its balances of payments was given by the Central Statistical Office in *Economic Trends*, No. 49 (November, 1957) and revised in No. 89 (March, 1961). Some other nations also prepare descriptions of their methodology which are usually issued by the office which publishes the tabulations. Thus, the methodology employed by France is found in: *La Balance des Payements, Etude Méthodologique*, published by the *Institut de la Statisque et des Etudes Economiques*, Paris, 1957.

Previous chapters have shown that the United Kingdom has made important contributions to balance of payments concepts and technology, as an examination of the early tabulations and a recent one, presented on Table 6.7, indicate. Modern balance of payments methodology owes a heavy debt of gratitude to British technicians and analysts for their contributions to this subject.

The IMF has made, and is continuing to make, determined efforts to standardize balance of payments methodology. Its task is a difficult one because the economic structure of its members differs and the methods appropriate to any one country do not necessarily meet the requirements of others. In addition, some nations had already established their methodologies prior to the organization of the IMF, had published time series of their tabulations and are reluctant to make changes.

TABLE 6.7

UNITED KINGDOM GENERAL BALANCE OF PAYMENTS, 1959-JUNE 1962
(in millions of pounds)

£ million

	1959	1960	1961	1961 Jan.–June	1961 July–Dec.	1962 Jan.–June
Current account						
1. VISIBLE TRADE						
Imports (f.o.b.)	3,613	4,100	4,006	2,080	1,926	2,027
Exports and re-exports (f.o.b.) ...	3,507	3,707	3,863	1,965	1,898	2,011
Total	−106	−393	−143	−115	− 28	− 16
INVISIBLES						
2. Government:						
debits	276	336	382	202	180	215
credits	43	49	44	27	17	26
3. Shipping:						
debits	619	701	713	359	354	361
credits	624	646	657	330	327	339
4. Interest, profits and dividends:						
debits	418	455	449	195	254	201
credits	682	695	696	337	359	395
5. Travel:						
debits	175	210	228	87	141	89
credits	153	188	206	88	118	97
6. Migrants' funds, legacies and private gifts:						
debits	95	96	96	48	48	47
credits	95	96	99	47	52	49
7. Other services:						
debits	312	343	366	186	180	178
credits	515	559	598	303	295	297
Total	+217	+ 92	+ 66	+ 55	+ 11	+112
CURRENT BALANCE	+111	−301	− 77	− 60	− 17	+ 96
Long-term capital account([1])						
8. Inter-government loans (net) ...	−117	− 91	− 14	+ 2	− 16	− 25
9. U.K. subscriptions to I.M.F., I.D.A. and European Fund	−236	− 10	− 9	—	− 9	—
10. Other U.K. official long-term capital (net)	—	− 1	− 19	− 19	− 13	− 6
11. Private investment:						
abroad (net)	−316	−312	−338	−200	−138	−170
in the United Kingdom (net) ...	+176	+221	+406	+184	+222	+156
BALANCE OF LONG-TERM CAPITAL	−493	−193	+ 26	− 27	+ 53	− 41
Balance of current and long-term capital transactions	−382	−494	− 51	− 87	+ 36	+ 55
Balancing item	− 23	+312	+ 80	+ 39	+ 41	+ 93
Monetary movements([1])						
12. Miscellaneous capital (net)	+ 33	+137	− 75	+ 67	−142	+ 87
13. Overseas sterling holdings:						
countries	+154	+376	−333	−187	−146	− 21
non-territorial organisations ...	+ 82	−156	+409	+ 3	+406	−173
14. U.K. balance in E.P.U.	+ 9					
15. U.K. official holdings of non-convertible currencies	+ 8	+ 2	+ 1	+ 1	—	—
16. Gold and convertible currency reserves	+119	−177	− 31	+164	−195	− 41
BALANCE OF MONETARY MOVEMENTS	+405	+182	− 29	+ 48	− 77	−148

([1]) Assets: increase −/decrease +.   Liabilities: increase +/decrease −.

Source: Great Britain, Central Statistical Office, *United Kingdom Balance of Payments, 1959-1962*, Cmmd. 1837, p. 9.

The methodology of the IMF is of special significance because it is followed by a large number of the member nations. United States methods are likewise significant due to the fact that, although the methodology of the United Kingdom is older, the preparation of *modern* balances of payments probably has received more attention in America than in any other country. In addition, the importance of the United States economy and the international role played by the dollar render the technology employed by this country of exceptional interest. The standard balance of payments of the United States, in the format as now published in the *Survey*, is presented on Table 6.8.

Commerce has recast its balance of payments in the IMF presentation form and these tabulations are published annually in the IMF *Balance of Payments Yearbook*. The United States balance of payments prepared under IMF classifications is presented on Table 6.9.

Tables 6.8 and 6.9 indicate that the presentation and classifications employed by the IMF differ in some particulars from those utilized by Commerce. In addition, definitions employed by the IMF and Commerce also vary. The tabulations prepared by countries using the IMF principles, therefore, cannot readily be compared with those of the United States as published in the *Survey*.

Differences between IMF and Commerce classifications and coverage. As far as coverage is concerned, the IMF tables exclude goods and services transferred under military aid as well as the counterpart grants themselves whereas Commerce includes them but shows them separately from other exports and grants. The Commerce tabulations do not include the undistributed profits of subsidiaries as investment income in the income account and their counterpart, reinvested earnings of subsidiaries, in the capital account whereas the IMF does.

Non-monetary gold constitutes a separate item on the IMF tabulations, but is included in the merchandise account by Commerce. The IMF places foreign diplomatic expenditures in the compiling country and those of international agencies in the

TABLE 6.8

UNITED STATES STANDARD GLOBAL BALANCE OF PAYMENTS,
1962 AND 1963 AS PRESENTED IN U. S. DEPARTMENT OF
COMMERCE, *Survey of Current Business*
(in millions of dollars)

Line	Type of transaction	All areas							
		1962			1963				
		Year	III	IV	Year	I	II	III ʳ	IV ᵖ
1	Exports of goods and services	31,329	7,322	8,185	na	7,651	8,777	7,680	na
2	Goods and services transferred under military grants, net	1,539	218	305	na	447	675	ʳ 215	na
3	Goods and services excluding transfers under military grants	29,790	7,104	7,880	31,603	7,204	8,102	7,465	8,832
4	Merchandise, adjusted, excluding military	20,479	4,888	5,146	21,902	4,945	5,678	5,184	6,098
5	Transportation	1,749	446	441	1,848	410	468	496	474
6	Travel	921	286	188	941	187	265	289	200
	Miscellaneous services:								
7	Private	1,475	370	393	1,511	372	373	373	393
8	Government, excluding military	184	49	49	204	49	51	50	54
9	Military transactions	660	127	209	632	164	241	ʳ 78	149
	Income on investments:								
10	Direct investments	3,050	646	1,059	3,158	778	695	659	1,026
11	Other private	800	201	213	909	210	226	227	246
12	Government	472	91	182	498	89	108	109	192
13	Imports of goods and services	24,964	6,466	6,312	26,118	5,919	6,553	6,955	6,691
14	Merchandise, adjusted, excluding military	16,145	3,960	4,181	16,962	3,915	4,223	4,305	4,519
15	Transportation	2,055	543	477	2,154	468	595	586	505
16	Travel	1,905	737	378	2,071	315	536	805	415
	Miscellaneous services:								
17	Private	436	114	108	434	103	107	114	110
18	Government, excluding military	400	143	99	421	91	84	150	96
19	Military expenditures	3,028	732	794	2,880	748	725	708	699
	Income on investments:								
20	Private	656	151	186	796	188	188	183	237
21	Government	339	86	89	400	91	95	104	110
22	Balance on goods and services	6,365	856	1,873	na	1,732	2,22ʳ	725	na
23	Excluding transfers under military grants	4,826	638	1,568	5,485	1,285	1,549	510	2,141
24	Unilateral transfers, net (to foreign countries (−))	−4,178	−826	−975	na	−1,086	−1,397	−872	na
25	Excluding military transfers	−2,639	−608	−670	−2,719	−639	−722	−657	−701
26	Private remittances	−491	−117	−143	−548	−130	−141	−132	−145
	Government:								
27	Military grants of goods and services	−1,539	−218	−305	na	−447	−675	ʳ −215	na
28	Other grants	−1,903	−434	−466	−1,907	−440	−815	−462	−400
29	Pensions and other transfers	−245	−57	−61	−264	−69	−66	−63	−66
30	U.S. capital, net (increase in U.S. assets (−))	−4,368	−496	−1,359	−5,733	−1,436	−2,399	−316	−1,582
31	Private, net	−3,273	−521	−1,083	−4,082	−974	−1,683	−250	−1,175
32	Direct investments, net	−1,557	−324	−538	−1,799	−501	−498	−154	−646
33	New issues of foreign securities	−1,076	−133	−461	−1,294	−596	−518	−184	−86
34	Redemptions	170	58	34	150	31	52	24	43
35	Transactions in outstanding foreign securities	−55	−15	49	43	−48	−64	56	99
36	Other long-term, net	−248	−34	33	−540	−11	−124	−119	−286
37	Short-term, net	−507	−73	−290	−642	61	−531	127	−290
38	Government, net	−1,095	25	−276	−1,651	−462	−716	−66	−407
39	Long-term capital	−2,133	−486	−660	−2,184	−563	−629	−438	−563
40	Repayments on U.S. Government loans, scheduled	617	115	213	649	126	131	163	229
41	Repayments and selldts, nonscheduled	666	471	142	325	25	34	241	25
42	Foreign currency holdings and short-term claims, net (increase (−))	−245	−75	29	−441	−50	−261	−32	−98
43	Foreign capital (lines 44–48), net (increase in U.S. Liabilities (+))	1,020	162	505	802	73	237	180	312
44	Direct investments in the United States	132	6	8	86	−18	36	56	12
45	Other long-term investments	139	−16	12	301	9	167	56	69
46	U.S. private short-term commercial and brokerage liabilities	−116	13	−55	5	−18	63	24	−64
47	U.S. Government liabilities other than interest-bearing securities	614	159	289	453	37	−19	ʳ 139	296
48	U.S. Government nonmarketable medium-term nonconvertible securities	251	.....	251	−43	63	−10	−95	−1
49	U.S. Government nonmarketable medium-term convertible securities	.....	.....	.....	702	350	152	175	25
50	Increase in short-term official and banking liabilities and in foreign holdings of marketable U.S. Government bonds and notes (decrease (−))	653	−188	309	1,880	ʳ 320	ʳ 918	187	155
51	Increase (−) in monetary reserve assets, including gold, convertible currencies, and IMF position	1,533	881	389	378	32	124	227	−5
52	Reduction in monetary reserve assets and increase in liquid liabilities including U.S. Government nonmarketable medium-term convertible securities (lines 49–51)	2,186	693	698	2,660	702	1,194	589	175
52a	Excluding increase in U.S. Government nonmarketable medium-term convertible securities (lines 50 and 51)	2,186	693	698	1,958	352	1,042	414	150
53	Errors and omissions and transfers of funds between foreign areas (receipts by foreign areas (−)), net	−1,025	−389	−742	−495	15	141	−306	−345
	Memorandum items:								
I	Increase in reported total foreign gold reserves and liquid dollar holdings.[3]	2,514	661	877	3,623	840	1,350	749	584
II	Through estimated net receipts from, or payments (−) to, the United States.[3]	2,128	681	680	2,691	687	1,178	574	152
III	Through other transactions.[4]	386	−20	197	932	153	172	175	432

Source: United States Department of Commerce, *Survey of Current Business.* Vol. 44, No. 3, (March 1964), p. 20.

TABLE 6.9

UNITED STATES STANDARD GLOBAL BALANCE OF PAYMENTS, 1957-1961
AS PRESENTED IN THE IMF *Balance of Payments Yearbook*
(In millions of dollars)

	1957 Credit	1957 Debit	1958 Credit	1958 Debit	1959 Credit	1959 Debit	1960 Credit	1960 Debit	1961 Credit	1961 Debit
A. Goods and Services	28,068	20,959	24,247	21,089	24,798	23,676	28,278	23,302	29,100	23,011
1. Merchandise f.o.b.	19,362	13,239	16,240	12,908	16,282	15,240	19,458	14,667	19,903	14,447
2. Nonmonetary gold	—	24	—	19	—	54	—	55	—	55
3. Freight on international shipments	911	760	654	781	622	861	693	963	664	927
4. Other transportation	1,088	809	1,018	855	1,024	898	1,012	1,025	1,021	1,064
5. Travel	785	1,372	825	1,460	902	1,610	968	1,744	975	1,747
6. Investment income	4,244	770	3,867	786	4,132	1,026	4,488	1,113	4,728	1,120
6.1. Direct investment	*3,676*	*319*	*3,143*	*328*	*3,317*	*416*	*3,621*	*483*	*3,718*	*466*
6.2. Other private	*363*	*250*	*417*	*319*	*466*	*329*	*518*	*358*	*631*	*386*
6.3. Government interest	*205*	*201*	*307*	*139*	*349*	*281*	*349*	*332*	*379*	*278*
7. Government, n.i.e.	642	3,422	569	3,666	654	3,354	693	3,302	771	3,216
7.1. U.S. military agencies	*372*	*3,165*	*296*	*3,412*	*302*	*3,109*	*335*	*3,048*	*406*	*2,947*
7.2. Other	*270*	*257*	*273*	*254*	*352*	*245*	*358*	*254*	*365*	*269*
8. Other services	1,036	563	1,074	614	1,182	633	966	433	1,038	435
8.1. Nonmerchandise insurance	*227*	*288*	*223*	*304*	*240*	*324*	*12*	*189*	*12*	*132*
8.2. Other	*809*	*275*	*851*	*310*	*942*	*309*	*954*	*304*	*1,026*	*303*
Net goods and services	7,109	—	3,158	—	1,122	—	4,976	—	6,089	—
B. Transfer Payments	101	2,472	94	2,483	64	2,545	66	2,631	59	2,926
9. Private	34	577	33	573	34	609	32	660	32	675
10. Central government	67	1,895	61	1,910	30	1,936	34	1,971	27	2,251
Net transfer payments	—	2,371	—	2,389	—	2,481	—	2,565	—	2,867
Net total (1 through 9)	6,566	—	2,618	—	547	—	4,348	—	5,446	—
Net total (1 through 10)	4,738	—	769	—	—	1,359	2,411	—	3,222	—
C. Capital and Monetary Gold	—	5,486	—	1,149	831	—	—	1,819	—	2,620
Nonmonetary sectors	—	4,377	—	4,009	—	2,816	—	4,594	—	3,643
11. Direct investment	—	3,186	—	1,880	—	2,181	—	2,645	—	2,210
11.1. In the United States	*235*	—	*169*	—	*280*	—	*315*	—	*311*	—
11.2. Abroad	—	*3,421*	—	*2,039*	—	*2,461*	—	*2,960*	—	*2,521*
12. Other private long-term	—	275	—	1,309	—	274	—	407	—	278
12.1. Liabilities	*234*	—	—	*17*	*471*	—	*289*	—	*393*	—
12.2. New issues and retirements of foreign securities	*179*	*597*	*85*	*955*	*95*	*624*	*100*	*575*	*123*	*510*
12.3. Transactions in outstanding foreign securities	—	*84*	—	*380*	—	*140*	—	*177*	—	*366*
12.4. Other assets	—	*7*	—	*42*	—	*76*	—	*46*	*82*	—
13. Other private short-term	42	—	151	—	—	8	—	437	—	229
13.1. Liabilities	*72*	—	*106*	—	*12*	—	—	*91*	*180*	—
13.2. Assets	—	*30*	*45*	—	—	*20*	—	*346*	—	*409*
14. Local government	....	....	....	....	....	....	....	....	....	....
15. Central government	—	958	...	971	—	353	—	1,105	—	926
15.1. Subscriptions to IDB and IDA	—	—	—	—	—	—	—	*164*	—	*172*
15.2. Loans extended	*687*	*959*	*550*	*1,150*	*987*	*995*	*603*	*1,040*	*1,274*	*1,766*
15.3. Other assets	—	*626*	—	*351*	—	*345*	—	*514*	—	*262*
Monetary sectors	—	1,109	—	2,860	3,647	—	2,775	—	1,023	—
16, 18. Liabilities	267	—	1,088	—	4,185	—	2,219	—	1,679	—
To IMF	—	*367*	*17*	—	*1,636*	—	*741*	—	—	*135*
U.S. Government long-term obligations	—	*52*	*31*	—	*686*	—	*127*	--	*505*	—
Long-term bank loans received	*9*	—	—	*8*	—	—	—	—	—	—
Short-term liabilities to other official institutions and banks	*564*	—	*805*	—	*1,626*	—	*1,557*	—	*1,235*	—
Other short-term liabilities	*313*	—	*245*	—	*237*	—	—	*6*	*74*	—
17, 19. Assets	—	1,376	1,772	—	—	538	556	—	—	656
IMF subscription	—	—	—	—	—	*1,375*	—	—	—	—
Other long-term assets	—	*350*	—	*152*	—	*181*	—	*164*	—	*335*
Short-term claims	—	*228*	—	*351*	—	*57*	—	*992*	—	*1,173*
Monetary gold	—	*798*	*2,275*	—	*1,075*	—	*1,702*	—	*857*	—
Net errors and omissions	748	—	380	—	528	—	—	592	—	602

Source: IMF, *Balance of Payments Yearbook*, Vol. 14, 1962.

government, not included elsewhere (n.i.e.) account and Commerce places them in private miscellaneous services.

The IMF presentation of the capital account shows, with a few exceptions, the domestic monetary and non-monetary sectors as the debtors or creditors, whereas Commerce classifies the capital account by broad categories of transactions with but little emphasis on the domestic sector.[24]

Net balance entries or "netting out." The entries on the capital accounts of both the United States presentations and those of other IMF members are "netted out," i.e., only the net credit or debit balances of the accounts are shown on the balance of payments. The unilateral transfers account on the United States tabulations, as presented by Commerce in the *Survey,* are also netted out but the United States tables in the IMF *Yearbook* show both the debit and credit entries to these accounts. Since the United States unilateral transfers credits are small, netting out does not greatly reduce the value of this account for analytical purposes. On the other hand, both unilateral transfers debits and credits for the other IMF member nations are important in many cases; consequently, they are both usually shown.

The capital accounts are netted out because the gross figures are not always significant and because only the net credit or debit balance are usually computed by firms and financial institutions under modern commercial accounting procedures.

The different classes of accounts. The balances of payments are sometimes divided into three parts, although these divisions are not always noted on the tabulations: the current account; transfers, unilateral transfers or donations; the capital account. Some nations include transfers in the current account category and have but two classifications: the current and the capital accounts.

The current account shows the transactions in goods and services, lines 1-23, Table 6.8; lines 1-8 on Table 6.9. The transfers account, lines 24-29 on Table 6.8 and 9-10 on Table 6.9 includes those transactions which take place without a quid pro

---

[24] Cf. IMF, *Balance of Payments Yearbook,* Vol. 14, 1962, note appended to the United States balance of payments.

quo of market value. The capital account reflects transactions in financial assets and liabilities, lines 30-50, Table 6.8; 11-16, Table 6.9.[25]

A similar but not identical division is utilized by the other social or national accounts and has become significant since the advent of Keynesian economics. Under the Keynesian system, it is important to distinguish between those segments of an economy which give rise to output, income and consumption from those which show savings and capital accumulations and those which represent the exchange (transfer) of funds. This tripartite division of the balance of payments renders the tabulation of greater use in the solution of some analytical problems which involve the other social accounts and is of more significance to statesmen in countries where the economy is directed or partially directed.

---

[25] Different meanings are sometimes attached to the term current account in commercial accounting practice. To avoid confusion, some balance of payments technicians have abandoned the classification of the accounts into current, transfer and capital transactions on their presentations. See: John P. Powelson, *op. cit.*, pp. 420-421.

7

Balance of Payments Methodology

The preparation of periodic balances of payments, relying more on actual data than on estimates, had to await the development of adequate government statistical services which, fortunately, have made great strides in the last two decades. The relatively recent publication by the International Monetary Fund (IMF) of the balances of payments of the large majority of its members attests to this fact as well as to the technical skill and ability of the officers and staff of this organization.[1] Thanks to the work of the League of Nations, the IMF, the United Kingdom, the United States Department of Commerce, and others, balance of payments methodology is now well established.[2]

Balances of payment have been more or less regularly prepared since the twenties by a number of nations, especially the United Kingdom, the United States, Canada, Yugoslavia, and the Scandinavian countries. As noted in previous chapters, the United Kingdom has been constructing balances of trade for several centuries. The early British tabulations embodied a considerable element of estimate and were based partly on previ-

---

[1] Cf. International Monetary Fund. *Balance of Payments Yearbook.* Washington: International Monetary Fund, published annually.

[2] Cf. *Note on Balance of Payments Statistics*, Report of the Subcommittee on Balance of Payments Statistics of the League of Nations Committee of Statistical Experts. Studies and Reports on Statistical Methods No. 9. Geneva, 1947; IMF, *Balance of Payments Manual.* Washington: International Monetary Fund, 3rd ed., July 1961. Before the IMF was organized, the balance of payments work of several countries and the League of Nations was already well developed and served as a foundation upon which the Fund was able to build. Among the technical works on the balance of payments see especially: John P. Powelson, *Economic Accounting,* New York: McGraw Hill Book Company, Inc., 1955.

ously existing tabulations such as customs house records, partly on questionnaires and special reports gathered on a sampling basis. The development of the modern balance of payments, in which estimates have been substantially reduced, had to await the development of other government statistics, especially those derived from exchange records, which followed World War II, and specially designed reporting systems.

With heavy reliance upon reports and statements prepared by others, and over which he has but limited control, the balance of payments economist is more of a statistician than an accountant. He has a certain choice, at times, between various sources which he could utilize and often must adapt those selected to his purposes. Each tabulation, statement or report received in the balance of payments office is the source, in part at least, of one or more entries on this statement or of adjustments to figures received from other sources. These entries are made according to standard commercial accounting principles and are carried as debits or credits to the several accounts.

Although there are many different kinds of source documents which are utilized in balance of payment construction, they may be classified conveniently into two broad groups: *the linked and non-linked debit and credit source systems.*[3]

The linked system derives its name from the fact that, *where the system is complete,* both the debit and credit entries for

<hr>

[3] The terminology, *linked and non-linked source systems* has been adapted from that developed in an unpublished thesis submitted for the degree of Master of Arts by a graduate student of the William Andrew Patterson School of Diplomacy and International Commerce of the University of Kentucky, Lawrence Bernard Wasserman, entitled "An Essay on Balance of Payments Construction and Interpretation," 1962, pp. 103-181. The French balance of payments statisticians use the terms accounting (*comptable*) and quasi-accounting (*quasi-comptable*) to characterize the French source documents. The accounting source documents (non-linked) include extracts from the records kept by the Treasury, bank note issuing institutions, the Exchange Stabilization Fund and those of certain banks. The quasi-accounting sources (linked) comprise those derived from exchange records such as license authorizations and declarations required by the exchange regulations. See: Ministère des Finances, Direction des Finances Extérieures, *Balance des Payements de l'Année 1960 entre la Zone Franc et les Pays Etrangers.* Paris, Imprimerie Nationale, no date, p. 141. The

given transactions on the balance of payments are derived from the same individual or group of source documents. The non-linked, on the other hand, is so termed because the debits and credits for the same transactions are found in separate and often unrelated documents. The linked system is sometimes termed the exchange record system because the sources utilized under it are generally derived from records created under exchange control systems. The non-linked system utilizes a wide variety of other government and private tabulations such as custom house records, bank and other financial institution reports, questionnaires and required business reports, among many others.

The linked system is rarely found in its pure form where exchange control records are the sole source of the data. These records are usually checked, complemented and adjusted by the use of some non-linked type source documents. As countries abandon or loosen exchange controls to return to convertibility, unless the exchange *records* are maintained, they move away from the linked toward a non-linked system. Many nations today use a combination of the two systems.

An assessment of the respective merits of the one or the other of these two systems is likely to be inconclusive, because the use of either system is seldom made on the basis of purely rational considerations. The balance of payments statistician, on the lookout for better source materials, generally uses those

---

French balance of payments statisticians likewise distinguish between two of their methods of drawing up these tabulations: the production account *(compte d'exploitation)* and the cash account *(compte caisse)* methods. The former is based on records of transactions showing the movement of goods, services, transfers and capital. The latter uses records indicating cash receipts and payments as well as those derived from payments agreements. According to the French authorities, the production account method is the more complete but less accurate of the two. Until 1960, the French balance of payments statisticians employed the cash account method. This method was modified in 1960 with the elimination of most exchange controls, and by the inclusion of the production account techniques. In other words, the French used a method based upon a linked source system until 1960 and after this date a combination of the linked and non-linked systems was employed. See: *Statistiques et Etudes Financières, Annuaire 1930-1959,* Part IX, "La Balance des Payements de la Zone Franc," December 1960, pp. 2076-2077.

which he has at hand or which others prepare for him. He welcomes a choice whenever he finds one; but his choice, like that of Hobson, is frequently limited to a specific type of record or no record at all.

Since there are so many different kinds of exchange control record and non-linked sources, it is impossible to select the system of any country and regard it as *representative*. The system employed by Ceylon has been selected to illustrate one form of the *linked,* and that of the United States as illustrative of one type of the *non-linked* systems.

The Ceylon system was chosen because this country follows closely the methodology recommended by the IMF, and that of the United States because of the size and number of this country's international transactions and the variety of sources utilized in the preparation of its balance of payments. Since few nations publish their sources and methodology in any detail, the choice of countries to illustrate the two systems is limited.

The Linked Debit and Credit System: Ceylon

Ceylon has been preparing balances of payments since 1931-1934.[4] With the inauguration of exchange controls applicable to non-residents of the Sterling Area in 1939 and their extension in 1948 to residents as well, it became possible for this country to utilize its exchange control records as sources of balance of payments data. Ceylon is a member of the Sterling Area and the exchange control system was originally based on those utilized by this institution.

Characteristics of the Ceylon system. Most of the transac-

---

[4] Cf. The *Administration Report* of the Ceylon Treasury prepared under the direction of the Financial Secretary. Colombo, Ceylon, 1936. The IMF maintains a training course for balance of payments statisticians of the member nations and utilizes a number of papers and documents in conjunction with its program. In addition, some of the students prepare papers as a part of their participation in the course. The discussion of Ceylon's system presented in this chapter is based on materials, specifically, material prepared by Chandra Dias, an economist in the International Finance Division of the Economic Research Department, Central Bank of Ceylon.

tions between residents of Ceylon and those of other countries are routed through its banking system and authorized exchange dealers. For this reason, the international business handled by the banks and dealers covers the greater part of Ceylon's foreign economic transactions. These records are, in some cases, incomplete and netted out. They are, therefore, supplemented and adjusted by the use of data derived from other sources.

Under 1948 legislation, the government has a virtual monopoly over foreign exchange transactions. Since much of Ceylon's international business is conducted in foreign currencies, especially sterling, all Ceylonese residents are required to turn over to the government, through banks and authorized dealers, their foreign exchange earnings and are given Ceylon rupees in exchange. Foreign exchange required by residents must be purchased from the same agencies. Since the banks and authorized dealers are subject to strict exchange control regulations, most international transactions are believed to be matters of record. These records, and the reports based thereon, form the sources of data for Ceylon's balance of payments.

Resident exporters and importers are required to obtain an export or import license before they can consummate a transaction. Others who require or earn foreign exchange in connection with their international business are either obliged to procure exchange licenses or to execute forms indicating the nature of the transaction envisaged. The purchases and sales of foreign exchange are reported on schedules called the Daily Purchase and Daily Sales Return, which are illustrated in abbreviated form on Tables 7.1 and 7.2.

Reports are specially prepared by government agencies covering all their international transactions. The most important are those involving government agency transactions under compensation agreements, P. L. 480, official gifts or grants in kind, contractor's services and capital.

Each exporter is required to fill out two additional forms which aid in the effective enforcement of the exchange controls and supply data essential for balance of payments purposes.

TABLE 7.1
CEYLON: EXCHANGE CONTROL RECORDS
THE DAILY PURCHASES RETURN*

Name of authorized dealer: _____Date_____

Type of transaction	Currency		Purchases
	Sterling	U.S. dollars	Indian rupees _____
1. Purchases against exports.			
2. Purchases of one foreign curency against the sale of another.			
3. Purchases covered by Form C.			
4. Purchases against travel of amounts below Rs 1,000/-.			
5. Miscellaneous purchases below Rs 1,000/-.			
6. Purchases from other authorized dealers.			
7. Purchases from Central Bank.			

* Simplified format. Source: See footnote 4.

TABLE 7.2
CEYLON: EXCHANGE CONTROL RECORDS
THE DAILY SALES RETURN*

Name of authorized dealer: _____Date_____

Type of transaction	Currency		Purchases
	Sterling	U.S. dollars	Indian rupees _____
1. Sales against imports.			
2. Sales of one foreign currency against purchases of another.			
3. Miscellaneous sales.			
4. Sales to other authorized dealers.			
5. Sales to the Central Bank.			

* Simplified format. Source: See footnote 4.

These forms include:

1. The name of the exporter and buyer
2. The name of the consignee
3. The country of final destination
4. A description of the goods and their full invoice value including deductions
5. Freight and insurance paid in Ceylon
6. The method by which the export proceeds will be recovered
7. The date when the proceeds will be recovered
8. Commissions and other direct remittances abroad
9. The name of the exporting vessel
10. Port of final discharge
11. Port of transhipment, if any
12. Quantity shipped and date of shipment

All applications for foreign exchange, for merchandise imports or others, are made on a form which includes the following information:

1. Amount of foreign exchange
2. Name and address of beneficiary
3. Method of payment
4. Name of vessel carrying the goods, if an import
5. Quantity and description of the goods
6. F.O.B. value of the goods, insurance and freight
7. Country of export

More and more business firms and individuals are conducting their operations on an open account basis and only need to purchase or sell foreign exchange to settle periodically their debit or credit balances. These periodic settlements include transactions with Maldive Island traders, certain rupee and foreign currency accounts, shipping, airline and some governmental transactions. To obtain the data thus netted out, those firms which trade on this basis are required to report all of their transactions, generally on a summary basis.

Ceylon conducts a considerable amount of international business in rupees, and transactions so financed might appear to lie outside the exchange regulations. Since rupee balances in non-resident bank accounts are convertible at the demand of the holders, the Ceylonese authorities also bring these transactions under the exchange regulations and they must be reported in sufficient detail for balance of payments purposes.

Statistical procedures followed in Ceylon. The data carried on the various exchange control documents are summarized on eleven reports which are submitted by the banks, authorized dealers and others to the Ceylonese balance of payments authorities. A list of these reports is presented on Table 7.3. A partial balance of payments is constructed from each and the eleven resulting statements are then consolidated. Each item on these reports is coded, punched on cards and tabulated to yield the global and regional figures.

Ceylon's balance of payments statisticians make a number of adjustments to the data recorded on the reports. Some of these figures include lump sum amounts which need to be broken down into their components. Other adjustments are required because certain transactions are not shown on the exchange control records but are derived from other sources. In addition, some recorded data may be incomplete and must be complemented by the use of other documents. Since an exchange control number is assigned to each transaction, these adjustments can be made readily by referring to the numbers on the documents supporting the reports.

Merchandise trade is the most important magnitude on the Ceylon balance of payments, and it is also the weakest from a statistical point of view. Several unexplained discrepancies remain between the merchandise figures carried on the balance of payments and those shown on the customs house tables. Many transactions between parent and subsidiary firms require no foreign exchange and fall outside the balance of payments reporting system. Although Ceylonese statisticians are studying the problem, satisfactory adjustments for all the discrepancies have not as yet been developed. Exports are reported mainly on a f.o.b. and imports on a c.i.f. basis. Due to the fact that some freight and insurance transactions are not reported to the ex-

TABLE 7.3

Reports of Transactions Utilized in Preparing Ceylon's
Balances of Payments

1) Transactions effected through the banking system:
   a) In foreign currencies:
      1. Daily returns of purchases and sales of foreign exchange submitted by the authorized dealers (The DP and DS returns.)
      2. Monthly statement of foreign currency operations of the Central Bank.
   b) In Ceylonese rupees:
      3. Daily returns of debits and credits to nonresident rupee accounts held by authorized dealers in the name of foreign bank branches and correspondents.
      4. Weekly returns of debits and credits to nonresident rupee accounts held by authorized dealers in the name of foreign individuals, institutions, and firms.
      5. Monthly statement of debits and credits to nonresident rupee accounts held in the books of the Central Bank.
2) Transactions effected through special accounts
      6. Quarterly statements of receipts and payments through Traders' Accounts.
      7. Quarterly statements of receipts and payments through Maldivian Traders' Accounts.
      8. Quarterly statements of receipts and payments through Shipping Accounts.
      9. Quarterly statements of receipts and payments through Sterling Company Accounts.
     10. Quarterly statements of receipts and payments through Retained Accounts.
     11. Quarterly statements of receipts and payments through Government Accounts.

change authorities, it has not been possible to adjust either merchandise exports or imports to a strict f.o.b. or c.i.f. basis.

The reinvested profits of direct investment companies located in Ceylon are not shown on the exchange control records and no means of incorporating them on the balances of payments has been devised as yet. Intercompany transfers and illegal transactions in violation of exchange control regulations also escape the exchange control records and do not find their way to the balance of payments statements. The errors and omissions, in spite of all discrepancies, is relatively small. The balance of payments of Ceylon for 1962, prepared from these records, is presented on Table 7.4.

TABLE 7.4

CEYLON: GLOBAL BALANCE OF PAYMENTS, 1962 (PROVISIONAL)
(In millions of Ceylon rupees)

	Credit	Debit
A. Goods and Services	1,995.4	2,130.3
1. Merchandise[1]	1,765.4	1,898.2
2. Nonmonetary gold	—	1.9
3. Freight and merchandise insurance	3.6	4.5
4. Other transportation	114.2	29.2
5. Travel	5.3	19.5
6. Investment income	19.4	62.4
Direct investment	0.7	45.0
Other	18.7	17.4
7. Government, n.i.e.	36.5	35.2
8. Other services	51.0	79.4
Net goods and services	—	134.9
Trade balance (1 and 2)	—	134.7
Net services (3 through 8)	—	0.2
B. Transfer Payments	47.4	36.5
9. Private	6.7	36.5
10. Central government	40.7	—
Net transfer payments	10.9	—
Net total (1 through 9)	—	164.7
Net total (1 through 10)	—	124.0

TABLE 7.4, CONTINUED

	Credit	Debit
C. Capital and Monetary Gold	110.0	—
Nonmonetary sectors	16.8	—
11, 12. Direct investment and other private long-term	—	1.2
Direct investment liabilities	—	*1.1*
Other liabilities	—	—
Assets	—	*0.1*
13. Other private short-term	—	4.8
14. Local government	—	—
15. Central government	22.8	—
Loans received	*45.9*	*6.1*
Other liabilities	—	*9.3*
Assets	—	*7.7*
Monetary sectors	93.2	—
16. Private institutions: liabilities	1.5	—
17. Private institutions: assets	3.5	—
18. Central institutions: liabilities	55.5	—
To IMF	*54.3*	—
Other	*1.2*	—
19. Central institutions: assets	32.7	—
IMF subscription	—	—
Other claims	*32.7*	—
Monetary gold	—	—
Net errors and omissions	14.0	—

[1] Exports mainly f.o.b.; imports mainly c.i.f.
Source: International Monetary Fund, *Balance of Payments Yearbook.* Vol. 15, 1958-1962, Ceylon.

As Table 7.4 indicates, the values are entered as either debits or credits on the tabulation. Balance of payments methodology, like that of commercial accounting, employs well established conventional rules for determining those items which are entered as credits and those entered as debits.

Principles used in debiting and crediting. Several approaches to balance of payments debiting and crediting are employed: the assets and liabilities, the receipts and payments, the claims and the export and import approaches. Since the assets and liabilities approach seems to be gaining in favor, it has been employed throughout this work.[5] According to this approach, the following rules are observed:[6]

1. Transactions which result in an increase in the tangible, intangible or financial assets of a nation are debits on its balance of payments; those which entail decreases are credits.

---

[5] For an explanation of the receipts and payments and the claims approaches to debiting and crediting see: Max J. Wasserman and Charles W. Hultman, *Modern International Economics: A Balance of Payments Approach.* New York: Simmons-Boardman Publishing Corp., 1962, pp. 47-49. Although many students have attempted to establish definite rules for debiting and crediting, no principles, completely satisfactory in all cases without any logical distortion, have as yet been discovered. Noting that the rules of debiting and crediting are common to all the social accounts, the IMF, in its *Balance of Payments Manual,* 3rd ed., 1961, p. 2, describes them in the following terms:

The social accounts have common rules of credit and debit for recording economic transactions. Credit entries are made for the provision of goods and services or of financial items, whether they are sold, bartered, or furnished without a quid pro quo; debit entries are made for the acquisition of goods and services or financial items, whether these items are purchased, obtained by barter, or acquired without a quid pro quo. For the first three types of transactions, the rules immediately result in equal credit and debit entries. For the two remaining types, a credit entry for goods and services or financial items is matched by a debit entry for a transfer payment, and vice versa. (In earlier editions of this Manual, the term "donation" was used instead of "transfer payment.")

The credit and debit aspects of economic transactions are often referred to as flows, particularly in systems of national accounts. In this Manual, however the term "transaction" is usually used even when only one aspect of a transaction is being considered. Accordingly, the Manual distinguishes only three basic types of transactions, i.e., transactions in goods and services, transfer payments, and transactions in financial items.

[6] Adapted from: Max J. Wasserman, Charles W. Hultman and Laszlo Zsoldas, *International Finance.* New York: Simmons-Boardman Publishing Corp., 1963, pp. 82-83.

2. Transactions which result in an increase in a nation's liabilities are credits; those which involve decreases are debits.

3. Every increase in an asset must be accompanied by a corresponding decrease in another asset or assets or an increase in one or more liabilities of equal total value.

4. Each decrease in an asset entails a corresponding increase in another asset or assets or a decrease in one or more liabilities of equal value.

5. An increase in a liability finds its counterpart in a decrease of one or more other liabilities or an increase in assets of corresponding value.

6. Every decrease in a liability carries a corresponding increase in one or more liabilities or decrease in assets of equal value.

Ceylon's linked debits and credits. Merchandise transactions, Table 7.4, line 1, carried on the reports listed on Table 7.3 are debits if they are imports, because they increase Ceylon's tangible assets. The counterbalancing credit entry or entries will depend upon the manner in which payment for the imports was made, and the point at which it was noted on the exchange control record. For example, it will depend upon whether this point was upon acceptance or payment of the financial instrument, by bank draft or by other means. If payment were made by bank draft, bank or commercial acceptance, the credit would be entered to private institutions — liabilities or assets, if the transaction were private; or to central institutions—liabilities or assets, if public, as presented on lines 16, 17, 18, and 19 of Table 7.4. These entries would be credits because they reduce Ceylon's monetary assets or increase its monetary liabilities.

An export of merchandise, line 1, Table 7.4, is entered as a credit because it decreases Ceylon's tangible assets. If reports indicated that payment was made in short-term capital, the counter-balancing debit would be made to private or central institutions—assets or liabilities (banks), because the payment decreased Ceylon's monetary liabilities or increased its monetary assets.

Where these reports show an export or import of non-monetary gold, line 2, Table 7.4, this account is debited if the transaction was an import, and credited if an export, for reasons stated above. Similar entries would be made from these reports to the short-term capital accounts, as in the case of other merchandise transactions, if the export or import were financed by such means.

Reports of transactions in services such as freight, passenger transportation, insurance and others, lines 3-8, Table 7.4, call for entries similar to those which apply to merchandise. Service exports are held to constitute reductions, and service imports increases in intangible assets.

Transfer payments, lines 9-10, Table 7.4, are a special case since they are neither assets nor liabilities. This account has been established to take the counter-entries to debits and credits to the other accounts where there is no quid pro quo of market value. It is no mere dummy account, set up because there were no others available for appropriate entries; it is essential if the balance of payments is to reflect the international transactions of a country.

Assume that Ceylon receives a grant from the United States for the purchase of road building equipment; the exchange records yield a debit to Ceylon's central institutions assets, for its assets are increased. At the same time a credit is entered to the transfer payments — central government, line 10, Table 7.4, reflecting the fact that this is a unilateral transfer.

When the road building equipment is received and payment made, the merchandise account is debited, because the equipment represents an increase in Ceylon's assets. The central institutions' assets account is credited, because the payment represents a decrease in its monetary assets. When a private Ceylonese citizen ships goods as a gift to his friends in the Maldive Islands, merchandise is credited, for the shipment is an export, and private transfer payments receives the counter-balancing debit.

Should the reports show that an American firm made a direct investment in Ceylon, private institutions—assets (line 17), would be debited since the transfer of funds increased Ceylon's private monetary assets. The direct investments and other private long-term account, line 11, Table 7.4, is credited because the transaction increases Ceylon's liabilities.

When the exchange reports show a short-term capital transaction involving the sale by a Ceylonese bank of sterling exchange forward to a resident importer, it is a debit to private institutions —assets account when the transaction is completed, since short-term monetary assets are increased by the acquisition of the forward sterling. Since the forward transaction is likely to be covered by the purchase of spot sterling which represents a decrease in Ceylon's short-term monetary assets, the counterbalancing credit would probably be made to private institutions — assets.

The purchase of gold for monetary purposes by the central bank, as indicated on the reports, entails a debit to central institutions — assets, monetary gold, line 19, Table 7.4 because Ceylon's assets in form of monetary gold are increased. The credit is entered probably to central institutions—assets, other claims, because the government's bank deposits (assets) abroad are decreased by the drafts drawn in payment for the gold.

The same principles are followed in making entries to the balance of payments from the eleven exchange control reports for the other types of Ceylon's international transactions. Ceylon's exchange controls are believed to be well enforced and there are but few transactions which escape them. Consequently, its balance of payments is probably relatively accurate, except for some errors in timing; and its construction involves no unsurmountable difficulties.

The Non-Linked Debit and Credit System: The United States

Where a nation does not have an extensive system of exchange records, it cannot use these records as sources for balance of payments tabulations. Under such circumstances it must have recourse to another method: the non-linked system. Where neither exchange control records nor other useful statistical tabulations and reports are available, a country must prepare balances of payments based largely upon estimates if it is to construct them at all.

If a nation has both extensive exchange controls and good statistical tabulations and reports, it can elect to use either one as the basic source of balance of payments data. In such cases, a country can employ either the one or the other as the principal source, usually checking the results against the source not primarily utilized.

The United States does not employ exchange controls, unless regulations governing transactions with certain Communist powers can be termed such a system. Its official balance of payments always has been based upon the non-linked source system of debits and credits. The United States is well provided with a comprehensive and relatively accurate system of statistical tabulations of wide coverage. It probably has more quantitative information on the operations and structure of its economy than any other country.

Goods and services. These accounts, lines 1-4, 13-14, Table 6.8, have as their source, the foreign trade tabulations of the Bureau of the Census. The tabulations used by Commerce are the Census general trade statistics. For imports, this classification includes general imports, composed of all goods entered into the customs territory of the United States during the period covered. For exports, they comprise shipments made by private parties and the government, as well as the re-export of imports which have not been processed. They do not include the export of goods shipped in transit to the United States for foreign destinations, military cargoes, gold, and small gifts.

Since the concepts underlying the Census tabulations of foreign trade differ from those employed by Commerce in its balance of payments work, the data are reclassified and adjusted before being utilized. The adjustments for coverage are among the more important ones made.[7] The Census tabulations of foreign trade are based upon export declarations and import entries filed by exporters and importers with the Customs authorities.

-----

[7] Details concerning the adjustments made by Commerce to the Census foreign trade tabulations are given in: U. S. Department of Commerce, *Balance of Payments of the United States, 1949-1952* (a Supplement to the *Survey of Current Business*). Washington: U. S. Government Printing Office, 1952, pp. 20-29.

Commerce distinguishes three types of military transactions: those made under grants, those made under the auspices of the Defense Department and which are paid by the purchaser, and the commercial procurement of military items. The first two of these are shown separately on the United States balance of payments while the third is carried in the merchandise account.

Since the first two of these transactions are not of a commercial nature, separate treatment is indicated. In addition, it might be argued that some military shipments have more in common with domestic than with foreign trade. They are made in part for the protection of the United States; and were they to be eliminated, this country would doubtless be obliged to spend more money on its military establishments at home.

Transportation account. This account, lines 5 and 15 on Table 6.8 includes the freight and fares paid for the international movement of goods and persons by ocean and inland waterways, air, rail, road, and pipeline. In addition, it comprises payments for the international exchange or rental of transportation equipment as well as the substantial port costs, charter hire and other expenses of transportation companies paid to foreigners. The entries to this account are made on the basis of the residence of the operator of the transportation facilities rather than the ownership or the flag of the equipment they utilize.

Commerce assumes that in any merchandise transaction, the importer pays the freight. When the transportation is supplied by a foreign exporter, as far as the importer is concerned, it is an international transaction. Since the merchandise trade is valued on an f.a.s. basis, this practice introduces no valuation problems in principle. Hence all foreign purchases of transportation from American companies and United States purchases from foreign operators enter into the transportation account.

Thus the data used in compiling the transporation account are obtained from the shipping operators rather than from the exporters or importers. Every quarter, Commerce receives a report from American shipping operators which provides the principal source of the entries to this account. These data are supplemented by estimates made on the basis of shipping data furnished by the Maritime Commission, the Department of Defense, data on the number of travelers provided by the Immigration and Naturalization Service. In addition, a number of questionnaires is furnished annually by the United States representatives of foreign transportation companies and, in some cases, by the governments of the countries involved.

The receipts and expenditures of the United States and foreign airline operators are derived from a quarterly questionnaire similar to that employed for ocean shipping. Where incomplete, the data carried on this form are supplemented by estimate. International rail receipts and payments are estimated from the reports submitted by the railroads involved as well as from reports furnished by the Canadian government on United States rail traffic with that country. International pipeline transactions are obtained from the reports of the few companies engaged in this business.[8]

The travel account. Lines 6 and 16, Table 6.8, include all expenditures made abroad by Americans, and those made in the United States by foreign travelers. All foreign travel expenditures are included in this account except the fares for travel between the country of residence and the first and last ports, which are entered in the transportation account. The expenditures of Americans on official missions abroad and of foreign residents on official business in the United States are not included in this account. Official travel of Americans is entered in miscellaneous services — government, and that of foreign residents in miscellaneous services—private account.

For purposes of preparing the estimates for this account, Commerce divides travel into three parts: the overseas, Canadian and Mexican categories. For the overseas category, the Immigration and Naturalization Service supplies a count of the number of persons entering and leaving the United States. Data showing the expenditures of these travelers are obtained from a postcard questionnaire distributed to travelers on a sample basis.

---

[8] Further information concerning the sources of data, including the forms used for the transportation account, and the adjustments made are given in: Commerce, *op. cit.*, pp. 31-45.

In the case of the Canadian category, the questionnaire method is also employed on both sides of the border through the cooperation of the American and Canadian authorities. For the Mexican category, travel receipts and expenditures are estimated by netting out the border dollar flows between the two countries.[9]

The miscellaneous services account. This account, lines 7-8, 17-19, Table 6.8 receives the entries of a number of services transactions. The miscellaneous services—private account includes principally the international transactions of firms in the communications, reinsurance, motion picture, engineering and contracting business as well as home office charges, royalties and fees of parent companies, other royalties together with foreign government representational expenses in the United States.

As a general proposition, the data required to elaborate this account, with the exception of foreign government representational expenses in the United States, are obtained by the use of questionnaires filled out by the companies concerned.

Foreign representational expenses in the United States include expenditures of foreign governments and international organizations in the United States for personal services, rents, utilities, other administrative and operational outlays together with the costs of real property.

Although it is sometimes considered undiplomatic to request information concerning foreign government representational expenses, this information is obtained from some governments and international bodies. Where this information is not available, Commerce estimates the expenditures on the basis of the number of offices and installations maintained and the number of personnel employed.

Certain transactions are not entered as miscellaneous services — private account because the required data are lacking. This is true of payments made directly to foreign firms by Americans, and the professional services of lawyers, accountants, performing artists and doctors of medicine.[10]

---

[9] See: Commerce, *op. cit.,* pp. 45-56.

[10] The forms used in the preparation of the miscellaneous services—private account, together with a detailed description of it, are given in: Commerce, *op. cit.,* pp. 56-66.

All overseas service transactions of the United States government are included in the miscellaneous services — government account with certain exceptions. These exceptions are receipts and payments for freight and shipping which are entered in the transportation account, and transactions involving income on government capital which are debited or credited to the income on investment—government account.

Other items included are: the purchase of land and buildings of a non-income producing character; the cost of foreign materials used in the construction of non-income producing land and buildings; expenditures for official travel abroad; some foreign aid transactions; personal expenditures of United States government personnel and payments, except subscriptions to international financial institutions, for participation in international organizations. Certain military miscellaneous services transactions are not carried in this account, but are listed separately.

The distinction between military and other government services transactions is made on the basis of the type of agency reporting rather than the nature of the transaction itself. Only a small part of the total cost of conducting United States military operations abroad is included, because many of these expenses are incurred in the United States and are domestic transactions. In addition and as a general rule, payments for most United States military operations abroad are considered to be domestic transactions.

The non-military or other receipts and expenditures entered on this account arise from the administration and operations of United States civilian agencies abroad. They include principally the Department of State, its embassies, ministries and consulates together with the costs of missions and conferences abroad; the Post Office Department; the Panama Canal Company and the Panama Railroad. The data required to elaborate the miscellaneous services — government account are obtained directly by Commerce from the governmental agencies involved.[11]

Some United States government aid and grant programs require the deposit, termed counterpart funds, by the recipient

---

[11] Cf. Commerce, *op. cit.*, pp. 66-71.

country to the credit of the United States, of a certain percentage of the grant in the form of local currency. Other transactions, notably some of those undertaken under Public Law 480, require a similar payment for the commodities shipped by the United States in the currency of the country assisted. These deposits and local currency payments are entered as debits, line 42, Table 6.8.

Income on investments. This account, lines 10-12, 20 and 21, Table 6.8 is classified as a service on both the IMF and Commerce tabulations because it represents a payment for the services rendered by capital. According to Commerce methodology, all interest, rents, dividends and branch profits paid or credited during the period covered are entered on the balance of payments after deductions for taxes paid in the foreign country. A distinction is made between private direct, other private and government receipts and payments of income. Reinvested earnings are not included as income on the United States balance of payments since they are not transferred to American residents. They are reported and shown annually, however, on more detailed tabulations on foreign investments which are supplements to the balance of payments accounts.

Bench mark data for the estimation of income on private direct investment are provided by the census of United States direct investments abroad and foreign direct investments in the United States taken periodically, most recently by Commerce in 1957 and 1959.[12] Data for the *current* tabulations of income from

---

[12] For the censuses of U. S. investments abroad and of foreign investments in the United States see: U. S. Treasury Department, *Census of Foreign-Owned Assets in the United States* and *Census of American-Owned Assets in Foreign Countries*. Washington: GPO, 1945 and 1947 respectively; U. S. Department of Commerce, *Foreign Investments of the United States* (a Supplement to the *Survey of Current Business*), and *U. S. Business Investment in Foreign Countries* (a Supplement to the *Survey of Current Business*) and *Foreign Business Investments in the United States* (a Supplement to the *Survey of Current Business*), Washington: GPO, 1953, 1960 and 1962 respectively. In addition, these censuses contain much information concerning the amount and operations of both United States investment abroad and foreign investment in the United States which is not shown on the balances of payments. The U. S. Department of Commerce's *Survey of Current Business* usually carries articles in the August and October issues of each year dealing with the amount and performance of international investment which supplement the balance of payments data.

direct investments are obtained by means of a quarterly questionnaire required by law from the parent firms or subsidiaries in the United States.

Estimates of United States private income received from foreign dollar bonds are made on the basis of tabulations of outstanding issues. Since the approximate total value of privately-owned foreign currency stocks and bonds is known from existing tabulations, an estimate of the income which they paid to Americans is made by applying an average rate of return to this total. Estimates of the income earned by United States residents on private long-term bank and commercial loans are prepared by applying an average rate of interest to the amount outstanding, as reported by banks and commercial companies.

Although the amount of private miscellaneous long-term assets, principally real estate, estates and trusts, owned abroad by American residents is large, the amount of income received from this property is believed to be small, and a nominal entry is made for it. Figures showing the value of United States private short-term claims on foreigners are collected regularly by the Treasury Department. An estimated rate of return on these investments is applied to this value to derive the income figure applicable to this category of investment. The amount of income paid by United States residents to the foreign owners of American portfolio investments is based on data compiled by the Internal Revenue Service from income tax returns, and also on estimates of interest paid on reported holdings of time deposits and other assets.

United States government income payments to foreigners represent principally the return on foreign government monetary reserve holdings in this country. The total official short-term obligations held in United States banks is reported by financial institutions to the Treasury and the current rate of interest on these holdings is applied to this total to derive the income paid. The estimated market value of long-term federal obligations held abroad is multiplied by the current yield for this type of obligation to estimate the income paid on this category of investment. The United States government income receipts from its foreign investments are reported to Commerce by the several federal agencies involved.[13]

Unilateral transfers. Lines 24-29, Table 6.8 present the movement of unilateral transfers. These are divided into government grants excluding military, other government grants, military transfers, pensions and private remittances. Prior to the advent of Lend-Lease in 1941, private unilateral transfers constituted the largest element of this account, but since that time, those of the government have been more important.

Data for unilateral transfers — government are furnished by reports which the applicable federal agencies make to Commerce as well as from published and unpublished reports of these organizations. For the most part, this account is composed of the value of government aid and grant programs. It includes all international transfers by United States government agencies in the form of goods and services, cash and capital assets which are not accompanied by a quid pro quo in one of these forms. Other unilateral transfers, not connected with foreign aid programs, such as federal pensions and annuities, claim payments, settlements, recoveries and refunds are carried in the government — pensions and other transfers account. Reparations and restitutions received from other governments are also included in this account.

Private United States resident individuals and organizations have been making unilateral transfers for many years. Commerce divides these transactions into two groups: personal and institutional remittances.

Personal remittances occur when United States residents send gifts of money and goods to family and friends residing abroad, and when they receive gifts and restitution payments from overseas. The source data underlying Commerce's estimates of these personal remittances consist, in part, of figures received from agencies known to be in the personal remittance business such as the American Express Company, banks, steamship and communication companies. Other data, such as the value of the

---

[13] For further details concerning the income account see: Commerce, *Balance of Payments of the United States, 1949-1952* (A Supplement to the *Survey of Current Business*). Washington: G.P.O., 1952.

remittances by postal money order, are provided by the Post Office Department. The Department of Labor likewise reports the number of Mexican workers employed in the United States. The Labor Offices of certain Caribbean countries cooperate by providing data showing the number of resident workers from their area which aids in estimating the remittances made by their nationals.

Commerce assumes that most of the parcel post shipments to and from certain European and Asiatic countries are merchandise unilateral transfers and records them as such. The data for these transactions are obtained from the Post Office Department. Data showing the receipt by Americans of unilateral cash transfers from foreign residents are obtained from certain foreign government sources.

A large number of American organizations make institutional remittances abroad. These include religious, missionary, educational, scientific, health and welfare institutions, among others. The Advisory Committee on Voluntary Foreign Aid of the Department of State reports the remittances made by those agencies registered with it. In addition, Commerce obtains data by correspondence indicating the remittances made by religious and secular institutions known to engage in this work.[14]

The capital account. A capital movement or transaction is defined as the change in the ownership of financial assets between residents and non-residents. The capital account is presented on lines 30-50, Table 6.8, and is divided into two major parts: United States and foreign capital. This division is made on the basis of the ownership of the capital involved: United States capital movements occur where foreign-owned assets are bought by American residents; foreign where United States-owned assets are purchased by foreign residents. The terms capital, capital assets and liabilities and international investment are held to be synonomous. These terms encompass all international claims such as bank deposits, bonds, loans, mortgages, drafts, acceptances,

---

[14] The forms used in, and additional information concerning, the preparation of the unilateral transfers account are given in: Commerce, *op. cit.*, pp. 72-78.

notes and intercompany accounts. They also include all equities in the form of securities, estates, foreign unincorporated branches, trusts, annuity contracts and real property held for the purpose of producing income.

Certain categories of assets which Commerce does not consider to be capital are: stocks of goods stored abroad but owned by residents; houses, summer homes, hunting lodges and the like, for the personal use of the owner; government installations abroad, such as military bases; and non-commercial property of non-profit institutions.

Short-term capital movements are frequently the counterpart of transactions in goods, services, unilateral transfers and long-term capital. They may also be autonomous, resulting from, for instance, interest rate differentials, exchange arbitrage and speculation. This account is divided between private and government capital. Private capital movements are held to comprise all except those in which the United States government is an active participant and which are classified as government capital. Capital transactions in which foreign governments participate are considered to be private capital unless the United States government is also an active participant.

A distinction also is made between long- and short-term capital. Long-term capital is defined as consisting of assets and liabilities of an indeterminate maturity (largely equities) or with a stated original maturity of more than one year from the date of issue. Short-term capital is that having a maturity of one year or less.

Direct investments are distinguished from others on the United States balance of payments. They are defined as companies in which the investors have an important voice in the management as well as the branches of parent firms. Both Commerce and the IMF use, as a rule of thumb, the ownership of twenty-five per cent or more of the voting stock of the firm as a test for important voice in management but other criteria are also employed, such as ownership of ten per cent of the voting stock of associate foreign companies.

The sources used for the direct investment account consist

largely of reports filed with Commerce by American parent companies and United States resident subsidiaries of foreign firms. These reports provide information covering intercompany accounts, home office accounts with foreign branches, and data showing the purchases and sales of foreign subsidiary securities by the parent company. Data for the construction of the account, transactions in the United States and foreign securities, are obtained from reports collected for the Treasury Department by the Federal Reserve Banks on the basis of figures provided by banks, brokers and dealers.

A total of six special forms is used by the Federal Reserve Banks to obtain data on all capital transactions other than direct investment. These reports comprise those covering: (1) transactions in all long-term United States and foreign securities, including marketable United States government bonds and notes; (2) United States banks' long-term claims on, and liabilities to, foreigners; (3) short-term claims on foreigners of United States banks, including items held for their customers; (4) United States banks' short-term liabilities to foreigners; (5) United States non-bank concerns' long- and short-term claims on, and liabilities to, foreigners; (6) foreign debit and credit balances of United States brokers and dealers.

The respondents are not required to report on transactions of less than a specified amount, usually $100,000 to $500,000. Data on long-term securities are reported on a transactions basis. For all other long-term portfolio and short-term capital, data on outstanding assets and liabilities are collected, and flows that enter the balance of payments are computed from changes in these outstanding amounts.

The new security issues in the United States item is compiled from information supplied by underwriters and financial services. These sources are supplemented by reports appearing in the press and the tabulations of the Securities and Exchange Commission. Banks and commercial firms report their other long-term assets and liabilities on the same forms as those used for the short-term capital described below.

Short-term assets and liabilities consist of deposits, bills,

United States government short-term securities, short-term commercial paper and accounts, and drawing rights on the IMF. The Federal Reserve Banks obtain data from banks, brokers, dealers, exporters, importers, and certain commercial concerns which form the basis for its reports on the movements of these items. These data are submitted to the Treasury Department and forwarded to Commerce. Since some liabilities are reported in foreign currencies, their values are converted to dollars by the use of a rate of exchange. To obtain the true change in the values of these items, the dollar values are adjusted for exchange rate variations.

Government long-term capital movements include all loans and credits of the government to foreign countries with a maturity of more than one year together with their reimbursement and United States borrowings by means of special non-marketable bonds. The more important of these capital transactions are subscriptions to the International Monetary Fund and the International Bank for Reconstruction and Development; credits extended by the Agency for International Development and the Export-Import Bank of Washington; certain remaining Lend-Lease transactions; surplus property credits; the repayment of government loans and credits by non-residents; and long-term credits extended by foreign governments to the United States. The information for the elaboration of this account is reported to Commerce by the several federal agencies involved.

The foreign short-term assets of the United States government consist of foreign currency deposits of United States governmental agencies, IMF drawing rights, foreign currency holdings and advance payments made by federal procurement agencies. United States government short-term liabilities to foreign countries include the Philippine deposits with the Treasury Department; those of other foreign governments with various federal agencies and foreign advances on military purchases in the United States. The data for both of these accounts are obtained from the several government agencies concerned with these operations.

The movements of non-monetary gold, as already noted, are

treated as any other merchandise export or import. Monetary gold is regarded by Commerce and the IMF as another form of short-term capital. Transactions in monetary gold are computed according to the formula recommended by the League of Nations Subcommittee on Balance of Payments Statistics which also has been adopted by the IMF. According to this formula:[15]

The excess of current gold production over non-monetary consumption (or vice versa) appears as a credit (debit) in the current account of the balance of payments, while an increase (decrease) in the monetary gold stock of a nation appears as a debit (credit) in the gold and short-term capital account. Since the difference between domestic production and consumption, on the one hand, and the change in the monetary gold stock on the other, is equal to the net international gold movement, the use of the suggested method does not result in any change in the balance of payments as a whole.

The source for the basic data on gold exports and imports is found in the Census foreign trade tabulations. The Federal Reserve Bank of New York collects data showing the earmarking of United States gold stocks for foreign government account. The Treasury Department provides tabulations showing its foreign gold purchases and sales. Changes in the United States gold stock are published regularly in the *Federal Reserve Bulletin* and the holdings of the Exchange Stabilization Fund in the *Treasury Bulletin*. The Bureau of the Mint reports statistics on gold production and consumption in the *Annual Report of the Director of the Mint*.[16]

Debiting and crediting under the United States non-linked system. The transactions method of debiting and crediting, employed in commercial accounting, whereby each transaction, or totals of like transactions, are entered on the books, is not employed in either the linked or the non-linked system. The data obtained from the United States source materials mentioned

---

[15] Quoted from Commerce, *op. cit.*, p. 113.

[16]. For additional information concerning the capital account see: Commerce, *op. cit.*, pp. 91-113.

above are edited, examined for accuracy, adjusted, collated with other relevant information and are then posted to the balance of payments worksheets. The worksheets are used to compile the detail of each account, or its supporting tables, and the final total is entered in the appropriate account on the balance of payments.

The non-linked system of debiting and crediting is based upon the same principles as those which apply to the linked and the reasons for a debit or a credit, as presented in the illustrative examples of Ceylon's linked system, apply equally to the United States non-linked system. The principal difference is that under the linked, the debits and credits are often both found on the same document or related group of documents, whereas under the non-linked, each document yields usually only one entry, either a debit or credit.

Under the non-linked system, the balance of payments statisticians are working somewhat in the dark, for while they know what entries a given document requires, they do not know where the counterbalancing entries are to be found or for certain if they have been reported on any source document. Where both the debit and credit entries are shown on the source document, the balance of payments statisticians have a greater feeling of certainty in their work.[17]

However, there are other disadvantages to the linked and certain disadvantages which pertain to the non-linked system, and it is difficult to determine which system is the better. This question is examined in the following chapter which considers the accuracy of balances of payments.

---

[17] The debit and credit illustrations used in this chapter are of the *source document type* as distinguished from the *transactions type*. Under the transactions type, each individual international transaction is considered as the direct source of a balance of payments entry. The transactions type is useful as a teaching device and is appropriate for textbook use. The transactions type, however, is not utilized in balance of payments practice and, therefore, is not realistic. For a discussion of the transactions type, with illustrative examples and a list of the principal types of debits and credits see: Max J. Wasserman and Charles W. Hultman, *Modern International Economics: A Balance of Payments Approach.* New York: Simmons-Boardman Publishing Corp., 1962, pp. 44-66.

8

The Accuracy of
Balances of Payments

The old Latin adage, *qui numerare incipit, errare incipit,* (he who starts to count, starts to err), characterizes one of the principal difficulties of all statistical presentation, or of all counting for that matter. All statistics are subject to error and the balance of payments is no exception. Together with the other social accounts, it is among the more difficult tabulations to elaborate. It summarizes in a few lines the hundreds of thousands of international transactions made by a large number of people and institutions in widely scattered areas. Although this chapter is devoted to the graceless task of pointing out the deficiencies and assessing the accuracy of this tabulation, the astonishing fact is that it has been possible to prepare reasonably reliable balances of payments at all.[1]

Basic Causes of Error and Tests for Accuracy

The importance of balance of payments accuracy to the economic analyst scarcely needs to be stressed. If the statement lacks validity he cannot do much reliable quantitative work in the international field or any field which relies upon data derived from this compilation. In a world of directed and partially-directed economies, imperfect balances of payments may lead to the promulgation of programs and policies which are based upon incorrect premises. The domestic and external economic policies

---

[1] A penetrating study of the accuracy of economic statistical presentations is given in: Oskar Morganstern, *On the Accuracy of Economic Observations.* Princeton: Princeton University Press, 1963.

adopted by many nations, especially since the end of World War II, bear witness to the influence exerted by inferences drawn from these tabulations.

Basic causes of balances of payments errors. Fundamentally, balance of payments accuracy rests upon the educational level and discipline of the population. If an educational system limits itself to the creation of an intellectual elite, while neglecting the mass of the population, the balance of payments economists may well be qualified, but they will experience difficulties in procuring the requisite, or accurate, data from the people. Lack of discipline means that requests for data either go unheeded or that reports are carelessly prepared.

The administrative capacity of the government is scarcely less important. A poorly administered government cannot hope to obtain the cooperation, either voluntary or mandatory, of the people in reporting their international transactions. When a country does not enforce its reporting of international transactions properly, its balances of payments are likely to suffer. Nations which have well administered and reliable income taxes are usually in a better position to command accurate reporting than those which do not have such a system.

All errors and inaccuracies should not be laid at the feet of the administration or the respondents; some are due to the carelessnesses of the statisticians who prepare the forms and questionnaires, devise the reporting system and process the data.

The quality and aggressiveness of a nation's accounting profession also play an important role in promoting accuracy by creating reliable bookkeeping sources for the data. Nations which had good general statistical services before undertaking the preparation of periodic and systematic balances of payments— as contrasted with sporadic estimates—have a headstart in this field. Frequently, balance of payments reporting represents but an extension of an already-existing system. As a general proposition, it is easier for directed economies to install balance of payments reporting systems than for those which rely more heavily on laissez-faire. The license applications, authorization requests and reports required of directed economies frequently form a good base for such systems.

Balance of payments inaccuracies can be divided into two broad groups: those which involve but one side of a transaction, either the debit or credit, and thus affect the errors and omissions account; and those which involve an entire transaction, both the debits and credits, and do not affect the errors and omissions account.

Tests of balance of payments accuracy. Although no tests have been devised as yet which enable one to measure the accuracy of balances of payments, a number of devices may be employed which provide some idea of their reliability. The balances of payments for any one period can be compared with those for preceding periods and any important unexplainable discrepancies noted. This procedure might be facilitated by preparing time series charts or by working out proportions between those accounts which are strongly related such as freight or transportation and merchandise exports and imports.

The magnitudes carried on a country's balances of payments can be compared with their counterparts on those of its trading partners and any unexplainable discrepancies noted. Some countries and the IMF publish revisions of data previously presented. The extent of the revisions can be ascertained and some idea of the accuracy of the tabulations obtained from the importance of changes made. However, the mere fact that a nation frequently revises its figures is in itself no indication that the statements are inaccurate. Some of the countries which prepare the best balances of payments revise them frequently and these revisions are one indication of concern about accuracy.

The size and movement of the errors and omissions account also afford some evidence concerning balance of payments accuracy. Where this account is large, where it shifts abruptly from a debit to a credit balance or vice versa, there may be grounds for questioning the accuracy of the tabulation. Balances of payments tabulations may also be compared with the other national accounts for consistency.

The task of gauging the accuracy of balance of payments

is complicated by general price movements in the country of compilation and its trading partners. Changes in the official pars of exchange, multiple pars and shifts in the terms of trade also render the task of estimating accuracy a difficult one.

No discussion of accuracy would be quite complete without a word on the problems of misrepresentation and "window dressing." In some cases, the temptation to falsify these statements may be great. Although there are apparently no reasons for presuming that the balance of payments of the free nations are deliberately false or misleading, some of the data which *underlie* these tabulations may have been falsified.[2]

Accuracy of the Linked Source System

Often the balance of payments statistician has no other choice than to accept either the linked or exchange record, or the non-linked, statistical reporting, system of debit and credit sources, for only one of the two may be available. Where a choice between the two can be made, he is likely to make his selection on the basis of considerations which center around the issues of coverage and accuracy.

Under these circumstances, he may use the system which seems best and to rely upon the other for purposes of checking and completion. Or he may employ a combined system by using non-linked sources for the construction of some accounts and the linked for the others. The errors and omissions, or unrecorded transactions account is apt to be smaller where the linked system is used, although a small errors and omissions account is, in itself, no guarantee of the accuracy of the tabulation.

Coverage and evasion. To provide a *complete* linked source system for balance of payments purposes, the exchange records must cover *all* transactions. Where a nation is short of foreign exchange or where these reserves are in precarious balance, a nation's exchange control system may well cover all international economic transactions. If the shortage is less acute, exchange

---

[2] Cf. Darrell Huff, *How to Lie with Statistics.* New York: W. W. Norton and Co., 1954.

controls are likely to cover fewer classes of transactions and may be applied only to capital movements. In such cases, the linked system is only of limited use. The data for transactions not subject to controls must be either obtained from some non-linked system sources or be estimated.

Experience during and since World War II indicates that even the best administered systems of exchange controls are evaded as the existence of black markets, in which foreign exchange is bought and sold illegally, bears witness. Unless detected, black market transactions do not find their way on balances of payments which then understate some of the accounts. In examining tabulations constructed under the linked system for accuracy, the analyst should first determine the extent to which exchange controls are well administered and then attempt to estimate the probable amount of evasion which takes place.

Timing and periodic settlements. Although the *proposed* date when an international transaction is to occur may be correctly stated on the exchange records, the *actual* time when it is finally consummated may differ. Where different reporting periods are involved, an error in timing results. If an exchange transaction is assigned a code number which is applied to all the documents involved, including those related to shipping and payment, it may be possible to correct some of these timing errors. Unless such a code system is installed, the linked sources balance of payments statisticians have difficulty in determining precisely when a transaction was finally consummated.

A problem which troubles balance of payments statisticians arises in the cases of firms which engage in periodic settlements of net balances rather than the liquidation of specific transactions as they occur. The accounts of subsidiaries with their parent firms are often settled at certain intervals when only the net debit or credit balance outstanding is liquidated. The firms which engage in this practice only pay or receive the amount of foreign exchange represented by the net balance; the individual transactions which took place are not recorded on the exchange documents. As more and more international business is handled on this basis and, as the open account method of financing foreign trade continues to grow in importance, problems of this sort are apt to increase.

Difficulties such as these can be obviated by requiring all firms which operate on a periodic settlement basis to file supplementary reports, showing in sufficient detail the transactions which took place during the period covered. However, such regulations may raise problems of compliance. Ceylon, as noted in the previous chapter, has successfully required firms which engage in periodic settlements to report all transactions instead of the net balance alone.

Respondent's errors and valuation. It would seem simple enough for the inhabitants of a country using exchange records to fill out the requisite documents correctly. Unfortunately, errors of many kinds creep into the documents. Similar mistakes, it should be noted, are also found in the best kept records under the non-linked system.

Although foreign exchange must be obtained for travel abroad where nations employ extensive exchange control systems, very few travelers know with exactitude, just how much they plan to spend abroad and for what purpose. Private personal remittances of both goods and funds which do not clear the banking system are often reported inaccurately or are not reported at all.

Problems of valuation are also frequent sources of inaccuracies. The previous chapter showed that Ceylon has had difficulty in separating the cost of imported and exported merchandise from insurance and freight in all cases. Where such difficulties exist, it is not possible to value merchandise exports and imports on an uniform c.i.f., f.o.b., or f.a.s. basis. In such cases the merchandise account may include some freight and insurance in its stated values.

Other problems of merchandise valuation are encountered. Since most countries utilize import, and but relatively few export, tariffs, the values of imports are more likely to be accurately stated than those of exports, especially in the case of ad valorem duties. Import documents form the basis for the assessment of duties and are subject to verification by the customs appraisers.

Several methods of pricing imports and exports are available and the trader may be at a loss to ascertain just what price to enter on the documents which he fills out. In addition, the importer may value his purchases at one price and so enter it on the exchange records, while the customs authorities may select another as the more accurate amount, or in closer conformity with the provisions of the customs tariffs. Under such circumstances the value desired by the balance of payments office may not be reported. Rebates and discounts are not always treated uniformly. Where the value of the imported goods is reappraised after entry, the change in valuation does not always find its way on the balance of payments.[3]

A certain amount of smuggling is found in all nations with import tariffs, and is especially prevalent in weakly administered countries, notably those where government corruption prevails. In the case of some countries where smuggling is known to be rife, the reported imports are adjusted to include smuggled as well as legally entered goods. [4]

The use of multiple or frequently shifted pars of exchange also affects the valuation of the items carried on the balance of payments. If one rate is applied to certain transactions and different rates to others, the values presented will lack homogeneity. Where a wide range of multiple rates is employed, the balances of payments are not likely to be very meaningful.

Capital transactions and classification. Capital transactions are among the more difficult to record completely under exchange

[3] An excellent account of the problems associated with the valuation of merchandise transactions is given by: Nicholas Michael Petruzzelli, "Some Technical Aspects of Foreign Trade Statistics with Special Reference to Valuation." *The Catholic University of America Studies in Economics, Vol. 17.* Washington: The Catholic University of America Press, 1946. Dr. Petruzzelli describes the various valuation methods employed by a number of countries and includes a large bibliography.

[4] China (Taiwan) reported total imports of $330.3 million in 1961 which included an adjustment for smuggled goods amounting to $700,000. See IMF, *Balance of Payments Yearbook,* Vol. 14, notes accompanying the balance of payments of China (Taiwan). The data for China's adjustment for smuggling are obtained in part from some of the stores and bazaars which are known to deal in smuggled goods.

controls. Some nations which regulate capital movements may also have relatively unstable currencies which tempt larger holders of capital to invest their funds abroad where the monetary system is more stable. Such transfers are likely to be made in evasion of the exchange controls. Some of them are made by devious means and are not easily detected.

Income earned on foreign investments may not be repatriated but left abroad on deposit or invested in other forms of property. Except in the case where both sides of such a transaction are reported, or where further investigation is made, the appropriate debits and credits may escape the balance of payments.

The classification of international transactions is of the very essence of the balance of payments; for, without it, meaningful tabulations of manageable size would be impossible. However, forcing the thousands of transactions into a limited number of categories may do violence to the nature of some of them and give rise to inappropriate listings. In addition, mis-classification is apt to occur in the case of borderline transactions or those which lend themselves to misunderstanding.

A transaction, which to all appearances is a private personal remittance and should fall in the unilateral transfers account, may in reality be the reimbursement of a loan. Through errors in reporting, the fares paid by travelers which should be entered in the transportation account may find their way in the travel account. Gifts bought by travelers abroad may at times be classified as merchandise imports and at other times as travel, depending on how they are reported. The reinvestment abroad of income earned from foreign investments may be listed either as income or as investment when it should have been carried in both accounts.

Exchange control and balance of payments concepts. Exchange controls are utilized primarily to preserve or increase a nation's foreign exchange reserves and to protect a fixed par of exchange, rather than to constitute a system of balance of payments source records. In those cases where the control records are being established at a time when a balance of payments office is already organized, it may be possible to persuade the exchange control authorities to arrange the records so that they will also be suitable for balance of payments purposes. Where exchange controls exist before the opening of the balance of payments office, it may be possible to persuade the exchange control officials to alter their records to make them more useful for purposes of this tabulation. However, experience indicates that once established, a set of records is only changed with difficulty.

The balance of payments statistician, therefore, often has to do the best he can with records prepared for other purposes. One of the problems which he faces is that of the correct interpretation of exchange control records, of converting control coverage into that employed by the balance of payments.

Accuracy of Non-Linked Systems: The United States Experience

Many of the inaccuracies which characterize balances of payments elaborated under the linked are sometimes found in those prepared under the non-linked system. These are principally errors of timing; coverage; inaccuracies which arise when firms net out their transactions in periodic settlements; the mistakes of respondents in filling out reports and questionnaires; problems associated with valuation; smuggling; the use of multiple exchange rates; unreported and misreported transactions; problems of classification; the utilization of reports prepared for other than balance of payments purposes. In addition, the use of the non-linked system gives rise to errors inherent in its own procedures.

A potential source of error of the non-linked system, stems from the fact that the entries are obtained from differing and often unrelated sources. A glance at the various sources employed by the United States bears witness to this conclusion. The balance of payments statistician who works with exchange documents may be able to check out the reported transactions by referring back to original license applications and other supporting papers. Where other tabulations, reports and questionnaires are used, as under the non-linked system, such checking and reference is seldom possible. Errors which are present in these records may, therefore, remain uncorrected.

Shortly after the large deficits appeared on the United States balance of payments in 1958 and after, a debate arose over the measure used by this country in determining the magnitude of the deficits.[5] As one result of this debate, a Committee was appointed at the instance of the President by the Director of the Bureau of the Budget to examine the adequacy and reliability of the United States balance of payments.

This Committee, the Review Committee for Balance of Payments Statistics, did not confine its attention to the problem of surplus and deficit measurement alone. According to its directive, the inquiry of the Committee was to cover: "basic conceptual problems, problems of presentation and analysis, and technical statistical problems of data collection, estimation, and related matters."[6]

Although substantial improvement has been made in the United States balances of payments over the past ten years, fur-

---

[5] The principal protagonists in this debate were the Treasury Department and the Department of Commerce. In several public addresses, Secretary of the Treasury Douglas Dillon criticized the measurement of United States deficits as being overstated. The accuracy of the calculated deficits was defended by Walther Lederer, Chief of Commerce's Balance of Payments Division. A summary of these debates is presented by Richard F. Janssen, "Figure Feud: While U. S. Wrestles with Payments Deficits, Economists Fuss Over How to Figure It," a feature article on the editorial page of the *Wall Street Journal* for October 31, 1963. This debate drew the participation of people outside the government, See: Wendell Gordon, "The Criterion for an Adverse Balance of Payments," *American Economic Review,* Vol. LIII, No. 1, Part 1, March 1963, pp. 139-141; H. N. Goldstein's reply, "The Criterion for an Adverse Balance of Payments," *American Economic Review,* Vol. LIII, No. 5, December 1963, pp. 1094-1101; and Wendell Gordon's reply to H. N. Goldstein, "The Criterion for an Adverse Balance of Payments: Reply," *American Economic Review,* Vol. LIII, No. 5, December 1963, pp. 1101-1103.

[6] Report of the Review Committee for Balance of Payments Statistics to the Bureau of the Budget, *The Balance of Payments Statistics of the United States: A Review and Appraisal.* Washington: United States Government Printing Office, 1965, Chapter 1.

ther improvement is required if this statement is to prove of maximum utility. During the same period of time, the international economic relations of this country have become more complex; the international role of the dollar more crucial and new types of transactions have emerged for which the present methods are inadequate.

The materials in this section are based on the findings and recommendations embodied in the *Report* issued by this Committee. Although the experience of the United States with the non-linked system can neither be held to be representative of this system in general nor as employed by any other country, it does illustrate some of the difficulties encountered by balance of payments statisticians when using it. In this context, it might not be amiss to note that the United States balance of payments takes its place, along with those prepared by the United Kingdom, Canada, and West Germany, among the more reliable and meaningful presentations.

The merchandise account. In terms of magnitude, the merchandise trade account is the most important component of the United States balance of payments. Merchandise exports, including military exports financed by grants, amounted to more than $25 billion, and imports to about $18.6 billion in 1964. The accuracy and adequacy of the merchandise figures transcend in importance most of the other problems which face the Commerce balance of payments statisticians.

This account is elaborated from the general foreign trade data prepared by the Bureau of the Census. In preparing its tabulations, Census apparently envisages primarily the industrial users of the statistics, tariff officials and students of foreign trade in goods. Although these data may adequately serve the requirements of these end-users, they are not well adapted to balance of payments purposes in respect to coverage, valuation, classification and accuracy.

The instructions for the preparation of export declarations and import entries, which form the basis of the foreign trade tabulations, are not consistent with balance of payments valuation principles. In addition, the instructions are not sufficiently clear to enable traders to understand what is wanted. The import entries for merchandise dutiable under ad valorem rates form the basis of the assessment of duties and are more accurate than the others.

Although the Census Bureau has taken several steps to improve the accuracy of its foreign trade tabulations, the errors on import entry and export declaration documents are not always caught and the process of editing the forms sometimes introduces new ones, principally of timing. Adjustments for some of the errors in valuation and changes in coverage are made by the balance of payments statisticians. These adjustments are frequently occasioned by the under-valuation of merchandise shipped between allied firms and the over-valuation arising from the inclusion of ocean freight.

The classification of military shipments under grants are inadequate in that it sometimes fails to distinguish between goods, services and the personal expenditures of American personnel abroad. Shipments of supplies by the United States military to military forces abroad are not held to fall within the category of international trade but as domestic transactions.

The Review Committee recommended that greater attention be paid by Census to balance of payments requirements and suggested that Census undertake studies to discover and measure the sources of errors in the valuation and coverage of the foreign trade data. It also found that the instructions for exporters and importers required revision so as to bring them to utilize valuation principles consistent with balance of payments purposes. The Committee suggested that the quality of the data be improved through better coverage and that revised tables with classifications more suitable for balance of payments and analytical uses be prepared.

The day-to-day operations of the Bureau of the Census, the Committee held, needed tightening and improving so as to raise the quality of the data which it prepares. The presentation of the foreign trade statistics required improvement for both analytical and balance of payments purposes. The classification of goods by end-use and the preparation of adequate historical series were strongly recommended. Finally, the Review Committee urged the Bureau of the Census to prepare a new descriptive statement covering the foreign trade figures and the procedures used in compiling them.[7]

The transportation account. The transportation account is one of the more important numerically of those in the services category. Transportation payments amounted to about $2.5 billion and receipts to $2.3 billion in 1964. Although air transport is of growing importance, ocean transactions were the largest components of this account in 1963, amounting to about 75 per cent of the total receipts and 70 per cent of the payments for the movement of goods and people.

Under United States procedures, the importer is assumed to have paid the freight with merchandise valued on a f.a.s. basis. The principal source of the data for this account consists of reports submitted by the operators of transportation facilities or their agents. The reports received from United States operators are, in the main, satisfactory; those from the American-based agents of foreign operators are not. In the case of some countries, the governments objected to the fact that transportation company agents filed reports on the operations of their principals. To avoid disclosure of these operations, nine governments agreed with Commerce to furnish a report of their operations. These reports do not supply enough detail to permit the preparation of ocean freight payments and receipts without considerable estimate.

Due to the failure of some American operators to file reports, the data received from them are supplemented by estimate. A number of assumptions are involved in these estimates, some of which may be of doubtful validity. Problems have also arisen by reason of the difficulties involved in identifying the operators of tramp and charter-hire vessels. In some cases the operator is not identified and no entry is made; in others the transaction is entered more than once.

Estimates of ocean passenger fare receipts are made by multiplying the number of travelers by average fares to which esti-

---

[7] For further details concerning improvements in the merchandise account see *ibid.*, Chapter 2.

mated shipboard expenditures are added. Those for air passenger fares are estimated by the use of a more complex formula. The assumptions underlying these estimates and the validity of the figures used in preparing them are subject to a considerable margin of error. The port expenditures of both airlines and ocean carriers are relatively large, are prepared on a basis similar to freight receipts and payments and are also subject to error.

The Review Committee recommended that Commerce utilize a variety of measures to improve the estimates of the transportation account such as more frequent contacts with reporters; making its reports from operators and agents mandatory rather than voluntary; periodic benchmark surveys. It suggested that Commerce insist upon receiving reports from the agents of foreign operators. The Committee also advocated greater international cooperation in the exchange of transportation data, information and concepts. Finally, it suggested that a pilot study should be undertaken in cooperation with Canada, to ascertain trucking company receipts and payments for the American-Canadian trade.[8]

The travel account. In terms of dollar value, the travel account does not loom large on the United States balance of payments. In 1964, payments for travel were estimated at $2.1 billion and receipts at slightly more than one billion. Although the travel account is one of the less reliable, its limited importance does not warrant the expenditure of large sums in its improvement. Noteworthy increases in the quality of the travel data would prove relatively expensive.

For purposes of the preparation of this account, travel is divided by Commerce into three categories: overseas, Canadian and Mexican. Overseas travel is estimated by multiplying the number of travelers by an estimated average expenditure per traveler. The number of overseas travelers is obtained from the Immigration and Naturalization Service and the average expenditures from a random sample questionnaire handed to travelers.

The rate of response to foreign travel questionnaires is too

---

[8] A more extensive treatment of the transportation account is presented in *ibid.*, Chapter 3.

low to inspire confidence in the estimates based on this sampling. In addition, the editing of the returned questionnaires, since it involves the elimination of extremely high and low reported expenditures, may introduce a downward or upward bias in the travel data.

The statistics covering travel with Canada are generally satisfactory and are prepared under a cooperative arrangement with the Dominion Bureau of Statistics. The Mexican travel data on the other hand, leave something to be desired. The estimates of travelers to the interior of Mexico and the United States are made in a manner similar to those for overseas travel and are subject to like errors. No figures are collected on a systematic basis covering the expenditures of "border crossers," or people who travel frequently between Mexico and the United States for short periods. Commerce assumes that American border crossers use dollars and Mexican crossers pesos; this assumption tends to overstate United States net travel payments.

In view of these shortcomings, the Review Committee suggested that an on-the-spot study of border crossers be made to establish a system of sampling the expenditures of both Americans and Mexicans who travel frequently between these countries. It recommended also that Commerce explore means of improving the quality of the sampling procedures employed for travelers to and from other areas than Canada and Mexico. The Committee proposed greater cooperation between Commerce and the statistical officers of other countries in the compilation of travel statistics.[9]

The miscellaneous services-private account. In 1964 the United States miscellaneous services-private account recorded about $1.8 billion in receipts and $425 million in payments. Given the relatively large number of components of this account, a wide variety of methods is employed in elaborating it. Since each of these many components is of relatively small value, the Review Committee felt that the estimation procedures utilized by Commerce called for no major revision.

---

[9] The travel account shortcomings and the means of its improvement are described in greater detail in *ibid.*, Chapter 3.

However, the Committee did suggest that Commerce explore the possibility of using benchmark surveys or other means of establishing the magnitude of the transactions which are not now covered. These transactions include commissions, patent royalties, licensing fees, together with fees for legal, accounting and managerial services.[10]

The unilateral services-personal account. The United States unilateral services-private transactions are reported on a net basis and in 1964 they amounted to $550 million. Except for a few categories, receipts from personal remittances are almost impossible to detect and measure. Many of the items now reported as unilateral transfers might belong in other accounts such as commodity purchases or tourism. Beginning in 1960, Commerce started to include as private unilateral receipts, the counterpart outpayments taken from the balances of payments of Austria, Canada, West Germany and the United Kingdom.

The Review Committee recommended that the possibility of including the private unilateral transfer payments figures reported by other countries be examined in view of including the appropriate parts of them among the United States receipts. It was of the opinion that the list of institutions reporting unilateral transfers presently utilized by Commerce was incomplete and should be supplemented by the Treasury list of tax exempt organizations, labor unions, universities and the smaller foundations. As a general proposition, the Committee held that, although this account was probably deficient in several respects, many of the defects were at present probably irremediable.[11]

The government transactions accounts. Since the outbreak of World War II, the government's role in international economic life has greatly expanded, especially in the fields of military operations, civilian grants and loans. During the period 1959-1963, the international costs of maintaining the United States military establishments abroad averaged $3 billion a year and the outflows of government grants and capital averaged $4.5 billion annually.

---

[10] *Ibid.,* Chapter 3.
[11] *Ibid.,* Chapter 3.

This increased activity has served to complicate the compilation and analysis of balance of payments statistics.

The personal expenditures abroad of United States military and civilian personnel are classified as international transactions and are recorded on the balance of payments. Parts of these expenditures are known with some accuracy; those made in PX's, commissaries and other military outlets, for example. Others are estimated, but the accuracy of these estimates, based upon small untested samples, cannot be determined. Likewise, no reliable gauge of the reliability of the receipts of military personnel has been devised as yet.

Military expenditures abroad for construction are not reported in a satisfactory manner and may be over- or understated since they are not always separated from the domestic expenditures of these contractors. Military receipts from sales overseas and transfers made under grants of United States military goods and services to foreign governments may also embody errors due to the difficulty in separating these items from commercial exports and in determining their value.

The measurement of government non-military grants presents difficulties in that many transactions not classified as grants, do in fact contain unmeasured grant elements. These are purchases of goods from other nations at prices above the world market; loans made at concessional rates of interest and small donations of private funds handled through government channels.

The valuation of grants under P. L. 480 has presented certain difficulties in compiling balance of payments statistics. Commodities shipped under this Act are often overvalued in balance of payments statistics when compared with their probable market value. This over-valuation amounts to as much as fifteen to fifty per cent in the case of some products. Errors are also introduced when these exports are valued by the exporting firms at prices which differ from those used by the government agencies involved.

The distinction made on the balance of payments between government short-term claims and foreign currency holdings is essentially arbitrary. On the other hand, there are but few conceptual or data problems related to long-term government outflows or receipts. Although new complexities have been introduced by the handling of foreign currencies acquired under P. L. 480, the reported data are believed to be of good quality.

Errors in timing have arisen in the case of the government financing of exports because some of these transactions are entered at different times on different records. In addition, lack of adequate data on the sources of commodities financed by loans and grants contributes to uncertainty in determining whether the expenditures were made in the United States or abroad.

With the increased balance of payments deficits which appeared in 1958 and after, the President, in August 1962, ordered the federal agencies to file reports semi-annually on their international transactions. These reports are reviewed by the Bureau of the Budget to determine whether or not all possible actions are being taken to reduce international payments and increase receipts. These reports are popularly known as the "gold budget" because they were established by the Bureau of the Budget in an effort to reduce the United States gold outflows.

The gold budget has had two effects on the balance of payments. First it has served to improve the quality of the agencies' reports showing their international transactions. Secondly, government agencies have desired to take credit to the greatest possible extent for reductions in foreign expenditures and for increases in receipts. This has resulted in the preparation of reports which do not always correspond to the principles of balance of payments accounting followed by Commerce.

To improve the accuracy and suitability of government reports for balance of payments purposes, the Review Committee made a number of recommendations:

1. Adapt gold budget reports to balance of payments purposes or reconcile them with the principles of this tabulation.

2. Prepare a new manual of methodology for the use of federal agencies in reporting their international transactions.

3. Improve the quality of the reporting system for international government transactions as well as of the reports

showing the receipts and expenditures of government personnel stationed abroad.

4. Show the export market value of all commodities shipped under P. L. 480 and other programs.

5. Show the country where the funds are actually spent in all reports of agencies engaged in the loan and grant business.[12]

Direct investment and related income. By the end of 1964, the book value of United States direct investment in affiliates abroad amounted to about $43 billion. On a depreciated replacement cost basis, the value of the properties involved would doubtless be far larger. In the same year, foreign direct investments in the United States had a book value of about $8 billion. United States income from direct investments, 1959-1963, averaged approximately $3 billion a year as recorded on the balance of payments and about $4.5 billion a year if the reinvestment of the undistributed earnings of foreign subsidiaries are included. Foreign direct investment in the United States yielded income to its owners abroad amounting to $500 million in 1963.

The Review Committee apparently found less fault with Commerce's statistics of direct investments and its income than it did with those of some of the other accounts. These statistics are largely compiled from reports submitted by American parents and foreign subsidiaries located in the United States. It noted that improvements in quality and coverage had been steadily made. The Committee did, however, find some room for the improvement of the direct investment and income accounts.

In view of the fact that data on direct investments form the basis for considerable analytical work, the Committee recommended that the coverage of the direct investment category include transactions in real estate since they are of increasing importance and are only partially recorded. Coverage could also be improved by continually modernizing the reporting forms so as to include new types of transactions and new entrants into the field as they arise.

Many respondents are confused by the reports which they

---

[12] For further details concerning the accuracy of the government accounts see *ibid.*, Chapter 4.

are required to submit. The quality of these reports could be strengthened, the Committee held, by more frequent contacts between reporters and Commerce personnel. Many of the reporters are working in the dark and do not always realize exactly what they should or should not include. The quality of their reporting could be improved, according to the Review Committee, if Commerce were to issue a manual of reporting instructions to all the respondents.

It also proposed that an Advisory Committee be established, composed of representatives of the various categories of reporters. Such a group, working under the aegis of Commerce, could help that Department keep abreast of new developments in the field as well as of reporting difficulties. The Committee also recommended more frequent direct investment censuses—every five years—to reduce the interval between them and to assure more reliable data.

At present, Commerce does not adjust its direct investment figures for unreported data, feeling that such adjustments might introduce an element of error into the final results. The Review Committee, nevertheless, was of the opinion that such adjustments should be made. It also held that more detailed industrial breakdowns of this account would prove useful by providing analysts with some much-needed information which is not available at present.

Commerce neither shows the undistributed profits earned by subsidiaries abroad nor the capital investment resulting from these retained profits on the balance of payments, although it does present these items in its special studies of American investment abroad. The Review Committee recommended that it regularly include these items as memorandum entries on its balance of payments presentations.

Since there is some confusion and overlapping between direct and portfolio investments, the Committee suggested that greater efforts be made to maintain the integrity of these two classifications. Commerce has much information on international investment in its files which it is unable to process at present due to a lack of personnel and funds. The Review Committee recom-

mended that Commerce should endeavor to publish this information. Finally, it suggested that greater international cooperation
in the preparation of these accounts might yield fruitful results.[13]

Other private and official capital and income accounts. Long-
term portfolio and short-term capital encompass a wide variety
of claims which arise from differing transactions and involve a
large number of American and foreign residents. In addition,
these holdings are heterogeneous as far as ownership, motivation,
importance and volatility are concerned. Consequently the preparation of satisfactory balance of payments presentations of their
movements involves difficulties.

The magnitude of these accounts has greatly increased during recent years. During the period 1959-1963, the reported net
annual outflow of United States private capital into foreign long-
term securities (other than direct investment in affiliated companies) averaged about $900 million a year. At the end of 1963,
American residents are estimated to have held about $13 billion
in these securities. Net outflows of United States short-term
capital have varied from a low of $80 million in 1959 to a high
of $1.5 billion in 1961. Foreign long- and short-term holdings in
the United States have likewise increased impressively during the
five years ending in 1963.

The primary responsibility for the collection of data on the
movements of long- and short-term capital rests upon the Treasury for which the Federal Reserve Banks act as data-gathering
agents. Figures showing foreign official holdings of assets in the
United States are accurately reported since the banks which hold
these accounts file reports of high quality. The reports do not,
however, separate the holdings of foreign monetary authorities
from those of other official financial institutions.

The data on securities transactions made by both American
and foreign residents are incomplete because some financial and
non-financial intermediaries are not adequately represented in
the reporting system. Errors of omissions and duplication arise
and the type of securities traded and their geographic break-

---

[13] See *ibid.*, Chapter 5 for additional information concerning the direct
investment account.

downs are sometimes inaccurately classified. The reports by banks on their private long- and short-term transactions are generally satisfactory but may embody some errors due to the fact that the nationality of the account holders is not always known. The data showing liabilities to, and the claims on, non-bank reporters are not as complete and precise as they should be and involve duplication and omission. Some transactions are not discovered by the present reporting system, such as investments in mortgages and real estate; estates, trusts and personal holding companies; minority interests in foreign business concerns.

The estimates of income on investment, both foreign in the United States and American investment abroad, embody inaccuracies of varying degrees of importance. These are due primarily to imperfect data showing the amount of these holdings and dubious assumptions concerning their yields. In addition, income on certain types of short-term claims is not included in the estimates.

The Review Committee made a series of recommendations to remedy these deficiencies. It proposed that Commerce and the Treasury Department take censuses or make surveys to establish benchmark data for long-term portfolio assets and private short-term claims and liabilities. Such benchmarks could assist in the review of the data collection system and provide better bases for estimating income from investments. The Committee thought that greater cooperation between the Federal Reserve Banks and the reporting units is required to yield more accurate figures.

It also recommended that the United States government seek broad cooperative arrangements with key countries and international organizations to obtain better coverage of particular types of capital movements. In addition, it suggested that Commerce make greater use of questionnaires to collect more reliable figures on transactions in foreign dollar bonds. Finally, the Committee proposed the use of greater detail in conjunction with the presentation of the capital and income accounts.[14]

---

[14] *Ibid.*, Chapter 6, presents additional comments on the other private and official capital accounts.

Tabular presentation. Although tabular presentation may not raise questions of statistical accuracy and reliability, tables may be misleading or have other shortcomings which render their modification desirable. The Review Committee found that the tabular presentations of the United States balances of payments were too complex and technically worded to be readily understood.

In view of the changing character of the international economic relations of the United States, Commerce has altered its balance of payments presentation and nomenclature from time to time. As a result, the tabulations lack stability and consistency. In addition, it is difficult to compare the figures shown on the balance of payments with similar series carried on other financial tabulations such as those of the Treasury and Federal Reserve Board. In the opinion of the Committee, some of Commerce's tables create analytical biases principally by netting out certain transactions.

Accordingly, it recommended a revision of Commerce's standard or main table as well as the summary, supporting and detailed tables. The Committee's proposed tabular presentation for the summary (standard) balance of payments is shown on Table 8.1; a selection of the recommended supporting and detailed compilations is given in Appendix B. The proposed summary table is designed to replace Commerce's standard table which will no longer be published if the Committee's recommendations are carried out.

The suggested summary table, although considerably shorter than Commerce's standard fifty line table, makes but few changes in the presentation of the merchandise trade or services accounts. It combines transport with travel and embodies the Committee's preference for the official settlements basis of measuring surpluses and deficits (discussed in Chapter 9) in preference to the type of liquidity measurement now employed by Commerce (Line J, Table 8.1).

The United States long-term capital account is organized by type of asset rather than by kind of holder (Line E).

A new line has been added which segregates all dollar assets

TABLE 8.1

Proposed Summary United States Balance of Payments Table (Period)
(In billions of dollars)

Type of transaction	1954	1955	1956	1957	1958	1959	1960	1961	1962	1963	Line
A. Goods and services, except transfers under military grants [net receipts (+)]	1.8	2.0	4.0	5.7	2.2	.1	3.9	5.6	5.1	5.7·	A.
A.1 Merchandise exports, adjusted	12.8	14.3	17.4	19.4	16.3	16.3	19.5	19.9	20.6	22.0·	A.1
A.2 Transport and travel receipts	1.8	2.1	2.3	2.8	2.5	2.5	2.6	2.7	2.8	3.0	A.2
A.3 Military receipts	.2	.2	.2	.4	.3	.3	.3	.4	.7	.7	A.3
A.4 Investment income and related receipts	2.4	2.6	2.9	3.1	3.1	3.4	3.6	4.3	4.9	5.1	A.4
A.5 Miscellaneous service receipts	.6	.7	.8	.9	1.0	1.0	1.1	1.1	1.2	1.3	A.5
A.6 Merchandise imports, adjusted	−10.4	−11.5	−12.8	−13.3	−13.0	−15.3	−14.7	−14.5	−16.1	−17.0	A.6
A.7 Transport and travel payments	−2.0	−2.4	−2.7	−2.9	−3.1	−3.4	−3.7	−3.7	−4.0	−4.4	A.7
A.8 Military payments	−2.6	−2.9	−2.9	−3.2	−3.1	−3.1	−3.0	−3.0	−3.0	−2.9	A.8
A.9 Investment income and related payments	−.4	−.5	−.6	−.7	−.7	−.9	−1.0	−.9	−1.1	−1.3	A.9
A.10 Miscellaneous service payments	−.5	−.5	−.6	−.6	−.7	−.7	−.7	−.8	−.8	−.8	A.10
B. Remittances and pension payments (net)	−.6	−.6	−.7	−.7	−.7	−.8	−.7	−.7	−.7	−.8	B.
C. U.S. Government grants and capital except military grants.	−1.6	−2.2	−2.4	−2.6	−2.6	−2.4	−2.8	−3.5	−3.7	−3.9	C.
C.1 Nonmilitary grants and long-term credits	−2.0	−2.3	−2.3	−2.6	−2.8	−2.7	−2.9	−3.8	−4.0	−4.1	C.1
C.2 Scheduled repayments of long-term credits	.5	.4	.3	.7	.5	.6	.6	.6	.6	.6	C.2
C.3 Foreign-currency balances and short-term claims [net increase (−)]	−.1	−.3	−.6	−.6	−.3	−.4	−.5	−.3	−.2	−.4	C.3
D. Foreign official capital except claims of monetary institutions [net increase in foreigners' assets (+)]	.0	−.1	.0	.3	.3	.4	.6	.4	.4	.3	D.
D.1 Investments and claims of foreign governments, except monetary institutions.	.0	.0	.0	.1	.0	.2	.2	−.1	.1	.4	D.1
D.2 Investments and claims of international non-monetary institutions.	.0	−.1	.0	.3	.3	.1	.4	.5	.3	−.2	D.2
E. Long-term private capital [net increase in U.S. assets (−); net increase in foreigners' assets (+)].	−.7	−.5	−2.0	−2.9	−2.6	−1.4·	−2.1	−2.2	−2.7	−3.3	E.
E.1 U.S. direct investments abroad	−.7	−.8	−2.0	−2.4	−1.2	−1.4	−1.7	−1.6	−1.7	−1.9	E.1
E.2 Transactions in foreign securities	−.2	.0	−.4	−.5	−1.3	−.7	−.7	−.8	−1.0	−1.1	E.2
E.3 Other U.S. investments abroad	−.2	−.3	−.2·	−.4	−.2	−.3	−.2	−.3	−.3	−.6	E.3
E.4 Foreign direct investments in the United States	.1	.2	.2	.2	.1	.2	.1	.1	.1	.0	E.4
E.5 Transactions in domestic securities	.1	.4	.3	.2	−.0	.6	.3	.3	.1	.2	E.5
E.6 Other foreign investments in the United States	.0	.0	.0	.0	.0	.0	.0	.0	.0	.1	E.6
F. Short-term private capital except claims of foreign commercial banks reported by U.S. banks [net increase in U.S. assets (−); net increase in foreigners' assets (+)].	−.6	−.2	−.2·	.0	−.2	.1	−1.6	−1.3	−.5	−.3	F.
F.1 U.S. claims on foreigners reported by U.S. banks	−.5	−.2	−.4	−.3·	−.4	−.1	−1.0	−1.1	−.3	−.7	F.1
F.2 Other U.S. claims on foreigners	−.2	−.0	−.1	−.0	.0	.0	−.4	−.4	−.2	.0	F.2
F.3 Foreign claims on the United States, except claims of foreign commercial banks reported by U.S banks.	.0	−.0	.3	.3	.2	.1	−.2	.3	.1	.5	F.3
G. Short-term claims of foreign commercial banks reported by U.S. banks [net increase (+)].	.0	.4	.4·	.1	.0	1.1	.1	.6	−.1	.4	G.
H. Net errors and omissions [net receipts (+)]	.2	.5	.5	1.2	.5	.4	−.8	−1.0	−1.1	−.3	H.
J. Balance settled by official transactions (sum of lines A through H, equal, with opposite sign, to sum of lines K and L.	−1.5	−.7	−.2	1.1	−3.0	−2.5	−3.5	−2.0	−3.3	−2.3	J.
K. Special intergovernmental transactions [net receipts (+)].						.4	.1	.7	.7	.3	K.
K.1 Advance repayments of long-term debt to the U.S.						.4	.1	.7	.7	.3	K.1
L. Reserve transactions [net increase in U.S. assets (−)].	1.5	.7	.2	−1.1	3.0	2.1	3.4	1.3	2.7	1.9	L.
L.1 U.S. holdings of gold, convertible currencies, and other reserve assets [net increase (−)].	.3	.0	−.3	−.8	2.3	1.1	1.7	.7	·.9	.3	L.1
L.2 IMF position [increase in drawing rights (−)]	.2	.1	−.6	−.4	.0	−.0	.4	−.1	.6	.0	L.2
L.3 U.S. liabilities to foreign official monetary institutions [net increase (+)]	1.0	.5	1.1	.1	.7	1.1	1.3	.7	1.1	1.6	L.3
Memoranda: The following transactions are not included in the table above:											
I. U.S. military grants (excluded from line C.1) and transfers under military grants (excluded from lines A.1, A.2, A.3, and A.5)	3.4	2.6	2.6	2.4	2.3	2.0	1.8	1.5	1.5	1.5	Memo: I.
II. Reinvested earnings of the foreign subsidiaries of U.S. firms (excluded from lines A.4 and E.1)	.7	1.0	1.2	1.4	.9	1.1	1.3	1.1	1.2	1.6	II.
III. Reinvested earnings of the U.S. subsidiaries of foreign firms (excluded from lines A.9 and E.4)	.2	.2	.2	.2	.2	.2	.2	.2	.2	.2	III.

Source: Report of the Review Committee for Balance of Payments Statistics to the Bureau of the Budget, *The Balance of Payments Statistics of the United States: A Review and Appraisal*. Washington: U.S. Government Printing Office, 1965.

held by international non-monetary institutions (Line D.2). The proposed table also lists changes in the short-term dollar claims of foreign banks as a separate major section (Line G). In addition, it carries foreign short-term non-bank *claims* as short-term private capital (Line F.3) instead of listing them as liquid United States *liabilities* as is the current Commerce practice.

The expression "increase in foreigners' claims or assets" is substituted for "increase in United States liabilities," and foreign dollar assets are classified according to type of holder rather than by the kind of United States debtor. Finally, the terms receipts and payments are employed in preference to credits and debits used on the Commerce presentations.

In the opinion of the Committee, the existing Commerce array of tables should be replaced by a new group: (a) a summary balance of payments, as illustrated on Table 8.1; (b) a set of detailed and supporting tables keyed to the summary table which develop the major components of the balance of payments in greater detail (see Appendix B). It recommended that Commerce should continue to publish quarterly balance of payments statistics and that they should appear, as at present, three months after the close of the quarter to which they apply. In addition, the Committee held that Commerce should publish a yearbook providing continuous data for several years and organized in a manner similar to the quarterly tables. The yearbook should also supply additional detail, both functional and regional. Finally, it suggested that the special annual articles published in the *Survey of Current Business* and the monthly tables presented in the *Federal Reserve Bulletin* and *Treasury Bulletin* should be reorganized and revised to achieve a more effective presentation of detail.[15]

As previously noted, the present United States balances of payments are among the world's best. They justifiably enjoy well-nigh universal respect both at home and abroad. In view of the findings of the Review Committee, one is led to pose the question: How accurate are the balances of payments of other

---

[15] The changes in tabular presentation recommended by the Review Committee are explained in some detail in *ibid.*, Chapter 10.

nations? The question almost answers itself. Those who examine or analyze these statements may be well advised to follow the Cartesian principle of *le doute méthodique* (methodical doubt) before drawing any conclusions from them.

Errors and Omissions and Transfers of Funds between Foreign Areas

This account, sometimes termed unrecorded transactions, appears on the balances of payments prepared by the use of both linked and non-linked sources and is presented on line 3, Table 6.8. It is purely a balancing item used where the debits are over- or understated with reference to the credits or vice versa.

Ordinarily, this account does not receive entries; it is computed by subtracting the total debits from the total credits or vice versa, of the other accounts. An exception to this general rule arises in the case of some countries which are at a loss to know in precisely what account to enter certain transactions. In such cases, they are sometimes entered directly in the errors and omissions account.

In Italy, for instance, certain short-term capital movements for which no reliable estimates are available, have been entered directly in the errors and omissions account. Estimates of the counterpart entries for Italian banknotes returned to Italian banks have been also included in this account, since the Italian authorities did not know whether these banknotes were used to finance transactions in goods and services or investments.[16]

In a certain sense, the term errors and omissions is too broad when applied to this account. It does not embody counterbalancing errors, i.e., those which affect equally both the debit and credit sides of a transaction. It also presents a net figure and does not show total magnitudes.

Although a small errors and omissions account is no guarantee of accuracy, a large one, relative to the gross international turnover, or one with considerable variation over time in magnitude or sign, is generally a danger signal. The IMF holds that

---

[16] Cf. Notes to Italy's balance of payments, IMF *Balance of Payments Yearbook*, Vol. 14.

where the errors and omissions account constitutes less than five or six per cent of the total exports and imports, the balance of payments submitted by a country may be held to be acceptable in the absence of other information to the contrary.

Errors and omissions on regional and bilateral presentations. Commerce distinguishes two broad categories of items which compose the errors and omissions account: those which arise solely on the bilateral and regional balances of payments and those which appear in the global compilations. Those in the first category arise when a resident, say of the United Kingdom (Sterling Area), liquidates a debt to a Latin American by sending him a dollar draft on a New York bank, which is ultimately deposited to the credit of a Latin American bank in the same financial institution. When the draft clears the New York bank, the balance of the Sterling Area and United Kingdom is decreased in this bank and that of Latin America increased by the same amount.

United States short-term liabilities to the Sterling Area and the United Kingdom are decreased (debits). However, there is no counterbalancing credit to this regional or bilateral balance of payments for no increase in United States exports of goods, services, unilateral transfers or capital to this area or country has taken place. United States liabilities to Latin America are larger, represented by an increase in the credits to the foreign short-term capital account. But, there is no counterbalancing debit, for no increase in United States imports of goods, services, unilateral transfers or capital from this region has occurred.

In the case of the *regional* balance of payments with the Sterling Area and the *bilateral* balance of payments with the United Kingdom, the errors and omissions account debits will be larger. The regional balance of payments with Latin America will show an increase in credits in the errors and omissions account.

The errors and omissions account on the United States *global* balance of payments will not be changed by these transactions, for the only account involved, short-term foreign capital, received equal debit and credit entries on this tabulation. Errors on the regional or bilateral statements also arise when the United States settles its accounts with one country in the currency of another, e.g., where it pays Canada for imports of wood pulp by means of a sterling draft on its London holdings.[17]

Errors and omissions on global presentations. The other type of errors and omissions affects both the global and regional balances of payments and occurs when but one side of a transaction, either a debit or credit, is duplicated, omitted, over- or understated. Transactions which American residents conduct directly with non-residents without benefit of an American intermediary, are an important source of errors of this kind. When a resident of the United States purchases real estate directly from an English owner, for example, and pays for it through banks which lie within the Commerce reporting system, the payment constitutes a credit to United States private short-term capital. But there is no counterbalancing debit to the long-term capital account (real estate), for the transaction is not ordinarily reported either by the English sellers or American purchasers to the United States authorities.

Errors of this type are likely to arise in conjunction with the direct transactions of residents with foreign principals in insurance; real estate; the purchase and sale of securities; the settlement of, or movements in, estates and trusts; professional services; industrial property; other services such as those of advertising agencies, market research firms and the like.

Errors and omissions frequently arise in conjuction with the evasion of foreign exchange controls. Assume that an exporter in a country using exchange controls arranges with a friendly American importer to evade the foreign country's controls by a procedure known as "underbilling." The exporter ships goods to the American importer worth $1,500 but bills him for but $1000. The transaction is put through the exporter's exchange control records as a merchandise export for the amount billed. When

---

[17] Some balance of payments statisticians hold that these *multilateral settlements* are not true errors and omissions. They simply cannot be separated from the others. They call attention to the fact that if data on these mulilateral settlements were available, regional and bilateral errors and omissions could be identified and corrected in the appropriate accounts.

the American importer remits the $1000, both ends of the transaction balance as far as the records go. Unless investigated and discovered, the exchange control authorities are satisfied.

Since he remitted but $1000 for goods worth $1,500, the American importer fulfills his end of the "deal" by depositing $500 in a New York bank to the credit of the foreign exporter under the exporter's name and country of residence. When the United States bank reports its foreign short-term capital movements, this transaction is included and the Commerce balance of payments statisticians credit foreign private short-term capital with $500. However, no counterbalancing debit to merchandise is entered since none was recorded. The credits to errors and omissions have increased thus by $500. The exporter has accomplished the objective of his evasion of the exchange controls by accumulating $500 to the credit of his account in New York.

During the period 1947-1949, when many of the United States trading partner nations were employing exchange controls, the errors and omissions account showed total credits of $3.1 billion. This large credit balance is believed to be the result of "hot capital" inflows to the United States from Europe made in violation of exchange controls. After the devaluation of the European pars of exchange of 1949, the errors and omissions credits decreased.[18]

Certain international transactions lend themselves to duplicate debits or credits. If funds are remitted through banking channels by a United States resident to an American traveling abroad by a draft on a foreign bank, United States private short-term capital receives a credit entry for the amount remitted. Under present reporting procedures, debits might be recorded for more than one of the following accounts: travel, merchandise imports, or unilateral transfers. The errors and omissions account debits would be increased by these duplications.[19]

---

[18] Hal B. Lary, *Problems of the United States as World Trader and Banker*. New York: National Bureau of Economic Research, Inc., 1963, p. 23.

[19] Commerce, *Balance of Payments of the United States, 1949-1951* (a Supplement to the *Survey of Current Business*), Washington: U.S. Government Printing Office, 1952, pp. 115-116.

Other errors and omissions often arise when balance of payments statisticians use records prepared for other than balance of payments purposes. Attention has already been drawn to the fact that the Census Bureau tabulations of exports and imports embrace a different coverage than that used for balance of payments purposes. These tabulations are consequently adjusted by Commerce to bring them to conform to its definitions. Although these adjustments are carefully made, some errors are almost certain to arise.

Revisions in balance of payments data and methodology sometimes increase the errors and omissions account. The Commerce Census of United States investments abroad taken in 1960 revealed that a previously published investment figure for 1957 was understated by about $400 million. When the revision was made by debiting the appropriate capital account for $400 million, no counterbalancing entry for this debit was found; consequently, the errors and omissions credits were increased by this amount.[20]

Walther Lederer, chief of Commerce's Balance of Payments Division, reports that, although efforts are being made to reduce the size of the errors and omissions account, new sources of errors appear almost as rapidly as the old ones are detected and eliminated.[21]

Errors and omissions arise from a variety of other sources. Where merchandise, services or unilateral transfers, for example, are over- or undervalued, while the means of payment are shown at their exact transaction value, either the debit or credit balance of the errors and omissions account will be affected.

---

[20] Philip W. Bell, "Private Capital Movements and the U. S. Balance of Payments Position." *Factors Affecting the United States Balance of Payments.* Compilation of Studies Prepared for the Subcommittee on International Exchange and Payments of the Joint Economic Committee, Congress of the United States. Washington: U. S. Government Printing Office, 1962, pp. 449-450.

[21] Walther Lederer, "The Balance of Foreign Transactions: Problems of Definition and Measurement." *Special Papers in International Economics,* No. 5, September 1963, Princeton: International Finance Section, Department of Economics, Princeton University, 1963, pp. 58-60, and Hal B. Lary, *op. cit.,* pp. 16-17.

If a transaction is shown as having taken place during one reporting period, while the means of payment, or the other side, at another, the errors and omissions account for both periods will reflect this fact (errors in timing).

Should a reporting system provide for incomplete coverage of a group of transactions, while the other side is more completely covered, errors will likewise arise. Some balance of payments statisticians provide for "cut offs" in their reporting requirements. Under such a procedure, transactions below a stated value level are not reported. Now if the other side of these transactions is reported in full, the errors and omissions account will mirror this omission.

Errors will likewise appear due to the failure of certain respondents to report, while the counterbalancing entries are reported. Adjustments for seasonal variations, applied to monthly, quarterly and semi-annual presentations, unless equally applied to both debits and credits, may also affect this account.

The errors and omissions account of one country does not necessarily find its counterpart in those of its trading partners and there is little or no relationship between this account on the balances of payments of the several nations. The problem of attributing errors and omissions to one or a group of accounts, although it is often useful for certain analytical purposes, is fraught with difficulties. This topic is discussed in Chapter 9.[22]

The Inadequate Representation of Licensing Investments

Although the inadequate representation of any type of transaction may not necessarily constitute an error in the strict sense of the term, such shortcomings do decrease the utility of the balance of payments. Licensing arrangements are inadequately presented on today's balances of payments and, in view of their large and growing importance, this defect calls for rectification.

---

[22] For further details concerning the errors and omissions account see: Commerce, *op. cit.*, pp. 115-117; Report of the Review Committee for Balance of Payments Statistics to the Bureau of the Budget, *The Balance of Payments Statistics of the United States: A Review and Appraisal.* Washington: U. S. Government Printing Office, 1965, Chapter 7.

It is easy to understand how licensing arrangements come to be poorly represented. A license to use a patent, copyright or other industrial property ordinarily involves the transfer of little, if any, capital. Since the balance of payments only carries value magnitudes, the mere transfer of a right (without a stated capital value) to exploit industrial property does not give rise to capital movements under present balance of payments definitions.

Although the value of the capital transferred under a licensing arrangement may not be stated, the revenue earned by such arrangements is often substantial. This revenue is generally reported and finds its way on the balance of payments. Unfortunately, it is not always entered in the same account. If it is reported to the balance of payments authorities as resulting from investment, it is entered in the income account. Where it is reported as royalties, it is entered on the miscellaneous services-private account. Under present procedures, the earnings from licensing are partially reported as income from investment and partially as a miscellaneous service transaction. It is thus impossible to ascertain from either the balance of payments itself, or its supporting tables, the total revenues resulting from licensing.[23]

This situation could be remedied without serious change in either the form of, or the concepts underlying, the balance of payments. The total revenue from licensing could be carried as

---

[23] Under present IMF and Commerce practice, revenues from licensing arrangements, where they arise from royalties on the use of industrial property or technology, are considered as a part of the miscellaneous services, rather than the income, account. This practice is based on the theory that entries to the income account should be restricted to factor returns. Royalties, under this theory, are held to constitute remuneration for the services of industrial property. The distinction is a fine one and breaks down in practice, for the balance of payments statistician has no way of knowing if the entries to the income account are discrete and include factor returns exclusively. From a practical point of view, it would be better to include the revenues arising from licensing as a part of income. This is the practice recommended by the Review Committee for Balance of Payments Statistics, See: Report of the Review Committee for Balance of Payments Statistics to the Bureau of the Budget, *The Balance of Payments of the United States: A Review and Appraisal.* Washington: U. S. Government Printing Office, 1965, Chapter 10.

a separate part of either the miscellaneous services or the income accounts and be labeled as such. In this way, the revenue earned and paid out as a result of licensing arrangements could be ascertained.

If it is not feasible for the owners to assign values to the rights transferred, the capitalized value of these arrangements made during a given period could be estimated by applying a rate of return to the income earned. Thus, if the income earned on their account amounted to $100 million, the rate of return was estimated at eight per cent, the capitalized value would stand at $1.25 billion. Knowledge of the estimated capital value of these arrangements would facilitate comparisons with that of other investments and be useful in the formulation of foreign investment policies.

A count of the number of licensing arrangements in effect made by residents for the benefit of non-residents and vice versa, could be carried at the bottom of the tabulation as a *memorandum account* not constituting an integral part of the balance of payments itself. The estimated value of these arrangements could likewise be shown as a memorandum account.

The use of memorandum accounts would neither alter this statement importantly nor serve to increase the errors and omissions account. The additional information would be of substantial value to both statesmen and analysts.

9

The Measurement of
Surpluses and Deficits

The concept of a surplus or deficit on the balance of payments *as a whole* is a mathematical impossibility. Since this statement is composed of debits and credits, by definition of equal magnitude, unless errors are present, it can show neither a surplus nor a deficit. It must balance. However, it is possible for any one account, or any group of accounts except the total of all accounts, to show a surplus of debits over credits or vice versa; it is seldom that each account or group balances exactly.

The term *surplus and deficit* originated in the history of this tabulation when only the merchandise accounts were included in it. Since exports and imports were but infrequently of equal magnitudes, favorable or unfavorable, surplus or deficit balances appeared. Until all the services, unilateral transfers and capital movements were included, the tabulation continued to show a surplus or deficit because certain transactions were omitted. Although the accounts carried today embrace virtually all international transactions, the historical terminology continues, sanctioned by the years and by usage.[1]

Were it possible to break with this tradition and employ expressions which more accurately described what is included under surpluses and deficits, the term "funds available for the defense of the par or rate of exchange," "the movement of selected

---

[1] Similarly and for the same reasons, a balance of payments is never in disequilibrium; it is always in equilibrium by definition. It may be necessary to take measures to augment or reduce the gold and short-term capital accounts, and this is what is usually meant by restoring balance of payments equilibria. The concept of balance of payments equilibrium, like that of surplus and deficit, rests on traditional usage.

short-term capital" or "financing accounts" would perhaps prove more accurate. What is called surplus or deficit is a matter of definition. Certain accounts are selected by analysts or the monetary authorities which can readily and conveniently be used to maintain the par or rate of exchange, measure the movement of international monetary reserves, finance transactions when the exchange earnings are insufficient. The accounts selected for these purposes are usually held to measure the surplus or deficit.

Short-term Capital Measures of Surpluses and Deficits

The measurement of surpluses and deficits is based upon a division of the balance of payments accounts into two groups: substantive, or above the line, and balancing, or below the line transactions. The deficit or surplus is presumed to arise in the above the line accounts and to be financed by those below the line. The selection of items to be carried above the line is a matter of choice, rather than of the essence of the transactions, and the definitions employed are strongly colored by national institutions and policies.

The balance on the substantive accounts is exactly equal to that on the balancing, but carries the opposite sign. Thus, if the balance on the former accounts amounted to +$2,000 million, that on the balancing would total −$2,000 million. Either the algebraic total of the substantive or the balancing accounts thus could be used to measure the surplus or the deficit. Custom dictates, however, that the balancing accounts are generally used for this purpose.

Historically, the balance of payments was created largely to measure surpluses and deficits, to shed some light upon the manner in which these balances arose and to show their significance for both domestic and external economic policy. Before the balance of payments included all international transactions, the measurement of surpluses and deficits was an easy matter. It consisted simply in the debit or credit balance on those accounts which were carried on the tabulation. Later, after all transactions were included, items such as specie, long- and short-term capital, were held to constitute the measure of the surplus or deficits as the early chapters of this book indicate.

Surplus and deficit determination has been associated historically with policy considerations. Surpluses and deficits have been used both to support and disprove Bullionist and Mercantilist doctrines; to justify or discredit monetary and banking policies as during Britain's Bullion Controversy (1797-1821); to develop appropriate policies with reference to the international flow of specie; to debate the wisdom of international investment policies; to show the relationships between the international flow of short-term capital, and the other accounts.

Although some of these policy considerations still remain, changes became manifest late in the nineteenth century and were accelerated after World War I and II. Domestic was separated then from international policies and the responsibility for international financial policy was transferred from the commercial banks and the banking system to the government. In addition, many governments endeavored to maintain international policies independent of those of other nations, while at the same time, they attempted to establish and enforce fixed pars of exchange.[2]

These developments took place at a time when economic systems, based more or less heavily on laissez-faire, started to give ground and to be replaced by partially-directed economic orders. Managed monetary systems, an integral part of the partially-directed economy, must take the international movements of specie and short-term capital into account. The advent of Keynesian economics, with its emphasis upon money and income, likewise brought policy matters, involving the measurement of surpluses and deficits, to the foreground.

The short-term capital accounts. Any capital asset may be defined as a reserve asset and, when netted against the appropriate liabilities, may be used to measure the surplus or deficit provided the nature of the accounts, the circumstances as well

---

[2] Cf. Walther Lederer, "The Balance on Foreign Transactions: Problems of Definition and Measurement." *Special Papers in International Economics*, No. 5, September 1963. Princeton: International Finance Section, Department of Economics, Princeton University, 1963, pp. 8-12.

as policy considerations, warrant it. The usual or normal accounts employed for this purpose, however, consist of liquid items such as gold and short-term capital assets together with holdings of foreign currencies. To measure the surplus or deficit, these accounts are netted against short-term liabilities of a similar type including the liquid claims of non-residents. The use of long-term capital inflows and unilateral transfer receipts as *balancing accounts* in surplus and deficit determination is treated in a subsequent section.

Gold is historically the reserve asset par excellence. When some nations were on a silver standard in the past, silver was also used for this purpose. Given its ready convertibility into other suitable reserve assets, *at a price*, it is still possible to count silver among international reserves and to use it in the measurement of surpluses and deficits. The relative volatility of the price of silver, however, renders it one of the less stable assets.

The inclusion of gold among the world's reserve assets requires no explanation for it is universally demanded and usually exchangeable for anything that is for sale. As a measure of surpluses and deficits, however, it has one characteristic which should be taken into account.

If all nations used the same measure of surpluses and deficits, identical balances of payments concepts and definitions, and comparable methodologies, the deficits of some nations would exactly equal the surpluses of the others. Gold however, introduces one complication into this comparison. The net addition to the world's monetary gold assets have averaged about $550 million annually during the past decade, but has varied considerably from year to year. This fact introduces an element of asymmetry in the international comparisons of surpluses and deficits, for the accretions to the monetary gold stocks of some countries do not find their counterparts in the monetary gold outflows of any others.

The short-term reserve assets usually used as a part of the measure of the surpluses and deficits include: deposits in foreign banks; holdings of short-term bank and commercial paper; foreign currency accumulations; short-term notes and other claims; certain obligations of foreign governments, regardless of term, especially those of the United States; drawing rights on the IMF; bonds of the International Bank for Reconstruction and Development (IBRD) and other non-monetary international organizations; remaining balances with the now-extinct European Payments Union (EPU).

To complete the measure of the net surplus or deficit, a nation's short-term liabilities must be deducted from these assets. The more important short-term liabilities are bank deposits; bank and commercial paper; liabilities derived from foreign owner-ship of a nation's currency; the counterpart of foreign holdings of notes and other short-term claims; the obligations to the owners of government notes and securities; IMF holdings of a nation's currency; liabilities for the deposits of the IMF, IBRD, and other international institutions; remaining debts to the EPU.

In many cases, the balance of payments presents only the net figures for these short-term assets and liabilities. These ac-counts are usually grouped under a certain classification system. They may be classified by the type of owner of the assets, by type of party upon whom the liability rests or by the nature of the assets and liabilities themselves. Some form of classification is necessary to bring the number of balance of payments accounts to manageable proportions.

Divergent or asymmetrical measures of surpluses and def-icits. There is but little symmetry in the type of short-term assets and liabilities used to measure national balance of payments deficits and surpluses. Each nation employs that measure which best suits its institutions and the structure of its economy and which is in accord with the economic policies which it pursues. Table 9.1 presents the principal items used in the definitions employed by twelve major industrial countries.

All the countries represented include changes in the gold and foreign exchange assets of monetary institutions in their measures of surpluses and deficits. The movements of the foreign exchange assets of private commercial banks are carried below the line by all the countries shown on the tabulation except the United States, Germany, and Japan. Holdings of these assets by

TABLE 9.1

Industrial Countries: Treatment of Major Items in National Definitions of Balance of Payments Surplus or Deficit[1]

| | Gold and Foreign Exchange Assets | | | Transactions with IMF | | Other Liquid Liabilities of: | | |
| | Monetary institutions | | Non-monetary sector | Subscriptions | Drawings and repayments[2] | Central monetary institutions | Commercial banks | Non-monetary sector |
	Central institutions	Commercial banks						
United States	b	a	a	b	b	b	b	b[3]
United Kingdom	b	b	a[4]	a	b	b	b	b[3,4]
Belgium-Luxembourg	b	b	a	b	b	b	b	a
France	b	b	b[4]	b	b	b	b	b[4]
Germany	b	a	a	a	a	b	a	a
Italy	b	b	a	b	b	b	b	a
Netherlands	b	b	a	b	b	b	b	a
Austria	b	b	a	a	a	b	b	a
Denmark	b	b	a	a	a	b	b	a
Norway	b	b	b[4]	a	a	b	b	b[4]
Sweden	b	b	a	a	a	b	b	a
Japan	b	a	a	a	a	a	a	a

[1] A "b" indicates that the item is included below the line and an "a" that it is included above the line.
[2] Covers drawings and repayments both by the country concerned and in that country's currency by other countries.
[3] Includes government obligations, but only a few private liabilities.
[4] Includes incomplete information on private assets and liabilities.

the non-monetary or non-bank sectors are treated as substantive or above the line assets by all countries except France and Norway.

Japan is the only country which does not treat changes in the liquid liabilities of central monetary institutions as balancing transactions. With the exception of the United States, movement of the liquid liabilities of commercial banks is treated in the same manner as asset holdings by all countries. The changes in the liquid liabilities of institutions in the non-monetary sector are held to be balancing transactions by all nations other than the United States, the United Kingdom, France and Norway. Thus the liquid liabilities of United States commercial banks and private parties are regarded as below the line transactions, while the assets are not. Transactions with the IMF, drawings and repayments, show considerable diversity in treatment, and are handled as above the line by some and below by other countries.

Japan and Germany employ the most extreme definitions of surpluses and deficits. Japan includes changes in its gross reserves as balancing transactions but excludes changes in its position with the IMF and all other liabilities, as well as commercial bank and other privately held assets. Germany applies a similar concept except that its balancing items include changes in the foreign liabilities of the Bundesbank which carries out virtually all of this country's transactions with the IMF.[3]

Allocation of the errors and omissions account. The errors and ommissions accounts present a thorny and unresolved problem in surplus and deficit measurement. Errors and omissions appear in varying degrees in all of the balance of payments accounts.[4] Unless some means is found of allocating this account to the others in a rational manner, it must be included either as a substantive or balancing item. As yet, no satisfactory method

---

[3] Cf. Poul Høst-Madsen, "Asymmetries Between Balance of Payments Surpluses and Deficits." IMF *Staff Papers* July 1962, pp. 187-195.

[4] An account of the sources of errors and omissions is given in: Walther Lederer, "Measuring the Balance of Payments." American Statistical Association, *1961 Proceedings of the Business and Economic Statistics Section,* 1962, pp. 42-44.

of dividing this item among the several accounts has been discovered.[5]

The allocation of errors and omissions to the above or below the line groupings is not a matter of indifference. Assume that the above the line accounts showed a balance of +$3,000 million, errors and omissions, amounting to +$500 million excluded. The balancing items would then read: errors and omissions, +$500 million, other balancing accounts, −$3,500 million, total deficit −$3,000 million. Had the errors and omissions been included in the above the line accounts, the balance on this group would have stood at +$3,500 million and the deficit at −$3,500 million excluding errors and omissions.

If it were possible to distribute correctly the errors and omissions with the result that +$250 million of it were allocated to the above, and +$250 to the below, the line transactions, the statement would read: Substantive accounts +$3,250 million, balancing −$3,250 million, deficit $3,250 million.

Since the principal source of errors and omissions in some countries lies in the substantive accounts, these nations are likely —provided they are aware of this situation—to include it in the above the line transactions. Others, feeling that the principal source is found in the balancing accounts, would probably place it in the below the line items.[6] Uniformity in the treatment of

---

[5] An unsuccessful effort to allocate the errors and omissions among the other accounts on the balance of payments was made by the late Ray Ovid Hall, who, when Chief of Commerce's Balance of Payments Division, did much to improve these statements. Hall's method was based upon incorrect assumptions and is not used. See: Ray Ovid Hall, "Some Neglected Relationships in the Balance of Payments." *American Economic Review*, Vol. XXXI, No. 2 (March 1941), pp. 81-86, and Ray Ovid Hall, *International Payments: A Science*. Washington: Privately published by the author and out of print, 1946.

[6] Philip W. Bell leans to the conclusion that United States errors and omissions tend to vary with the movement of its private short-term capital, but his results, based on a correlation analysis, are admittedly inconclusive. See: Philip W. Bell, "Private Capital Movements and the U. S. Balance-of-Payments Position." *Factors Affecting the United States Balance of Payments*. Eighty-seventh Congress, second session, Joint Committee Print. Compliation of Studies Prepared for the Subcommittee on International Exchange and Payments of the Joint Economic Committee. Washington: U. S. Government Printing Office, 1962, pp. 395-481.

this item among the several nations, does not appear to be a likely prospect. Thus the errors and omissions account will doubtless continue to plague balance of payments analysts, distorting both the above and below the line balances. Balance of payments literature offers few guides concerning the proper placement of this account.

Policy considerations involved in surplus and deficit determination. The decision whether to include a given account as a part of a nation's surplus and deficit measurement is not necessarily an arbitrary one. The defense of the rate of exchange has passed from the hands of the commercial banks to the government and its financial institutions. Consequently, the government can only include among its net assets available for this purpose, those reserve items which it possesses, finds available, can borrow or which it can readily preempt.

Since a nation's surplus or deficit position is usually given some publicity, there are also public relations considerations involved in its measurement. Large deficits cast discredit upon a currency and lead to speculative pressures working to lower the rate of exchange. If these deficits persist, the government may feel constrained to devalue its par of exchange and find itself under pressure from both within and without to do so. Substantial surpluses can lead to speculation tending to increase the rate of exchange in terms of other currencies. They also invite the feeling on the part of its trading partners, that the par of exchange is undervalued and needs to be revalued upward.

Underdeveloped nations, desirous of attracting foreign aid grants, may find it desirable to show the largest deficits possible. Others in a highly competitive export position, showing a surplus and fearing the development of pressures to revise their pars of exchange upward, might find it convenient to use measures which minimize the size of their surpluses.

When a nation runs a persistent surplus or deficit, its statesmen may be led to take corrective measures. These measures may run from mild attempts to promote merchandise and services exports or imports, the inflow or outflow of investment capital, to more drastic schemes involving currency inflation or deflation or the installation of import and exchange controls. The means used to measure surpluses and deficits, therefore, are matters of high national policy.

Since gold and foreign exchange assets held by the government and its financial institutions are readily available for the defense of its currency, most nations are likely to include them as measures of its reserve holdings. Where a nation either has, or can readily obtain, control over the liquid foreign exchange assets of its commercial banks, it may feel justified in including these assets in computing its reserve position. In fact, many nations have banking legislation which permits such appropriation either directly or indirectly.

Among other devices, countries have used the facilities of the forward exchange market to shift the commercial banks' foreign exchange holdings to the central bank or vice versa. The German Bundesbank has utilized forward exchange transactions to sell dollars to the commercial banks, with a forward commitment to reacquire the dollars at the same rate, three months later. The Italian official exchange office, Uffici dei Cambi, has provided Italian commercial banks with large amounts of dollars through similar swap transactions.[7]

Private non-bank holdings of gold and foreign exchange are not as easily preempted by the government as are bank assets. Of the twelve industrial countries listed on Table 9.1, only two of them, France and Norway, feel that these assets are available to the government if required. Of course, in periods of great need, as was the case with the United Kingdom and the Netherlands at the outset of World War II, governments can obtain possession of these assets by vesting. Indeed, even long-term securities were vested in both governments by such legislation.

IMF drawings rights and repayments are regarded by six of the twelve countries listed on Table 9.1 as a part of their

---

[7] Cf. Oscar L. Altman, "Recent Developments in Foreign Markets for Dollars and Other Currencies." IMF *Staff Papers*, March 1963, pp. 55-58; Paul Einzig, *The Euro-Dollar System: Practice and Theory of International Interest Rates.* New York: St. Martin's Press, Inc., 1964, pp. 112-122.

reserve assets and since recourse to the IMF has often been used, this classification seems appropriate policy to these nations. However, it would be well for those countries which so classify them to distinguish the gold from the credit tranche drawings. Recourse to the use of the gold tranche is quasi-automatic; the use of the credit tranche must be negotiated with the Fund and is not automatic.

IMF subscriptions give rise to drawing rights on the Fund. The debits for subscription payments to the IMF are offset by credit entries for gold and national currency payments to this institution. Where both the subscription and the liabilities counterparts are thus placed below the line, surpluses and deficits are neither increased nor decreased by this practice.

It also suits the policies of some nations to regard the bonds of the IBRD as a reserve asset, although these bonds are long-term obligations. Where this practice is followed, these bonds are placed in the same category as the short- and medium-term obligations of the United States as to stability of price and security. Most nations, however, do not include these bonds as reserve assets.

When the EPU was in operation, members of that organization included changes in their debit and credit balances as below the line items. When the EPU was dissolved, the major debtor nations entered the repayments above the line, but the major creditor countries showed them as balancing transactions. The policy considerations which led to this asymmetric treatment are not clear.

The treatment of liquid liabilities generally is based on the same policies as their liquid asset counterparts are. There are, however, exceptions to this practice. Both the United States and the United Kingdom regard the liquid liabilities of commercial banks and the non-monetary sector as balancing items, but the former holds the assets of these institutions to be above the line items. It believes that commercial bank and non-bank *liabilities* affect its international liquidity. Since its government cannot easily preempt the *assets* of the commercial banks or non-monetary parties, it does not regard it as appropriate policy to include them among its reserve assets.[8]

Effect of divergent treatment of liquid assets and liabilities. If all nations used the same accounts, identically defined and constructed, to measure their surpluses and deficits, and if all transactions were equally timed, total deficits would exactly equal total surpluses of all nations for any given period. Since differences exist among them in the choice and nature of the balancing items, as well as in timing, asymmetries appear in world deficits and surpluses. Table 9.2 presents these asymmetries for the twelve industrial nations listed on Table 9.1 for 1959, 1960, and 1961.

TABLE 9.2

EFFECTS OF SOME MAJOR ASYMMETRIES IN THE CLASSIFICATION OF
VARIOUS BALANCE OF PAYMENTS ITEMS, 1959-61[1]
(In billions of U.S. dollars)

	1959	1960	1961
Transactions in monetary gold	700	335	570
Transactions with the IMF[2]	−248	−42	−409
Change in assets of commercial banks of Japan and Germany	−419	91	−351
U.S. liabilities to private non-bank and international non-monetary organizations	−320	−225	−630
Other items[3]	−514	−457	−215
Total effect[4]	−801	−328	−1,035

[1] No sign indicates that the item contributes to an excess of surpluses, and a minus sign that it contributes to an excess of deficits.

[2] The U.K. subscription in sterling, as well as in gold, to the International Monetary Fund (IMF) in 1959 has been omitted from this item, because it was specifically allowed for in the official evaluation of the balance of payments for that year as a special factor affecting surplus or deficit.

[3] Partial estimate covering only changes in post-EPU claims and government short-term assets not included in reserves.

[4] This calculation disregards all asymmetries between surpluses and deficits that result merely from defective statistics. In practice, the purely statistical asymmetries can be quite significant.

Source: Poul Høst-Madsen, "Asymmetries Between Balance of Payments Surpluses and Deficits." IMF *Staff Papers,* July 1962, p. 195.

[8] Cf. Poul Høst-Madsen, *op-cit.,* pp. 187-190.

The asymmetric measures used by these twelve countries tended to exaggerate the deficits, for each of the years examined. In 1961, total deficits amounted to over one billion dollars. Some of the balancing items listed are thought to have but a temporary or non-recurrent effect. These are transactions with the IMF which may be expected to balance out in the longer run, EPU debits and credits which will disappear over time and the temporary German repayments for armaments. The remaining items appear to be of a more permanent and recurring nature.[9]

The basic and over-all balance method. To avoid the problems of definition associated with the more conventional measures of surpluses and deficits and to attain uniformity, analysts have turned in increasing numbers to the basic and over-all balance as a substitute. According to this concept, balance of payments accounts are divided into two major groups: those which measure the basic balance and those which measure the over-all balance.

The accounts usually included in the basic balance are merchandise and services, unilateral transfers and long-term capital. Those classified in the over-all category include short-term capital, monetary gold, and errors and omissions. The basic balance includes the so-called fundamental transactions and the over-all, the means of financing them. Table 9.3 presents the basic and over-all balances of the United States for 1963.

A number of advantages are claimed for the basic balance measure:

1. It separates transactions which are subject to trends over time from those which are not.

2. It separates volatile and erratic transactions from those which are relatively stable.

3. It separates transactions which respond to broad economic forces from those which are sensitive to short-term changes in credit conditions and expectations or which respond more or less passively to the balance on other transactions.

In spite of these advantages and its growing popularity,

---

[9] Poul Høst Madsen, *op. cit.*, pp. 195-197.

it appears doubtful that this concept will be adopted by all nations. It does not suit the policy considerations of some countries, and these will probably continue to use either their present measures or modifications of them. Nevertheless, this concept serves a useful broad analytical purpose, especially where international comparisons are involved.[10]

The definitions of basic and over-all balances presented here are employed, sometimes with certain modifications, by many analysts. Some students include types of volatile long-term capital in their over-all, rather than basic balance. Other introduce categories called open market capital and official compensatory financing between the basic and over-all balances, while some provide differing breakdowns of government transactions.

Certain analysts employ the term basic balance to indicate above the line accounts as presented on the analytical tabulations of all countries. Under this usage, the basic balance ceases to have any definite meaning since it varies from nation to nation according to the items which it carries above and below the line. As used in this work, and as it is more generally employed, the basic balance is used to characterize a different concept of surplus and deficit measurement which aims at bringing uniformity to the measurement of these magnitudes.

In recent years, Commerce has introduced, on an experimental basis, balance of payments presentations embodying the basic balance concept. The Commerce tabulations do not correspond, however, to the generally accepted definition of basic balance. Its calculations include in the basic category, certain types of private short-term capital as well as errors and omissions. On Table 9.3, the Commerce presentation has been altered to conform to the standard definition of basic balance by including these two accounts in the over-all, rather than basic,

---

[10] For example, Walter Salant and his associates put the basic balances to good use in making balance of payments projections and international comparisons. See: Walter S. Salant, Emile Despres, Lawrence B. Krause, Alice M. Rivlin, William A. Salant and Lorie Tarshis, *The United States Balance of Payments in 1968*. Washington: The Brookings Institution, 1963.

TABLE 9.3

UNITED STATES: BASIC AND OVER-ALL BALANCES, 1963[1]

(In millions of dollars)[1]

Basic transactions

Balance on goods and services	5,485
Remittances and pensions	− 812
U.S. government grants and capital	−3,789
Private long-term capital	−3,053
Basic Balance	−2,169

Over-all items

Advance repayments on U.S. government loans	325
Advance payment on U.S. military exports	359
Sale of non-convertible, non-marketable securities	− 43
Sale of convertible, non-marketable securities	702
Changes in U.S. and foreign short-term capital	− 637
Changes in U.S. short-term liabilities and foreign holdings of U.S. government bonds and notes	1,580
Changes in U.S. monetary reserve assets	378
Errors and omissions	− 495
Over-all Balance	2,169

[1] In its basic and over-all balance of payments analysis, Commerce includes among the basic items, errors and omissions and certain forms of private short-term capital. These items have been eliminated from the basic balance on this table and included in the over-all. In addition, Commerce gives the reader a choice of including the following items in either the basic or over-all balance: advance repayments on U.S. government loans, advance payments on U. S. military exports, sale of convertible and non-convertible, non-marketable securities (Roosa bonds). These items have been placed definitely in the over-all category on this table.

Source: Computed from data presented in the *Federal Reserve Bulletin*, Vol. 50, No. 6, (June 1964), p. 799.

balance. In addition, this table places definitely in the below the line group the sale of both convertible and non-convertible United States Government bonds, advance repayments of loans and advance payments on military exports.

Table C.3, Appendix C, presents a comparison of the over-all balances for some twenty countries as well these balances for certain groups of countries, including the EEC. The footnotes to this table present several different definitions of the over-all balance.

Extraordinary Measures of Surpluses and Deficits

The short-term capital measures of surpluses and deficits described in the preceding section may be termed the standard or *ordinary* means of determining this balance. Some nations live beyond the means provided by their foreign exchange earnings derived from commercial transactions. Other countries may have over-valued rates of exchange or economic problems which hold back exports and encourage imports. They must, therefore, find ways of acquiring the funds, or the "income" to sustain their international standards of living.

Public finance uses the term ordinary budget to characterize those which include the usual, normal or ordinary receipts and expenditures. The term extraordinary budget is applied to those which include unusual receipts and payments which can be regarded as having an exceptional character. Thus France, shortly after the end of World War I, constructed an ordinary budget to receive the receipts and expenditures arising from the normal operations of the Republic. The heavy and exceptional expenses associated with the reconstruction of its war-damaged territory and some of the reparation payments receipts used to finance these operations, were carried in a separate, extraordinary budget.

Borrowing from public finance, the term *extraordinary* measures of surpluses and deficits can be applied to balance of payments analysis. These extraordinary measures include official unilateral transfers and special government borrowing to finance balance of payments deficits.

Official unilateral transfers as surplus and deficit measures.
The analytical balance of payments of Korea for 1962, presented
on Table 9.4, illustrates the use of official unilateral transfers
as a measure of surpluses and deficits. Section D of this table,
representing the algebraic sum of Korea's goods and services,
private transfer payments and errors and omissions, may be
regarded as its substantive or above the line transactions. Sections E and F, net central government aid received and monetary
movements, may be held to be the below the line or balancing
transactions. The net deficit is shown by Section D or the sum of
sections E and F.

A number of countries, principally underdeveloped and
recipients of aid from the industrial nations, employ this extraordinary measure of surpluses and deficits at the present time.
The highly industrialized Allies of the United States during
World War II and the Marshall Plan countries after this war,
ran balance of payments deficits which could well have been
measured by this technique.

Other extraordinary measures of surpluses and deficits. For
many years now, Brazil has lived beyond its commercial earnings
of foreign exchange. It has employed a number of devices to
meet its deficits. Its balance of payments for 1962 is presented
on Table 9.5. Although Brazil uses an extraordinary measure of
surpluses and deficits, it might well have included below the
line certain items shown above it. As indicated on its balance of
payments, line G and H, swaps and deferred payments together
with other official monetary movements, apparently constituted its
measure. Private short-term capital, section E, consisting of commercial and other private assets and liabilities is counted as an
above the line or substantive item and apparently does not form
a part of Brazil's surplus and deficit measurement.

Similarly, Export-Import Bank loans to the private sector,
local and central government loans, P.L. 480 cruzeiro liabilities
to the United States government (section B), are held to be
substantive rather than balancing although the central bank
loans (section H) are thought to be balancing. Under other

TABLE 9.4

KOREA: ANALYTIC BALANCE OF PAYMENTS, 1962[1]
(In millions of U.S. dollars)

A. Goods and Services	
Receipts	
Merchandise f.o.b.	54.8
Foreign military forces	84.7
Other government, n.i.e.	5.8
Other services	17.9
Total	163.2
Payments	
Merchandise f.o.b.	−388.5
Freight and insurance on imports	−36.9
Other aid services	−6.1
Other services	−21.9
Total	−453.4
Net Payments	−290.2
B. Private Transfer Payments and Miscellaneous Capital	
Relief goods from private institutions	12.3
Other transfer payments	24.2
U.S. loans to private sector	2.2
Other capital	−6.5
Total	32.2
C. Net Errors and Omissions	−3.6
D. Total (A through C)	−261.6
E. Net Central Government Aid Received	
U. S. surplus agricultural commodities	201.0
Other relief grants	0.2
Drawings on U. S. Government loans	1.7
Trade credits on U. S. surplus agricultural commodities	3.9
Hwan/won liabilities arising from purchases of U.S. surplus agricultural commodities	6.0
Counterpart funds used by U. S. Government and UNKRA	−1.2
Total	211.6
F. Monetary Movements	
IMF accounts	—
Payments agreement liabilities to Japan	5.2
Claims on UN forces in Korea (increase−)	—
Other short-term assets, net (increase−)	44.8
Monetary gold (increase−)	—
Total	50.0

[1] The annual data in this table are taken from the basic tables in this and previous *Yearbooks.* They are rearranged by the Fund staff to facilitate analysis. No sign indicates credit; minus sign indicates debit.
Source: IMF, *Balance of Payments Yearbook,* Vol. 15, Released November 1963, Korea.

TABLE 9.5[1]

BRAZIL: ANALYTIC BALANCE OF PAYMENTS, 1962
(In millions of U.S. dollars)

A. Goods, Services, and Transfer Payments	
Exports f.o.b.	
Coffee	643
Value at 1958 prices	872
Difference between value at current prices and value at 1958 prices	−229
Cotton	112
Cocoa	41
Other exports	418
Total exports	1,214
Imports f.o.b.	−1,304
Trade balance	90
Freight and merchandise insurance	−99
Investment income	−129
Other services	−91
Transfer payments (including U. S. Government grants	1
Total	−408
B. Long-Term Capital (including P.L. 480 cruzeiro liabilities)	
Direct investment in Brazil	69
Export-Import Bank loans to private sector (net)	
Other private	88
Local government loans received (net)	
Central government loans received (net)	
P.L. 480 cruzeiro liabilities to U. S. Government	−12
Other central government	
Total	145
C. Total (A plus B)	−263
D. Net Errors and Omissions	−137
E. Private Short-Term Capital	
Commercial bank liabilities	−2
Commercial bank assets	−9
Other private	23
Total	12
F. Total (C through E)	−388
G. Swaps and Deferred Import Payments	
Swap transactions	46
Deferred import payments	128
Total	174
H. Other Official Monetary Movements	
Central bank loans received (net)	119
IMF accounts	−18
Payments agreements	7
Other short-term liabilities	−36
Other short-term claims (increase−)	83
Monetary gold (increase−)	59
Total	214

[1] Data for 1962 were reported in this form by Brazil's Superintendency of Money and Credit. No sign indicates credit; minus sign indicates debit.
Source: IMF, *Balance of Payments Yearbook*, Vol. 15, July 1963, Brazil.

policy considerations, it would have been possible to hold these items as balancing rather than as substantive.[11]

Columbia has employed a somewhat similar method of surplus and deficit determination to that used by Brazil, as Table 9.6 shows. The deficit on its substantive accounts amounted to $94.7 million in 1961. The balancing accounts included import and other credits, $41.3 million; other monetary movements, $62.6 million; errors and omissions, —$9.2 million; total, $94.7 million.

The official compensatory financing and the special official financing concepts. The use of unilateral transfers and other extraordinary means of measuring surpluses and deficits illustrated by the cases of Korea, Brazil, and Columbia represents an application of the official compensatory and special official financing concepts. These concepts were developed by the IMF in the early days of its balance of payments work but were abandoned in 1954.

According to the concept of official compensatory financing certain other accounts, in addition to the conventional gold and foreign exchange movements, are used to measure the deficit or surplus. Under this measure, the balancing items include:

1. International reserves
   a. Monetary gold
   b. Short-term official assets abroad
   c. Long-term assets

---

[11] The classification of accounts shown on Table 9.5, an analytical presentation, was made by the IMF staff. See footnote 1 to Table 9.5. The handling of the valuation of Brazil's coffee exports constitutes another interesting feature of its balance of payments. The value of Brazil's coffee exports is shown both at current and 1958 prices, but the current prices are used in surplus and deficit determination. A similar practice is followed by the other Latin American coffee-producing countries. In this context, the balance of payments of Venezuela is of interest. The transactions of the oil companies in Venezuela constitute the larger part of this country's international transactions. On both the standard and analytic balance of payments of this country, the transactions of the oil companies are shown separately from those of the other sectors of the economy. See: IMF, *Balance of Payments Yearbook*, Vol. 15, February 1964, Venezuela.

    d. Liabilities to official and bank institutions other than the IMF and IBRD

2. Liabilities to the IMF and IBRD
3. Official transactions in outstanding long-term obligations of the reporting country
4. Long-term official loans for balancing transactions
5. Official grants.

The official compensatory financing concept is the broadest of the extraordinary measure of surpluses and deficits. In addition to unilateral transfers and special import credits, it includes long-term official loans contracted for balance of payments purposes. Table 9.7 section F, illustrates this concept as applied by the Latin American countries in 1947.

Special official financing is generally undertaken by governments, or at their instigation, for other than balance of payments purposes to meet certain international financing requirements

TABLE 9.6

COLUMBIA: SUMMARY ANALYTIC BALANCE OF PAYMENTS, 1961
(in millions of U.S. dollars)

Balance on goods and services, private and government capital	−94.7
Import and other credits	
Private import credits	−17.1
Commercial bank's short-term liabilities	2.6
Bank of the Republic loans (net)	55.8
Total	41.3
Other monetary movements	
Commercial banks' foreign assets	− 6.6
IMF accounts	65.0
Central institutions other net claims	14.4
Monetary gold increase	−10.2
Total	62.6
Errors and Omissions (net)	− 9.2

Source: Adapted from IMF, *Balance of Payments Yearbook*, Vol. 14, February 1963, Columbia.

TABLE 9.7

Financing of Transactions of Latin America with
Rest of World, 1947[1]
(In millions of dollars)

	Total
A. Goods and Services and Private Donations	
Trade balance (f.o.b.)	472
Nonmonetary gold, net	50
Investment income, net	−580
Transportation and insurance, net	−516
Foreign travel, net	27
Other services, net	−65
Private donations, net	−7
Total	−619
B. Private Capital, net	
Direct investment liabilities	280
Other long-term capital	−18
Short-term capital, net	174
Total	436
C. Special Official Financing, net	
Donations	24
Loans received	110
Amortization and other repayments	−93
IMF, IBRD gold and dollar subscriptions	−67
Total	−26
D. Surplus or Deficit (−) of Above Items	−209
E. Errors and Omissions, and Multilateral Settlements	−214
F. Compensatory Official Financing, net	
Repurchase of foreign debt and debt settlements	−177
Loans received or extended (−)	−199
IMF advances	31
U.S. Stabilization Fund loans	100
Other foreign exchange liabilities	69
Foreign exchange holdings	−279
Monetary gold holdings	878
Total	423

[1] No sign indicates credit; minus sign indicates debit.
Source: IMF, *Balance of Payments Yearbook;* 1938, 1946, 1947, p. 60.

as they arise. Forms of special official financing include the financing of the amortization of the foreign-owned segment of the public debt or its repayment at maturity; the payment of subscriptions to the IMF and IBRD; reparation payments; bank loans to finance international trade; contributions for relief; Export-Import Bank loans; IBRD loans. One use of this concept, that by the Latin American countries in 1947, is shown on line C. of Table 9.7.

Although the IMF abandoned its official compensatory financing measurement of surpluses and deficits, it is far from dead. This concept facilitates the international comparison of deficits and surpluses by the use of a uniform definition. Many nations continue to use these concepts which present interesting future possibilities.[12]

Measurement of United States Surpluses and Deficits

Ever since large deficits appeared on the United States balances of payments in 1958 and after, the nature of its current measure of surpluses and deficits has been debated by both analysts and statesmen alike.[13] The principal charge against the present method of determining these magnitudes has been that it is not realistic and that it exaggerates the size of the actual deficit.

This charge is a serious one. Leaving aside for the moment the all-pervasive question of applicability, an exaggerated measure of deficits could lead the United States government to adopt corrective measures which might not be necessary. Indeed, this government has already taken a variety of steps to restore its balance of payments equilibrium. None of them has restricted international commerce to any great extent, but if the *apparently* large deficits persist, some measures might be taken which could have serious repercussions.

In addition, large published United States balance of pay-

---

[12] For a critique of these concepts see: Fritz Machlup, "Three Concepts of the Balance of Payments and the So-Called Dollar Shortage." *Economic Journal* (March 1950), pp. 46-48.

[13] See Chapter 8, note 5.

ments deficits serve to cast discredit upon the stability and security of the dollar, to cause foreigners and their governments to lose confidence in it, to breed speculation against the dollar and lead to United States gold outflows. To a world where bits of information, news interpretations and rumors play such a large part, the foreign exchange markets are especially sensitive to small indications of a currency's strength or weakness. Speculation against the dollar, runs on the United States gold stock, heavy gold purchases on the free gold markets have already appeared. The dollar must, it is argued, like Caesar's wife, be above all suspicion.

The current United States measure. The current United States measure of surpluses and deficits is apparently based on the theory that these magnitudes differ for reserve and for non-reserve centers. As a reserve center, the United States is not likely to run out of dollars, because it is the source of this international reserve currency. A non-reserve center, on the other hand, runs this risk.

The principal dangers to the dollar arise from speculation against it which might work to reduce its exchange value and to bring other nations to demand gold for their official dollar holdings. The United States must, therefore, be in a position to defend the rate of exchange of the dollar and to maintain the international liquidity of its currency.[14]

Considerations such as these have doubtless prompted Commerce to adopt a form of liquidity measure of its balance of payments surpluses and deficits. The United States short-term liquidity position is the best measure, according to Commerce, of its ability to defend the dollar. A non-reserve center might adopt some type of quantitative measures of its surpluses and deficits such as those based on the volume of gross or net for-

---

[14] Oscar L. Altman, in a study of the size of United States deficits and gold losses, found a relationship between the size of the deficits and the gold outflows. This finding tends to refute the notion that foreign monetary authorities have preferred gold to dollars as a reserve asset in recent years. See: Oscar L. Altman, "Quelques Aspects du Problème de l'Or." *Cahiers de l'Institut de Science Economique Appliquée,* Series R, No. 7 (October 1962), Paris.

eign exchange holdings. Such measures would be in order for these countries because they depend upon the amount of foreign exchange which they hold or can command to continue to trade in periods of deficits.

The measure in current use by Commerce is composed of two groups of assets and liabilities:

1. Short-term official and banking liabilities and foreign holdings of marketable United States government bonds and notes

    a. Foreign private holders including banks, international and regional organizations, but excluding the IMF

    b. Foreign official holders

2. United States monetary reserve assets

    a. IMF position

    b. Convertible currencies

    c. Gold

TABLE 9.8

UNITED STATES: ANALYSIS OF BALANCE OF PAYMENTS
EXCLUDING MILITARY AID, 1963
(millions of dollars)

A. Balance on regular types of transactions	−3,301
B. Balance on special government transactions	1,343
C. Balance on regular and special government transactions	−1,958
D. Balance C excluding sale of non-marketable medium-term convertible government securities	−2,660
E. Balance C including sale of non-marketable medium-term convertible government securities	−1,958
F. Increase in short-term official and banking liabilities and in foreign holdings of U.S. government bonds and notes.	1,580
G. Decrease in U.S. monetary reserve assets	378
H. Sale of non-marketable medium-term convertible government securities (including in lines B and C)	702

Source: Adapted from data presented in: Walther Lederer, "The Balance of Payments in 1963." *Survey of Current Business*, Vol. 44, No. 3 (March 1964), pp. 16-17.

The deficit on the United States balance of payments for 1963 as measured by these items is presented on Table 9.8. The above the line items are shown in three groups: the balance on the regular transactions (line A), that on the special government transactions (line B) and the balance on both the regular and special transactions (line C). The below the line accounts, however, are computed on this table for only one of these groups, the balance on the combined regular and special transactions (line E). The deficit for 1963 thus computed stood at $1,958 million. Had it been calculated for the regular transactions alone, it would have stood at $3,301 million, and the items carried in the special transactions group would then be considered as balancing accounts.

The regular transactions include the normal, recurrent operations of the United States and exclude special government transactions. These latter transactions comprise unusual and non-recurrent items such as the repayment of loans made by the United States to foreign governments; advance payments made by foreign governments to the United States for military exports; sales of non-marketable, medium-term, convertible and non-convertible securities denominated in dollars and foreign currencies. Under Commerce practice, errors and omissions are included in the regular transactions and are regarded as a substantive rather than a balancing account.

The deficit for 1963 was computed under two concepts: one excluding the sale of non-marketable, medium-term, convertible United States government securities (the so-called "Roosa bonds") and the other including these securities. This dual measure of the deficit was adopted by Commerce to satisfy: (a) those government officials and analysts who felt that the Roosa bonds were long-term securities and did not belong in the computation of the deficit; and (b) those who felt that, since these bonds were convertible into dollars on four days notice, they were in effect, short-term securities and belonged in the calculation of the deficit.

Critique of the allocation of individual accounts. The critique of the Commerce measurement of surpluses and deficits takes two forms: the allocation of the individual accounts between the above and below the line categories and criticism of the concept as a whole.[15]

Some analysts believe that the errors and omissions account, because it finds its principal source in the short-term capital accounts, should be placed below the line as a part of the measure of surpluses and deficits.[16] In 1963, this account amounted to −$495 million. Had it been included as a balancing instead of substantive item, the deficit on the combined regular and special transactions would have amounted to −$1,463 million instead of −$1,958 million including the Roosa bonds.

Commerce includes the deposits of international and regional institutions, except the IMF, among the balancing items. Critics of this practice point out that international institutions such as the IBRD, for example, are not likely to withdraw completely these deposits on short notice. It is, therefore, incorrect to include them among the liquid liabilities. In 1963, these deposits decreased by $225 million. If these withdrawals were included in the above the line transactions, instead of below, as these critics recommend, the deficit would have stood, in 1963, at −$2,183 million instead of −$1,958 million with the Roosa bonds included.[17]

Commerce includes as a balancing item, the change in United States liquid liabilities to foreign *private* banks and other holders, but excludes their counterpart, United States private liquid asset claims on foreigners. On the other hand, Commerce nets its *official* short-term assets against its official short-term liabilities. This results in an asymmetric treatment of official and private short-term assets and liabilities. If private short-term liabilities are regarded as balancing items, the critics argue, the

---

[15] All of the figures employed in this section have as their source: Walther Lederer, "The Balance of Payments in 1963." *Survey of Current Business*, Vol. 44, No. 3 (March 1964), pp. 14-23.

[16] Cf. Hal B. Lary, *Problems of the United States as World Trader and Banker*. New York: National Bureau of Economic Research, 1963, pp. 137-146.

[17] Cf. Poul Høst-Madsen, *op. cit.*, pp. 189-190.

corresponding assets should also be placed in this category.[18]

Apparently Commerce takes this position because United States liquid liabilities to foreign commercial banks can be relatively easily preempted by the central banks and thus turned into demand claims against the United States gold supply. In fact, some of the foreign central banks keep some of their official dollar holdings in the form of foreign dollar deposits of their commercial banks. The assets of United States commercial banks and other private holders cannot easily be preempted by American authorities and are thus not readily available for the defense of the dollar.

This explanation appears plausible. However, upon close examination, it loses some of its validity. Some of the deposits of foreign commercial banks and other holders in the United States are time deposits and are not subject to demand withdrawal. The foreign banks also keep a substantial fraction of the counterpart to their own domestic dollar deposits in the form of deposits in the United States banks, especially their Euro-Dollar deposits. These deposits in the United States are the cover against their domestic dollar liabilities on the Euro-Dollar Market and are not usually subject to immediate withdrawal.

Other private short-term assets include credits extended by American banks to their foreign customers. American banks expect their depositors, especially those to whom they have extended credit, to maintain a certain fraction of their deposits intact which is not customarily subject to withdrawal. On the other hand, the foreign deposits of American banks and others are not liquid in their totality. Some of them represent advance

---

[18] This is essentially the position taken by Wendell Gordon. See: Wendell Gordon, "The Criterion for an Adverse Balance of Payments." *American Economic Review*, Vol. LIII, No. 1, Part 1 (March 1963), pp. 139-141. A reply to Wendell Gordon was made by: H. N. Goldstein, "The Criterion for an Adverse Balance of Payments: Reply." *American Economic Review*, Vol. LIII, No. 5, pp. 1094-1101. See also Wendell Gordon's reply to H. N. Goldstein: Wendell Gordon, "The Criterion for an Adverse Balance of Payments: Reply." *American Economic Review*, Vol. LIII, No. 5, pp. 1101-1103.

payments on United States exports and capital outflows.[19]

In addition to the critique of Commerce's allocation of specific items to either the substantive or balancing category, a number of analysts have taken the entire Commerce concept of surplus and deficit to task. The liquidity concept used by Commerce is held by these analysts to be inappropriate for the world's most important reserve center. It does not represent adequately the balance of payments position of such an institution.[20]

Three alternative concepts to that employed by Commerce have already been proposed: the sensitivity to monetary policy, the exchange or open market and the official settlement concepts of surpluses and deficits. To complete this discussion, a fourth concept, the basic and over-all balance is proposed here.

Alternative measures: the sensitivity to monetary policy concept. In espousing such a liquidity definition, Commerce is apparently of the opinion that the speed with which internationally invested funds can be used to defend the dollar is an essential feature of any calculation of the surplus and deficit. If all liquid claims against the dollar were to be exercised at once, or in a short period of time, then the speed with which the United States can mobilize its resources is of paramount importance. If such an eventuality does not appear probable, the basic logic of Commerce's position is subject to question.[21]

As an alternative to the Commerce measure, Hal B. Lary (formerly chief of the Balance of Payments Division of that agency and now Associate Director of Research of the National Bureau of Economic Research) has proposed the use of the "sen-

---

[19] For a defense in depth of Commerce's allocation of accounts as balancing items see: Walther Lederer, "The Balance on Foreign Transactions: Problems of Definition and Measurement." *Special Papers in International Economics,* No. 5 (September 1963). Princeton: International Finance Section, Department of Economics, Princeton University.

[20] Cf. Hal B. Lary, *op. cit.,* pp. 137-148. In the materials prepared by the IMF staff (unofficial) for use in conjunction with its balance of payments training program, attention is drawn to the fact that the difficulties of expressing the surplus or deficit of the reserve centers by means of a single figure, which can be used as a guide for policy, are almost insuperable.

[21] Cf. Hal B. Lary, *op. cit.,* pp. 146-148.

TABLE 9.9

UNITED STATES: BALANCE OF PAYMENTS SURPLUSES AND DEFICITS, 1960-1961
BASED ON SENSITIVITY TO MONETARY POLICY CONCEPT (LARY)
(In billions of dollars)

ITEMS TREATED AS MAKING UP THE
"BALANCE ON BASIC TRANSACTIONS"

		1958-1959 (average)	1960-1961 (average)
1.	U.S. *payments, recorded*	28.4	30.2
2.	Imports of goods and services	22.1	23.1
3.	Remittances and pensions	.8	.9
4.	U.S. government grants and credits	3.1	3.7
5.	U.S. private long-term capital	2.5	2.5
6.	U.S. *receipts, recorded*	24.5	28.9
7.	Exports of goods and services	23.3	27.6
8.	Repayments on U.S. government loans	.8	1.0
9.	Foreign long-term investment in U.S.	.4	.4
10.	*Balance on items listed above*	−3.9	−1.2

ITEMS TREATED AS "SENSITIVE
TO MONETARY POLICY"

11.	Gold and convertible currency holdings of U.S. monetary authorities	1.5	1.2
12.	Liquid liabilities to foreign and international monetary authorities	1.2	1.2
13.	Liquid liabilities to foreign and commercial banks and other private or international holders	1.0	.8
14.	U.S. private short-term capital[a]	−.1	−1.4
15.	Unrecorded transactions, net	.4	− .6

[a] Less changes in foreign commercial credits to the United States.

NOTE: Detail may not add to totals shown because of rounding.

Source: Hal B. Lary, *Problems of the United States as World Trader and Banker*. New York: National Bureau of Economic Research, 1963, p. 141. Reproduced by permission of the National Bureau of Economic Research.

sitivity to monetary policy" concept. According to this basis, international transactions are divided between those which are relatively sensitive to monetary policy actions and those which are not.[22] Table 9.9 shows the United States balance of payments as presented under this concept.

Lary conceives of monetary policy as that which affects the conditions under which capital can be borrowed or loaned; differential taxes or other terms established on the market between domestic and foreign borrowers and lenders; any intervention by the authorities in the foreign exchange market.

The items placed below the line are those which are held to be sensitive to monetary policy and which are the responsibility of the authorities. They include: gold and the convertible currency holdings of the authorities; liquid liabilities; the movement of private United States short-term capital and errors and omissions or unrecorded transactions.

The items placed above the line and less directly subject to monetary policy include those which respond to the general influence of basic economic forces, military and political policies. They include, as Table 9.9 shows, the movement of goods and services, unilateral transfers, United States private and government long-term capital. This presentation is a form of the basic balance.

According to Lary, the items sensitive to monetary policy reflect the ability of the monetary authorities to induce either an inflow of funds or to curtail an outflow. Under this concept, private United States short-term assets are included as balancing instead of substantive transactions as under the Commerce concept. The sensitivity to monetary policy basis shows different magnitudes for surpluses and deficits than those used under Commerce's liquidity measure. During the period 1958-1959, the Lary concept showed an average deficit of $3.9 billion and Commerce $3.6 billion; during 1960-1961, Lary's method showed a deficit of $1.2 and Commerce's, $3.2 billion.

Alternative measures: the exchange or open market balance

---

[22] See: Hal B. Lary, *op. cit.*, especially pp. 148-160.

concept. Walter R. Gardner, formerly chief of the IMF's Balance of Payments Division and later Deputy-Director of its Research and Statistics Department, has proposed an "exchange-market analysis of the United States balance of payments." Gardner suggests the use of this concept as a measure of the balance of payments surpluses and deficits of the United States. The analytical balance of payments prepared under the exchange or open market balance concept is presented on Table 9.10.[23]

Gardner defines the basic balance as consisting of market goods and services together with direct investments and non-commercial transactions (unilateral transactions, military expenditures and government interest receipts). Another category, open market transactions, is introduced as a substantive account consisting of portfolio securities, short-term capital and errors and omissions.

The exchange market balance, comprising the basic balance and open market capital, may be regarded as the measure of the United States surplus or deficit. The final category, compensatory financing, which is equal to the exchange market balance, shows how the surplus or deficit was financed. This category includes: United States loans, IMF dollar assets, other official dollar assets and gold.

Gardner is apparently of the opinion that it is wise to divide the basic balance into two parts, the one dealing with less volatile transactions such as merchandise, services, unilateral transfers, and the other dealing with more volatile long- and short-term capital movements excepting direct investment. In 1958-1959 the Gardner method showed a larger deficit than the Commerce calculations; in 1957 and 1960, smaller ones.

A similar proposal has been advanced by Professor Robert Triffin of Yale University and is presented on Table 9.11.[24]

---

[23] Walter R. Gardner, "An Exchange-Market Analysis of the U. S. Balance of Payments." IMF *Staff Papers*, Vol. VIII, No. 2 (May 1961), pp. 195-211.

[24] Robert Triffin, "The Presentation of the U.S. Balance of Payments Statistics, General Comments." American Statistical Association, *1961 Proceedings of the Business and Economic Statistics Section*, Washington, 1962, pp. 51-57.

TABLE 9.10

UNITED STATES: BALANCE OF PAYMENTS SURPLUS AND DEFICIT, 1960
BASED ON EXCHANGE MARKET BALANCE CONCEPT (GARDNER)
(In billions of dollars)

A. Market Goods and Services	
1. Exports	19.4
2. Imports	−14.7
3. Trade Surplus	4.7
4. Net Services (excl. item C)	1.7
Total item A	6.4
B. Direct Investment	−1.6
C. Noncommercial Transactions (excl. item G)	
1. Military expenditures	−3.0
2. Government aid abroad	−2.8
3. Government interest receipts, etc.	0.3
4. Private transfers	−0.6
Total item C	−6.1
D. Basic Balance (A through C)	−1.3
E. Open-Market Capital (excl. item G)	
1. Portfolio securities, etc.	−0.4
2. Short-term	
(a) Assets	−1.2
(b) Liabilities to	
(i) Commercial bank	0.1
(ii) Other	
3. Net errors	−0.9
Total item E	−2.4
F. Exchange-Market Balance (D + E)	−3.7
G. Compensatory Financing	
1. U.S. loans	0
2. IMF dollar assets	0.7
3. Other official dollar assets	1.3
4. Gold	1.7
Total item G	3.7
For comparison with Item G above	
Department of Commerce balancing item	3.8

Source: Walter R. Gardner, "An Exchange-Market Analysis of the U. S. Balance of Payments." IMF *Staff Papers*, Vol. VIII, No. 2, (May 1961), p. 206.

TABLE 9.11

UNITED STATES: BALANCE OF PAYMENTS SURPLUS AND DEFICIT, 1960
BASED ON BASIC BALANCE AND OPEN MARKET CAPITAL (TRIFFIN)

(In billions of dollars)

			1960
1.	I.	*Gross Current Account Surplus*	7.9
2.		A. Conventional current account	3.1
3.		B. Military exports under grants	3.0
4.		C. *Plus* military expenditures	1.8
5.	II.	*U.S. Military Programs and Basic Capital Exports*	9.2
6.		A. U.S. Government	7.6
7.		1. Military programs	4.8
8.		a. Export financing	1.8
9.		b. Dollar settlements	3.0
10.		2. Economic programs:	2.8
11.		a. Export financing	2.2
12.		b. Dollar settlements	0.6
13.		B. Direct investment (net)	1.7
14.		1. U.S. capital	1.7
15.		2. Foreign capital (−)	——
16.	III.	*Basic Balance:* I-II	−1.3
17.	IV.	*Open Market Capital*	2.7
18.		A. U.S. capital	2.2
19.		B. Foreign capital	−0.2
20.		1. Dollar holdings	——
21.		2. Other	−0.2
22.		C. Errors and omissions	0.6
23.	V.	*Official Settlements:* III-IV	−4.0
24.		A. U.S. gold and convertible currency holdings	−1.7
25.		B. International institutions:	−1.0
26.		1. IMF capital subscription	——
27.		2. Dollar holdings (−)	−1.0
28.		C. Foreign monetary authorities' dollar holdings (−)	−1.2

Source: Robert Triffin, "The Presentation of U.S. Balance of Payments Statistics, General Comments," in American Statistical Association, *1961 Proceedings of the Business and Economic Statistics Section,* Washington, 1962, Table I, p. 56. Reproduced by permission of the American Statistical Association.

Triffin's basic balance includes goods and services, unilateral transfers and direct investment in a manner somewhat similar to Gardner. His category, open market capital, however, differs from that employed by Gardner (see Tables 9.10 and 9.11). He does not include Gardner's group, exchange market balance. Instead of using the compensatory financing concept of showing how the deficit was financed, he utilizes official settlements for that purpose. The official settlements indicate the steps taken by the authorities to close the balance. In 1960 the Triffin measure indicated a larger deficit than that of Commerce; in 1958 and 1959, smaller ones.

Alternative measures: the official settlements concept. The Review Committee for Balance of Payments Statistics (discussed in Chapter 8) recommended a change from the present liquidity measure of surpluses and deficits to that of "balance settled by official transactions." This official settlements measure would include, below the line, the following items regarded as financing the transactions carried above the line:

A. Reserve transactions
    a. Changes in the United States monetary authorities' holdings of gold and convertible foreign currencies
    b. Changes in the net United States creditor or debtor position in the IMF
    c. Changes in total United States liabilities to foreign official monetary institutions
B. Special intergovernment transactions.

Table 8.1, line H, and Appendix B, Table B.10, present the United States balance of payments utilizing the official settlements method of surplus and deficit determination. Table 9.12 indicates the difference in the magnitudes of the surplus and deficit, 1954-1963, as measured under this and the Commerce concept. The official settlements method tends to minimize the deficits and to exaggerate the surpluses when compared with the current Commerce method.

The official settlements concept differs principally from that employed by Commerce in its treatment of the short-term capital movements. Commerce places the *private* short-term assets of American residents above and the *private* short-term liabilities of American banks and other residents below the line. The official settlements basis carries *all* private short-term capital transactions above the line. Its treatment of private short-term capital is thus symmetrical. Under both concepts, the *official* short-term capital movements are included as balancing transactions. In addition, as Appendix B, Table B.10 shows, the official settlements method uses a different classification, detail and organization of the accounts from those employed by Commerce.

A number of considerations led the Review Committee to adopt its concept. The monetary authorities of each country have the responsibility of maintaining stable exchange rates and private individuals and firms are not in this business. The official settlements concept gives recognition to this fact.

TABLE 9.12

UNITED STATES: COMPARISON OF BALANCE OF PAYMENTS SURPLUSES AND DEFICITS, BASED ON OFFICIAL SETTLEMENTS AND LIQUIDITY CONCEPTS
(In billions of dollars)

	Official Settlements Basis (1)	Commerce Liquidity Basis (2)	Difference (Col. 1 minus Col. 2) (3)
1954	—1.5	—1.5	0
1957	+1.1	+0.5	0.6
1959	—2.5	—4.2	1.7
1963	—2.3	—3.3	1.0

Source: *Report of the Review Committee for Balance of Payments Statistics.* Washington: U. S. Government Printing Office, 1964, Chapter I.

The proposed new classification of accounts is based upon the nature of the foreign holder, rather than on the nature of the assets which he holds. This avoids making the difficult distinction between liquid and non-liquid assets and liabilities which has led to many intergovernmental agency disputes in recent years.

Under both the official settlements and the Commerce methods, errors and omissions are placed above the line. Since this statistical discrepancy is thought to originate principally in the private short-term capital accounts, this grouping is more logical under the official settlements concept, where both of these accounts are considered as substantive. With the Commerce classification, some short-term capital movements are placed above and others below the line and the errors and omissions account could not logically be placed in either group alone.[25]

Alternative measures: the basic and over-all balance concept. The measurement of surpluses and deficits for a reserve country such as the United States offers almost insuperable difficulties. It is doubtful whether any *single* measure of these magnitudes could meet all of the requirements of policy makers and analysts. In this dilemma, analysts are turning more and more to the concept of the basic and over-all balance which was described in an earlier section of this chapter. In some respects, this concept offers the best, or perhaps the least objectionable, measure which international economists have thus far devised.

Of all the measures, the basic balance embodies the smallest element of judgment. Less a criterion of international liquidity than some others, it is better suited to a reserve center where liquidity is less a matter of concern than is the defense of the rate of exchange. Separating transactions subject to trends and broad economic changes from those which are erratic and subject to short-run movements, it makes a logical grouping for the several balance of payments accounts.

The comparison of surpluses and deficits of the several nations forms a part of the basis of one of the policy-making and analytical purposes served by the balance of payments. The basic balance is better suited to this goal than any other for, if universally used, it would facilitate international comparisons. Since the defense of the exchange value of the dollar is the problem of American policy-making officials, it would be useful in this connection, if the United States international

---

[25] Cf. *Report of the Review Committee for Balance of Payments Statistics*, Washington: U. S. Government Printing Office, 1964, Chapter 9.

economic performance could be gauged against that of the other nations. This observation also applies to the international reputation or the standing of the dollar which can then be judged in comparison with that of other leading currencies.

These advantages, coupled with the growing popularity of this measure, commend it to the serious consideration of balance of payments statisticians responsible for the preparation of the United States compilations. Regardless of what measure is ultimately adopted, more and more attention is likely to be paid to the basic and over-all concept by analysts and policy-makers both at home and abroad.

10

Balance of Payments Disequilibria: Reserves and Exchange Market Policies

Ordinarily, the balance of payments of any nation, for any period of time, is not in equilibrium with the debits and credits on the *above the line transactions* of approximately equal amount. *Disequilibrium*, temporary or persistent, is the rule. The imbalance on the substantive accounts is settled in the short-run by drawings on, or additions to, the balancing accounts. Even in the long-run, where equilibrium is attained by the play of economic forces, official intervention or both, the funds which restore the balance are channeled through these accounts.

The international reserves, which form the balancing accounts, afford the necessary cushion or time to permit a nation to attain equilibrium. The longer the period required to restore balance, the larger reserve holdings should be.

International reserves are accumulated during periods of balance of payments surpluses and drawn down when deficits occur. It is, therefore, elementary good policy to accumulate sufficient reserves in times of surpluses to tide over the lean years of deficits. As will be noted later, the actual reserves on hand are not the only criterion of a nation's capacity to meet deficits. Other means are available for this purpose. They are provided by the exchange and capital markets of the world.

A distinction is sometimes drawn between reserves and working balances. Such a distinction is generally made on the basis of time. Working balances are created to handle the day-to-day excesses of payments over receipts. Reserves are established to cope with situations where payments exceed receipts over longer periods. The reserve concept is broader and includes working balances within its category.

The Concept of Liquidity

Reserves must be liquid, that is, readily exchangeable into either gold or some other currency acceptable to a nation's trading partners or to its sources of financing. The term liquidity is rather loosely used in international economics and its precise meaning must often be inferred from the context in which it is used. It generally has one of two broad meanings. It may refer to the ability of a nation to defend its rate of exchange or to continue temporarily to trade during a period of balance of payments deficit. The term is also employed to indicate the adequacy of the total amount of reserves available to sustain growth in international trade. This chapter treats the former use of the term; the latter usage is discussed in Chapter 12.

International liquidity is only needed by those nations which have fixed rates of exchange. Where freely floating or flexible rates are used, balance of payments equilibrium is attained by means of fluctuations in the rate and, except in cases of dire emergency, no reserves are needed. In addition, where the fixed rates are frequently changed—as was the case with many countries during the thirties—but relatively small reserves are required.

Where deficits occur under flexible rates of exchange, the rate falls in terms of those of other countries; prices of exported goods decrease; those of imported goods rise; the cost of investment overseas rises and that of capital inflows drops. Equilibrium in the balance of payments is restored by the play of these forces. Balance of payments surpluses are reduced by an increase in the rate of exchange in terms of other currencies, which produces the opposite price and cost effects. Where fixed rates of exchange are changed frequently, similar effects are produced but may be slower to appear.

Definition of liquidity. According to Thomson's *Dictionary of Banking,* liquid assets, sometimes called floating assets, comprise cash and other property which "undergo conversion into cash viz., stock, sundry debtors and bills receivable." They are distinguished from fixed assets acquired for use in business such as plant and equipment. Liquid assets are distinguished from fixed on the basis of the *function* to which they are put rather than their *nature.* Thus machinery is a fixed asset in a factory, but it is a liquid asset to the firm which manufactures machinery for sale. In the first case, it is the asset the firm employs to set up or engage in business. In the second, it is the asset which the firm uses in its trading operations.[1]

Thomson's definition referred to a domestic situation where but one currency is used. In the case of his definition, liquid assets consist of currency or other assets which may be readily converted into currency. The claims on these assets are also stated and satisfied in the same currency. In international economic relation assets may be held in the currencies of several nations, and the claims must be liquidated in currencies satisfactory to the claimant. The United Kingdom, for example, as the metropolis (reserve center) of the Sterling Area can hold some of its reserves in sterling and satisfy some claims of other members of the Area in this currency. Where the claimants must pay non-members in currencies other than sterling, other currencies must be provided.

Thus the definition of liquid asset employed in international economics is based on the acceptability of this asset as a means of settling international debts. Before government central banks started to play their present role in international payments, and

---

[1] R. W. Jones, *Thomson's Dictionary of Banking: A Concise Encyclopaedia of Banking Law and Practice.* New York: Philosophical Library, Tenth Edition, 1952, p. 384. Liquidity must be distinguished from solvency. *Financial solvency* refers to the ability of a debtor to satisfy claims against him when they fall due. *Total solvency* refers to a situation where a debtor has enough assets, valued at their current market price, to meet all of his obligations. See: Walther Lederer, "The Balance on Foreign Transactions: Problems of Definition and Measurement." *Special Papers in International Economics,* No. 5, (September 1963), Princeton: International Finance Section, Department of Economics, Princeton University, 1963, p. 9, n. 2.

where international transactions were handled through the medium of the commercial banks, gold (and to a much less extent silver) constituted the principal liquid asset. After the central banks took over the responsibility for international settlements, deposits in these banks or their notes, were used as liquid reserves by other banks, both domestic and foreign. The international acceptance of central bank deposits and notes depended upon their ability to convert demand obligations into gold. Through the use of deposits in these central banks, national currencies were convertible into international media of exchange.[2]

This system, sometimes held to constitute a form of the gold exchange standard, employed central bank credit as a supplement to, or a substitute for, gold as the international currency. The central banks of the large financial centers thus became international bankers' banks. In addition, the international assets held by some central banks frequently served as reserves against their own *domestic* demand liabilities. In this way, international and domestic reserves commingled.[3]

The terms liquidity and reserves are often used interchangeably and are sometimes held to be but two aspects of the same thing. Technically, however, *liquidity*, in the international sense, refers to the characteristics or qualities of an asset which enable it to be instantly transferred into a generally accepted currency used in international transactions. *Reserves*, on the other hand, are those assets which possess these characteristics or qualities. The distinction is a fine one and is, of course, a matter of definition. As used here, the terms liquidity and reserves are used interchangeably.

Liquidity and equilibrium. Equilibrium on the exchange market differs from economic equilibrium in the international economic relations of a country. Equilibrium in the one does not imply that a similar situation exists in the other. The mere fact

---

[2] Cf. Robert Triffin, "The Return to Convertibility: 1926-1931 and 1958- ? or Convertibility and the Morning After." Banca Nationale del Lavoro, *Quarterly Review*. Rome: March 1959, pp. 6 ff.

[3] Walther Lederer, *op. cit.*, pp. 7-12.

that the supply and demand relationships of the exchange market are in balance does not necessarily mean that the economies of the trading partners are likewise in balance. At a given price on the grain exchange, the demand and supply for wheat may be in equilibrium, but this does not necessarily mean that all the traders who bought and sold at that price are also in balance.

An equilibrium rate of exchange is, therefore, not necessarily one which will bring a nation's international position into balance. Ragnar Nurkse has pointed out that equilibrium can be obtained at varying levels of income and employment. He defines the *true* equilibrium rate of exchange as one which maintains the external accounts of a country in balance without large unemployment at home. It is only where an economy is operating at its maximum potential with full employment that exchange market equilibrium can be used to measure international equilibrium.[4]

International equilibrium cannot be sustained unless the exchange market is also in balance. Unless rigidly fixed at a given point, the rate of exchange is likely to move up or down in terms of other currencies. These movements affect the ability of an economy to export and import and have repercussions on resource utilization. If the reserves are inadequate and recourse must be had to international borrowing, these transactions will likewise have an impact on international equilibrium.[5]

When an economy is not in a state of international equilibrium, the amount of its reserve assets and the exchange market stability of its currency are bound to be affected. International disequilibria generally causes a shrinkage of reserves and downward pressure on the rate of exchange. Although international

[4] Ragner Nurkse, "Conditions of International Monetary Equilibrium." *Essays in International Finance,* No. 4 (Spring 1945), International Finance Section, Department of Economics, Princeton University. Reprinted in Howard S. Ellis and Lloyd A. Metzler, *Readings in the Theory of International Trade.* Philadelphia: The Blakiston Company 1950, pp. 3-34. See especially pp. 4-16.

[5] Walther Lederer, *op. cit.,* pp. 16-18.

and exchange market equilibria are different concepts, they are very closely related.

This relationship is strengthened when international reserves are combined with domestic reserves and used as backing for demand liabilities of the central banks. This situation prevails in many countries, and, where it is found, the volume of money and credit in circulation (unless countered by government action) depends to a greater or lesser extent upon the movements of a nation's balance of payments. The volume of money tends to increase in periods of balance of payments surplus and to decline when deficits prevail.[6] Where foreign trade constitutes a large percentage of the gross national product, the dependence of money supply on foreign trade is especially marked. Of course, this tendency can be countered by appropriate money management.

Unless offsetting policies are pursued, an increase in international liquidity may be expected to exert upward pressures on demand, employment and (sometimes) prices. Such increases, on the other hand, may also create greater temporary maneuverability to chronically deficit countries and thus tend to prolong their balance of payments disequilibria. A reduction in international liquidity is likely to have the opposite effect and intensify pressure on deficit countries.[7]

A balance of payments basic disequilibrium (see Chapter 9) is not the only force operating to increase or decrease the total volume of reserves and liquidity. Speculation, either working against or favoring a national currency, can serve to alter these amounts. Should speculation develop either for or against a national currency, the monetary authorities will usually take steps to protect the rate of exchange.

Assume that speculation against the dollar develops in Switzerland. The United States takes steps to protect the exchange value of the dollar by selling Swiss francs against dollars,

---

[6] See: Max J. Wasserman, "The New Ethiopian Monetary System." *The Journal of Political Economy,* Vol. LIV, No. 4, (August 1946), pp. 358-362.

[7] IMF, *Annual Report, 1963-1964.* Washington; IMF, 1964, pp. 26-27.

thus drawing down its holdings of this currency and reducing its total reserves. Of course, the United States must either possess, or have access to, Swiss francs to carry out these transactions. Now assume that speculation in favor of the dollar and against the Swiss franc develops in Switzerland. The United States might then buy Swiss francs against dollars and increase its reserve holdings of this currency.

Lack of confidence in a particular currency, the preference of monetary authorities for gold or the desire of these authorities to maintain a customary proportion of reserves in gold, can all contribute to change the composition of a nation's reserve holdings. Should France, for example, lose confidence in the dollar, this nation might exchange its dollar holdings for gold or other currencies. If its confidence in the dollar remains unimpaired, but monetary authorities feel that the proportion of dollars to gold in their reserve holdings have risen too much, France might also be led to exchange some of its dollars for gold.

Liquidity and the rate of exchange. Most international transactions take place through the short-term capital accounts which form a part of the reserves. Even those transactions which involve the exchange of goods for goods, goods for capital and the like—partial or complete barter—are often put through the short-term capital accounts as a matter of procedure. These accounts form a sort of pool which is fed by exports and drained by imports. In addition to providing a mechanism through which other transactions take place or are financed, short-term capital accounts have a life of their own; they are bought and sold for other than financing purposes. They are widely traded by banks, foreign exchange dealers, and businessmen as a source of profit possibilities, as short-term investments or as a hedge for other transactions (forward market). Such trading does not necessarily reflect changes in the basic balance. It does, however, affect the demand and supply functions of a country's currency and those of the other nations involved.

Other forces act on these functions as well. The Euro-Dollar market where foreign banks accept deposits in dollars, pounds and other non-domestic currencies—the dollar deposits are usually covered by deposits in United States banks—creates demand and supply for the currencies utilized and affects the reserve position and the rate of exchange of the countries whose money is involved.[8] The reserve center currencies are in a somewhat special situation for there is additional demand for their currency on the part of those nations using it for reserve purposes.

When the responsibility for exchange rate stability passed from private to central banks and the government, a line was drawn between the operations in short-term assets and liabilities and the function of the control of the rate of exchange. Financial operations, except in those countries engaging in substantial amounts of government international transactions, are largely in the hands of the private sector. Responsibility for maintenance of the rate of exchange falls on the shoulders of the government or its central bank.

Reserve and non-reserve centers. The liquidity problems of the reserve centers are somewhat different from those of other financial capitals of the world. A reserve center is a capital market where a group of countries deposit or invest some of their international reserves and/or whose currency is used as an international payment medium by others. The United Kingdom, France, Portugal and the United States are the four reserve centers of the world. The first three are such centers principally by virtue of the fact that they are the headquarters of three monetary areas: the Sterling, Franc and Escudo Areas. The United States is a reserve center mainly because the dollar is the most important reserve medium. Many of the nations which use America as a reserve center, carry on their international

---

[8] See: Paul Einzig, *The Euro-Dollar System: Practice and Theory of International Interest Rates.* New York, St. Martin's Press, Inc., 1964; Oscar L. Altman, "Foreign Markets for Dollars, Sterling and Other Currencies." IMF *Staff Papers*, Vol. X, No. 1 (March 1963), pp. 48-96; Alan R. Holmes and Fred H. Klopstock, "The Market for Dollar Deposits in Europe." Federal Reserve Bank of New York *Monthly Review*, Vol. 42, No. 11 (November 1960), pp. 197 ff; Norris O. Johnson *Eurodollars in the New International Money Market*, New York: First National City Bank, no date; Paul Turot, "Le Marché des Capitaux à Court Terme en Europe et l'Euro-Dollar." *Banque*, Paris, April 1961, pp. 215 ff.

trade in their own currencies. The United States is not the metropolis of a monetary area.[9]

The fact that the dollar, pound, franc, and escudo are widely used as reserve assets by other countries adds another dimension to the demand for these currencies. The demand for these exchange media is thus not limited to that of importers, borrowers and others who require these currencies to finance their transactions. The demand for dollars and certain other currencies is also augmented by operations of the Euro-Dollar Market. London, Paris and Lisbon use gold and dollars as their reserves, not only for their own international transactions, but for their liabilities to the other members of the Area as well. Reserve-wise, these areas are not self-sufficient units; they must rely on other currencies to maintain their liquidities.[10]

The Composition of Reserves

The balance of payments does not measure the *total* amount of reserves available to a country. It only shows the periodic additions or subtractions to the balance of payments accounts

---

[9] For a brief description of these monetary areas and an explanation of the reasons for not considering the United States as such an institution see: Max J. Wasserman and Charles W. Hultman, *Modern International Economics: A Balance of Payments Approach.* New York: Simmons-Boardman Publishing Corp., 1962, pp. 167-186, especially footnote 2, p. 168.

[10] During World War II, the overseas members of the Sterling Area accumulated almost $15 billion in reserves in London which the United Kingdom spent on its war effort. At the conclusion of the war, the overseas members started to draw on these reserves to finance their imports. This was the period of Britain's "unrequited exports" which constituted a severe drain on this country's liquidity. As a result, the United Kingdom was forced to negotiate a $3.75 billion loan in the United States to tide it over these difficulties. In addition, it was obliged to ration the drawings of some of the overseas members of the Area on their London Reserves. France, too, experienced difficulties during the years following the war. As metropolis of the Franc Area, it supplied much of the foreign exchange needed by the overseas members for a number of years after the conclusion of this conflict. Since the French balance of payments was in deficit during many of these years, France had recourse to borrowing from the United States, seeking credits from the EPU and drawings from the IMF to meet its obligations. See: Max J. Wasserman and Charles W. Hultman, *op. cit.*, pp. 168-180.

selected to determine the movement of the surplus or deficit. These accounts do not necessarily constitute reserves. A country might employ a narrow or wide measure of surpluses and deficits which is either smaller or larger than the actual reserve available to it. A variety of items are included in the reserves and this

TABLE 10.1

INTERNATIONAL RESERVES, POTENTIAL RESERVES, AND RESERVE
SUBSTITUTES OR SUPPLEMENTS
(All items are net and unconditional unless otherwise specified)

A. Short-term reserves and potential reserves

1. Owned reserves
    Gold
    Short-term financial assets
    Quasi-short-term assets such as medium-term U.S.
      bonds and notes
    Preempted private short-term assets—conditional

2. Drawing rights potential reserves[1]
    Gold tranche drawing rights on the IMF
    Credit tranche drawing rights on the IMF—conditional

3. Borrowed potential reserves
    Credits extended by private foreign residents—
      conditional
    Credits extended by foreign governments and official
      financial institutions—conditional

B. Long-term portfolio reserves and potential reserves (most
    direct investments excepted)

1. Owned long-term assets

2. Long-term credits extended by foreign governments
    and private parties—conditional

---

[1] Drawing rights on the IMF are determined by a member's quota and holdings of its currency. Total IMF drawing availabilities consist of its subscriptions as augmented from time to time, borrowing and deposit arrangements.

C. Reserve substitutes or supplements
   1. Official unilateral transfers—conditional
   2. Certain private unilateral transfers—conditional
   3. Transactions on the forward markets
   4. Reciprocal currency agreements (swaps) between official central banks including the BIS—conditional
   5. Medium-term bonds denominated in dollars and foreign currencies—conditional[2]
   6. Prepayment of military exports—conditional
   7. Reparations, damages, indemnities, tributes and other claims—conditional

---

[2] These are often called Roosa bonds.

The *Annex Prepared by Deputies* to the *Ministerial Report of the Group of Ten*. Washington, IMF, August 10, 1964, Appendix II, Tables I-III, pp. 17-21, presents a somewhat different classification of reserves from that shown on this table. The classification employed in this *Report* shows the following categories:

A. Reserves

1. Gold and foreign exchange

   Gold
   Foreign Exchange
2. Other

   IMF gold tranche
   Special U. S. bonds
   Swaps used by other party
   Miscellaneous

B. Credit facilities

1. Assured

   Swaps unactivated
   IMF standbys
   Other credit lines
2. Subject to negotiation

   Other IMF tranche
   Potential credit lines

---

concept varies from nation to nation and over time.[11] Reserves may be simply defined as those net assets, or their substitutes,

---

[11] History records some strange and even grisly examples of the type of "assets" which have been used by countries in desperate need of them. During World War II, one nation was so hard pressed for reserves that it extracted the teeth of the executed inmates of its concentration camps for the gold in the dental work to augment its thin gold holdings. It also confiscated as much of the gold in the banks of the countries which it occupied as it was able. In addition, it appropriated bonds, stocks, and other capital instruments which it sold, wherever it could, to supply additional reserves. Many nations have imposed, or attempted to impose, indemnities and reparation payments upon their defeated enemies to build up their reserve holdings. These payments were especially substantial at the end of the Franco-Prussian War of 1870-1871 as well as at the end of World Wars I and II.

actually and potentially available to a country for the defense of its rate of exchange and to counterbalance balance of payments deficits.

Classification of reserves. Table 10.1 presents a classification of reserves, potential reserves, reserve substitutes or complements. This classification has been made as broad as possible so as to include the modern instruments employed on the exchange market to support the national currency. The reserves actually used by any country at a given time would ordinarily not involve all of those listed on this table. Each country selects those items which are available to it, useful for its objectives and appropriate for its policies.

The reserve items may be divided into reserves, potential reserves and reserve substitutes or complements. Reserves consist of those assets which are actually in existence when needed, such as government-owned capital or capital which belongs to others but which the government can preempt or vest in itself. Potential reserves do not necessarily exist at any given moment, but can be created by borrowing or the exercise of drawing rights on the IMF. Reserve substitutes or complements are items which are not reserves in the strict sense of the term, but which can act in the place of reserves or perform some of the functions usually associated with reserves. They might be termed quasi-reserves and they consist of unilateral transfers, transactions on the forward markets and swap arrangements between government central banks. All of the items listed on Table 10.1 are net. Gross reserve assets cannot be counted upon in time of need, for some of their counterpart liabilities might mature or be called by their foreign owners.

Some reserve items are classified as unconditional and others as conditional. Unconditional reserves are those which the authorities are free to use without restriction or negotiation. Owned reserves, credit tranche drawing rights on the IMF, and transactions on the forward markets are either actually or virtually unconditional. Conditional reserves usually are restricted and generally must be negotiated. The restrictions and the negotiations involve certain conditions which the user must meet in order to obtain the reserves. Borrowing, preemption and IMF credit tranche drawing rights are of this nature.[12]

Short-term reserves and potential reserves. This category, line A on Table 10.1, is divided into owned reserves, drawing rights potential reserves, and borrowed potential reserves. *Owned reserves* are those the title to which is vested in the government, the central bank, other official financial institutions including those held by commercial banks for the account of the government. These assets are, of course, immediately available to the monetary authorities.

Gold, constitutes the oldest (with the possible exception of silver) of all reserve media and ranks highest on the list of desirable reserve assets. There is, however, insufficient gold available for it to constitute the sole reserve asset. In addition, the annual accretions to the world's monetary gold stock, at its present official United States price of $35.00 per fine troy ounce, are too small to sustain the increasing requirements of all nations.

Holdings with an original stated maturity of one year or less are generally defined as *short-term financial assets.* Wherever stock or other markets exist where credit or other capital instruments are freely traded, medium- and long-term capital assets may possess liquidity, but they possess it sometimes at a price. Where these markets prevail, these instruments can usually be readily sold, but the holder can seldom be certain of the price which he will receive.

Some medium- and long-term capital instruments may be purchased by governments within a year or less of their maturity dates. Such capital, although it is classified as long-term by definition, is really short-term. To classify securities and notes

---

[12] A discussion of the various types of conditions faced by countries using this kind of reserves is given in J. Marcus Fleming, "The Fund and International Liquidity." IMF *Staff Papers,* Vol. XI, No. 2 (July 1964), pp. 177-178. Fleming divides these conditions into three types: (a) conditions relating to policies which confront a country such as the stipulations of the IMF Agreement; (b) conditions relating to the policies which a country should pursue in order to obtain these reserves, such as the balance of payments programs to follow and (c) conditions relating to the period for which the reserves may be used.

according to the number of days which they have to run before maturity, rather than by stated original maturity, would impose an almost impossible task upon the balance of payments statisticians. However, in taking inventory of its reserve assets, a government might take the period before maturity of these items into account in analyzing its net reserve position.

Certain medium-term United States notes and bonds held by foreign governments are usually classified by these governments as short-term assets. Commerce, in its balance of payments work, also classifies them as short-term. In view of their security and price stability, this classification seems appropriate. These reserves are termed *quasi short-term assets* on Table 10.1.

Assets held by private firms, individuals, and banks, to which the government may take title by a variety of means, are called *Preempted short-term reserves* (conditional). Through appropriate legislation, decrees or executive orders, the government may oblige the owners of these assets to surrender them for compensation. Through forward and open market operations, enough pressure may be put on banks to bring them to surrender these assets to the central bank in exchange for domestic currency. By means of change in reserve requirements, bank interest and rediscount rates and other forms of financial pressure, a government may bring the private owners of these assets to sell them. In some cases, assets classified as commercial bank holdings, may in reality belong to the government, which is conducting some of its reserve operations through the medium of these banks.

Drawings on the IMF consist in the purchase from this institution of the currency of another member or members against the currency of the nation making the drawing. Drawings thus contribute to the IMF currency holdings of those countries having recourse to its resources and to decrease those of the nations whose currency is withdrawn or purchased. All purchases and repurchases are made at the par values of the currencies concerned. Drawings may not be used as cover for forward transactions, speculation or large and sustained capital transactions, although some exception to the latter have been made. The IMF holdings of a member's currency determine in part that member's position with the organization; its future drawing possibilities; the charges to be paid for the use of the Fund facilities and the obligation to repurchase its own currency with that of the other members at some future date.

The rights of members to draw on the IMF, are termed *drawing rights potential reserves*. These rights are divided into two categories: the gold and the credit tranche which are determined by a member's quota and its position with the IMF.

The quota of a member is equal to its subscription as determined by the IMF in accordance with the member's population, reserve holdings, income and product, international trade, among other factors. As a general matter, the Fund applies the principles of ability to pay and potential need for reserve assistance in determining the amount of member subscriptions. The subscriptions of the individual members may be either increased or decreased at the instance of the IMF with the consent of the member or at the instance of the member itself with the agreement of the Fund. Provision is also made for increasing or decreasing the quotas of all members simultaneously and the Fund has already availed itself of this prerogative by augmenting all the quotas by fifty per cent. Future increases in all member's subscriptions are not improbable in the foreseeable future.

Twenty-five per cent of a member's quota or ten per cent of its net official holdings of gold and dollars, whichever is the smaller, is payable in gold. The balance must be paid in its own currency. The gold tranche derives its name from the fact that it is determined by the amount of the subscription payable in gold. The credit tranche refers to drawing rights above the gold tranche.

The IMF position of a member consists of the relationship between its quota and the Fund's holdings of its currency. The gold tranche position is defined as a member's quota minus the IMF holdings of its currency (if the result is positive). This tranche includes the member's "net credit position" or that part of its gold tranche position which exceeds twenty-five per cent of its quota. A member is held to be drawing on the credit tranche when the drawing increases the Fund's holdings of its currency by more than its quota. The credit tranche consists of an amount equal to two hundred per cent of the quota less the Fund's holdings of its currency unless a waiver of conditions is obtained.[13]

The *gold tranche drawing rights* are virtually unconditional for, in the language of the IMF, a member is given "the overwhelming benefit of the doubt," in utilizing this facility. The gold tranche must be utilized, however, for making payments consistent with the provisions of the IMF Agreement. Drawings in the *credit tranche* are subject to conditions which increase in severity with the amount of the outstanding drawings.[14]

Certain exceptions to the total amount of drawings allowed are made in the case of the compensatory financing of export fluctuations. This type of financing provides an additional drawing facility, normally not exceeding twenty-five per cent of a member's quota, if its earnings from exports fall short of the normal amount. Various other conditions are also imposed under these compensatory financing arrangements.[15]

Since 1952, members of the IMF have been able to negotiate stand-by drawing arrangements in anticipation of future needs. Under these arrangements a member, sensing future needs for Fund assistance, makes advance drawing arrangements with it. Then if the need arises, the member is able to draw upon the Fund up to the amount negotiated without further consideration by the IMF. Each stand-by arrangement is a separate negotiation and each carries its own period of validity, terms and conditions which must be in accord with the IMF Agreement, policies, rules and regulations. A charge of one-half of one per cent is made for a stand-by arrangement which is refunded against

---

[13] Cf. J. Marcus Fleming, *op. cit.*, pp. 180-185. The drawing rights are defined in the Articles of Agreement of the IMF, especially Articles V, VI, and VII. They are further governed by the Rules and Regulations of the IMF, especially Sections D, E, J, I, and K. See: IMF, *By-Laws, Rules and Regulations.* Washington: International Monetary Fund, 24th issue (July 1964), pp. 15-44.

[14] J. Marcus Fleming, *op. cit.*, pp. 180-185.

[15] See the Report by the IMF, *Compensatory Financing of Export Fluctuations.* Washington: IMF, February 1963.

charges for any drawings made under it. As a general proposition, the terms of the stand-by arrangements correspond to those in effect for the tranche upon which the member proposes to draw.

Drawings on the IMF involve a service charge of one-half of one per cent on all drawings. In addition, further charges are made for the Fund holdings of a member's currency in excess of its gold tranche. These charges begin at two per cent per annum and rise in proportion to the amount of foreign exchange drawn and the length of time that the member's currency is held by the IMF. With a number of exceptions and under certain conditions, a member may be required to repurchase a certain part of the Fund's holdings of its currency. Usually, a member is obliged to repurchase the amounts drawn within a period of from three to five years after the drawing has occurred.[16]

In addition to owned reserves, many nations have the power to borrow at short-term from governments, official and private financial insitutions. These borrowing facilities, *borrowed potential short-term reserves*, are not reserves in the strict sense of the term because they may, or may not, be available whereas owned reserves are. Since they are frequently used, they should be included in any calculation of a nation's ability to defend its exchange rate and to trade where balance of payments deficits occur. These assets are, of course, conditional.

Some of these short-term credits, notably those extended by the Export-Import Bank of Washington, are tied and their proceeds must be spent in the lending country unless exceptions are granted. The monetary areas commonly extend short-term credits to their members. In the Sterling and Escudo Areas, the overseas members have often granted credits to the metropolis; in the case of the Franc Area, the metropolis has usually extended

---

[16] Cf. IMF Articles of Agreement, Article V, Section 7 and Schedule B; IMF *Rules and Regulations,* Section I. A brief but authoritative description of the Fund's operations is given in IMF, "Introduction to the Fund." *Finance and Development* (The Fund and Bank Review), a Quarterly Publication of the International Monetary Fund and the International Bank for Reconstruction and Development. Washington: Vol. I, No. 1. (June 1964), pp. 3-14.

credits, until recently, to the overseas members.[17]

When the defense of the exchange rates was in the hands of the commercial banks, borrowing from private sources to supplement lean reserves was more common than it is today. Nevertheless, *credits extended by private foreign residents* are a source of supplementary reserves and should be included in a listing of these potentialities. Such reserves are conditional.

It is customary for central banks to extend short-term credits to one another for purposes of the mutual defense of their currencies and these credits constitute conditional reserves. They are here termed *short-term credits extended by official financial institutions.* The sale of United States medium-term obligations to central banks (which are commonly held to be short-term by foreign governments) belong in this category. Cooperation between central banks is on the increase today for they have come to realize that the movement of the rates of exchange of other currencies is of importance to them.

Long-term portfolio reserves and potential reserves. It is not customary to regard long-term portfolio assets and potential assets as liquid items forming a part of reserve holdings. As liquidity is commonly understood, long-term holdings are not liquid or are only liquid at a price. If the need is sufficiently great, however, the long-term assets may be sold to acquire foreign currencies even though their liquidation may entail a capital loss.

The previous chapter has shown that extraordinary balance of payments surpluses and deficits are measured in part by the use of long-term borrowing. The British and the Dutch governments vested some of the long-term assets of their private residents to acquire badly needed foreign exchange during World War II. They should, therefore, be included in any complete inventory of reserves.

Direct investments are not grouped in this category because the sale of such assets involves far more than the mere exchange

---

[17] Cf. Max J. Wasserman, Charles W. Hultman and Laszlo Zsoldos, *International Finance.* New York: Simmons-Boardman Publishing Corp., 1963, pp. 246-267.

of long-term capital for foreign currencies. These investments consist of branches and subsidiaries abroad. They would have to be liquidated, or ownership transferred from domestic to foreign residents, in order to utilize them for liquidity purposes. Involving the plans of business, their sale would raise problems of business rights and have an important impact on both the internal and external economies. The liquidation of these investments would be the desperate act of a country facing grave problems of national liquidity.

By and large, governments are not large holders of *owned long-termed assets* and those which they do hold are more frequently obligations of foreign governments and the IBRD rather than the bonds and equities of private enterprise. Where governments do hold a portfolio of foreign securities, they can be liquidated to acquire foreign currencies.

A government borrows on the long-term abroad for two principal reasons: it may not be able to obtain short-term accommodation on advantageous terms and the balance of payments disequilibrium may be of long duration which cannot be bridged by short-term credits.

There have been many examples of *long-term credits extended by foreign governments and private parties* to assist other nations in times of balance of payments difficulties. One recent example, important by reason of its size and implications, was the United Kingdom loan for $3.75 billion extended by the United States in the fall of 1945. This long-term loan, made under the Anglo-American Financial Agreement, was designed to provide the United Kingdom with dollars to meet its short-term obligations which members of the Sterling Area had accumulated during World War II.[18] There are other instances of less sizable long-term government loans to cover short-term obligations. In addition, occasions have arisen where governments have borrowed from private financial institutions and banking syndicates

---

[18] For a succinct account of the Anglo-American Financial Agreement and the operations which it sustained see: Raymond F. Mikesell, *United States Economic Policy and International Relations.* New York: McGraw-Hill Book Company, Inc. 1952, pp. 171-179.

to meet their needs for reserves or to halt gold outflows.[19] Insurance companies, foundations and eleemosynary institutions constitute an important source of these private long-term funds. Borrowed long-term capital is a conditional form of international reserves.

Reserve substitutes and supplements. Some facilities which governments employ to maintain liquidity in the short-run are not properly classified as reserves, but may be regarded as reserve substitutes or supplements. Like international borrowing, these conditional "assets" do not appear in any inventory of reserves until the actual transactions take place. They are widely used to obtain foreign currencies and should be carried in any complete list of reserve availabilities.

A number of nations living beyond their international payments means, including many undeveloped countries, utilize *official unilateral transfers* as a potential, albeit highly conditional and aleatory, sources of additional reserves, as a glance at the analytical balance of payments presented on Table 9.4 reveals. If these potential sources of assets were not available, a large number of countries would have to modify their international standards of living.

A number of countries and organizations including the United States, the United Kingdom, France, the United Nations, the Columbo Plan countries, the Overseas Development Fund of the European Economic Community (EEC) are engaged in the unilateral transfers business. The U.S.S.R. and Communist China apparently prefer the use of long-term loans at low interest rates to carry out their "foreign aid" programs.

Unilateral transfers present one solid advantage to the

---

[19] One noteworthy instance of this type of borrowing arose in 1895 when the United States arranged to float a long-term bond issue under onerous terms with a banking syndicate organized by J. P. Morgan and Company and August Belmont and Company (representing the Rothschild banking interests abroad). The proceeds of the loan were used to halt United States gold outflows, acquire foreign currencies and defend the exchange rate. The banking syndicate took full financial advantage of the Treasury's plight in that year and of its inability to obtain suitable accommodation elsewhere. See: Alexander Dana Noyes, *Forty Years of American Finance.* New York: G. P. Putnam's Sons, 1909, pp. 234-256.

recipient countries in that such *largesse* need not be repaid. The acceptance of these transfers does, however, pose some problems for the recipient countries which some of them, apparently, do not always realize. The unilateral transfers extended by the United States are tied at present, that is, the proceeds of these grants must be spent in this country. Those of some other countries may not be tied *de jure*, but they are *de facto*, while some have no ties at all. The unilateral transfers of international institutions are generally not tied and this constitutes one of the advantages of this type of aid to the recipient nations.

The balance of payments unilateral transfers account includes private as well as official transactions of this type. *Certain private unilateral transfers* are of a similar reserve substitute character to those in the official category. However, all private unilateral transfers do not belong in this group. The United Jewish Appeal in the United States, and similar donations to Israel made by private residents of other nations are an important example of this type of reserve substitute.

These private unilateral transfers have been employed by Israel to balance its international accounts and this nation has come to rely upon them to maintain its international standard of living. Such reserve substitutes are conditional. Immigrant remittances, private gifts to family and friends abroad, payments made by religious, charitable, scientific, educational, health and welfare organizations to their missions overseas do not fall in this category. They are above, rather than below, the line international transactions.

Another form of reserve substitute or supplement, *transactions on the forward markets*, has been used for some time by several nations and is widely employed by the United States today. The use of the forward facilities is confined largely to exchange rate problems, and this market can only be used in the short-run (three to six months usually). These transactions are generally utilized for one or more of the following purposes:

　　1. To bring the spot rate to lie within the limits imposed
　　by the IMF Agreement (one per cent above or below
　　par)

2. To correct undesirable changes in either the spot or forward rates or to bring these rates to a desired level

3. To correct premiums or discounts on the forward rates

4. To discourage speculation in a nation's currency

5. To discourage leads and lags in the purchase and payment for imports, i.e., advanced or retarded imports, pre-payment or late payment, in anticipation of a rise or a fall in the rate of exchange of the currency required.

The forward market may be used where a country is short of reserves to accomplish the purpose at hand, or where the reserves are adequate, but the use of forward market facilities are preferred in any specific case. Forward transactions must, of course, be paid at maturity unless they are "rolled over" and they may or may not be covered by simultaneous transactions in spot or by the use of other hedging facilities. The use and mechanism of the forward market it described in the following section where the recent United States experience on this market is discussed.[20]

Before World War II, central banks and governments frowned on the use of the forward markets. Many of them felt that such use was speculative and that it was inappropriate for an official institution to have recourse to these facilities. Others held that the use of the forward markets tended to interfere with the freedom of the exchange markets and constituted an unwarranted incursion into the free market mechanism. Some were of the opinion that recourse to such transactions was an indication of weakness and should not be used by official financial institutions.[21]

These attitudes have changed since World War II and

---

[20] The classic or standard work on forward exchange is Paul Einzig, *A Dynamic Theory of Forward Exchange.* London: Macmillan and Company, Ltd., 1961. This book represents a revised edition of Einzig's previous study, *The Theory of Foreign Exchange,* originally published in 1937. In conjunction with the mechanism and uses of this market see: especially pp. 17-120.

[21] Cf. Paul Einzig, *op. cit.,* pp. 381-545.

many nations are now using the forward facilities. This market constitutes a valuable weapon in the arsenal for the defense of the currency. It can often be effectively used as either the principal, or an auxiliary, instrument for this purpose and present policies point to an increasing employment of this market. It thus takes its proper place in the list of available reserve and reserve substitutes.[22]

After the substantial deficits which appeared on the United States balances of payments in 1958 and after, official financial institutions started to demand gold in exchange for some of their heavy dollar holdings. To reduce these outflows, the Federal Reserve Bank of New York made *reciprocal currency agreements (swaps) with official central banks, and the Bank for International Settlements (BIS)*. Other countries have also utilized these reciprocal or "swap" agreements.[23]

Under these arrangements, for example, the Federal Reserve Bank of New York acquires the right to draw up to a specified amount on the Bank of France. In exchange, the Bank of France receives the right to draw a specified amount of dollars on the Federal Reserve Bank of New York. These arrangements are usually made at a determined rate of exchange for a short period, three to six months, on a stand-by basis. If these reciprocal credits are needed, the Bank of France credits the Federal Reserve deposit account with the agreed amount of francs and the Federal Reserve Bank of New York credits that of the Bank of

---

[22] The use of the facilities of the forward exchange market by the Treasury and the Federal Reserve System during the dollar exchange rate crises of 1961 and 1962 is given in Charles A. Coombs, "Treasury and Federal Reserve Foreign Exchange Operations." *Monthly Review* of the Federal Reserve Bank of New York, Vol. 44, No. 9 (September 1962), pp. 1138-1153.

[23] The use of the term "swaps" to designate these reciprocal currency agreements might result in some confusion for the term is also employed to characterize forward covered by spot exchange transactions. In the latter case, the forward exchange is held to be "swapped" against the spot cover and this employment of the term swaps is the traditional one. The use of the term swaps to designate reciprocal currency agreements is appropriate, however, in the context of forward exchange, for the credits exchanged under these arrangements do in fact constitute the cover or the swap for forward commitments.

France with the agreed amount of dollars. Both countries are obliged to reverse the transaction on a specified date at the agreed rate of exchange. Each country thus has hedged against the risk of devaluation of either currency.

Credits are subject to call and use on two days notice, after consultation. The foreign currency obtained by each party is deposited in time deposits or invested in credit instruments earning indentical interest on each side. Each swap arrangement is usually renewable, or may be rolled over, upon the agreement of both parties.

These agreements are frequently made to enable either of the parties to meet forward obligations. They are thus often tied to the forward market operations of one or both parties and form an integral part of a country's use of these facilities. If a country's forward rate is at a premium in terms of another currency, it could sell the premium currency forward without spot cover to correct the situation. Where its forward rate is at a discount, it could buy the other currency forward and correct the disparity without recourse to the spot market. If it bought or sold forward with spot cover, the purpose of the operation— the correction of a forward premium or discount—might be defeated.

Where both the spot and forward rates are rising or falling, the situation can often be corrected by recourse to the forward market alone in the expectation that the spot rate would follow. Or it could operate solely on the spot market in the hope that the forward would be corrected. The United States has had recourse to the forward markets because it lacked the foreign currency reserves to operate on spot and did not wish to involve its monetary gold stock.[24]

Although swap arrangements are a conditional reserve substitute, they afford an effective method of defending the rate of exchange in readily reversible situations. They are widely employed by the United States at the present time. Often employed in conjunction with swap arrangements, *medium-term*

---

[24] Cf. Charles A. Coombs, *op. cit.*, pp. 1146-1150.

bonds denominated in dollars and foreign currencies, the Roosa bonds, constitute another conditional reserve substitute or supplement of increasing popularity since 1961. Swap arrangements are employed for exchange market situations which are quickly reversible. Where the situation is not readily reversible within a short period, the United States Treasury may issue bonds with maturities falling within a two to five year period, denominated in dollars or a foreign currency, and sell them to foreign monetary or banking authorities against their currencies or dollars.

Where a foreign central bank is accumulating excessive amounts of dollars and there is danger that they may be presented for redemption in gold, the Treasury and Federal Reserve System often sell these bonds to central banks to "mop up" the excess dollar holdings. The bonds used for these purposes are usually denominated in the appropriate foreign currencies, although they may be in dollars, at the choice of the foreign monetary authority in question.

In recent years, the United States has availed itself of the *prepayment of its military exports* to other countries as a type of conditional reserve substitute. These prepayments are a specialized form of reserve substitute in that they apply only to a specific period and to those countries which have purchased military equipment. The military exports must be paid by the importing country; the prepayment merely advances the date. Thus they do not represent any net addition to a nation's reserves; they merely make funds available earlier than the agreement originally specified.

Some countries are in a position to collect *reparations, damages, indemnities, tributes and other claims* which arise from war, acts of foreign individuals or governments, the seizure or nationalization of the property of other nationals or governments and the like. Payments arising from such claims are generally settled by treaty or agreement. Sometimes they are voluntary, as in the case of the payments made to Israel by West Germany in indemnification for the damages sustained by European Jews. These reserve substitutes are usually highly conditional and are only available to those countries which have sustainable or enforceable claims on foreign countries for such payments. They cannot be classified as reserves in the strict sense of the term. Since they do serve the purpose of reserves in those cases where they are available, they may be properly included in an inventory of reserve substitutes.

Under the investment guarantee program of the Agency for International Development (AID), the guarantee contracts with American investors stipulate that the damaged private parties, upon reimbursement by the United States, turn over their claims against the foreign country involved to the United States government. Any collections which this country makes as a result of the invocation of these guarantees should be placed in this category of reserves substitutes.

The role played by the more conventional forms of reserves such as gold, short- and long-term foreign assets, international borrowing facilities, IMF drawing rights and preempted private holdings is already well known and is available in a number of authoritative works. The publications of the IMF including its *Annual Reports of the Executive Directors,* the *Annual Reports on Exchange Restrictions,* the *International Financial News Survey,* the *Staff Papers* and the review, *Finance and Development,* published in cooperation with the IBRD, are invaluable sources of information on the current management of reserve holdings. The more recent developments, especially those since March 1961, involving the less conventional forms of reserves, potential reserves, reserve substitutes and supplements are less well known. The rest of this chapter, therefore, is devoted to an examination of these recent developments.

Recent Reserve Practices and Policies

In the *Annex Prepared by Deputies to the Ministerial Statement of the Group of Ten,* a group established under the auspices of the IMF to review the stability and adequacy of the international payments system, the new developments in reserve practices and policies were characterized as follows:

> In sum, a country's liquidity is no longer solely measured by the level of its reserves in the form of gold and

reserve currency balances (primary reserves). There is now a variety of ways in which monetary authorities can, if needed, replenish their balances of the currencies used for operations. Primary reserves are thus supplemented by a broad spectrum of other resources and facilities. At one end of this range come "other reserves" of only slightly less liquidity but of unquestioned availability; at the other end of the range are negotiated credits, including those which will only be available when an international institution is satisfied that the borrower will employ effective adjustment processes to correct his deficit.[25]

The enlargement of the concept of reserves has not been the only change which has characterized the international payments scene since 1960. Another important development has been the growth of close cooperation among the central banks, monetary authorities and international financial institutions in the solution of balance of payments, exchange rate and monetary gold problems. Although there has always been some cooperation in these matters, the present arrangements surpass anything seen in the past.

This cooperation probably results from a realization that, as far as international payments are concerned, all nations must either hang together or they will hang separately.[26] The problems of the United States monetary gold assets, for example, are not

---

[25] *Ministerial Statement of the Group of Ten and Annex Prepared by Deputies.* Washington: IMF, August 10, 1964, p. 8. The group of Ten derives its name from the fact that it consists of the representatives of the ten countries participating in the General Arrangements to Borrow of the IMF.

[26] In the voluminous literature on the subject, see especially Fritz Machlup, "Plans for the Reform of the International Monetary System," *Special Papers in International Economics,* No. 3 (August 1962). Princeton: International Finance Section Department of Economics, Princeton University, 1962; "International Monetary Arrangements: The Problem of Choice," *Report on the Deliberations of an International Study Group of 32 Economists.* Princeton: International Finance Section, Department of Economics, Princeton University, 1964; *Ministerial Statement of the Group of Ten and Annex Prepared by Deputies.* Washington: IMF, August 10,

the exclusive concern of this country; they are that of all countries which use the dollar as a part of their international reserves.

A new dimension in reserve policies and practices. In an
address before the annual convention of the American Bankers
Association on September 25, 1962 in Atlantic City, New Jersey,
Under Secretary of the Treasury for Monetary Affairs, Robert
V. Roosa, stated:

> The new initiatives have taken the form of a new set
> of arrangements under which the United States, for the first
> time in a generation, is dealing directly on the foreign ex-
> change markets, in a great enlargement of the resources
> available through the IMF, and in the application of cooper-
> ative arrangements to the London gold market. Taken to-
> gether, an entirely new dimension has been added to our
> international financial system.[27]

The operations to which Under Secretary Roosa referred
are sometimes termed the "financial component in the outer
perimeter defense of the dollar" in contrast to the inner defenses
which involve the productivity, competitiveness, stability and
growth of the economy.[28] Other countries have long employed
exchange market intervention as a means of defending their
currencies. They are obliged to so intervene as the rates of exchange near the IMF permitted floors and ceilings. Previously,
the United States relied upon the convertibility of official holdings of dollars into gold as its exchange market safeguard and

---

1964; IMF Staff, *International Reserves and Liquidity.* Washington: IMF,
1958; Robert V. Roosa, *The Beginning of a New Policy* (remarks at the
monetary conference of the American Bankers Association, Rome, Italy,
May 17, 1962) and *Banking and the Balance of Payments* (remarks at
the annual convention of the American Bankers Association at Atlantic
City, N. J., September 25, 1962), both reprinted in *Factors Affecting the
United States Balance of Payments,* compilation of studies prepared for
the Subcommittee on International Exchange and Payments of the Joint
Economic Committee of the United States, 87th Congress, 2nd Session,
Joint Committee Print. Washington: U. S. Government Printing Office,
1962, pp. 327-332 and 333-340, respectively.

[27] Robert V. Roosa, *op. cit.,* p. 338.

[28] Robert V. Roosa, *op. cit.,* p. 327.

was satisfied to let the other nations intervene to maintain the spot rate.[29]

The programs utilized by the United States since 1961 have been mainly designed to afford time during which this country could apply more fundamental measures to eliminate its balance of payments deficits. The United States held no reserve of foreign currencies until March 1961. Consequently there was no opportunity to support the dollar through spot sales of foreign currencies as the European monetary authorities have done as a matter of customary practice. Only gold could be used to support the rate and the dwindling gold reserves rendered such support of doubtful value. United States gold reserves had declined from over $24 billion in 1949 to about $17.5 billion in 1961.

It was, nevertheless, clear that unless some effective measures were taken, the gold stock would doubtless continue to decline as long as the balance of payments deficits persisted. In addition to purely national considerations, the United States had the responsibility of assuring the official gold convertibility of the dollar, the key currency of the world's payment system. The United States was thus forced to have recourse to transactions on the forward market, and to reciprocal credit arrangements or swaps.

The United States operations in defense of the rate of exchange were not unilateral actions. They represent a part of the cooperative effort of treasuries and central banks on both sides of the Atlantic to create a first line of defense against disorderly speculation in the foreign exchange markets and in defense of the United States stock of monetary gold.

Speculation can and does play an important and useful role in maintaining markets where foreign traders and financial institutions can readily buy and sell foreign exchange. The market also establishes the going rates of exchange. In addition, speculation helps to correct temporary deviations of spot and

---

[29] The IMF Agreement only requires members to maintain their *spot* rates of exchange within one per cent of parity; they are not obliged to maintain the *forward* rates at any designated level. See Article IV, Section 3.

forward rates from the levels appropriate to underlying payment trends.

When combined with political and economic uncertainties, speculation can at times seriously unsettle the foreign exchange markets and prove a disruptive force. In periods of exchange market anxiety, sharp declines in the spot or forward rates may generate greatly exaggerated speculative fears. This volatile market is peculiarly subject to rumor; it sometimes transforms bits of information and misinformation into predictions of impending catastrophe. In such periods, the market may yield to grossly exaggerated selling and buying with cumulative effects upon the spot and forward rates.

Until March 1961, the role of the United States on the foreign exchange markets was essentially passive. Although foreign central banks defended their own currencies, they were under no obligation to defend the dollar. When pressures on the dollar developed, its rate tended to fall toward the floor. The United States preferred to allow the dollar rate of exchange to be determined by market forces and to the unilateral decisions of foreign monetary authorities.

Since 1958, successive balance of payments deficits in the United States have brought large gold losses and excessive accumulations of dollar reserves by other nations. Rumor of the possible devaluation of the dollar, by raising the price of gold above $35.00 per fine troy ounce, generated a wave of heavy speculation against the dollar in 1960. In 1961 the late President Kennedy "spiked" these rumors by his pledge to maintain the gold price of the dollar at all costs. In addition, he announced a policy for restoring United States balance of payments equilibrium. However, the dollar remained vulnerable to speculative activity and market shocks which made their appearance in massive proportions in March 1961.[30]

Reserve policies following the mark and guilder revaluations of 1961. During the week-end of March 4, 1961, the German

[30] Cf. Charles A. Coombs, "Treasury and Federal Reserve Foreign Exchange Operations." *Federal Reserve Bulletin*, Vol. 48, No. 9 (September 1962), pp. 1138-1140.

government announced the upward revaluation of the mark by five per cent and shortly thereafter the Dutch government proclaimed a similar change in the guilder. Although the new pars were doubtless fully justified, they touched off a severe wave of speculation on the exchange markets of the world.[31]

Many foreign exchange traders felt that these revaluations would be followed by a similar change in the Swiss franc although this feeling was not justified by the Swiss balance of payments deficit situation. In four days more than $300 million worth of currencies were transferred into Swiss francs in anticipation of this projected upward revaluation. The Bank of England suffered heavy reserve losses.

The governors of central banks attending the March 1961 monthly meeting of the Bank for International Settlements (BIS) in Basle (Basle Group) announced that they were cooperating to meet this speculative threat and they extended more than $900 million in credits to the Bank of England. The dollar had not been seriously touched by the first wave of speculation, but the central banks had excessive accumulations of dollars which posed a threat to the United States monetary gold reserves. This was the start of the Basle cooperative credit agreements to aid currencies under speculative attack.

Since speculators also anticipated a second revaluation of the German mark, a heavy flow of funds into Frankfurt developed with the resulting increase in the Bundesbank's holdings of dollars. Non-German residents with commitments to pay marks and Germans anticipating the receipt of foreign currencies, sought to hedge these forthcoming transactions by recourse to the forward market. A premium on the forward mark and a discount on the forward dollar developed rapidly and rose to nearly four per cent. These forward transactions are an example of the "leads and lags" taken by traders with future commitments, to anticipate shifts in the rates of exchange.

Since forward cover was expensive and only available in limited quantities, commercial hedging resulted in demands

---

[31] Charles A. Coombs, *op. cit.*, pp. 1140-1143.

for spot marks to cover future mark commitments and to German private borrowing of dollars in New York and on the Euro-Dollar Market. Under an agreement between the Bundesbank, the Federal Reserve Bank of New York, acting as agent for the Treasury, undertook the forward sale of marks in New York. This decision was taken to provide an ample supply of forward marks and to drive the premium on them down to a level of one per cent.

These forward sales were covered by the agreement of the Bundesbank to supply marks to the Treasury at the same rate that the marks had been sold by the Treasury. For its part, the Treasury agreed to supply the Bundesbank with dollars, should they be required, under similar terms. These arrangements marked the inauguration of the Treasury-Federal Reserve reciprocal currency agreements or swaps. In this way, the Treasury's forward commitments were covered against the possibility of loss. Under these arrangements, the Treasury sold over $118 million marks equivalent forward for delivery in three months and stemmed a large part of the speculative inflow of dollars into Germany. Following this operation, the market demand for forward marks declined.

When these forward contracts matured, the spot dollar rose as a result of the demand for dollars needed to repay the Treasury under the forward mark contracts. Coordinated intervention in the spot market by the Treasury and Bundesbank also helped to strengthen the spot dollar. After confidence in the dollar had been restored, the forward premium on the mark was allowed to rise somewhat, to mitigate commercial demand for cover. By early December of 1961, the forward mark commitments of the Treasury had been fully liquidated.[32]

Likewise, during 1961 the flow of dollars into Switzerland, the Netherlands and Italy created similar pressures on the dollar. In the case of Switzerland, the attraction of the Swiss franc stemmed from speculative belief in a possible upward revaluation of this currency and the notion that this franc might prove a safer haven for funds than the dollar. The inflow of this "hot"

---

[32] Charles A. Coombs, *loc. cit.*

capital into Switzerland masked a deficit on the Swiss balance of payments. Consequently, forward transactions in Swiss francs appeared to offer a quickly reversible solution. The Treasury sold Swiss francs forward, the Swiss National Bank furnished the Treasury cover in the form of a line of credit against the issue by the Treasury of three-month certificates of indebtedness denominated in Swiss francs.

Early in 1962 the Swiss franc started to weaken as a result of Switzerland's large current account deficit. The National Bank of Switzerland needed dollars to meet the deficit and the Treasury was able to liquidate much of its forward Swiss franc commitments and to receive some gold as well. Similar operations were carried out by the Treasury in Dutch guilders and Italian lira during 1961.[33]

In carrying out these transactions, the Treasury first relied upon the limited resources provided by its Stabilization Fund. To provide a wider base for the exchange market operations, the Federal Open Market Committee authorized the Federal Reserve Bank of New York to undertake open market transactions in foreign currencies.[34]

During 1961, the Treasury and Federal Reserve operations were closely coordinated. The Federal Reserve swap network was increased between 1962 and 1964. The volume of these reciprocal currency arrangements from its inception in 1961 through August 31, 1964 are presented on Table 10.2. The existence of the network exerts a strong stabilizing influence on both the gold and foreign exchange markets. Traders and speculators realize that the United States could mobilize large sums to counter any offensives against the dollar.

Policies following the assassination of President Kennedy, 1963. One of the more striking examples of the new dimension in reserve policies occurred following the assassination of President

---

[33] Details of these transactions are given in Charles A. Coombs, *op. cit.,* pp. 1145-1146.

[34] The text of the Authorization Regarding Open Market Transactions in Foreign Currencies is given in the *Federal Reserve Bulletin,* Vol. 48, No. 9 (September 1962), pp. 1150-1153.

TABLE 10.2

Federal Reserve Reciprocal Currency Arrangements (Swaps)
August 31, 1964

Institution	Amount of total facility in millions of dollars	Term of arrangements in months
Bank of France	100	3
Bank of England	500	12
Netherlands Bank	100	3
National Bank of Belgium	50	6
Bank of Canada	250	12
BIS	150	6
Swiss National Bank	150	6
German Federal Bank	250	6
Bank of Italy	250	6
Austrian National Bank	50	12
Bank of Sweden	50	12
Bank of Japan	150	12
Total	2,050	

Source: Charles A. Coombs, "Treasury and Federal Reserve Foreign
Exchange Operations." *Monthly Review* of the Federal Reserve
Bank of New York, Vol. 46, No. 9 (September 1964), p. 162.

Kennedy on November 22, 1963. This sad event touched off a
wave of speculation on the exchange markets of the world. The
Federal Reserve stepped in instantly with offers of most foreign
currencies in large amounts on the New York market at rates
prevailing just before the tragedy. As the market realized the
size of the potential Federal Reserve operations, calmness was
restored.

Although most of the European markets were closed at the
time of the assassination, telephone contacts were made with
the officials of the principal European central banks. Arrangements were made for both sides of the Atlantic to intervene in
the event of speculative developments. As the news of these
arrangements spread on the foreign exchange markets, trading
remained quiet and orderly at stable rates.

In the following months the Federal Reserve Bank continued to intervene in the forward markets to influence the timing and the direction of short-term capital flows between money market centers. The Treasury expanded its issues of medium-term foreign currency denominated securities. These securities were sold to foreign central banks to provide foreign currency cover for forward and spot transactions. They provided the United States with the time necessary to meet market contingencies. Table 10.3 shows the amounts of these bonds issued up to August 31, 1964.

TABLE 10.3

UNITED STATES TREASURY BONDS DENOMINATED IN FOREIGN
CURRENCIES (ROOSA BONDS), AUGUST 31, 1964

Issued to	Foreign currency	Equivalent in millions of dollars
Austrian National Bank	Austrian schillings	50.3
National Bank of Belgium	Belgian francs	30.1
German Federal Bank	German marks	628.2
Swiss National Bank	Swiss francs	257.3
BIS	Swiss francs	69.5
Total		1,035.4

Source: Charles A. Coombs, "Treasury and Federal Reserve Foreign Exchange Operations." *Monthly Review* of the Federal Reserve Bank of New York, Vol. 46, No. 9, (September 1964), p. 164.

Before his death, President Kennedy had made a stand-by arrangement with the IMF amounting to $500 million, the first which the United States had contracted. In February 1964 the first drawing under this arrangement was made for $125 million equivalent in German marks and French francs. The foreign currency proceeds of this drawing were sold to other member countries for their use in making repayments to the IMF. At that time, the IMF's holdings of dollars equalled the dollar portion of the United States subscription and the IMF could no longer accept dollars in repayment of members' drawings.

In the months following November 1963 until February

1964, the Federal Reserve-Treasury operated in marks, guilders, Canadian dollars, Belgian and French francs, lira, kroner and yen. Certain aspects of these transactions are noteworthy.

The first instance of the refunding of the swap arrangements occurred in the case of German marks. Since the forward transactions in marks did not appear to be quickly reversible, the Federal Reserve and the Treasury, in line with their policy of reserving swap transactions for quickly reversible situations, refunded the credits extended by the Bundesbank into two year, medium-term, Treasury obligations denominated in marks.

The Canadian $500 million wheat sale to the Soviet Union introduced new foreign exchange problems of a technical character. The sales contracts between the Soviet Union and the international grain companies which handled the transaction, called for payment in United States dollars. However, these companies had to purchase the wheat in Canadian dollars. As a result of these transactions, the Canadian dollar moved to a premium vis à vis the United States dollar.

Fearing a flow of arbitrage funds, the United States and Canadian authorities intervened to eliminate the forward premium on the Canadian dollar. They hoped to reduce the covered interest arbitrage incentive in favor of Canada. The Federal Reserve Bank of New York bought Canadian dollars spot and sold them forward against United States dollars. The Canadian dollar resources required for these operations were acquired by a drawing on the Federal Reserve swap line with the Bank of Canada.[35]

Gold pool transactions. The largest and most important center for free market transactions in gold, the London gold market, reopened in 1954.[36] The annual flow of gold to this market usually

---

[35] For a more complete description of these foreign exchange transactions see: Charles A. Coombs, "Treasury and Federal Reserve Foreign Exchange Operations and the Gold Pool," *Federal Reserve Bulletin*, Vol. 50, No. 3 (March 1964), pp. 294-304.

[36] A description of the London gold market is given in "The London Gold Market," *Quarterly Bulletin* of the Bank of England for March 1964. An excerpt of the salient parts of this article was reprinted as a special supplement to the *Monthly Review* of the Federal Reserve Bank of New York, Vol. 50, No. 3 (March 1964).

exceeds the combined industrial and speculative demands for the metal by a wide margin. The lower limit of the free market price of gold should be about $34.83, derived from the United States parity price of $35.00 per fine troy ounce less the Treasury charge of $0.0875 and the shipping costs between New York and London of about $0.08. The upper price limit is determined by the Treasury charge and the shipping costs and is approximately $35.17.

In the long-run the London price of gold is heavily dependent on central bank demand and ultimately on the purchases by the United States Treasury. In the short-run, the price of gold is subject to speculative demands and the flow of new gold from South Africa and other sources. In October 1960, a temporary short-fall of gold production, coupled with heavy speculative demand and aggravated by market uncertainties, culminated in a rise in the price of gold to approximately $40.00 per ounce. The Bank of England, with the support of the United States monetary authorities, intervened in the market on a substantial scale, and brought the price down to more appropriate levels.

In October 1961, United States authorities approached the BIS group of central banks with a proposal to establish a central bank selling arrangement which would share the burdens of intervention to stabilize the London gold market. The United States, the central banks of Belgium, France, Germany, Italy, the Netherlands, Switzerland and the United Kingdom cooperated in this effort. They undertook to supply agreed proportions of such gold sales as the Bank of England, acting as agent for the group, determined to be necessary. The United States share of this gold pool amounted to fifty per cent.

With the stabilization of the gold price, in December 1961, the pool was de-activated. Early in 1962, a gold buying arrangement was made with the same end in view by the same countries. Under this arrangement, the Bank of England acted as agent for the group; each member agreed to assume a certain proportion of the purchases made by this Bank. After the stabilization of the gold price, these arrangements were also de-activated.

The gold pool today consists of two kinds of arrangements: a selling and a buying arrangement, each active or inactive as conditions require. These programs have effectively stabilized the free market price of gold and held it within the customary range. Speculative demand has diminished, more gold has gone into official reserves and confidence in the international payments system has been reinforced by the operations of the gold pool.[37]

Reserve policies March-August, 1964. The period March-August 1964 was characterized by improvements in the balance of payments position of many of the major trading nations and a decline in the volume of international gold transfers. Nevertheless, both bilateral and multilateral credits were again called on to stabilize the exchange markets and to preserve the gold and foreign exchange reserves of the major trading nations. In addition, the gold pool operations maintained the price of gold within reasonable limits.

Official trading on the foreign exchange markets by the Treasury-Federal Reserve and foreign central banks was active in sterling, marks, Swiss francs and Canadian dollars to curtail short-term money flows arising from speculation and interest arbitrage. The Treasury issued $474 million worth of medium-term bonds denominated in foreign currencies and redeemed $200 million of the outstanding issues for a net addition of $274 million. These bonds were issued to obtain additional foreign currencies for exchange market operations and to refund swap arrangements.

The stand-by arrangement with the IMF was renewed for another year and the United States drew a total of $250 million in foreign currencies during January-August 1964. Since the Fund's dollar holdings were too large to permit nations to repay their drawings in this currency, these foreign currency drawings

---

[37] Cf. Charles A. Coombs, "Treasury and Federal Reserve Foreign Exchange Operations and the Gold Pool." *Federal Reserve Bulletin*, Vol. 50, No. 3 (March 1964), pp. 304-307.

were exchanged against dollars held by other countries to facilitate repayments to the IMF.[38]

United States transactions in marks and lira during this period show how the United States now responds to the ebb and flow of payments imbalances and reveal a new aspect of the role of the dollar as an international reserve currency. During the winter months of 1963-64, the German balance of payments showed a large surplus and the Italian, a substantial deficit. This situation brought about a weakening of the lira and a strengthening of the mark against the dollar.

The United States intervened in the exchange markets, with the cooperation of the German and Italian authorities, to stem the rise of the mark and halt the decline of the lira. The Bank of Italy drew dollars from the Federal Reserve and the Federal Reserve drew marks from the Bundesbank under the respective swap arrangements. The subsequent exchange market operations in marks and lira served to dampen disturbing market pressures.

The Italian government also drew marks from the IMF, exchanged them with the United States against dollars and the United States used the marks to liquidate a part of the credits which the Bundesbank had extended under an earlier swap arrangement. Italy's sale of marks to the United States served to reduce its obligation to this country.

The Treasury also repaid $200 million in lira bonds which it had issued to the Bank of Italy in 1962 and sold $200 million equivalent in mark-denominated bonds to the Bundesbank. In effect, the medium-term foreign currency bonds acquired by the Bank of Italy were exchanged for a usable asset by the Bundesbank as Italy's balance of payments shifted into a surplus position. The Bank of Italy sold $200 million in gold to the United States Treasury to replenish its dollar reserve holdings. This gold was immediately sold to the Bundesbank thus recognizing the fact the "Italian deficit and the German surplus

---

[38] Charles A. Coombs, "Treasury and Federal Reserve Foreign Exchange Operations." *Monthly Review* of the Federal Reserve Bank of New York, Vol. 45, No. 9 (September 1963), p. 167.

were, to a considerable extent, opposite sides of the same coin."
This gold transaction illustrates another aspect of the pivotal
role of the United States in the world payments mechanism.[39]

The role of the United States on the foreign exchange markets was both described and predicted by a group of officials of
central banks in 1963 in the following terms:

> Even after the United States has regained equilibrium
> in its payments accounts, certain countries will from time
> to time move into a strong creditor position which will, in
> turn, expose the United States, as banker for the interna-
> tional financial system, to the risk of net drains upon its
> gold stock. We have previously suggested that informal
> understandings should be sought whereby the creditor
> countries might attempt, either through greater flexibility
> in their gold policy or through more extensive use of for-
> ward exchange and related operations, to avoid causing a
> net drain upon the United States gold stock. To round out
> such a system of minimizing net gold losses by the United
> States as a result of pronounced surplus and deficit positions
> in other countries, the United States might also find it
> useful on occasion to provide the creditor country with an
> investment outlet for its surplus in the form of special bonds
> denominated in the creditor's currency.[40]

Concluding observations. The transactions on the foreign
exchange markets which the United States and several European
countries have carried out since 1961 have served to enlarge the
conventional concepts of reserves, reserve management and policies. Although the principal beneficiary has doubtless been the
United States, these arrangements have proved of direct and
indirect value to those nations which participated in them. The
direct benefit has been the stabilization of exchange markets and

---

[39] Further details concerning exchange market operations during this
period are given in Charles A. Coombs, *op. cit.*, pp. 162-172.

[40] C. A. Coombs (Federal Reserve Bank of New York), M. Iklé
(Banque Nationale Suisse), E. Ranali (Banca d'Italia), and J. Tüngeler
(Deutsche Bundesbank), "Conversations on International Finance." *Monthly
Review* of the Federal Reserve Bank of New York, Vol. 45, No. 8 (August
1963), p. 120.

the damping effect which they have exerted on brusque and volatile fluctuations in the rate of exchange. The indirect benefit derives from the greater stability of the international payments system. Nations other than those which have participated in these transactions have also benefitted from these latter results.

These arrangements and transactions have had the signal advantage of protecting the United States monetary gold stock. It is indeed fortunate that they have redounded to the advantage of the United States for, in 1961 when heavy pressures developed against the dollar, this country did not possess any foreign exchange reserves. Its only reserve at that time was its monetary gold stock.

Although some of the devices employed have been used before and may be regarded as traditional, their method of application to recent problems is novel. Transactions on the forward market are traditional with traders and, even if not conventional, they have been widely used in the past by central banks as well. The use of forward exchange in conjunction with reciprocal currency agreements as cover is new as are the agreements themselves. The medium-term Treasury bonds denominated in foreign currencies are also a novelty.

These devices have gained time which is essential to permit the orderly balancing of a nation's international accounts. They are especially well adapted to mitigate the effects of speculation, window dressing, leads and lags, heavy in- and outflows of short-term capital on exchange rates and forward discounts and premiums.

Table 10.4 presents the official reserves and credit facilities of the world as they stood in December 1958 and June 1964. The total amount of these reserves and quasi-reserves amounted to almost $87 billion in June 1964, an increase of almost $20 billion or 29 per cent since December 1958. About three-quarters of the reserves and credit facilities in June 1964 consisted of owned reserves in the traditional form of gold and foreign exchange; one-fourth of the total was represented by other assets and credit facilities. The new reserve facilities have been of growing importance in the international payments system and present indications point to their continued growth in the future.

It seems clear that confidence in the United States economy and in the measures which this country has taken to reduce the balance of payments deficits have been essential ingredients in the mix of exchange market policies which the United States has employed. If the United States deficits persist and if the dollar becomes more redundant, it is doubtful if they will continue to prove adequate. More fundamental measure will then be necessary. These topics are explored in Chapter 11.

TABLE 10.4

OFFICIAL RESERVES AND CREDIT FACILITIES
DECEMBER 1958 AND JUNE 1964
(In millions of dollars)

	December 1958	June 1964	Change 12/58-6/64
Gold	38,030	40,480	+2,450
Foreign exchange	19,340	25,240	+5,900
IMF gold tranche position	2,560	3,890	+1,330
Roosa bonds	0	950	+ 950
Federal Reserve swaps	0	2,050	+2,050
IMF credit tranche position	7,290	14,120	+6,830
Total	67,220	86,730	+19,510

Source: J. Dewey Daane, Member, Board of Governors of the Federal Reserve System, *International Liquidity and All That*. Paper read before the Southern Finance Association, Atlanta, Georgia, November 13, 1964.

11

The Automatic Adjustment of Balance of Payments Disequilibria

The small size of balance of payments deficits and surpluses in relation to the magnitude of the movement of the other accounts is one of the interesting features of this tabulation. This fact suggests that there are either (a) strong relationships among the several accounts themselves, (b) forces set in motion by international commerce which tend to bring the accounts into balance, (c) government intervention has directed the economy along paths which have promoted balance of payments equilibrium or (d) a combination of these factors which has achieved this result. The object of this chapter is to explore some aspects of these four possibilities.

The Automaticity of Economic Forces

Many international economists hold that balance of payments disequilibrium sets forces in motion which tend to restore the balance automatically. Others, with their eyes on practice and less inclined to place faith in economic theories, maintain that these forces no longer operate in the modern world. Strangely enough, there is truth in both of these apparently opposing points of view.

Origins of the theory of automaticity. Ever since the Physiocrats developed their ideas of natural law and order, later economists have been seeking the natural laws which these French economists declared would automatically control economic life without the necessity of government intervention.[1] The Physiocrats represented the revenge of the French agricultural landlords against Mercantilism which, with its ban on the export of grain, had seriously injured French farmers. In combating Mercantilist doctrine, the Physiocrats maintained that agriculture was sufficiently strong to succeed without any special consideration. They held that the government should abolish all regulation of economic life. In this way, they hoped to be rid of the favoritism shown industry and trade and to place agriculture on an equal footing with these sectors.[2]

Since Mercantilism, or the Regulated System, had reigned in France for about one hundred and fifty years at the time of the Physiocrats, the people had never known an unregulated economic order. The Physiocrats, therefore, had to answer this question: how could an economy function, or function satisfactorily without government control? The answer they provided was based on the theory that economic life, like physical life, generated laws which would control the economy in the absence of governmental regulation. Projecting this theory against the background of philosophical naturalism and the discovery of new laws in the natural sciences, their timing was excellent.

An unregulated system controlled by the play of natural economic laws would be far superior, they thought, to a man-made artificial system. All that was needed was to attain such a system was to *laissez-faire, laissez passer*, literally in the language of their day, to allow people to manufacture and trade

---

[1] See especially the work of the Physiocrat, Mercier de la Rivière, *L'Ordre Naturel et Essentiel des Sociétés Politiques.* Edgard Depitre, editor, in the *Collection des Economistes et des Réformateurs Sociaux de la France.* Paris: Librairie Paul Geuthner, 1910. The original edition of this work was published without the name of the author (whose full name was Paul-Pierre le Mercier de la Rivière de Saint-Médard) in London by Jean Nourse, bookseller and in Paris by Desaint, bookseller, in 1767.

[2] Norman J. Ware, "The Physiocrats: A Study in Economic Rationalization." *The American Economic Review,* Vol. XXI, No. 4 (December 1931), pp. 607-619.

freely.[3] The Physiocrats themselves discovered very few economic laws which have survived the test of time.[4]

In this context, it is interesting to note that the theory of the automatic regulation of the economy through the free play of economic forces was invented to use as an argument to combat Mercantilism. In seeking a propaganda weapon to use in destroying the Mercantile system, the Physiocrats hit upon a basic principle which was destined to play an important role in political economy in the future.

The development of economic laws. With the fall of the ministry of Turgot who had tried to employ some Physiocratic principles, and the publication of Adam Smith's *Inquiry into the Nature and Causes of the Wealth of Nations* in 1776, the death knell of the Physiocratic movement was sounded. Adam Smith, who spent some ten months in Paris where he became familiar with the doctrines of the school and with several members of it as well, was a strong partisan of laissez-faire. He fathered few economic principles, and it remained for his successors to discover the laws which govern the operations of economies.

The laws of economics can control both the domestic and the international economies. While they were allowed to operate, they guaranteed a more or less automatically controlled economic system. It appears that many nations now oppose the automatic regulation of the economic system and prefer either a directed or partially-directed economy. Curtailing the free play of economic laws, however, does not necessarily discredit them or prove that they cannot operate.

Automatic adjustment of the international economy. Although the regulation of the economic system by natural laws was probably neither widely known nor accepted before the Psysiocrats, some forces in economic life were held to operate automatically. The Mercantilists thought that a favorable bal-

---

[3] Auguste Oncken, *Die Maxime Laissez-faire, Laissez-passer,* Berne, 1886.

[4] The standard work on the Physiocrats is Georges Weulersse, *Le Mouvement Physiocratique en France de 1756 à 1770.* Paris: Félix Alcan, 1910. A brief but penetrating analysis of the Physiocratic movement is given by Henry Higgs, *The Physiocrats.* London: Macmillan and Co., 1897.

ance of trade would be liquidated by the inflow of specie from deficit countries. They also espoused the ideas, formulated much later by the followers of Lord Keynes, that additions to the monetary stock arising from specie inflows raised the economic level and could serve to increase prices.[5]

It remained for the Scottish philosopher, David Hume, with his price-specie-flow mechanism, to suggest the idea of automatic adjustment of balance of payments disequilibria.[6] Hume's theory, which applied exclusively to specie, was extended to include paper money by David Ricardo.[7] According to a corollary to this theory, balance of trade surpluses are automatically adjusted by the movement of money, exchange rates and prices. This analysis has been extended to include the automatic adjustment of the balance of payments by changes in interest rates and income as well. In addition, a new dimension has been recently added to this body of theory, the concept of feedback or the amount of international receipts which a given payment engenders.

The automatic adjustment operation. In the absence of official intervention and controls, the automatic adjustment of the balance of payments will be operative. The results of this adjustment are not always deemed satisfactory or in accord with government policy. The balance of payments may be in equilibrium at low levels of employment and economic activity. The adjustment process may move too slowly or too quickly. It may generate inflows or outflows of funds where the authorities hold that the opposite movements would be more desirable.

The fact that governments prevent the free movement of exchange and interest rates, prices and income from impinging

---

[5] Perhaps the two best works on the Mercantilists are: Gustav Friederich von Schmoller, *The Mercantile System.* New York: P. Smith, 1931 and Eli Filip Hecksher, *Mercantilism.* New York: Macmillan and Co. (rev. 2nd ed., edited by E. F. Söderland), 1955.

[6] David Hume, "Of the Balance of Trade," in his *Political Discourses* (1752), as quoted in A. E. Monroe, *Early Economic Thought.* Cambridge, Mass.: Harvard University Press, 1924, pp. 325 ff.

[7] David Ricardo, *Principles of Political Economy and Taxation.* E. C. K. Gonner, editor. London: George Bell and Sons, 1891, pp. 117-122.

on the payments balance indicates that government officials believe that these forces operate. Governments, when they intervene in this process, usually tailor their intervention to these principles. Tariffs, import quotas, exchange controls, exchange rate pegging and interest rate adjustments operate with, or on, the forces of adjustment. Were measures taken which did not utilize these principles, the efforts would probably fail to attain their objectives.

Adjustment of Balance of Payments by Movements in Exchange Rates and Prices

The automatic adjustment of balance of payments disequilibria by means of changes in exchange rates and prices are considered together in this section because of their similarity. The movement of exchange rates serves to restore equilibrium through its effect on the prices of imports, exports and investment. Likewise, changes in prices affect the rates of exchange.

Characteristics of the exchange rate adjustment process. The automatic adjustment of the balance of payments by shifts in exchange rates has been a part of the theoretical body of economics ever since the Bullion Controversy raged in England, especially between 1800 and 1815. It formed a part of the purchasing power parity doctrine, believed to have been first formulated by Henry Thornton in 1802.[8]

The manner in which exchange rates restore equilibrium is well known. Stated in its simplest terms, the theory holds that a nation's balance of payments deficit brings about a decrease in its reserve supply and an increase in that of its trading partners. At the same time, the deficit country's demand for the currency of other nations increases and surplus countries' demand for the deficit country's currency declines. Its rate of exchange is thus forced downward by the play of these demand and supply functions on free exchange markets. A balance of payments

---

[8] Henry Thornton, *Inquiry into the Nature and Effects of Paper Credit of Great Britain.* (London: 1802). Philadelphia: Reprinted by James Humphreys for Mathew Carey, 1807.

surplus has the opposite effects and forces the exchange rate upward.

Where a nation's rate of exchange rises in terms of that of others, the prices of its exports increase and those of its imports decrease. Exports fall off, imports rise, and the surplus which brought about the rise in the rate of exchange is reduced. A fall in a country's rate of exchange has the opposite effect and reduces the deficit by checking the volume of exports and increasing that of imports.

The historical past is replete with instances where various countries have taken advantage of the faculty of the exchange rate to stimulate exports, imports and investments or to hold them in check. During the thirties, the world witnessed efforts on the part of many nations to vanquish the Great Depression by establishing rates of exchange which undervalued their currencies to foster exports and reduce imports. During World War II and the years immediately following, when the European belligerents badly needed imports and had little to export, rates which overvalued the currency were the order of the day. The use of multiple exchange rates represents a selective effort to encourage the export and import of some goods and to discourage that of others.

Exchange supply and demand functions. The supply of any nation's foreign exchange is a function of its demand for that of its trading partners. Where an American resident purchases silk textiles from a mill in Lyons, France, he has a demand for francs. To pay for the transaction, he exchanges dollars for the required francs. The French supply of dollars is thus increased in proportion to the American's demand for francs.

The demand for any country's currency is in part a derived and in part a direct demand. The residents of any country demand the currency of others because they desire their goods, services and investments. This part of their demand is derived from that for the goods, services and investments in question. Another segment of the demand for foreign exchange stems from speculators who desire the currency itself to use in their opera-

tions rather than for the purchase of other things. This demand
is direct. The supply of any currency is a composite supply. The
United States supply of sterling, for example, is derived from
the British industries which use sterling to make payment for
imports of United States goods, services and capital. It is a
composite of the supply, provided by many different industries
and services in exchange for foreign currencies to pay for imports.

The supply of any country's currency is derived in part from
credit. Banks sell foreign exchange which they do not possess
by borrowing it from abroad. As noted in the previous chapter,
the Treasury-Federal Reserve carries out many of its exchange
market operations on the basis of credit extended by swaps or
Roosa bonds.

Foreign exchange demand and supply elasticities. The foreign exchange demand and supply functions are price elastic
or inelastic in varying degrees. The demand price elasticity is
derived from that of the goods for which the exchange is
required. The supply price elasticity is derived from that of the
supply conditions, including cost, of the goods purchased with
the exchange. Throughout this chapter, the term elasticity refers
to price, rather than income, elasticity.

Where a nation produces few goods and services, it is relatively easy to determine the elasticity of the demand for its
foreign exchange. If it produces a wide variety of goods and
services, the determination of the demand elasticity becomes
virtually impossible.

The elasticities of demand and supply for foreign exchange
are of importance in determining whether a freely floating or
flexible rate will move within a narrow range or be subject to
wide variations. Where the demand and supply elasticities are
high, the rate tends to move within narrow limits; where they
are relatively inelastic, the range of variations may be large.

The ability of the rate of exchange to correct a balance
of payments disequilibrium is in part dependent upon demand
and supply elasticities. For changes in a nation's exchange rate
to be effective in restoring payments balance, the value of its

imports must decline more than that of its exports. Where its demand for imports is inelastic, a drop in the rate of exchange may reduce the quantity imported only slightly. This slight decrease may be offset by the higher prices of the imports resulting from the lower rate of exchange. If foreign demand for its exports is also inelastic, the country's total receipts may drop, because the volume demanded increases but slightly when prices decline. Where such perverse elasticities prevail for a deficit country's exports and imports, balance of payments equilibrium might be more easily restored were the rate of exchange to rise.

Stable and unstable rates of exchange. The problem of the ability of flexible exchange rates to restore balance of payments equilibrium may be approached by examination of their stability or instability. *Stable rates of exchange usually serve to correct deficits and surpluses; unstable rates may operate to aggravate the problem.* An exchange market situation where unstable exchange rates prevail is shown on Figure XI.1. Table 11.1 illustrates a similar situation but utilizes other magnitudes than those presented on Figure XI.1.

Table 11.1 shows that as the German mark increases in value in terms of dollars from six to two marks per dollar, and that of the dollar declines in terms of marks from $.167 to $.500, the quantity of dollars demanded increases while the supply of marks declines. Such a situation can give rise to a backward

TABLE 11.1

GERMAN DEMAND FOR UNITED STATES DOLLARS

Exchange rate in marks per dollar	Quantity of dollars demanded	Quantity of marks supplied	Exchange rate in dollars per mark
6	900	5,400	$.167
5	950	4,750	.200
4	1,000	4,000	.250
3	1,050	3,150	.333
2	1,100	2.200	.500

sloping supply curve for marks similar to that shown on Figure
XI.1. This curve declines from left to right and intersects the
demand curve from below to the right. The usual or normal
currency supply curve moves upward from left to right and

FIGURE XI.1

BACKWARD-SLOPING FOREIGN EXCHANGE FUNCTION

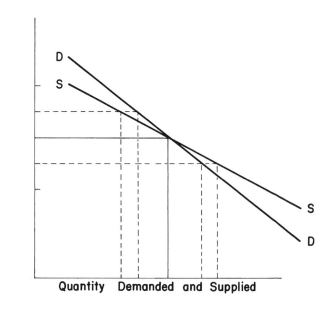

Exchange Rate of German Marks in Terms of Dollars

Quantity Demanded and Supplied

intersects the demand from above and to the left and is illustrated on Figure XI.2.

Such situations represented result in unstable exchange rates. As the price of marks increases in terms of dollars, the quantity

FIGURE XI.2

FOREIGN EXCHANGE DEMAND AND SUPPLY

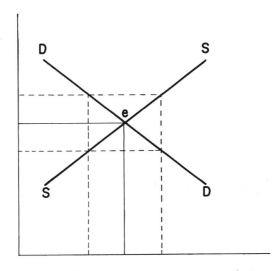

Exchange
Rate of
German
Marks in
Marks per
Dollar

Quantity   Demanded   and   Supplied

of marks supplied declines and the demand for dollars increases. Normally, the quantity of foreign exchange demanded would decline with an increase in price and that supplied would increase as shown on Figure XI.2. In the case illustrated on Figure XI.1, if the mark rate in terms of dollars were to fall below the equilibrium rate, the amount of mark exchange demanded would exceed the amount supplied. The rate of exchange would continue to fall and equilibrium would not be established. Were the mark rate to rise above the equilibrium rate, the amount of marks supplied would exceed the amount demanded and the rate would continue to rise. This is an unstable situation where changes in the rate of exchange could not establish balance of payments equilibrium. Such a situation is found where the supply curve slopes backward and the demand for exchange is inelastic.[9]

Effects of the forward and Euro-Dollar Markets. The theory of the automatic adjustment of balance of payments equilibria via the rate of exchange was elaborated about a century and a half before the Euro-Dollar Market was established and before the forward market assumed the importance which it has today. The operations of these two institutions do not necessarily invalidate the theory, but they do suggest that they should be taken into account when defining it.

The effects of changes in the forward rates may be reflected on the balance of payments. Large forward premiums on foreign currencies are often added and discounts subtracted from the prices which importers quote their domestic purchasers. They serve to discourage or encourage imports. The premiums arise usually in times of balance of payments surplus; the discounts in periods of deficit. In this way the movement of forward exchange exerts a stabilizing effect on the balance of payments.[10] Thus the forward rate participates in the automatic adjustment

---

[9] Max J. Wasserman, Charles W. Hultman and Laszlo Zsoldos, *International Finance*. New York: Simmons-Boardman Publishing Corporation, 1963, pp. 224-227.

[10] Paul Einzig, *A Dynamic Theory of Forward Exchange*. London: Macmillan and Co., Ltd., 1961, pp. 217-218.

of balance of payments disequilibria.[11] In this respect, it has similar effects on the balance of payments as the spot rate and should be incorporated in the theory. This topic is further explored in a subsequent section of this chapter.

Although transactions on the Euro-Dollar Market are carried out at the prevailing rates of exchange, forward and spot, the Market offers an alternative to the more conventional forms of foreign trade financing. This institution affects the dollar and other exchange rates in a variety of ways. It provides a large available supply of dollars and other currencies for forward cover on spot transactions. The Market serves to increase or decrease the amount of foreign exchange available. The rates of interest prevailing in the Market for borrowed funds are frequently attractive so that borrowers have recourse to it in preference to their national markets. Loans which cannot readily be financed at home are often accommodated in it.

Where exchange market dollars are transferred into Euro-Dollars, the supply of the former is reduced and upward pressure is exerted on the dollar rate. The Euro-Dollar Market may bring downward pressure on the dollar rate when the dollar facilities of this market are used to finance transactions instead of those available on the conventional exchange market. The higher interest yield of this market than on United States deposits tends to induce Euro-Dollar holders to retain them, thereby reducing the sales outlets for dollars.[12]

The large supply of Euro-dollars available is a potential source of selling pressure against the dollar rate of exchange. This pressure is multiplied because of the substantial amount of dollar borrowing and re-lending transactions which a given

[11] In addition to recognizing the stabilizing influence which movements in both the spot and forward rates exercise on balance of payments, Paul Einzig notes that these movements may have destabilizing effects as well. The destabilizing effect stems from the shifting relations between exchange rates and prices. The relationship is not solely unilateral with prices affecting exchange rates, but bilateral with exchange rates reacting on prices as well. See: Paul Einzig, *op. cit.*, pp. 205-213, 223-224.

[12] Cf. Paul Einzig, *The Euro-Dollar System: Practice and Theory of International Interest Rates.* New York: St. Martin's Press, Inc., 1964, pp. 87-88.

dollar deposit sustains. Each borrower can, temporarily at least, sell the dollars which he has borrowed. Since the Euro-dollars do not constitute a subtraction from the dollars available from American banks, but an addition to them, they tend to exert an unfavorable influence on the dollar rate of exchange.

In addition, the Euro-Dollar Market has a tendency to divert pressure from the forward to the spot rates in the case of speculative trading against the dollar. The dollar rate of exchange is also affected by the interest rates prevailing on the Euro-Dollar Market. Where these rates are higher than those in the United States, they tend to provoke investment funds outflows and have a depressing effect on the dollar rate of exchange. Where they are lower, the opposite effects are noted.[13]

This market complicates the role of the rate of exchange as an automatic restorer of balance of payments equilibrium, by affording an additional means of financing foreign trade and a supplementary source of demand and supply for currency, especially dollars. On balance, as Einzig has pointed out, the market probably reinforces the balancing role of the rate in times of normal exchange market activity, but exerts a destabilizing role in periods of speculative activity.[14] The relationships of this market to rates of exchange, and to the balancing role of the rate, needs to be further explored and the theory of the automatic adjustment of balance of payments imbalance may need to be modified as a result of these findings.

Rationale of fixed exchange rates. The adverse effects of certain types of demand and supply elasticities and the nature of some foreign exchange supply curves are among the reasons which have led nations to prefer fixed exchange rates to flexible ones. Exchange rates are closely linked to domestic price levels and movements. Where a government seeks to prevent inflationary rises or deflationary declines in prices, the rate of exchange should also be controlled. If it is not, one factor will be free and the problem of control thereby aggravated. The use of over- or undervalued rates of exchange is, of course, impossible with

---

[13] Paul Einzig, *op. cit.*, pp. 88-93.
[14] Paul Einzig, *op. cit.*, p. 94.

flexible rates. While such rates run counter to the IMF Agreement and most industrialized nations frown on their use, some countries may be tempted to use them in time of emergency or crisis.[15]

The preference for fixed rates must be indeed a strong one, for the price for their use is high. Fixed rates involve the use of reserves and the defense of the rate of exchange with all the difficulties associated with these measures. The use of fixed exchange rates does not, of course, prove that balance of payments disequilibrium cannot be restored by movements of flexible rates of exchange. It merely establishes the fact that, at present, most governments prefer not to rely upon this form of the automatic adjustment mechanism.[16]

Characteristics of adjustment by price changes. In its simplest terms, the theory of the automatic adjustment of balance of payments via prices holds that, during periods of balance of payments deficit, money flows out of circulation and bank reserves, thereby reducing the volume of money and credit in circulation. If there is no counterbalancing effect on employment, resource utilization and output, prices are likely to decline. Balance of payments surpluses, by increasing the volume of money and credit in circulation, tend to have the opposite effect. This mechanism rests upon the quantity theory of money.

As far as the movement of banking reserves is concerned, money flows can only affect prices where the domestic banking reserves include substantial proportions of foreign currency. The marriage of foreign and domestic reserves in the banking system is the prevalent practice in most countries. Some nations, like the United Kingdom, separate foreign from domestic re-

---

[15] Some economists favor the use of flexible exchange rates. In the extensive literature in support of these rates see especially, Milton Friedman, "The Case for Flexible Exchange Rates," *Essays in Positive Economics.* Chicago: The University of Chicago Press, 1953, pp. 157-203.

[16] For a penetrating analysis of the relative merits of fixed and flexible exchange rates see, especially: George N. Halm, "Fixed or Flexible Exchange Rates?" *Factors Affecting the United States Balance of Payments.* Compilation of Studies Prepared for the Subcommittee on International Exchange and Payments of the Joint Economic Committee, 87th Congress, 2nd Session, Joint Committee Print. Washington: U. S. Government Printing Office, 1962, pp. 255-285.

serves. The Bank of England maintains domestic reserves for the Issue Department and the foreign reserves of the United Kingdom are held in a separate Exchange Equalization Account. In such cases, the flow of foreign exchange will not necessarily serve to affect prices automatically. The Federal Reserve System divorces domestic from foreign reserves, for the System holds neither metallic gold nor foreign exchange as reserve against its demand obligations. India, which has joined domestic and foreign currency in its banking reserves, is now moving to separate the two.

One of the more noteworthy examples of the operation of price movements, and their limitations, in effectuating balance of payments equilibrium was that of the West African Currency Board. This Board issued West African pound notes for what were formerly Nigeria, the Gold Coast, Gambia and Sierra Leone. The West African Currency Board kept all of its reserves in sterling securities. Thus, the reserves of the West African pound were composed entirely of foreign exchange (sterling); and the amount of notes issued tended to be a function of the combined balance of payments surpluses and deficits of the member countries of the system.

However, the amount of money in circulation in these countries did not vary precisely with their balance of payments surpluses and deficits. Apparently, there was a minimum below which the monetary stock did not decline. The operations of the Marketing Boards in stabilizing the prices of the principal commodities of the area often countered the effects of change in reserves. The movements of the population in and out of the tribal economies in periods of prosperity and depression also tended to check the effects of foreign exchange flows.[17] Thus in a near-perfect example of the price-specie-flow-mechanism in its mod-

---

[17] See Andreas Prindl, *The West African Currency Board: An Analysis of a Colonial Monetary System.* Lexington, Kentucky: unpublished dissertation for the doctorate in international economics, University of Kentucky, June 1964. The West African Currency Board, founded in 1912, is now practically defunct and its remaining affairs are administered by a single official at the Bank of England.

ern paper money form, the West African system did not operate exactly according to model.[18]

The price effects of balance of payments disequilibria have another aspect. Some analysts hold that where a country is importing more goods than it is exporting, the domestic stock of goods tends to increase. Unless a corresponding change takes place in the money and credit in circulation, a drop in prices may follow. This will discourage imports and encourage exports and reduce the balance of payments deficit. A surplus, due to an excess of exports over imports, is corrected by the movement of goods and prices in the opposite directions. This aspect of the theory has but limited application. It can only be used in the case of those countries which continue to produce regardless of price and market situations. Highly industrialized nations customarily tailor their industrial output to prices and markets.

Exchange rates, prices and disequilibrium. The automatic adjustment of balance of payments imbalances is fostered by the movements in *both* the rate of exchange and prices; the two factors tend to reinforce each other in attaining this result. The sequence of causality generally postulated for these two related theories is that which prevails in the purchasing power parity doctrine. This theory holds that prices rise or fall first and then the rate of exchange falls or rises, thus counteracting the price change and bringing prices into line internationally.[19] The French economist, Albert Aftalion, in an empirical study of leads and lags between prices and exchange rates

---

[18] Perhaps another qualification should be made to the equilibrating role of prices. If balance of payments equilibria were restored by the movement of prices, there would be a tendency toward an international level of prices. As a matter of fact, the purchasing power parity theory in its absolute form affirms that there is such a tendency. James W. Angell has pointed out, however, that the tendency toward the international equalization of prices is limited to those homogenous goods which are traded internationally and that all prices are not equalized in this manner. See James W. Angell, *The Theory of International Prices.* Cambridge, Mass.: Harvard University Press, 1926.

[19] Probably the best known exposition of the purchasing power parity theory is that presented by Gustav Cassel, *Money and Foreign Exchange After 1914.* New York: The Macmillan Co., 1922.

in Europe, discovered that during World War I and until 1921 this sequence was followed. However, between 1921 and 1924, the chain of causality was reversed; the fall in European exchange rates preceded the rise in prices by a period of several months.

These findings led Aftalion to reject the purchasing power parity theory as invalid and to elaborate a psychological theory in its place. According to the purchasing power parity theory, the rise in prices led directly to a decline in rates of exchange. According to Aftalion, the rise in prices was preceded by monetary inflation. This inflation was a continuing process; future increases in money were anticipated and discounted in advance by traders on the foreign exchange markets. The causality started with falling exchange rates which, in their turn, provoked a rise in prices. Thus, rates of exchange, far from always moving up or down in response to price changes, were in themselves a frequent cause of price changes.[20] Under Aftalion's thesis, the rate of exchange is not necessarily an equilibrating force; but one which could make for disequilibrium in price relationships.

The fact that the rate of exchange does not always serve to equalize prices between any two nations was brought out in a comparison of French and United States wholesale prices and the movement of the dollar-franc rate of exchange, 1919-1926. The findings of this study indicate that the rate of exchange did not fall far enough during the French inflation of that period to equalize French and American prices. It showed, further, that as inflation progressed, the decline of the franc vis à vis the dollar was increasingly less proportionate to the rise in French prices.[21]

Such findings do not necessarily disprove the theory of the automatic adjustment of balance of payments imbalances by

---

[20] Albert Aftalion, *Monnaie, Prix et Change*. Paris: Receuil Sirey, 1927, pp. 9-96, 250-349. Paul Einzig also calls attention to the reciprocal effect of changes in prices on exchange rates and movements in exchange rates on prices. See his *A Dynamic Theory of Forward Exchange*. London: Macmillan and Co., Ltd., 1961, pp. 211-212.

[21] Max J. Wasserman, "The Compression of French Wholesale Prices During Inflation, 1919-1926." *The American Economic Review*. Vol. XXVI, No. 1 (March 1936), pp. 62-73.

movements in exchange rates and prices. They do, however, indicate that it may be more of a general tendency than a rigorous theory applicable at all times and places.

Exchange rates, prices and the forward and Euro-Dollar Markets. Probably the most widely accepted theory of forward exchange is that formulated by Lord Keynes. It is known as the interest parities (or parity) theory. This theory stresses the varying rates of interest obtainable on short-term capital in various countries and affirms that the forward rate is determined by the differences in interest rates in any two countries. The interest differential is generally expressed as a percentage per annum. The theory holds that the actual forward rate fluctuates around this basic differential in accordance with the supply and demand for forward exchange. Interest parities may be said to condition the equilibrium level of the forward rate.[22]

The interest parities theory of forward exchange has been found unsatisfactory by some students who have substituted a form of the purchasing power parity theory to explain the determination of this rate. They hold that where the inflow and outflow of reserves is divorced from the banking system, as in the case with the British Exchange Equilization Account, the purchasing power parity theory can not be applied to the spot rate; the forward rate then reflects the purchasing power parity of the pound. The weakness of this theory lies in the fact that it fails to explain precisely how the forward rate follows purchasing power parity when the spot rate does not.

Another application of the purchasing power parity theory to forward rates has been made in the case of over-and undervalued exchange rates. Where a fixed spot rate of exchange is over- or undervalued, it is not established at its purchasing power parity. In this case, the purchasing power parity of the currency

---

[22] A concise history of forward exchange theories is given in Paul Einzig, *A Dynamic Theory of Forward Exchange.* London: Macmillan and Co., Ltd., 1961, pp. 132-143. An exposition of the interest parities theory is presented by Einzig in *op. cit.*, 143-205. One of the many difficulties associated with the interest parities theory stems from the fact that there are not one, but many different interest rates which may operate to determine the parities. See Einzig, *op. cit.*, pp. 148-161.

is expressed by the forward rate. The differential between the spot and the forward rates measures the amount of over- or undervaluation.[23] The interest parities and the purchasing power parity theories of forward exchange are sometimes combined into a single theory. The spot rates are held to be determined by the purchasing power parity of the currency; the forward rate by the interest parities theory. Under this approach, the forward rate is a purchasing power rate modified by interest differentials.

Einzig divided the effects of forward exchange into two broad groups: the direct and the indirect. The direct effect of a forward discount is similar to that of a drop in the spot rate. If spot French francs stand at $.2025 (4.938 francs per dollar) while the ninety-day forward franc is at $.1825 (5.479 francs per dollar), the forward franc is at a discount and the forward dollar at a premium, of two cents (compared with spot). French importers, unwilling to take a speculative risk and buying dollars forward to cover their import payment obligations to the United States, pay more for forward dollars, thereby increasing the cost of their imported goods.

The price of the forward dollar is the cost of this currency to French importers who desire to avoid taking a speculative position in this currency. Of course, those who do not cover could acquire spot dollars and reduce the cost of their imports. If these importers were able to pay for their American imports in francs, the United States exporters would then cover their future franc receipts by the sale of francs forward and would add the discount on the francs which they would receive to their export selling prices.

Under a discount on the forward franc, American importers of French goods would pay less for them. They would use the low franc forward rate instead of the higher spot in computing the net cost of the imported French merchandise. Where the French forward franc is at a premium, the cost of French imports

---

[23] Einzig apparently rejects both the interest parities and the purchasing power parity theories as complete explanations of forward rates and substitutes a dynamic theory in their place. See his *op. cit.*, especially pp. 275-283.

of American goods would be less and that of American imports of French goods would be higher.[24]

These direct effects of forward discounts and premiums could be countered by their indirect effects. A discount on a nation's currency causes interest rates to rise by stimulating the activity of rival markets for funds—the foreign markets. These foreign markets draw capital from the domestic market in the countries whose forward exchange is discounted, thus curtailing the amount of credit available to industry.[25]

The effect of the increase in interest rates and the curtailment of credit tend to exert downward pressures on prices. Forward premiums have the opposite effects on interest rates and prices to those occasioned by discounts. Forward discounts and premiums thus tend to reinforce or counter decreases and increases in the spot rates, as the case may be, and to dampen or increase the effects of changes in spot on interest rates and prices.[26]

Although the Euro-Dollar Market has a profound influence on both the spot and forward exchange markets, it is difficult to generalize these effects. This market both adds funds to, and draws funds from, the conventional exchange markets. In addition, it provides an alternative to these conventional markets by providing another method of financing international transactions.

The effects of this market on exchange rates depends largely upon the source of the Euro-Dollars. The existence of the Euro-Dollar Market exerts a fairly steady downward pressure on the dollar rate of exchange, but not necessarily on those of other countries. On the other hand, speculation against the dollar may be diverted from the exchange to the Euro-Dollar Market, thus easing the pressure on the dollar rate of exchange.

On balance, Einzig is apparently of the opinion that it is difficult to state definitely whether or not the Euro-Dollar Market makes for more or less stable exchange rates. Under normal exchange market conditions, he feels that this market exerts a stabil-

---

[24] Paul Einzig, *op. cit.*, pp. 212-213.
[25] Paul Einzig, *op. cit.*, pp. 187-204.
[26] Paul Einzig, *op. cit.*, p. 213.

izing effect; under abnormal conditions, a destabilizing effect.[27] Until more information on this market is available and more analytical conclusions have been drawn, its precise effects on the automatic adjustment of the balance of payments by means of exchange rates should be deferred. As matters now stand, the impact of the Euro-Dollar Market on this theory is doubtless more pronounced in the case of the dollar than in that of other currencies.

Most modern industrial nations have partially directed economies in which the regulation of price movements represents the keystone of economic policy. The stability of the domestic economy is heavily dependent upon steady price levels. Balance of payments equilibrium can not always be maintained where prices vary according to free market forces. Changes in the monetary stock, arising from the increase or decrease in reserves, are no longer always permitted free play in affecting the volume of circulating media. A wide variety of methods is used to control credit including the regulation of interest rates, reserve requirements, quantitative and qualitative controls.

There is little doubt but that balance of payments equilibrium tends to be restored by price movements in the manner indicated by the theory. However, this tendency is held in check by government countermeasures. It would be erroneous to conclude from this fact alone that the theory is invalid.

Adjustment by Changes in Interest Rates and Income

Although the movements of interest rates and income are related, they are not as closely associated as exchange rates and prices in the balance of payments equilibrating process. They are grouped together in this section principally as a matter of organization.

Characteristics of adjustment by interest rate changes. Changes in the rate of interest affect balance of payments sur-

---

[27] Paul Einzig, *The Euro-Dollar System: Practice and Theory of International Interest Rates.* New York: St. Martin's Press, 1964, pp. 87-94.

pluses and deficits principally, but not exclusively, through their impact on the movements of the capital and income accounts. Changes in these rates generally exert a weaker influence on balance of payments maladjustment than movements of prices or exchange rates, which affect other international transactions importantly as well as capital and income.

The theory of the automatic adjustment of balance of payments equilibria via movements in the rates of interest holds that balance of payments deficits are reduced by increases in these rates and surpluses by declines. A deficit is followed by an outflow of capital, thereby reducing the volume of bank reserves and loanable funds. Unless there is a corresponding change in the demand for loans, the rate of interest will tend to rise.

This increase in interest rates will make the capital market more attractive to funds abroad seeking investment outlets and will be followed by an inflow of capital. This inflow, by increasing a nation's international receipts, serves to reduce the deficit and restore equilibrium. A balance of payments surplus means that funds are entering the country: increasing the supply of bank reserves and loanable money; depressing the rates of interest and promoting in turn an outflow of funds with a resultant reduction in the surplus. In addition, a deficit in any country is likely to be matched by surpluses in others where interest rates will face downward pressures. There will, therefore, be a tendency for capital from surplus nations to move to deficit countries in response to higher interest rates.

This bald statement of the theory ignores many important details and exceptions. Among the exceptions to the theory the following may be noted: (a) the currency which flows in and out of a country as a result of surpluses and deficits does not always affect the supply of loanable funds; (b) demand for funds may rise with increases in the supply of capital and fall when the supply drops; (c) there is not a single rate of interest in any country, but several; (d) demand and supply are not the only factors acting on the rate of interest, there are many others; (e) the in- and outflow of currency has other impacts than those on the supply of capital, such as those on production, income and prices; and these may counter or increase the balancing effects of interest rates.

Nevertheless, this theory does emphasize the role of the rate of interest in the establishment of equilibrium in the balance of payments. This aspect has long been recognized by governments and central banks which have frequently used their control over interest rates to assist in restoring balance of payments equilibria. Control of the bank rate has been the standard device which the Bank of England has employed ever since the full gold standard days, to control gold flows and reduce balance of payments surpluses and deficits. The success of Britain's policy, and similar policies employed by other nations, is a good index of the validity of this theory.

Interest rates and the forward markets. The part which interest rates play in balance of payments adjustment assumes that capital flows from low to high interest rate countries. In this international flow of capital, the investor may run the speculative risk of changes in rates of exchange. If an American makes a short-term investment in French notes or bills, he takes a chance that the franc exchange rate will not decline in terms of dollars. If it does decline, the interest earned may be reduced, wiped out, or a net loss on the transaction may be sustained.

The forward markets offer a hedge against such possibilities and serve to mitigate this speculative risk. In addition, where the foreign currency involved in an international investment transaction is at a forward discount, the actual interest earnings are increased if the transaction is covered. Where the foreign currency is at a forward premium, the interest earned is reduced if the exchange risk is hedged. Thus the forward market may either reduce, increase or maintain level the profits arising from foreign interest differentials. Foreign currency discounts serve to encourage the migration of capital while premiums discourage it. On balance, the development of the forward markets has probably increased the international mobility of capital by rendering foreign markets more attractive to those who fear speculative exchange risks. They have not operated to prevent those who are inclined to take this risk from making foreign investments.[28]

The forward markets are of importance from yet another point of view. Rates of interest and the capital markets in almost all countries are now subject to government or central bank regulation. These markets offer a partial escape from such regulations by reducing the exchange risk when investing in alternative markets abroad, thereby making international investments more attractive. By helping to free capital movements from the grip of national controls and eliminating the speculative risk inherent in these transactions, the forward markets facilitate the automatic adjustment of balance of payments disequilibria via the movements of interest rates and thus tend to reinforce the applicability of this theory. They also serve to foster the integration of the capital markets of the world, the international leveling of interest rates, the spread over wider areas of the supply and demand for capital. Local conditions affecting interest rates such as national regulations, differences in the marginal efficiency of capital, variations in the loan risk element and other factors will doubtless persist for a long time to come, however. On the other hand, should national capital markets ever integrate, interest rate differentials may cease to play their role in balance of payments adjustment. Insofar as the forward markets promote this integration, they operate, ever so little, to mitigate the role of interest rates in the restoration of balance of payments equilibria.[29]

The Euro-Dollar Capital Market. In contrast with the *na-*

---

[28] The doctrine of comparative advantage rests, in part, upon the immobility of the factors of production. The greater international mobility of capital fostered by the forward markets and the Euro-Dollar Market serves to attenuate slightly the basic postulate upon which the theory rests. The increased mobility of labor and business establishment promoted by the Common Market further slightly weakens the validity of the theory. The continued growth of institutions such as these will render the theory less and less generally valid.

[29] The effects of the forward markets on interest rates, capital markets and balance of payments are far more complicated than those indicated in the highly simplified account presented here. Einzig has described and analyzed these effects in considerable detail in *A Dynamic Theory of Forward Exchange,* especially pp. 123-293.

tional capital markets, the Euro-Dollar Market is an *international* capital market.[30] Indeed, the desire to escape national controls, customs, economic and political conditions were among the several causes underlying the formation of this institution.[31] The Euro-Dollar Market is not a subsidiary market; it is a capital market in its own right. In addition, it is also a foreign exchange market.

The interest rate structure of this institution resembles that found on national capital markets. In other words, it has not one, but many somewhat interdependent interest rates. The rates vary according to the type of transaction, risk, credit-worthiness of the borrower, time, competitive market conditions, among others.

The rates in this Market are not stationary, but vary over time. Some, but not all, of the rates are lower than those found on the national capital markets. The interest on time deposits in the United States, however, has been lower than those prevailing in the foreign banks operating in it. The low rates for certain types of loans and its relative freedom from regulation, largely account for the Market's success and rapid growth. The rates, for certain types of loans, are even lower than some of those found in the United States. As a matter of fact, many American banks through their branches overseas, as well as American firms and their foreign subsidiaries, borrow on this market.[32]

The lower rates which prevail on it are explained, in part, by the fact that the banks which operate on it are apparently satisfied with a smaller margin of profit. Since the transactions are usually very large, these small margins yield a substantial total profit.[33] This market operates largely outside national banking and foreign exchange regulations which likewise fosters a low interest rate structure.

---

[30] Cf. Paul Einzig, *The Euro-Dollar System: Practice and Theory of International Interest Rates.* New York: St. Martin's Press, Inc., 1964, pp. 75-86 and Norris O. Johnson, *Eurodollars in the New International Money Market.* New York: National City Bank, (no date), pp. 12-21.

[31] Norris O. Johnson, *op. cit.,* pp. 5-7, 17-21.

[32] Paul Einzig, *op. cit.,* pp. 39-41.

[33] Norris O. Johnson, *op. cit.,* p. 5, states that a transaction of between $500 million and one billion is regarded as an odd lot.

The Euro-Dollar Market is essentially a short-term credit institution handling loans of a maturity of one year or less. Recently, some intermediate loans of two to three years maturity have been negotiated on it and the institution shows some signs of becoming a market for intermediate as well as short-term credit. Thus far, it has not handled long-term capital requirements in the form of bond flotations with maturities of from ten to thirty years. In the opinion of some students, this is one of its principal shortcomings.[34]

In respect to the relationship between short-, intermediate- and long-term capital requirements, the Euro-Dollar Market follows the practices prevalent on many European capital markets. Short-term loans are frequently renewed time and time again so that they are often *de facto* intermediate- or long-term obligations. The many restrictions on long-term capital found in Europe account, in part, for the development of this practice.[35]

Interest rate adjustment and the Euro-Dollar Market. The automatic adjustment of balance of payments disequilibria via interest rates is today somewhat complicated by the growth of the Euro-Dollar Market. It has now attained substantial size; the Bank for International Settlement estimates its net deposits at $5 billion and its foreign exchange at $2 billion for a total of $7 billion in 1964. This represents a gain of $4 billion in six years.[36] The supply of dollars on this market stems in large part from United States balance of payments deficits since 1950. Additional funds from the capital markets of Europe, Canada and Japan have also served to spur its growth.

---

[34] Cf. Norris O. Johnson, *op. cit.*, pp. 17-21.

[35] See Norris O. Johnson, *op. cit.*, pp. 18-21. The exceedingly brief discussion of the Euro-Dollar Market presented in this chapter cannot begin to do justice to either the nature or the significance of this new institution. Paul Einzig in *op. cit.*, presents a detailed description and analysis of the operations of this market. Norris O. Johnson's work embodies a less detailed analysis of the institution but presents clearly its significance.

[36] Thirty-fourth *Annual Report* of the BIS. These figures are also used by Norris O. Johnson, *op. cit.*, p. 8 and by Gilbert Mathieu, "Les 'Euro-Dollars' et les 'Euro-Devises' Représent Actuellement plus de $30 Milliards de Francs." *Le Monde* (a weekly periodical published in Paris), Vol. 17, No. 835 (October 15-October 21, 1964), p. 9.

The existence of this institution adds another dimension to the problem of balance of payments adjustment. Figure XI.3 shows the flow of capital between countries A, B and C. Capital flows between these countries from those with the lower to those with the higher rates of interest. The forces acting on this flow are double in nature. The surplus country "pushes" capital out by its relatively low rates of interest while the deficit country "pulls" it in by reason of its higher rates.

FIGURE XI.3

INTERNATIONAL CAPITAL FLOWS WITHOUT EURO-DOLLAR MARKET

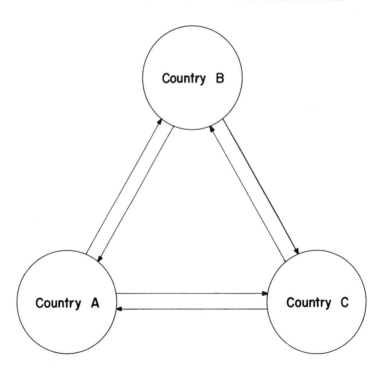

Figure XI.4 illustrates the capital flow between these countries and among them and the Euro-Dollar Market. It would be theoretically possible to regard this market as just another "country" thus adding but a single new area to the international capital flow. There is one difficulty, however, with this point of view. Although it may be a capital market, it is not an economy. It deals with financial flows but not capital embodied in goods as a factor of production.

FIGURE XI.4

INTERNATIONAL CAPITAL FLOWS WITH EURO-DOLLAR MARKET

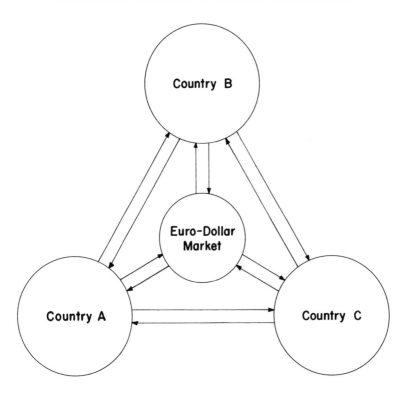

The essential point of the matter is that it presents an ever-present alternative to capital markets in other countries where certain types, but not all, of loans can be accommodated. In spite of the fact that it is perhaps the freest (from regulations and restrictions) in the world, it is not open to everyone. Small transactions are not welcomed and the use of its facilities by either borrower or lender is limited to those who know it, understand it, and who have the appropriate financial connections. It is a limited and specialized market which has not replaced the more conventional national capital markets.

It would thus appear that the Euro-Dollar Market does not substantially impede the capital flows between national capital markets which form an essential part of the theory of the adjustment of balance of payments disequilibrium via interest rates. The institution does not invalidate this theory, although it may attenuate its action somewhat and limit its field of applicability. Apparently some types of capital flow back and forth from national capital markets to the Euro-Dollar Market for a wide variety of reasons of which interest rate differentials are but one. Since some interest rates are habitually lower on this market than on others; differentials, although they may accelerate or decelerate flows, may be of less importance than other factors. ·

Although many reasons account for the formation of the Euro-Dollar Market, one of the more important, in addition to low interest rates, is found in the unsatisfactory character of many European markets. They apparently are not particularly well adapted to foster substantial rates of economic growth and do not meet the growing demands of European businessmen. The success of the Euro-Dollar Market is attributed in part to the fact that it has contributed toward meeting business requirements.[37]

---

[37] The Treasury Department made an excellent survey of European capital markets for the Joint Economic Committee, especially those in Belgium, France, Germany, Italy, Sweden, the United Kingdom and Switzerland. See: Materials Prepared for the Joint Economic Committee, Congress of the United States, 88th Congress, 2d Session, Joint Committee Print. *Economic Policies and Practices: A Description and Analysis of Certain European Capital Markets* (paper No. 3). Washington: U. S. Government Printing Office, 1964.

Limitations on the role of interest rates. The heavy foreign borrowing by means of bond issues, notes and loans on the United States market bears witness to the fact that European capital markets do not meet the needs of expanding business on that continent. About one-half of all foreign long-term bonds sold publicly in major countries, 1961-1963, were floated in the United States.[38] Lower interest rates prevailing in this country were but one reason underlying recourse to this market. In some cases higher rates of interest were paid by the foreign borrowers in the United States than those quoted (but not always in effect) in their own country. The rates paid by these foreign borrowers in the United States were also frequently substantially higher than those paid by American borrowers.[39]

Lower interest rates are but one of several factors which prompted foreigners to borrow on the United States markets. Among the others, lower underwriting costs, availability of funds, the general acceptability of the dollar and accessibility may also be cited.[40] The growing recourse to the United States long-term capital market by foreigners doubtless prompted the Kennedy administration to seek an interest equalization tax in an effort to reduce the balance of payments deficits.[41]

The rate of interest is only one of several factors which determine the international flow of capital in response to balance

---

[38] "Foreign Long-Term Borrowing in the United States." *Business Conditions,* a Review by the Federal Reserve Bank of Chicago, September 1963, p. 9.

[39] "Investment Characteristics of New Foreign Capital Borrowed in the U. S." *Economic Review.* Federal Reserve Bank of Cleveland, June 1964, pp. 4-11.

[40] Federal Reserve Bank of Cleveland, *op. cit.,* p. 11.

[41] On the influence of comparative interest rates on foreign borrowing in the United States see especially: Paul Meek, "United States Investment in Foreign Securities (Excluding Canadian and IBRD Issues)." Chapter X in Raymond F. Mikesell (ed.), *U. S. Private and Government Investment Abroad.* Eugene, Oregon: University of Oregon Books, 1962, pp. 241-269; and Philip W. Bell, "Private Capital Movement and the U. S. Balance of Payments Position," in *Factors Affecting the United States Balance of Payments.* Compilation of Studies Prepared for the Subcommittee on International Exchange and Payments of the Joint Economic Committee, Congress of the United States, 87th Congress, 2d Session, Joint Committee Print, Washington: U. S. Government Printing Office, 1962, pp. 401-481.

ts deficits and surpluses. Although these other factors tant, they apparently do not seriously hamper the effec-)f the rate in performing this function. There is sufficient eviu⌐ ⸗ at hand, especially the employment of interest rates by central banks as balance of payments equilibrating forces, to sustain the theory.

For a long time now, government monetary authorities in many countries have not allowed rates of interest to be determined at all times by the play of free market conditions. Rates of interest have been controlled by these authorities to act as a brake on, or to spur, expansion, to counter contraction, to reduce balance of payments surpluses and deficits among other objectives. The fact that interest rates often act under man-made circumstances, to restore balance of payments equilibrium, does not disprove the theory. On the contrary, these man-made actions follow the dictates of the theory and constitute strong evidence in support of its validity.

Characteristics of adjustment by changes in income. Prior to the publication of Lord Keynes' *General Theory of Employment, Interest and Money* in 1936, many economists were wont to follow Say's Law of Outlets which ascribed a neutral or facilitating role to money in the economy. Goods exchanged against goods; money was but the medium of exchange and the standard of value employed in the transactions. Keynes showed that money, as it moved in circulation, activated the economy and generated income as it was spent and re-spent. An injection of money into the circulating stream had a multiplier effect on income, raising its level by a multiple of the amount injected. A leakage of funds out of the purchasing stream had the reverse effect and income was reduced by a multiple of the amount withdrawn.[42] Although

---

[42] It is interesting to note that the Scottish financier, John Law, in his efforts to convince the Regent of France to establish a royal bank, formulated in 1716, some of the basic postulates upon which the income effects of exports and imports rest. See his *Premier Mémoire sur les Banques, Présenté à son Altesse Royale Monseigneur le Duc d'Orléans, Régent de France.* Paris (circa) 1716. Reproduced in Eugène Daire, *Economistes Financiers du Dix-Huitième Siècle,* Paris: Chez Guillaumin et Cie., Libraires, 1851, pp. 517 ff.

Keynes did not work out the multiplier effects of foreign trade, some of his followers did.[43]

The foreign trade multiplier represents an extension and development of Keynes' domestic national income multiplier. Since this latter theory is well-known and is available in many introductory economics textbooks, it is not repeated here. Both the domestic and foreign trade multiplier theories are complex and have been interpreted in various ways by several authors. The following statement represents a highly simplified version of it in one of its accepted forms.

The multiplier is generally presented by first showing its operation in a closed economy (one without foreign trade, without government spending and taxes). With a given marginal propensity to consume (MPC), injections of primary expenditures of 100 per unit of time would finally augment national income by $\frac{100}{1\text{-MPC}}$. In this simple economy, what is not consumed is saved. Therefore, the marginal propensity to save (MPS) equals 1-MPC, and the multiplier can be expressed as $k = \frac{1}{\text{MPS}}$.

In an open economy (one with foreign trade), new dimensions are added to the problem: leakage through imports (M), which is in addition to the leakage through savings (S); and an injection, exports (X), in addition to the investment injection (I). Some of the newly injected purchasing power arising from exports leaks out through both savings and imports in an open economy and $C + M + S = 1$. The multiplier in an open economy is $k = \frac{1}{\text{MPS} + \text{MPM}}$ and the multiplicand involves exports in addtion to investments (I). Income (Y) is increased or decreased by

---

[43] The theory of the foreign trade multiplier has been the work of a number of economists. See especially: Fritz Machlup, *International Trade and the National Income Multiplier*, Philadelphia: The Blakiston Co., 1943. Reprinted by Augustus M. Kelley, New York, 1961; Lloyd A. Metzler, "The Transfer Problem Reconsidered." *Journal of Political Economy*, Vol. 50, 1942, pp. 397 ff; James Meade, *The Balance of Payments*. Oxford University Press, 1951, chapters 3-7, 15 and 18.

the action of the multiplier as computed by the equation $dY = k$ $(dI_d + dI_f)$, when I_d is domestic investment and I_f is foreign investment (X-M).

If the marginal propensity to save is $\frac{1}{4}$, in a closed economy, then $k = \frac{1}{\frac{1}{4}} = 4$. In an open economy with the same marginal propensity to save and a marginal propensity to import of $\frac{1}{8}$, $k = \frac{1}{\frac{1}{4} + \frac{1}{8}} = 2.67$. In the closed economy an injection during a given period of $100 million would increase income by $400 million ($4 \times 100) and in the open economy by $267 million ($2.67 \times 100).

In an open economy, a nation trades with others and its exports and imports have foreign repercussions or tertiary effects. The export (injections) of one country constitute the imports (leakage) of others. The leakages of one country flow back in the form of injections to its trading partners and the injections of any nation occasion leakages in others. The amount of the foreign leakages which flow back as injections depends, in part, upon the foreign marginal propensity to import (MPM). Leakages stimulate the economy of the nations which receive them as injections and generate a return flow.[44]

This theory assumes that injections and leakages will not work themselves out through changes in price or be countered by shifts in the rate of exchange. All the other variables which might affect the operation of the multiplier are held constant. In addition, the exposition presented here leaves several other relevant factors out of consideration for purposes of simplification. Finally,

---

[44] Cf. Gottfried Haberler, "A Survey of International Trade Theory." *Special Papers on International Economics*, No. 1, September 1955. Princeton: International Finance Section, Department of Economics and Sociology, Princeton University, 1955, pp. 30-48. Haberler's work presents a succinct but authoritative summary of the principal features of the multiplier analysis. A longer exposition in depth of the theory is presented by Fritz Machlup, *op. cit.*, An excellent, non-mathematical description of it is given in John Parke Young, *The International Economy*. New York: The Ronald Press Company, 4th ed., 1963, pp. 125-141. A highly realistic discussion of it is given by Thomas C. Schelling, *International Economics*. Boston: Allyn and Bacon, Inc., 1958, pp. 197-226.

there is more than one concept of the multiplier. Some prefer a period analysis of injections and leakages, while others view it as either spontaneous or as a continuum.

Regardless of the assumptions and the method of formulation, balance of payments disequilibria tend to be automatically adjusted through the multiplied income effects of the out- and inflow of funds resulting from foreign export-import transactions. A rise in exports increases income. Some of this increase, in response to the marginal propensity to import, will in turn result in larger imports, thus tending to balance the international accounts. An increase in a nation's imports causes a leakage of income and reduces its ability to import in the future.

Through the foreign repercussions or tertiary effects, the increased exports of a country, which are the imports of its trading partners, reduce the capacity of these partners to import further and thus tend to restore balance. On the other hand, increased imports, which are the exports of its trading partners, increase the income of these partners and in turn result in larger imports on their part.

Under the foreign trade multiplier analysis, it is customary to divide transactions into two groups: autonomous and induced. The autonomous transactions are those which take place by reason of price, style, increased industrial utilization, innovation and the like. The induced are those which occur by reason of income changes at home and abroad.

Like the national income and product accounts, the multiplier theory deals with real goods and services rather than with financial flows. For this reason, in part, it holds that $Y = C + I_d + I_f + G$, where Y represents income, C consumption, I_d domestic investment, I_f foreign investment and G government expenditures. This is also part of the rationale which holds that $I_f = X - M$. However, it is possible to conceive of the multiplier in terms of money flows or flows of funds rather than goods. Under such an approach, the movement of goods is set aside and interest focused on the movement of funds. Here the multiplier deals with the movement of funds as represented by the unilateral transfers and capital accounts and leaves exports and imports out of the equation.

The balance of the unilateral transfers and capital accounts is exactly equal to that on the current account and the value of foreign investment (I_r) is the same under either a goods or funds approach. The use of the flow of funds analysis, could conceivably lead to a theory of the *net multiplier effect on foreign economic transactions.*

The net multiplier effect is based on the postulate that payments counterbalance receipts and vice versa from whatever source they arise, whether classified as autonomous, induced or not. The net cash flows are measured then by the balance of payments surplus or deficit on the unilateral transfers and capital accounts. The net multiplier effect, under this concept, consists of this surplus or deficit times the sum of the marginal propensity to import and to save. The multiplier effects on the heavy United States deficits on these accounts prevailing from 1958 to 1964 serve to explain in part, the persistent unemployment and the relatively slow rate of growth of the American economy during this period.

The forward and Euro-Dollar markets and adjustment by income changes. The theory of the automatic adjustment of balance of payments surpluses and deficits by means of income changes assumes that imbalances are not corrected by changes in the rates of exchange. It should be noted, however, that all international income flows must pass through a rate of exchange and this assumption must also be carried to the forward rates. To the extent that a good forward market renders the international exchange of funds more efficient, these markets can be held to contribute to the effectiveness of the income flow mechanism of balance of payments adjustment.

The Euro-Dollar Market is essentially a short-term market. In what is perhaps the most widely accepted form of the multiplier theory, short-term capital movements are not included. In addition, the movement of much short-term capital is not autonomous; it is induced. Short-term capital movements are often merely a result of transactions on the current account. To include them, in addition to exports and imports, would be double counting. According to this general view, then, the Euro-Dollar Market may be presumed to have but little effect on the automatic adjustment of balance of payments equilibrium by changes in income.

However, the Euro-Dollar funds are used for a wide variety of purposes—for the financing of imports, among others. Since this market, by adding another means of financing international transactions, facilitates the international flow of funds, it may aid in adjustment of balance of payments equilibrium through changes in income. It also tends to foster savings by providing investment opportunities. The investments which flow to this institution are leakages from the source country and conversely, the Euro-Dollar funds which flow into other countries constitute new injections for them.

Funds, however, are not converted into capital goods in the Euro-Dollar Market; they must be so converted in a country if they are converted at all, for this institution is not an economy. From this point of view, the Euro-Dollar Market forms a part of the mechanism through which the international movement of funds is channeled. Far from invalidating or weakening the theory of the automatic adjustment of the balance of payments by means of changes in income, the Euro-Dollar Market tends to strengthen it by making the international flow of funds more efficient. This market serves as a way around the blocks and bars in the form of government regulations and private conventions which hamper the movement of investment capital between the national markets. The theory and equations which illustrate its mechanism, therefore, stand as usually stated, and need not be substantially modified by the operations of the Euro-Dollar Market.

The balance of payments effects upon income are not allowed any more free play in modern partially-directed economies than are exchange rates, prices and interest rates. The effects of increasing and decreasing incomes, from whatever source, can be parried by a host of government actions, principally by measures of monetary and fiscal policy. Here again, government action usually follows the principles involved in this theory. Thus when the economy does not operate according to theory because of government intervention, this fact does not disprove it. On the contrary, it is perhaps its strongest support.

Feedback

Feedback is the latest addition to the family of balance of payments adjustment theories but is of a somewhat different character than the older members. It refers to the flow of funds in the opposite direction which given payments or receipts engender. If an American firm invests $100,000 in its foreign subsidiary which in turn uses $80,000 of the investment to purchase equipment from the parent or another American firm, this purchase is termed feedback. Another instance of feedback occurs where Americans purchase, say, coffee from Brazilians and the dollar proceeds are used by Brazilians to purchase machine tools in the United States.[45] Feedback is generally expressed in terms of percentages. Thus in the first case mentioned above, the feedback was eighty per cent.

Characteristics of feedback. Feedback may be said to constitute a form of quantitive expression of the relationships among the several accounts on the balance of payments. These relationships have been long recognized but have only recently been measured. The feedback analysis does not attempt to work out the chain of causality which explains why a given flow of funds will result in a counter-flow; it merely measures the relationship without attempting to explain how it occurred.

Feedback is of interest to government policy makers for it enables them to estimate the amount of foreign aid funds which will return in the form of exports. In addition, it helps them estimate such matters as the in- and outflows engendered by foreign aid for the domestic and foreign port and other expenses which foreign and American vessels carrying exports under this program might incur.

---

[45] A discussion, with examples, of negative and positive feedback is given in: Walter S. Salant, Emile Despres, Lawrence B. Krause, Alice M. Rivlin, William A. Salant and Lorie Tarshis, *The United States Balance of Payments in 1968.* Washington: The Brookings Institution, 1963, pp. 15-18.

Where exports are tied to loans and grants, the feedback is chained to the outflow. Some private business arrangements also provide for *tied feedback*. Where a parent firm requires its subsidiaries to purchase equipment from it or where manufacturers of equipment oblige the users to utilize supplies which they produce, the resulting feedback is likewise tied.

The geographical sources of imports and outlets for exports are important in its analysis. Feedback to the United States is likely to be less pronounced from those countries which accumulate dollar reserves than from those countries which are in the habit of spending all of their foreign exchange earnings.

The feedback matrix. The feedback mechanism may be illustrated by the use of a matrix similar to that shown on Table 11.2. This table shows the feedback of a three-country world, countries A, B and C. Country A invests $1,000 in country B which in turn imports goods from country A valued at $700 and from country C at $300. Country A also invests $1,000 in country C which in turn imports goods from country A valued at $600 and from country B worth $400. The feedback ratios for country A's investments are seventy per cent for those in country B and sixty per cent for those in country C.

TABLE 11.2

SUMMARY—HYPOTHETICAL FEEDBACK MATRIX
(in dollars)

Exports from	Imports into country A	B	C
Country A	0	700	600
Country B	0	0	400
Country C	0	300	0

The process, of course, does not stop with the first round. If the assumption is made, for the sake of simplicity, that country A retains all of its foreign exchange earnings, in the second round country B, which had earned $400, spends seventy per cent of it in country A for a total of $280, and thirty per cent in country C for a total of $120. Country C spends, in this round, sixty per cent of its total earnings of $300 in country A for $180, and forty per cent in country B for a total of $120. Similar calculations are made for each round of spending until the original sum invested is exhausted.

Using appropriate assumptions and estimates, the feedback ratio can be computed for actual or projected situations. One important use of this technique was made by Walter S. Salant and his associates in projecting the United States balance of payments for 1968.[46]

Partial feedback analysis. The many difficulties associated with the preparation of general analyses of feedback have led some students to prepare partial analyses of it. In addition, analysts and policy-making officials often desire to observe the impact of specific transactions upon the balance of payments position. Partial analyses of feedback, restricted to specific transactions, are consequently prepared. One such study was made by the Department of Commerce for use in the *President's 1961 Tax Recommendations* and was published as a part of the *Hearings* on these recommendations.[47] Table 11.3 reproduces some of the data presented in this study.

This study was made in conjunction with Congressional hearings on tax credits on depreciable property and improvements in the federal income tax. It examines the amount of feedback in the form of United States exports which direct investments in American manufacturing subsidiaries abroad fostered during 1959-1960. As Table 11.3 shows, this specific feedback, in terms of gross exports, varied from 10.6 per cent in the case of Europe to 48.0 per cent in the countries classified as the rest of the world. For the world as a whole, the percentage of direct

---

[46] Walter S. Salant, et al., *op. cit.*, pp. 276-277 especially. Salant and his associates employed modifications of the matrix prepared by Whitney Hicks of Stanford University while he was working at the Agency for International Development. The estimates prepared by Hicks constitute developments of those made earlier by Karl Shell and Richard Cooper of the Council of Economic Advisers.

[47] *Revenue Act of 1962. Hearings Before the Committee on Finance, United States Senate, Eighty-seventh Congress, Second Session, on H.R. 10650.* Part I, April 2, 1962, Washington: U. S. Government Printing Office, 1962, pp. 183-193.

investment represented by gross exports was 22.7. If the net exports, that is total exports minus imports, are used, the percentages vary from 4.1 in the case of Europe to 47.8 for the rest of the world and 19.0 for the world as a whole.

These percentages seem relatively low when compared with the results of a general analysis prepared by Whitney Hicks of Stanford University for AID. His findings show the feedback of United States exports in 1960, expressed as a percentage of imports, to be: Canada, 72.64; dollar Latin America, 63.19; non-dollar Latin America, 45.31.[48] Walter Salant and his associates call attention to the fact that Hicks' figures were derived from a trade rather than a payments matrix. After a critical examination of Hicks' data, Salant and his associates are apparently of the opinion that they understate the feedback ratios.[49] As might be expected, both the ratios shown on Table 11.3 and those in the Hicks study are higher for the non-reserve accumulating countries than for those where reserves are built up.

TABLE 11.3

RATIOS OF MANUFACTURING SUBSIDIARIES' EXPORTS
TO UNITED STATES TO UNITED
STATES PARENT COMPANIES' INVESTMENT, 1959-1960
(In percentages of parent company investment)

	Gross Exports	Net exports (gross exports minus imports)
Canada	20.9	17.7
Europe	10.6	4.1
Latin America	42.0	41.5
Rest of the World	48.0	47.8
World	22.7	19.0

Source: Adapted from *Revenue Act of 1962. Hearings Before the Committee on Finance U. S. Senate. 87th Congress, 2nd Session on H.R. 10650.* Part I, April 2, 1962. Washington: U. S. Government Printing Office, 1962, p. 187. (Table prepared by the Department of Commerce.)

[48] Cited by Walter S. Salant, et al., *op. cit.* p. 276.
[49] Walter S. Salant, et al., *op. cit.,* p. 277.

Several American parent firms have prepared types of partial feedback analyses. Some of these were presented before the House of Representatives Ways and Means Committee in the spring of 1961 to support the continuation of certain tax deferrals.[50] These studies compared new capital investments in American subsidiary firms with the resulting receipts from dividends and exports. As a general proposition, these analyses show that the feedback ratios were over 100 per cent in some cases. Since these studies were directed at obtaining a continuation of certain tax concessions, it is conceivable that they were not entirely objective.[51]

The period analysis used in many feedback analyses, especially those of the matrix type, is satisfactory as a laboratory technique. The feedback process, outside the "laboratory," is, however, not a matter of periods; it is a continuum. *In the long-run, a nation's receipts equal its payments minus those amounts retained by its trading partners for reserve and working balance purposes including funds retained by the Euro-Dollar Market.* For payments to non-industrialized, underdeveloped nations, the feedback ratio approaches 100 per cent, for these areas do not accumulate reserves. The reserve accumulating, more industrialized nations present a feedback ratio of less than 100 per cent over periods of time; less by the proportion which receipts set aside as reserves and balances bears to payments.

---

[50] *Hearings* under the Revenue Act of 1962 cited in Note 47, p. 183.
[51] See: *Hearings* under the Revenue Act of 1962 cited in note 47, pp. 183-186.

12

The International Payments System

The present international payments system is less the result of formal agreement among nations than a process of evolutionary change from earlier systems. When considering the substitution of some other system for the present one, it is important to bear this fact in mind. Since the current system was not constructed by international negotiation and agreement, it appears somewhat unlikely that it will be succeeded by one installed by such procedures. *Natura non fecit saltum* (nature makes no leaps).

Types of International Payments Systems

Leaving primitive systems and the silver standards aside, the various monetary systems which have been employed are the gold coin; the gold bullion; the gold exchange; the international gold bullion and the paper standards. The present international payments system has been termed the gold, the dollar, the foreign and the mixed exchange system. Although the term *mixed exchange*, which implies the use of gold and various forms of foreign exchange, appears to describe best the present institutions, common usage seems to indicate a preference for the term *gold exchange system*. Consequently this term is used here to designate the present payments mechanism.[1]

The gold coin standard. Under the gold coin or full gold

---

[1] Under the older gold exchange standards, gold is usually readily available for international payments. With the possible exception of the United States, gold is not readily available today for international payment. The term gold exchange standard is applied to the present system largely because gold constitutes an important fraction of the reserves held by the principal industrial nations and is available from the United States as an ultimate means of payments on official demand.

standard, the standard monetary unit is a defined quantity of gold. Other forms of metallic or paper money which circulate along with the standard coin are freely convertible into and maintained at parity with it. Prior to World War I, most industrial nations used the gold coin standard. Residents were free to hoard and deal in gold; they could obtain it on demand from their treasuries or central banks and gold was widely employed as a means of international settlement. All foreign exchange paper issued by countries on this standard was freely convertible into gold. Given the almost universal preference for gold as a store of value and medium of exchange and its stability as a standard of value, the gold coin system of international payments rested upon a solid foundation.[2]

The par of exchange between two countries on the gold coin standard was established by the proportion of fine gold embodied in the standard monetary unit of each country. The former British pound sterling contained 4.8665+ times as much fine gold as the United States dollar and the par of exchange was £1 = $4.8665 or $1.00 = £0.2503+. The rate of exchange fluctuated around the par but was limited in its movement by the gold export and import points. These points were determined by the costs of shipping gold and were not fixed but varied as these costs changed. The rate of exchange could not exceed the upper gold export or the lower gold import point. Ordinarily, foreign transactions were settled by the use of bills of exchange; it was only when the gold points were reached that gold flowed in or out of a country.

The gold bullion or bar standards. The gold bullion or bar standards are generally employed by nations which lack sufficient gold to maintain the gold coin standard. It has often been an intermediate one used by countries on paper money which desire to return to the gold coin standard in the foreseeable future. Should the world ever return to the gold standard, the gold bullion would doubtless prove the only practical one. It is doubtful that there is sufficient gold, as well as large enough

---

[2] See: William Howard Steiner and Eli Shapiro, *Money and Banking*. New York: Henry Holt and Company, 1941 (revised ed.), pp. 46-53.

accretions to the world's monetary stock, to sustain a universal gold coin standard without reductions in the volume of money outstanding.

The essential feature of the gold bullion standard lies in the fact that other forms of currency and foreign exchange are not freely convertible into gold in any amount demanded. Other forms of money are only convertible into gold in "wholesale" quantities. Gold could further be economized by restricting conversion solely to international settlements while not authorizing conversion for domestic purposes.

Were the world to use such a standard, monetary authorities of user nations would no longer be plagued by questions concerning the stability of currencies employed as international reserves. Nations whose currency was used as a reserve medium, would not be constrained to follow the disciplines imposed by considerations of international confidence.[3]

The pars of exchange were established under the gold bullion standard similar to those under the gold coin standard. The gold points also operated to limit the fluctuations in the rate of exchange at least for the larger transactions. As under the gold coin standard, gold only flowed in or out of a nation when the gold points were reached.

The gold exchange standards. Gold exchange standards were devised as a means of permitting colonies and overseas territories to continue the use of their national currencies, usually silver, for their domestic transactions while trading internationally in terms of gold. The territories using this standard kept their international reserves in the form of deposits in the central banks of the mother country and made their foreign trade arrangements, international payments and receipts in terms of the currency of this center.

These central bank deposits constituted both the reserves of the colonies' domestic currency as well as their international reserves. Under such conditions, there was a strong tendency

---

[3] Cf. William Howard Steiner and Eli Shapiro, *op. cit.*, pp. 50-53, and Rollin G. Thomas, *Our Modern Banking and Monetary System*, New York: Prentice-Hall, Inc., (2nd ed.), pp. 38-44.

for their domestic money supply to be a function of their balances of payments. The money supply often increased with surpluses and declined with deficits. When silver was abandoned in favor of paper money as the domestic circulating medium, the system was continued. Domestic and international reserves were likewise deposited in the central bank of the mother country and international transactions were arranged and settled in terms of this center's currency. Given the dependence of the domestic money supply upon the balance of payments, these forms of the gold exchange standards were termed the *automatic* type.

During the twenties, the gold exchange standard in its *managed* form was adopted by several European industrial countries, as a step toward the adoption of the gold coin or bullion standard, which was, however, never taken. These countries used paper and token money for their domestic circulation and gold for their international transactions. They kept a part of their reserves in gold and convertible foreign exchange in their central banks and a part on deposit in the monetary centers of full gold standard countries, especially the United States and the United Kingdom. Similar to the gold bullion standards, gold was usually available for international transactions. Domestic paper money was not, however, generally redeemable in gold.

In contrast to the automatic types, the central banks did not allow inflows and outflows of gold and foreign exchange to affect the volume of domestic money in circulation unless it accorded with their policy objectives. The volume of money in circulation was controlled by the banks, often independently of balance of payments results.[4]

The international gold bullion standard. The United States is the only country which has used this standard. It is a monetary system loosely linked to gold which lies somewhere between the other forms of the gold and the paper standards. Under this standard, no gold circulates in the United States; residents are forbidden to hold or trade in gold at home or abroad; paper, silver and token money is not redeemable in gold to private holders. Foreign governments, their central banks and other

---

[4] See: Rollin G. Thomas, *op. cit.*, pp. 38-44.

official financial institutions may, however, obtain gold on demand from the Treasury in exchange for dollars, if such demands are for legitimate monetary uses. The Secretary of the Treasury, with the approval of the President, is authorized to pay gold out to meet official demands; but he is not obliged to do so. As a matter of policy, the Treasury has honored all such demands to date.[5]

Under the international gold bullion standard, the par of dollar exchange is established by the Treasury gold price of $35.00 per fine troy ounce. There are no gold points to limit fluctuations in the dollar rate of exchange. Until 1961, the United States government did not intervene in the exchange market to stabilize its rate of exchange, but left these operations to the foreign central banks. Foreign transactions are ordinarily settled by the use of credit instruments.

The paper standards. During the depression years of the 1930's almost all nations abandoned the forms of the gold exchange standards which they had been using. Their domestic circulating media consisted of paper and metallic token coins backed by reserves of diverse composition. For the most part, domestic reserves consisted of government obligations, gold and foreign exchange. For international reserves, gold and foreign exchange were used. The over-issue of paper money and inflation of greater or lesser severity characterized many of these paper standards.

Official pars of exchange were usually established and in some cases they were changed from time to time to bring them into line with the prevailing (and frequently rising) price levels. In some cases, the rates of exchange were allowed to float freely; in others they were pegged by central bank intervention on the foreign exchange markets. With the advent of World War II, most nations established exchange controls giving the central banks monopoly over dealings in foreign exchange. Under these controls, the par constituted the official rate and, theoretically

---

[5] Max J. Wasserman, Charles W. Hultman and Laszlo Zsoldos, *International Finance: Theory, Practice, Institutions.* New York: Simmons-Boardman Publishing Corporation, 1963, pp. 16-18.

at least, the rates of exchange were inflexible and not allowed to float freely.

Gold, under these paper standards, was not employed in exchange transactions or in liquidating foreign business contracts. It was used, however, to meet large balance of payments deficits accumulations as they arose from time to time. During the late 1930's and the World War II years the United States monetary gold stock increased to a maximum of $24.6 billion in 1949 as a result of these settlements.

Foreign exchange controls were sometimes well and sometimes poorly enforced. In many nations, black markets in foreign exchange developed as the fixed pars became less and less realistic in the face of over-issued paper money and rising prices. In some cases these black markets were later tolerated and became gray markets; and finally, some of them were given official recognition.[6] Balance of payments deficits were held in check as much as possible by controls; and if shortages of international reserves occurred, recourse was had to international borrowing, drawings on the European Payments Union and the International Monetary Fund and foreign aid receipts.

During the period of exchange controls, many currencies were not freely convertible into all others. With the post-World War II improvements in balance of payments positions, controls were relaxed and most European currencies became largely convertible by 1958. The international payments system gradually underwent changes leading to the development of the present system.[7]

The Present International Payments System

The present international payments system is the heir of all the monetary systems which preceded it. Its immediate predecessors are the paper systems of the 1930's and the World War II

---

[6] See the case of France in 1948 as described by: Norman Crump, *The A B C of the Foreign Exchanges.* London: Macmillan and Co., Ltd., 1958 (12th ed.), pp. 234-235.

[7] Max J. Wasserman, Charles W. Hultman and Laszlo Zsoldos, *op. cit.,* pp. 18-25, 235-240.

years. In the post-World War II period several new dimensions were added to the paper money standards of the time: (1) the IMF was established; (2) the United States consistently ran balance of payments deficits, 1950-1964, in every year except 1957, thus contributing to the growth of the international reserves of some of its trading partners; (3) the forward markets underwent substantial development; (4) the Euro-Dollar System grew into a large short-term capital and foreign exchange market; (5) the EPU and its successor, the European Monetary Agreement (EMA), kindled the spirit of international monetary cooperation and (beginning in 1961) this spirit increased substantially; (6) the concept of international reserves was extended by use of the forward facilities, swaps, and by Roosa bonds.

Characteristics of the system. The circulating media of almost all countries today are the notes of governments and central banks, silver and token coins. This money is not redeemable in gold and is a form of credit money.[8] Paper money is backed by reserve of gold, government obligations and foreign exchange and may be said to be partially covered by something of value. These notes circulate because of this reserve, confidence in the integrity and stability of the government and the public requirement for some sort of medium of exchange and standard of value.

The fact that paper money is no longer subject to the gold discipline constitutes both a disadvantage and an advantage, and is of importance to the international payments system. The disadvantages are attributable to the ease with which this money can be over-issued, especially to meet budgetary deficits. Its advantages stem from the fact that the monetary system is not subject to the vagaries of gold production, hoarding and the

---

[8] The silver certificates of the United States are redeemable in silver dollars. United States gold certificates state on their face that they are redeemable in gold, but they do not circulate and it is unlawful for a private citizen to hold them. They are used as reserves by the Federal Reserve Banks, but they are not redeemable in gold by the Treasury at the present time. In some parts of the world, notably the Middle East and Africa, the coins, mostly silver of some other countries continue to circulate. In some of these areas, the silver Maria Theresa dollar continues to be used. These dollars are no longer an official currency of any nation, but are coined by mints and private firms for both governments and individuals.

gold market as well as the relative ease with which it may be managed. The principal impact of paper money upon the international monetary system lies in the relation of the volume outstanding upon prices and foreign exchange rates.

Today, most of the industrialized nations manage their paper money carefully. The volume of notes issued is regulated with reference to the price level; economic contractions, expansion and growth; interest rates; employment and the utilization of resources. Care is taken so that the money supply will not become redundant and to preserve a determined ratio with reserves. All nations, however, do not utilize such sophisticated techniques of money management, and in some countries its over-issue is chronic with inflation and the deterioration of its external position as results.[9]

The use of a country's paper money for purposes of external payments depends upon two factors: convertibility and acceptability. Convertibility means that a currency is readily exchangeable into others. Acceptability refers to the willingness of foreigners to take the currency in payment or in exchange for theirs.

Under conditions of relatively free convertibility, there are great differences in the external acceptability of national currencies. By and large, the degree of acceptability depends upon the government's reputation for monetary integrity; the volume of foreign business transacted; the supplies of goods, services and capital available and the market for imports. Ordinarily, exporters prefer to be paid in their own currency because they must meet their expenses in their own money; and by so doing, they avoid taking exchange risks.

Under the present international payments system, several currencies have emerged as international media of payment: principally the dollar, pound, French franc and escudo. The

---

[9] Cf. M. S. Szymczak, *Monetary Policy in A Free Economy*. An address at the School of Banking, University of Wisconsin, Madison, Wis., August 29, 1950. Reprinted, in part, under the title "The Constructive Role of Monetary Policy" by Paul A. Samuelson, Robert L. Bishop and John R. Coleman, *Readings in Economics*. New York: McGraw-Hill Book Company, Inc., 1955, pp. 118-128.

dollar and pound have achieved this position because they are the two principal reserve currencies of the world and because of the highly developed financial institutions which prevail in their respective countries. In addition, the pound is both the money of account and of payment of the Sterling Area. The French franc and escudo derive their international status in part from the fact that they are the money used in the Franc and Escudo Areas. Due to Swiss monetary stability and the wide use of Swiss banking facilities, this currency is gaining in general acceptability. The German mark and the Dutch guilder, by reason of the increasing volume of trade and their strong balance of payments positions, are also becoming of increasing importance as media of international settlement. Most of the other currencies are of but limited use in international trade.

Where countries have a currency that is little known and traded, foreign transactions are often carried out by the use of other more acceptable exchange. The dollar and pound are widely employed by other nations as a substitute for their own monies in foreign transactions. Within a monetary area, the currency of the center is usually employed in this manner.

Composition of reserves. There is insufficient monetary gold available and accretions to monetary stocks are too small to warrants its use as the exclusive owned domestic and international reserve component. This void is filled by the use of foreign exchange in various forms, principally bank deposits. The dollar and pound are by far the most widely employed currencies for reserve purposes. Table 12.1 shows the total owned reserve holdings of selected countries and areas at the end of 1963 including gold, foreign exchange and IMF gold tranche positions.

Total owned reserves as defined on this table amounted to almost $70 billion largely held by the industrial countries, especially those of Europe and the United States. There is substantial difference in the amount of reserves owned by different regions. Some areas, like Latin America and other underdeveloped regions, tend to live from hand to mouth accumulating small reserves. There is also considerable variation in the proportion of gold in the reserve holdings. Thus, the proportion is high in

TABLE 12.1

TOTAL OWNED RESERVE HOLDINGS, SELECTED COUNTRIES
AND AREAS, 1963[1]

(In billions of U.S. dollars)

	Total Reserves	Gold	Foreign Exchange	IMF Gold Tranche	Gold Percentage of Total
All countries	69.25	40.21	25.10	3.94	58.1
Industrial countries	48.37	34.53	10.52	3.33	71.4
Industrial Europe	23.72	15.34	6.76	1.62	63.4
Other Western Europe	5.56	2.10	3.25	.21	37.7
Latin America	2.79	1.17	1.51	.11	41.9
Middle East	2.11	.74	1.31	.06	3.6
Other Asia	3.56	.62	2.90	.04	17.4
Other Africa	.95	.07	.86	.03	7.4
United States	16.84	15.60	.21	1.04	92.6
United Kingdom	3.15	2.48	.17	.49	78.7
France	4.91	3.18	1.28	.45	64.8
Germany	7.65	3.84	3.26	.55	50.2
Switzerland	3.08	2.82	.25	—	91.6
Italy	3.28	2.34	.71	.23	71.3
Japan	2.06	.29	1.59	.18	14.1

Totals may not add due to rounding.

[1] At end of fourth quarter, 1963. Total holdings include gold, IMF gold tranche and foreign exchange.

Source: IMF, *International Financial Statistics.* Vol. XVII, No. 8 (August 1964), pp. 15-17.

the case of Switzerland and the United States and low in the case of Japan, Asia and Africa. For all countries, gold constituted 58.1 per cent of the total owned reserves at the end of 1963.

The United States dollar is the principal component of foreign exchange reserves and constitutes 49.5 per cent of the total foreign exchange held, as indicated on Table 12.2. Sterling amounted to 31 per cent of foreign exchange holdings and was owned principally by the other Sterling Area countries. United Kingdom foreign exchange assets are composed largely of dollars.

The gold tranche position with the IMF does not constitute as yet a significant share of these reserves.[10]

TABLE 12.2
COMPOSITION OF OFFICIAL AND BANK GROSS FOREIGN EXCHANGE ASSETS, 1962[1]
(In percentages of total official gross assets)

	Dollars	Sterling
All countries[2]	49.5	31.2
Latin America	69.7	− 2.7
Continental Europe	56.7	12.2
United Kingdom	99.7	—
Other Sterling Countries[2]	4.5	94.7
Rest of the World[2]	52.3	13.0

[1] At end of second quarter 1962.
[2] January 1962.

Source: IMF, *International Financial Statistics*, Vol. XVI, No. 1 (April 1963), p. 23.

As explained in Chapter 10, reserves are needed with fixed rates of exchange to sustain a nation's trade in periods of balance of payments deficits and to defend the rate of exchange. The foreign exchange component must meet certain standards. It should be fully convertible; stable in value; widely demanded; issued by countries of high monetary stability and with well organized exchange, money and capital markets. And above all, the foreign exchange utilized must have the weight of custom and traditional use behind it. The employment of foreign exchange should impose a severe discipline upon both the supplying and the using nations.

The International Monetary Fund. The inauguration of the IMF in 1946 marked an epoch in the history of the international payments system. The creation of the Fund served to institu-

---

[10] The composition and the level of reserves is treated in: IMF, *International Reserves and Liquidity*. Washington: IMF 1958, pp. 40-66.

tionalize many aspects of the system and to give it a somewhat official stamp of approval by virtue of the formal agreement of the member nations.

In addition, the creation of the IMF opened a period of international monetary cooperation. The pre-World War II systems were characterized by individual and unilateral actions on the part of the participating nations. Some countries followed from time to time a beggar-my-neighbor policy by maintaining undervalued rates of exchange in an effort to boost their exports at the expense of those of its trading partners. Unilateral actions were taken often without regard for either the interests of other nations or of the payments system as a whole.

These policies came to a virtual end when the IMF opened its doors. The Fund Agreement embodied a code of financial conduct which must be followed by all members on pain of denial of the use of the Fund's resources or expulsion. "Fighting rates of exchange" are outlawed; the established pars are to be respected and only changed under specified conditions. Convertibility is fostered and impediments to trade are to be minimized. The members agree to maintain currency stability and to avoid discriminatory practices. In addition, the Fund provides a forum for the discussion of problems of exchange and payments, aids in the solution of the problems of its individual members while working to improve the whole system of payments. It gathers and publishes a wealth of statistical and other information, including the balances of payments of some seventy-five countries.[11]

The question of fixed versus flexible rates of exchange was decided at the Bretton Woods meeting in 1944 in conjunction with the elaboration of the Fund Articles of Agreement. The proponents of fixed rates prevailed and the establishment of the Fund served to institutionalize these rates and to give them international sanction. The rates were, however, not rigidly fixed.

---

[11] A concise history of events leading to the preparation of the IMF Articles of Agreement is presented by Charles L. Merwin, "The Road to Bretton Woods." *Finance and Development* (The Fund and Bank Review). Vol. 1, No. 2 (September 1964), pp. 59-64.

Spot rates are permitted to vary by as much as one per cent above and below par and provision is made for changing the pars when the need arises. No such restrictions apply to forward rates. The movement above and below the pars of exchange permitted by the Agreement is reminiscent of the gold points of the defunct gold standards. The Agreement thus provides for some flexibility in the rates of exchange.

In exchange for the members' agreement to these disciplines, the Fund provides an additional source of liquidity in the form of drawing rights. These rights, which were described in Chapter 10, broaden and give greater flexibility to the international payments system. The IMF may be said to preside, in a limited way, over the operation of the payments system.[12]

The era of international cooperation in the payments system inaugurated by the IMF was reinforced by the General Arrangements to Borrow (GAB) signed by ten of the larger industrial members of this institution. Beginning in 1961 it was further strengthened by the programs of mutual assistance in the defense of exchange rates and by the gold pool arrangements. These developments, outlined in Chapter 10, indicate a realization of the interdependence of nations in the payments system and a desire to work together to make it function effectively in the interests of all.

The foreign exchange markets. An international payments system can be no better than the exchange markets through which it operates. Before the emergence of the present payments system, some European countries, especially the United Kingdom, had highly developed exchange markets. Those of the United States, however, left something to be desired — especially for a country whose currency was destined to play a key role in the system. Since the end of World War II, the European and

---

[12] A brief description of the Fund's activities is presented by the unsigned article, "Introduction to the Fund." *Finance and Development* (The Fund and Bank Review). Vol. 1, No. 1, (June 1964), pp. 3-14.

American markets have undergone further development.[13]

The exchange markets are buttressed by the national and Euro-Dollar money markets where the funds necessary for a system which functions largely on credit are available. The money markets of the United States are unsurpassed while those of Europe are not as well adapted to meet the exacting requirements of the payments system as they might be. The essentials of good exchange and money markets lie in the savings, the institutions which mobilize these savings and in freedom from unwarranted interference and control, both public and private. The exchange markets deal in both private and public funds. Public funds are used to finance both private and public transactions.

The volume of savings is a function of many variables. One of the more important of these is the disposable income of the inhabitants and its distribution. Strong exchange markets, therefore, are likely to exist in countries where income levels are high and evenly divided. The mobilization of these savings depends in part upon the nature of the institutions charged with this work and in part upon the confidence of the public in the stability of these institutions as well as in the currency and the government.

Foreign exchange markets, like money markets, offer a tempting field for regulation, both public and private. The New York foreign exchange market is relatively free; those in other industrial countries are frequently controlled by both government regulation and private convention. This may hamper their activities and restrict their effectiveness. There is a price on

---

[13] For a description of the United Kingdom foreign exchange markets see Norman Crump, *op. cit.*, and Walter Bagehot, *Lombard Street: A Description of the Money Market*, with a New Introduction by Frank C. Genovese. Homewood, Illinois: Richard D. Irwin, Inc., 1962. A description of the New York foreign exchange market is presented in Alan R. Holmes, *The New York Foreign Exchange Market*. New York: Federal Reserve Bank of New York, 1959 and Robert V. Roosa, *Federal Reserve Operations in the Money and Government Securities Markets*. New York: Federal Reserve Bank of New York, 1956. A discussion of the French foreign exchange market is presented in André de Lattre, *Les Finances Extérieures de la France*. Paris: Presses Universitaires de France, 1959, pp. 101-124.

exchange and money market freedom, however. Where markets are free, speculation is apt to be rife. While speculation serves to broaden the market, it may prove to be a disruptive factor at times. Speculation often operates against a national rate of exchange and renders the government's task of maintaining stable exchange rates more difficult. The existence of disruptive speculation is the price which must be paid for freedom.[14]

The development of extensive forward markets in some of the important trading nations is one of the features of the present international payments system. By providing a hedge against exchange rate fluctuations, it facilitates trade and renders the whole payments system less hazardous. In addition, in recent years it has provided facilities which some governments have employed in defending their rates of exchange. The forward market is subject to restrictions similar to those which prevail on the spot markets and is conditioned by like factors.[15]

The shortcomings of the European capital and exchange markets helped pave the way for the formation of the Euro-Dollar Market. This market is not primarily an exchange, but rather a short-term capital market. However, many international transactions are financed by funds derived from it; and it supplements the forward market by making cover more readily obtainable.[16] Improvements in the capital and foreign exchange markets

---

[14] Paul Einzig has presented an excellent picture of the modern foreign exchange market in its historical setting. See: *The History of Foreign Exchange*. London: Macmillan and Co., Ltd., 1962.

[15] See: Paul Einzig, *A Dynamic Theory of Forward Exchange*. London: Macmillan and Co., Ltd., 1961.

[16] On the Euro-Dollar Market see: Paul Einzig, *The Euro-Dollar System: Practice and Theory of International Interest Rates*. New York: St. Martin's Press, Inc., 1964; Norris O. Johnson, *Eurodollars in the New International Money Market*. New York: First National City Bank, no date; Alan R. Holmes and Fred H. Klopstock, "The Market for Dollar Deposits in Europe," *Monthly Review*, Federal Reserve Bank of New York, Vol. 42, No. 11 (November 1960), pp. 197-202; Oscar L. Altman, "Foreign Markets for Dollars, Sterling and Other Currencies," *Staff Papers*, IMF, Vol. VIII, No. 8 (December 1961), pp. 313-352; Oscar L. Altman, "Recent Developments in Foreign Markets for Dollars and Other Currencies," *Staff Papers*, IMF, Vol. X, No. 1, pp. 48-96.

make for a more effective international payments system and lessen the necessity for any drastic overhaul of it.

Operation of the system, liquidity and management. Importers and exporters carry on their business, both foreign and domestic, usually in the currency of their own country. An importer pays for the merchandise which he imports, and the exporter is paid for the goods he exports, *ultimately* in their own currencies. Since at least two different currencies are usually involved in an international transaction, some means must be found of exchanging one for the other. The importer generally purchases the required foreign money needed to pay for his purchases from a bank or some other intermediary, and the exporter sells the foreign money which he has received likewise to his bank or some other intermediary. Foreign trade is generally financed by the domestic banking system of each country involved.

To insure that importers can always find the foreign currencies necessary to consummate their transactions, the banks and dealers need an adequate supply of them. This supply is made available largely by the country's exports. Should imports exceed exports and the banks run short of exchange, they will appeal to the central bank which will then draw on its reserves accumulated from periods of export surpluses. If no reserves are available, the country must borrow, obtain the exchange by other means or cease importing until the earnings from exports again permit it to buy abroad.

This situation only prevails in the case of fixed pars and rates of exchange. Where flexible or freely floating rates are employed, reserves are not required, because the movement of the rates themselves automatically adjusts the imports and exports so as to attain equilibrium (see Chapter 11).

As used in this chapter (see also Chapter 10), the term "international liquidity" refers to the adequacy of the reserves to continue to finance any expansion which foreign trade might undergo in the future. If international liquidity is adequate, trade will continue to flow freely and to expand. If it is inadequate, imports, and consequently exports, will have to be cut. Where there is too much liquidity, inflation and the disruption of world trade are likely to follow.

Tables 12.1 and 12.2 indicated the total amount of owned reserves, and their composition, which have served recently to maintain liquidity. Between 1958 and 1963, the total amount of these reserves increased sixteen per cent. Gold reserves grew by $2.1 billion, claims on the United States by $5.1 billion, those on the United Kingdom fell by $0.2 billion, the IMF gold tranche position was augmented by about $1.4 billion and other items increased by $0.8 billion. Almost sixty per cent of the total increase in owned reserves was in the form of dollars. The growth in liquidity sustained an increase in foreign trade in the five years, 1959-1963, of forty percent; from $107 to $155 billion. The value of world trade has nearly tripled since 1950.

The gold added to reserves, exclusive of the Soviet Union, has come from new production and Soviet sales. The new gold production in 1963 amounted to $1,360 million and sales by the Soviet Union in that year were $550 million, for a total of $1,910 million. The rest of the reserves added in that year came from changes in the IMF gold tranche positions and foreign exchange, principally dollars.[17]

The foreign exchange added to the total world reserves comes from deficits on the balances of payments of those nations whose currency is used for this purpose. For the immediate post-World War II years, 1946-1949, the United States ran surpluses on its balances of payments, thus contributing to the "dollar shortage" of those years, restricted world trade and the maintenance of barriers to trade. Beginning in 1950, as Table 12.3 indicates, this country had deficits in every year except 1957. These deficits attained substantial proportions beginning in 1958 and served to augment the small reserve holdings of America's trading partners. The net deficits, 1946-1963, amounted to $20.3 billion and those between 1950 and 1963, to $28.4 billion. The deficits of other countries, especially the United Kingdom,

---

[17] J. Keith Horsefield, "International Liquidity," *Finance and Development* (The Fund and Bank Review), Vol. 1, No. 3 (December 1964), pp. 173-175.

TABLE 12.3

UNITED STATES BALANCE OF PAYMENTS SURPLUSES AND DEFICITS, 1946-1963

(in billions of dollars)

1946	1.6
1947	4.9
1948	1.0
1949	0.2
1950	−3.6
1951	−0.3
1952	−1.1
1953	−2.1
1954	−1.5
1955	−1.1
1956	−1.0
1957	0.4
1958	−3.5
1959	−3.8
1960	−3.9
1961	−2.4
1962	−2.2
1963	−1.9
Totals	−20.3

Source: 1946-1959: *The International Position of the Dollar.* Committee for Economic Development, May 1961, p. 33; 1960-1963 *Survey of Current Business,* June 1964, p. 12.

contributed likewise to the growth in reserves as did also, but to a lesser extent, the increases in the IMF gold tranche positions.

If every country which had a balance of payments surplus insisted on being paid in gold, foreign trade would be restricted by the reserves held in gold. Conversely, if every creditor country were satisfied to accept the currencies of its trading partners, and did not ask for gold, international liquidity could expand indefinitely with resulting inflation and the disruption of world trade. The operation of the present international payments system lies somewhere between these two extremes.

If no nation ever had a balance of payments surplus or deficit, there would be no need for reserves. Were deficits and surpluses small, temporary or seasonal, the need for reserves would be minimal. On the other hand, if half of the countries had deficits while the other half had surpluses, there would be a cumulative need for reserves and liquidity.[18]

The management of international liquidity is essentially a political problem somewhat disguised in *technical* clothing. It is largely based upon the national interests of many sovereign nations, their concepts of advantage and disadvantage, their rights and responsibilities. The system is managed by the market; by a network of operating practices, policies and attitudes of a customary character; by international consultations and discussions which are termed "international monetary cooperation" and by the collective work of the IMF. This mixture of management techniques has grown and changed considerably over time, especially since the end of World War II, and further changes in it are likely.

The present policies and practices followed in the management of the system mirror the interests of countries and groups of countries. Changes in practices and policies, therefore, will involve the existing balance of national and regional advantages. For these reasons, the problems of reserves and liquidity are not essentially *technical*, but political; they greatly affect the interests of the nations which participate in the system. The problem of the improvement of, or changes in, the

---

[18] J. Keith Horsefield, *op. cit.*, pp. 175-176.

system must, therefore, be judged on political grounds as well as on considerations of technical efficiency.[19]

Reforms of the International Payments System

In the last few years, the problems of the international payments system have been the object of intensive study on the part of academic economists, national and international monetary authorities. This study has been prompted by the various shortcomings of the system, especially the fears of a "crisis of liquidity" where the growth of international reserves proves inadequate to sustain the increase in world trade. In addition, it has been more than two decades since the system was studied in the years immediately preceding the Bretton Woods conference. Agreement seems general that the system should again be subjected to study.[20]

The setting of the problem. According to the *Report on the Deliberations of an International Study Group of 32 Economists* (hereinafter called the Group of 32), three major problems of the international payments system may be distinguished:(1) payments adjustment, (2) international liquidity, (3) confidence. These three problems are interdependent.[21]

The object of the accumulation of international reserves is to cushion or finance balance of payments deficits and to

---

[19] Oscar L. Altman, "The Management of International Liquidity," IMF *Staff Papers,* Vol. XI, No. 2 (July 1964), pp. 216-245. For an interesting account of the development of the international payments system, see: Robert Triffin, "The Evolution of the International Payments System: Historical Reappraisal and Future Perspectives," *Princeton Studies in International Finance,* No. 12. Princeton: International Finance Section, Department of Economics, Princeton University, 1964.

[20] J. Keith Horsefield, *op. cit.,* pp. 172-173.

[21] *International Monetary Arrangements: The Problem of Choice, Report on the Deliberations of an International Study Group of 32 Economists,* hereinafter referred to as the *Report of the Group of 32.* Princeton: International Finance Section, Department of Economics, Princeton University, 1964, p. 24. This group was formed as a result of statements said to have been made by Secretary of the Treasury Douglass Dillon at a press conference during the Annual Meeting of the IMF on October 2, 1963. Secretary Dillon announced plans for two studies of the international payments system to be made by the Group of Ten (the governments of the ten industrial countries which agreed to the General Arrangements to Borrow

protect the rate of exchange. Adjustment on the other hand refers to the process by which payments imbalances are reduced or eliminated. The standard or classical method of balance of payments adjustment was explained in Chapter 11 where it was also noted that modern governmental authorities are reluctant to allow these automatic adjustment mechanisms free play. Short-term capital movements provide both the means through which the adjustment process takes place, the reserve cushion and the means by which deficits are financed. Where foreign exchange forms the basis of the international payments system, the management of short-term capital impinges strongly on the operation of the adjustment process.

Under the present system, policies may be applied which weaken the adjustment process. The deflation process in deficit countries may be held in check by the use of expansionary measures designed to maintain employment. A surplus nation may prevent the inflow of funds from having the inflationary effects which adjustment requires. Due to the downward rigidity of wages, adjustment works better in surplus countries than in those which are running deficits. When compared with the automatic gold standard, the present international payments system tends to weaken the automatic adjustment of balance of payments disequilibrium.[22]

Since there is insufficient gold stock and production, demand

in Paris in December 1961) and by the IMF. When asked whether or not economists outside of government and international organizations would be heard, Secretary Dillon is reported to have replied that these economists "have had their say." Three academic economists heard these remarks and felt challenged to embark on a study of their own. A group was formed which met first at Princeton in December 1963. A more formal group was then organized which met in Bellagio, Italy, January 17-23, 1964. The object of these meetings was not to obtain agreement, but to air and exchange views on the question of the operation of the international payments system and means for its improvement. *Report of the Group of 32*, pp. 5-23. The economists participating in the deliberations at Bellagio represented ten countries: the United States, United Kingdom, France, Belgium, Italy, the Netherlands, Switzerland, Japan, Canada and Sweden. *Report of the Group of 32*, p. 108.

[22] *Report of the Group of 32*, pp. 25-28. It should be noted that all of the members of this group did not necessarily agree with all of the observations made in the *Report*.

for additional reserves has been met largely by claims on the United States and the United Kingdom and by IMF drawings. The problem of liquidity stems from the fear that increases in these reserves cannot be relied upon to sustain the future growth of international trade with prices held at stable levels.[23]

The problem of confidence applies to all monies and monetary systems, domestic as well as international. In the early days of banking, when bank notes and deposits were not completely covered by gold, confidence in the ability of bankers to redeem these liabilities in gold on demand was essential to the successful operation of the banking system. The development of central banks, the lenders of last resort, aided the operation of the system by promoting confidence in it.

Since the liabilities of a nation under the international payments system are not fully covered by gold, the problem of confidence also arises in conjunction with this system. Unlike domestic systems, there is no central bank bankers' bank to act as a lender of last resort. The IMF, as at present constituted, can come to the aid of the central banks in a limited measure, but it is not a true bankers' bank. Confidence in the reserve currencies is essential to the smooth functioning of the international payments system.[24]

The problem of confidence is complicated by the fact that additional foreign exchange reserves can only be earned by surplus countries at the expense of deficits in those countries whose currencies are used as reserves. Unless the efficiency of the system is improved, and if more and more reserves in the form of foreign exchange are required, the deficits of the reserve-supplying nations will necessarily have to continue and the

---

[23] *Report of the Group of 32*, pp. 28-33. See also: Fritz Machlup, "Plans for Reform of the International Monetary System," *Special Papers in International Economics*, No. 3, August 1962. Princeton: International Finance Section, Department of Economics, Princeton University, 1962, pp. 5-7.

[24] *Report of the Group of 32*, pp. 34-36. See also: Sir Donald Mac-Dougall, "The Dollar Problem: A Reappraisal." *Essays in International Finance*, No. 35, November 1960. Princeton: International Finance Section, Department of Economics, Princeton University, 1906, pp. 25-27, 62-76.

As far as the United States is concerned, and *except for its* accumulated short-term liabilities of these nations will grow.[25] *gold reserve,* these continuing deficits and growing liabilities need not be a matter of great concern *provided the rate of growth of the American economy is at least as large as those of reserve-accumulating countries.* In the last analysis, leaving gold out of account, these liabilities are but claims on United States goods, services and capital. If its rate of growth is sufficient, these claims will not impose any great hardship upon this country.

Other problems involved, in addition to that of liquidity, are the decline of the gold stock in the United States and the continued convertibility of the principal foreign exchange reserve asset into gold. In view of the shortcomings of this system, academic, governmental and international institution economists have subjected it to intensive study and have elaborated plans for its reform.[26] The some fifteen plans for reform fall into four major groups: the semi-automatic gold standard, centralization of international reserves, multiple currency reserves and flexible exchange rates.[27]

The semi-automatic gold standard. This proposed reform of the international payments system envisages a return to a modified form of the gold coin or bullion standards. It is advocated by some economists who lack confidence in the ability of political authorities to control the payments system. In addition, certain protagonists of this reform stress the lack of discipline provided by the present system to force deficit and surplus coun-

---

[25] Cf. Fred H. Klopstock, "The International Status of the Dollar," *Essays in International Finance,* No. 28, May 1957. Princeton: International Finance Section, Department of Economics and Sociology, Princeton University, 1957, pp. 7-26; Peter B. Kenen, "Reserve-Asset Preferences of Central Banks and Stability of the Gold-Exchange Standard," *Princeton Studies in International Finance,* No. 10. Princeton: International Finance Section, Department of Economics, Princeton University, 1963, pp. 1-70; Robert Z. Aliber, "The Management of the Dollar in International Finance," *Princeton Studies in International Finance,* No. 13. Princeton: International Finance Section, Department of Economics, Princeton University, 1964.

[26] *Report of the Group of 32,* pp. 24-65.

[27] *Report of the Group of 32,* pp. 66-106 and an unsigned article (written by Herbert Bratter), "Plans for Increasing International Liquidity," *Banking,* April 1964, pp. 45-46, 130-131.

tries to take appropriate corrective measures. This failure leads to cumulative surpluses and deficits. Finally, many of them hold that other programs of reform either fail to grapple with these problems or create other difficulties.[28]

Under the semi-automatic gold standard, nations fix their pars of exchange in gold; buy and sell it at fixed rates; bring their domestic monetary supply to move in the same direction as changes in the gold reserves and in an amount proportional to changes in these reserves. To insure that there is sufficient gold to sustain the system, its price will be increased by an amount sufficient to permit the United States to use it to liquidate its liabilities to foreign monetary authorities as well as to lend enough to the United Kingdom to pay its sterling liabilities. After this, the price of gold remains fixed.[29]

Changes in the gold reserves under this standard bring about shifts in the rates of interest which induce balancing movements of short-term capital. In addition, movements in the money supply and interest rates reduce or increase total effective demand for goods and affect wages and prices. In this way payments imbalances are not permitted to accumulate or be postponed. Gold replaces foreign exchange currency reserves while its

---

[28] Among the proponents of the various forms of this system see: Jacques Rueff, "The West is Risking a Credit Collapse," *Fortune*, Vol. LXIV, July 1961, pp. 126-127, 262, 267-268 and Michael Heilperin, "Monetary Reform in an Atlantic Setting," *International Payments Imbalances and Need for Strengthening International Payments Arrangements*. Hearings before the Subcommittee on International Exchange and Payments, Joint Economic Committee, U. S. Congress, 87th Congress, 1st Session. Washington: U. S. Government Printing Office, 1961, pp. 331-340. See also Heilperin's statement in the *Report of the Group of 32*, pp. 115-116. General de Gaulle, in a press conference held in Paris on February 4, 1965, is reported to have said that he favored the use of a gold standard in place of the present gold exchange standard. He sketched the shortcomings of the gold exchange standard and stressed the facility which it gave key currency countries to continue to run balance of payments deficits without taking corrective action. General de Gaulle emphasized the fact that key currency countries could make direct investments abroad under the gold exchange standard without having to worry about ensuing balance of payments deficits. Non-key currency nations do not enjoy this advantage and the gold standard would put both key and non-key currency countries on

increased price brings forth sufficient additional supplies to sustain the growth in foreign trade.[30]

This program, although it may prove economically feasible, runs counter to the political trends of the day toward greater government control over economic life. The manner in which the automatic features of the proposed international payments system fit into the directed aspects of the economy is not clear. It is questionable, especially for nations where international trade represents a large percentage of national income and product, if it is possible to allow a semi-automatic system of payments to operate within a framework of other controls. Since the adoption of any reforms to the international payments system involves major political considerations, the prospects for the adoption of the semi-automatic gold standard do not appear to be especially bright.

Centralization of international reserves. Proponents of this plan stress the fact that, unlike domestic monetary systems, the international payments system has no central banks' bank. They also underline the haphazard and fortuitous nature of the present system. Further, its mechanism is slow and cumbersome. The use of national currencies as reserves interferes with needed adjustments in the pars of exchange by the nations whose cur-

---

an equal footing in this regard. He did not specify which form of the gold standard he preferred and seemed to favor the position taken by Jacques Rueff rather than that taken by his Finance Minister Valéry Giscard d'Estaing at the Tokyo meeting of the IMF in 1964. See the French text of General de Gaulle's remarks as reported in *Le Monde* Sélection Hebdomadaire, Vol. XVIII, No. 85 (February 4-10, 1965), p. 2, togehter with the comments in the same issue of *Le Monde* by Sirius and Pierre Drouin and the editorial, "Les Jalons" all on p. 1.

[29] Sir Roy F. Harrod is apparently a partisan of an increase in the price of gold. Among his several contributions to this topic see: Sir Roy F. Harrod, "Imbalance of International Payments," IMF Staff Papers, Vol. III, No. 2 (April 1953), pp. 1-46; "Plan for Restoration of Full Gold Convertibility of the Dollar Together with a Revision of the Gold Content of the Dollar," *Gold Reserve Act Amendments,* Hearings Before a Subcommittee of the Committee on Banking and Currency, 83rd Congress, 2nd Session, March 30, 1954. Washington: U. S. Government Printing Office, 1954, pp. 128-129 and "Europe and the Money Muddle," *Economic Journal,* Vol. LXVIII, September 1958, pp. 538 ff.

[30] *Report of the Group of 32,* pp. 74-81.

rency is so utilized. The best remedy for these defects lies in the creation of an international central monetary authority such as an expanded IMF (XIMF) or some other international central banking institution. They usually claim that none of the other proposed reforms would accomplish the desired results as effectively.[31]

Under the plans for the centralization of international reserves, each major reserve-holding country agrees to keep a part, at least, of its reserves in the form of sight deposits with the XIMF or some other international reserve institution. The gold value of these deposits would be guaranteed and ultimately most international reserves held in this form. Some gold might be owned; but under some forms of this plan, gold is to be converted into deposits. The present capital subscriptions to the IMF would be replaced by these deposits and the Fund's lending power thereby increased. When the XIMF acquired the assets of its members and created deposit liabilities, it could adjust these reserves to meet the requirements of growth and eliminate the instability of the present system.

The Fund would induce members to deposit their reserves by the offer of a gold guarantee of their value and by the payment of interest on them. The volume of reserves could be increased or decreased by the XIMF through open market operations in the member countries; by lending members short-term funds; by the provision of overdraft facilities to members and the purchase of IBRD bonds. Member countries would not be

---

[31] Among the several proponents of different types of this system see: Robert Triffin, *Gold and the Dollar Crisis*, New Haven: Yale University Press, 1960 and "Statement," *Employment, Growth and Price Levels,* Hearings Before the Joint Economic Committee, Congress of the United States, 86th Congress, 1st Session, Part 9A. Washington: U. S. Government Printing Office, 1959, pp. 2905-2954; Maxwell Stamp, "The Fund and the Future," *Lloyds Bank Review*, 1958, pp. 1-20 and "Changes in the World's Payment System," *Moorgate and Wall Street*, Spring 1961, pp. 3-22; A. C. L. Day, "Memorandum of Evidence," Committee on the Working of the Monetary System (Radcliffe Committee), *Principal Memoranda of Evidence*. London: H. M. Stationery Office, 1960, Vol. 3, pp. 75 ff; James W. Angell, "The Reorganization of the International Monetary System: An Alternative Proposal," *The Economic Journal*, Vol. LXXI, December 1961, pp. 691-708.

prevented from making balance of payments adjustments through appropriate policies and needed changes in exchange rates.[32]

In addition to overcoming the disadvantages of the gold-foreign exchange reserve system now in use, the centralization of reserves would provide a type of bank for central banks to use in time of need. This bank would operate on the international front much as national central banks do in supplying domestic credit flexibility and assisting in the maintenance of confidence.

Some economists feel that while an XIMF might be desirable in the future, it is not practical at the present time and difficulty would be encountered in negotiating it. They suggest that many of the objectives of an XIMF could be attained by transforming Fund drawing rights into transferable deposits. Others have proposed a system whereby the IMF deposits are created by voluntary transfer of gold, foreign exchange or both to the Fund. These deposits are to be used by other members when in need in a manner similar to drawing rights. Other students of the question have proposed that the IMF tie programs of aid to underdeveloped countries to its normal functions, and thereby expand its reserve-creating functions while aiding in economic development.[33]

If one regards the international banking system as similar to the domestic system, there may be considerable merit in the proposals for an XIMF or some other form of international central bank. The principal objection to an XIMF or similar institution is lack of responsibility to higher authority. Domestic central banks are responsible to other government authorities who, in their turn and in democracies, are responsible to the people. The responsibility of an XIMF, or other similar institution, is diffused among the members. It is often said that when one is responsible to so many, one is responsible to no one.

Further, would the institution be dominated by a few of its more influential members? Would the large number of newly-emerging nations, with their special desires and requirements, unduly influence the institution? Finally, how many nations

---

[32] *Report of the Group of 32*, pp. 81-87.
[33] *Report of the Group of 32*, pp. 87-88.

would be willing to surrender substantial control over their currency, banking, domestic and international economies to such an institution? Proposals for an XIMF may be sound from the economic point of view, but they also appear to raise difficult problems in *political* economy. The creation of such an institution might have to be hedged by so many escape clauses, qualifications and limits to its authority that it might not prove effective.

Multiple currency reserves. Partisans of multiple currency reserves for the international payments system point to the fact that the use of dollars and sterling places an undue burden on the United States and the United Kingdom. It also permits these two nations to run balance of payments deficits without taking prompt corrective measures. Although they must defend their exchange rates, these nations can continue trading without fear of running out of reserves, since their own currency constitutes, in part, their reserve.

They also hold that the present system is haphazard and does not guarantee adequate reserves. Since it does not offer either adequate adjustment facilities or certain access to additional reserves, it could impede the growth of world trade, the maintenance of full employment and stable prices. Partisans of multiple reserves suggest that no other change in the payments system would be as effective as this reform.[34]

Under the multiple currency reserve plan, monetary authorities of the reserve accumulating countries would gradually

---

[34] Steps toward the implementation of the multiple currency reserve system have already been taken. In 1961, the United States started to add foreign currency holdings to its gold reserve stock and has continued this development (see Chapter 10). The General Arrangements to Borrow signed by ten large industrial members of the IMF, represent another step in this direction, especially along the lines of a suggestion made by Dr. Edward M. Bernstein, formerly Director of Research of the IMF and now a private consultant. In addition to Bernstein, Xenophon Zolotas, Executive Director of the IMF and the late Per Jacobsson, formerly Managing Director of the IMF, have also supported this plan in one or more of its several forms. See: Xenophon Zolotas, *Summary Proceedings of the Twelfth Annual Meeting of the Board of Governors of the International Monetary Fund, 1957,* p. 42 and *Summary Proceedings of the Thirteenth Annual Meeting of the Board of Governors of the International Monetary Fund, 1958,* p. 91; Per Jacobsson, quoted in "Fund Report at ECOSAC,"

diversify their foreign exchange holdings until they hold a mix-ture of the foreign currencies of several nations and gold rather than gold, dollars and sterling as at present. The governments of the countries whose currencies are thus held would agree to buy and sell gold freely, to guarantee the gold value of their currencies and to supply short-term credit instruments for sale to the reserve holding nations.

The policies of the countries participating in the plan are to be coordinated so as to avoid destabilizing and abrupt changes in the composition of their reserve assets. They should agree to raise the foreign exchange part of their reserves when such a change is held to be desirable; to acquire the currencies of nations which run deficits and cooperate in the implementation of balance of payments adjustment procedures.[35]

Some partisans of this plan feel that the rate of increase in the reserves needed to sustain the growth of world trade, stable prices and employment can be settled by agreement on the part of the participating countries. They think that nations would be able to regulate their domestic policies with less fear of foreign repercussions than under the present system. These proponents are also of the opinion that such a plan could be installed with a minimum of negotiation and disruption to the present payments system.

Others fear that the substitution of one currency for another in the reserves, if made suddenly, might serve to disrupt the

---

International Financial News Survey, IMF, Vol. XIII, No. 16 (April 28, 1961), pp. 124-126 and *Summary Proceedings of the Sixteenth Annual Meet-ing of the Board of Governors of the International Monetary Fund, 1961*, pp. 27-29, 157-158; Edward M. Bernstein, "The Adequacy of United States Gold Reserves," *American Economic Review, Papers and Proceedings*, Vol. LI (1961), pp. 439-446 and *International Effects of U. S. Economic Policy*, Joint Economic Committee, United States Congress, 86th Congress, 2nd Session, Study Paper No. 16. Washington: U. S. Government Printing Office, 1960, pp. 85-86 and "The Problem of International Monetary Reserves," *International Payments Imbalances and Need for Strengthening International Financial Arrangements*, Hearings Before the Subcommittee on International Exchange and Payments, Joint Economic Committee, United States Congress, 87th Congress, 1st Session. Washington: U. S. Government Printing Office, 1961, pp. 107-137.

[35] *Report of the Group of 32*, pp. 91-92.

system. Accordingly, they desire to institute a *composite reserve currency unit* to avoid such substitutions and to maintain uniformity in reserve holdings. According to this form of the plan, reserve holding countries would agree to maintain a fixed proportion of their reserves in these units and in gold. Under this proposal the IMF would act as the custodian for the deposit of those currencies included in the units and their gold value would be guaranteed by each participating country.

At the present time, the multiple reserve currency plan in one of its several forms seems to have the best chance of adoption of the several proposed schemes. It apparently entails the least change in the current payments system and, as its partisans have indicated, it involves relatively simple international negotiation and agreement in order to be placed in operation. As a matter of fact, since the United States started to hold foreign currency reserves in addition to gold, and with the IMF General Arrangements to Borrow, the present international payments system appears to be moving in this direction.

Flexible exchange rates. One group of economists holds that the reserve problems of the present international payments system can be solved by the use of flexible or freely floating exchange rates in place of the present fixed rates. The use of such rates would eliminate the need for reserves, because balance of payments surpluses and deficits are automatically adjusted by the free movement of these rates. Flexible rates have a particular appeal to those economists who place reliance upon the ability of economic laws to regulate the economic system satisfactorily (see Chapter 11); who lack confidence in the ability of governments to bring about balance of payments adjustments

---

[36] Fritz Machlup, who has devoted considerable study to this topic, lists twenty-one economists who have written on it. See his: "Plans for the Reform of the International Payments System," *Special Papers in International Economics*, No. 3, August 1962. Princeton: International Finance Section, Department of Economics, Princeton University, 1962, pp. 56-58. Among the economists subscribing to some form of flexible exchange rates and writing English, see: Milton Friedman, "The Case for Flexible Exchange Rates," *Essays in Positive Economics*. Chicago: University of Chicago Press, 1953, pp. 157-201; John Burr Williams, *International Trade Under Flexible*

and to strong partisans of economic liberty and laissez-faire. This plan has probably the widest support among economists who favor any of the reform programs.[36]

Partisans of flexible exchange rates point out that fixed rates mean that balance of payments adjustment must be achieved through changes in employment, domestic price levels, or by barriers to international commerce. Fixed rates also permit balance of payments deficits to be temporarily countered by drawing on the accumulated reserves. For these reasons, adjustment under the present international payments system is not always effective. In addition, fixed rates tend to force nations to either deflate or inflate to match parallel developments on the part of their trading partners. Alternatives to flexible rates, they hold, are not as satisfactory.[37]

Balance of payments disequilibria would be adjusted under this proposal by the free play of exchange rates in increasing or decreasing the international prices of goods, services and capital as the occasion demands. Under an extreme form of this plan, the rates are to be completely free; government authorities would not intervene in the exchange market. Certain groups of nations, acting together, which desired to maintain fixed rates, could be allowed to do so among themselves, but must utilize flexible rates in their trade with non-members of the group.

Partisans of this system suggest that it would give the authorities greater liberty to employ monetary and fiscal policies for purely domestic goals. They maintain that the system will not necessarily impede foreign trade by fostering fluctuations in the rates of exchange. Foreign traders would have the forward market at their disposal to hedge their transactions and avoid taking speculative exchange risks. In general, its supporters do

---

Exchange Rates. Amsterdam: North-Holland Publishing Company, 1954; James E. Meade, "The Case for Variable Exchange Rates," *Three Banks Review,* No. 27 (September 1955), pp. 3-27 and "The Future of International Trade and Payments," *Three Banks Review,* No. 5 (June 1961), pp. 15-38; W. M. Scammell, *International Monetary Policy.* London: Macmillan and Co., Ltd., 1957; Lloyd W. Mints, *Monetary Policy for a Competitive Society.* New York: Macmillan and Company, 1950.
[37] *Report of the Group of 32,* pp. 94-95.

not believe that speculation under this system will be any more disruptive than under the present one. Should speculation prove too disturbing in any particular case, then governments might be justified in intervening in the market to re-establish stability.

There are various forms of flexible exchange rates. Under one, intervention of the monetary authorities is ruled out as long as the exchange rate moves within certain defined upper and lower limits. When these limits are reached, then the authorities could intervene to bring the rates back within the ceiling and floor. Under another type, the authorities are allowed to intervene in the market from time to time as necessity dictates, even where the rates do not reach an upper or lower limit. An alternative form envisages fixed rates of exchange for certain short, defined periods of time, but freely floating rates in the longer run. In this way, some of the advantages of the flexible rates is assured, while preserving room for partially managed rates.[38]

Some of the objections which were voiced against the semi-automatic gold standard apply to a system of flexible rates of exchange. Partisans of *dirigisme* are not likely to take kindly to the scheme. Some feel that the automatic adjustment of economic life via the free play of economic forces has been given sufficient test to indicate that it does not invariably provide entirely satisfactory results. The way in which free exchange rates fit into a system of partially-directed economies has not been worked out. Certain opponents think that freely floating rates will create as many problems as they solve. Others hold that the destabilizing influence of speculation has not been given the weight which it deserves by the proponents of the system. The reaction of today's forward markets to freely floating rates has not been ascertained. Forward cover might prove unobtainable or only obtainable at high prices. If this were to be the case, the system would put an excessive burden on foreign traders and investors.

Finally, it should be pointed out that the world has already had considerable experience with flexible rates of exchange. The hyperinflation in Germany, 1919-1923, when the mark fell to about three trillion to the dollar, is a case in point. The French

---

[38] *Report of the Group of 32,* pp. 98-99.

experience with flexible rates, 1919-1926, when prices rose by about 700 per cent and the franc dropped from about five to forty to the dollar, is another. Aftalion has pointed out that while exchange rates may move to equalize prices at times, when inflation becomes severe, exchange rates may provoke domestic price changes.[39] Flexible exchange rates have operated satisfactorily under the gold standards. Under paper standards—and all nations are on paper standards today—the experience has not been as good.

Finally, both the IMF and the Ministers and Governors of the ten countries participating in the General Arrangement to Borrow have recently taken definite positions against the use of flexible rates.[40] After some debate at Bretton Woods, the question of fixed versus flexible rates was settled in favor of the former. Perhaps the question was not settled for all time, but the present international payments system has been based on fixed rates ever since and the prospects for a change in this now customary practice do not appear promising.

Position of the IMF. In Chapter 3 of its *Annual Report for 1963-1964,* the IMF pointed out that the international payments system has sustained a signal expansion in the world economy since the end of World War II. The dollar played an important role in the growth of international reserves during this period as sterling did in the years before this war. The system has also shown adaptability to changing circumstances as well as capacity for improvement. Among the improvements, the development of new sources of liquidity has been noteworthy, especially those of a bilateral, regional and multilateral character.[41]

The *Report* notes that additional sources of liquidity will be required to sustain future growth in international trade with-

---

[39] Albert Aftalion, *Monnaie, Prix et Change.* Paris: Receuil Sirey, 1927, especially pp. 9-96, 250-349.

[40] *Annual Report of the International Monetary Fund, 1963-1964,* pp. 29-30; *Ministerial Statement of the Group of Ten and Annex Prepared by Deputies,* August 10, 1964, p. 1. The ten nations are: Belgium, Canada, France, West Germany, Italy, Japan, the Netherlands, Sweden, United Kingdom and United States.

[41] IMF *Annual Report for 1963-1964,* pp. 32-33.

out inflationary or deflationary effects and to permit full resource utilization. The Fund has already contributed toward these goals but the payments system in the future is likely to require greater use of these facilities than the Fund's present resources permit. The IMF Articles of Agreement provide for reviews of its quotas every five years.[42] The next quinquennial review of these quotas is scheduled for 1965 and the Fund proposes to consider the possibility of their increase on over-all or selective basis or a combination of the two.

Increased gold tranche positions, which amounted to about $3.9 billion in 1964, only serve to augment member's drawing rights nominally. These increased drawing rights are counterbalanced by a corresponding decrease in national gold reserves resulting from the required gold deposits in the IMF. The important increase in liquidity is contributed by the credit tranche positions which amounted to about $14 billion in 1964. Higher quotas will also increase the resources and liquidity of the Fund itself. In examining the question of quota increases, the IMF proposes to give special attention to that part of the members' subscriptions which are payable in gold because these payments reduce the liquidity of the members at the same time that they increase that of the Fund.

In addition to examining the question of quotas, the IMF also proposes to undertake a study of the General Arrangements to Borrow which expire in October 1966 and come up for review in 1965. These Arrangements may be continued, discontinued or increased. In its studies, the Fund proposes to consider the virtually unconditional gold and the conditional credit tranche drawing rights in view of developing new means of augmenting the former.[43]

Position of the Group of Ten. The Group of Ten of the General Arrangements to Borrow in its *Ministerial Statement* expressed confidence in the present international payments system as a foundation on which to build for the future. They did, however, voice the fear that the future supply of gold and foreign

---

[42] Articles of Agreement of the IMF, Article III, Section 2.
[43] IMF, *op. cit.*, pp. 34-39.

exchange might prove inadequate for world needs. Accordingly, they authorized a study of the payments system by their Deputies.[44]

The *Annex Prepared by Deputies* (to the *Ministerial Statement*) underlines the relationships existing between the balance of payments adjustment process and liquidity, and outlines the appropriate adjustment tools at the disposition of national governments. To clarify these questions further, the Ten asked Working Party 3 of the OECD to conduct a study of "how member countries, individually and collectively, and compatibly with the pursuits of their essential internal objectives, could in the future preserve a better balance of payments equilibrium and achieve a faster and more effective adjustment of imbalance."[45]

The *Annex* goes on to point out that the payments system is in a constant state of evolution with gold the basic asset. The increase of the foreign exchange components of international reserves has been a gradual process growing out of spontaneous practices rather than a planned and considered change. In addition, it called attention to the role played by the development of international monetary cooperation. The IMF has played a key part in this cooperation and its role has been further augmented by the General Arrangements to Borrow. In the international payments system, according to the Deputies, private liquidity should not be overlooked for the effective working of the system depends in part upon private working balances.

A nation's liquidity is no longer measured solely by the level of its reserves in the form of gold and foreign exchange. There are other facilities at the disposition of monetary authorities (see Chapter 10). To improve international liquidity and to provide for future growth, the Deputies found that, although gold will continue to be the ultimate reserve asset, the dollar has greatly contributed to the growth of international liquidity and there is no immediate prospect of any other currency assuming the functions of an international reserve currency.

They also agreed that while IMF credit facilities and those

---

[44] Group of Ten, *op. cit.*, pp. 1-2.
[45] Group of Ten, *op. cit.*, p. 5.

of a bilateral character will continue to play an essential part in financing imbalances, the need may be felt in the future for some additional kind of reserve asset. The recently developed swaps and ad hoc support operations have been effective in maintaining orderly conditions of international payments; but, in their opinion, there is no single unique manner in which the increasing requirements for liquidity must be met. The Deputies held that the present consultative machinery should be fully utilized and provision made for still closer cooperation by multilateral review and appraisal under a system of "multilateral surveillance."[46]

The *Annex Prepared by Deputies* concludes by making a series of recommendations:

1. Since the flow of new gold into monetary channels is not likely to prove adequate for the liquidity needs of the future, efforts should be made to discourage speculation in gold which checks this flow.

2. Existing stocks of gold should be allowed to play their proper role in the international monetary system.

3. Given the success which cooperation has already had, further developments in the form of multilateral surveillance should be encouraged.

4. Multilateral surveillance should include the exchange of information, mutually reinforcing actions and should apply to private as well as public operations.

5. A new reserve asset, created according to the over-all need for reserves is needed.[47]

6. The gold tranche or other similar claim on the IMF which

---

[46] *Statement of the Group of Ten*, p. 9. The precise meaning attached to "multilateral surveillance" is not at present clear and doubtless will not be clarified until such a plan is put into actual operation. In French, the term implies a greater degree of supervision and control than in English.

[47] Although the Group of Ten is careful not to specify the exact type of reserve asset contemplated, it might be worth noting that Dr. Edward M. Bernstein has proposed a "reserve unit" equivalent to a gold dollar which consists of a defined proportion of the currencies of eleven nations (the Ten plus Switzerland). The proportion represented by the currency of each nation depends upon the present role of each currency in the

is capable of enlargement, should be accepted as a type of reserve currency.

7. The use of Roosa type bonds should be continued and be placed under the scrutiny of multilateral surveillance.

8. Consideration should be given to the role which long-term credits might play in bolstering the payments system.

9. Fund quotas, both generally and on a selective basis, should be increased.

10. The IMF should give special attention to the problems created by the partial payment of subscriptions in gold.

11. Studies should be made by the countries of the General Arrangements to Borrow in the light of the proposed increase in Fund quotas.[48]

Although but little has been written on the subject, the possibilities of improvement of the mechanism of the payments system appear to offer promise. Banks, exchange dealers and other financial institutions are constantly endeavoring to increase the speed and reduce the costs of making international payments. These improvements increase the velocity of circulation of international payments media. They operate to make existing reserves more efficient and to increase their effective, if not their absolute, size. At least one private research organization has studied the problem in some detail and has prepared a series of findings and recommendations for the improvement of the international payments mechanism.[49]

France and the gold standard. On February 11, 1965, French Finance Minister, M. Valéry Giscard d'Estaing, delivered a lecture at the Faculty of Law of the University of Paris in which

---

payments system and each country's position in world trade and investment. Under Bernstein's proposal, each participant is free to hold any type of reserves it desires, but gold holdings must be matched by equal amounts of the new reserve units. The system would be administered by trustees. His plan would be put into effect gradually so as not to increase reserves suddenly. Bernstein feels that his reserve units would permit the reserves of all nations to grow as the need arose. Unsigned article (written by Herbert Bratter), "Plans for Increasing International Liquidity." *Banking,* April 1964, p. 46.

[48] *Statement of the Group of Ten,* pp. 8-14.

[49] Spindletop Research Inc., Iron Works Pike, Lexington, Kentucky.

he said that the important states *(les grands états,* presumably the ten countries of the General Arrangements to Borrow,) should agree to pay their international obligations in gold instead of reserve currencies. In the meantime France proposed to commence international payments in gold. Thus France, although recommending the international adoption of some form of the gold standard (apparently a gold bullion standard supplemented by composite reserve units), was taking unilateral action to apply it immediately.

M. Giscard d'Estaing continued by stating that France proposed to convert its dollar holdings into gold except for $660 million representing its long-term debt to the United States and an additional $200 to $400 million for working balances. At the beginning of 1965, France's holdings of dollars amounted to approximately $1.3 billion. It is likely, therefore, that France will convert between $200 and $400 million into gold in the near future. Presumably, it will continue to demand gold for official holdings of dollars as its holdings of this currency grow.

France is running a surplus on its balance of payments; the offer to pay its international short-term obligations in gold is, therefore, not very meaningful since it has no such obligations to meet at present. M. Giscard d'Estaing stated, however, that France would continue to pay out gold even if a deficit appeared.

Should France continue to run a surplus while the United States shows a deficit and demands redemption of its future official dollar accretions in gold, the consequences for the United States gold stock and the present international payments system could be serious. If the United States continued to pay out gold against official dollar holdings, it would be but a question of time until its monetary gold stock was reduced to the statutory level of twenty-five per cent of the outstanding Federal Reserve notes. If continued long enough, and without appropriate counter-action, the United States could conceivably be drained of substantial quantities of gold. Such a possibility does not appear likely, for well before it occurred steps would doubtless be taken by the Group of Ten and the Basle Group to forestall it, to amend the present or install some alternative international payments system. France's unilateral action and recommendations do, however, pose something of a threat to the present payments system.

As indicated in footnote 28 of this chapter, General de Gaulle does not approve of the present international payments system. He appears especially troubled by the fact that it permits the United States to continue to run balance of payments deficits, to invest abroad, without taking appropriate corrective action. However, the United States balance of payments deficits dating from 1950, have served to build up the reserve holdings of its European trading partners. Without these deficits, the international financial position of many nations would not be in their present relatively satisfactory state.

In addition, the United States deficits stem principally from its foreign aid programs and its long- and short-term capital outflows. The military and civilian grant programs have been a part of the United States contribution to the containment of Communism and the preservation of the free world. Its investment, although resented by some countries apparently for nationalistic or competitive reasons, serves to increase the product and income of the recipient nations and to promote their continued economic growth. The elimination of United States deficits through a reduction in these two accounts would mean the end of these endeavors. What nation is both prepared and willing to assume these tasks should the United States curtail its aid programs and foreign investment? It should also be noted that the reduction of payments imbalances is as much the responsibility of surplus as of deficit nations, as the recent upward revaluations of the mark and guilder bear witness.

Finally, as long as the dollar continues to be the principal reserve currency and other nations require increasing amounts of reserves, the United States is likely to incur balance of payments deficits of between one and two billion dollars a year. As things now stand, the present large deficits should doubtless be reduced, but their complete elimination should not be undertaken without consultation with the principal reserve-holding countries on a multilateral basis.[50]

The balance of payments and the international payments system. As earlier chapters have indicated, rudimentary international payments systems antedated the first attempts to construct balances of trade by many centuries. However, as trade developed and problems of international payments arose, the need for balances of trade, accounts and payments became more pressing. Balances of payments gradually developed in response to this need. Each improvement in this tabulation came either as a result of the pressing need for further information concerning the operations of the system, or to help the partisans of the various theories of trade imbalances to bolster their positions and arguments.

The balance of payments and the international payments system thus grew together. In a certain measure, the balance of payments may be said to be the outgrowth of payments imbalances and the international payments system. Of course, international payments have and can continue to operate without the benefit of balances of payments. A nation can keep track of its reserve position by the simple procedure of recording the movements of gold and foreign exchange. Such elementary record keeping, however, yields little information concerning the sources of the movements of these reserves and does not provide either analysts or statesmen with very helpful guides for policy. The modern balance of payments presents much information

---

[50] M. Valéry Giscard d'Estaing's lecture was reported in two articles in *Le Monde* Sélection Hebdomadaire (a weekly newspaper published in Paris), Vol. XVIII, No. 852, pp. 1 and 4. See also the comment, *Un Nouveau "Corset,"* by Pierre Drouin and the editorial on President Johnson's opposition to the gold standard, *Le Rendez-Vous,* both in the same issue of *Le Monde* on pp. 1 and 4 respectively. *Le Monde* calls attention to the fact that M. Giscard d'Estaing chose an academic audience to voice his views in a manner similar to that selected by the late General Marshall to announce the Marshall Plan (Harvard University Commencement, June 1947). *Le Monde* also mentions the strange *contretemps* which led M. Giscard d'Estaing's audience (which apparently approved his remarks) to "boo" the mention of Jacques Rueff, a strong supporter of the gold standard, and to applaud that of Robert Triffin, an avowed opponent of this standard.

concerning international commerce and the operations of the payments system as they affect individual countries and groups of countries such as monetary areas. It is an indispensable diagnostic tool. Without these compilations, the payments system could not possibly function as well as it does.

The role of the balance of payments in the operation of the system places great responsibility upon these tabulations and underlies the need for their steady improvement. Past improvements have aided in the development of trade and the payments system. The first ameliorations required lie in the field of accuracy and reliability. In addition, better means of relating the balance of payments to other quantitative data would be helpful. It could serve a useful purpose if it were more closely coordinated with other statistical series.

It would be naive, and run counter to the lessons of the history of this statement, to assume that it has reached its ultimate state of perfection and development. Balance of payments statisticians of the present and future face a challenge to perfect and coordinate their work to make the tabulation more useful.

With the international payments system, the full circle of the balance of payments as analyzed here is complete. Starting with the growth of trade in fourteenth century England, the study ends with the present international payments system. In this circle of development, the balance of payments has proved its value by presenting an indispensable macro-economic picture of external economic operations.

BIBLIOGRAPHY

Section I: History

Allen, R. G. D. "Statistics of the Balance of Payments," *Economic Journal,* March 1951, pp. 179-196.

Allen, R. G. D. and Ely, J. Edward. *International Trade Statistics.* New York: John Wiley and Sons, Inc., 1953.

Anderson, Adam. *An Historical and Chronological Deduction of the Origin of Commerce from the Earliest Accounts.* London: J. Walter, 1787.

Bacon, Nathaniel T. "American International Indebtedness," *Yale Review,* November 1900, pp. 265-285.

Badger, Donald T. *The Balance of Payments: A Tool of Economic Analysis.* Doctoral dissertation at George Washington University, 1951.

Barbon, Nicholas. *A Discourse Concerning Coining the New Money Lighter, In Answer to Mr. Locke's Considerations About Raising the Value of Money.* London: R. Chiswell, 1696.

Barbon, Nicholas. "A Discourse of Trade," (1690), *A Reprint of Economic Tracts,* Jacob H. Hollander (ed.). Baltimore: John Hopkins Press, 1907.

Beer, Max. *Early British Economics from the XIIIth to the Middle of the XVIIIth Century.* London: George Allen and Unwin, Ltd., 1938.

Bell, John Fred. *A History of Economic Thought.* New York: Ronald Press, 1953.

Bland, A. E., Brown, P. A., and Tawney, R. H., (eds.). *English Economic History: Select Documents,* 2nd ed. London: G. Bell and Sons, Ltd., 1915.

Bourne, Stephen. "The Growing Preponderance of Imports over Exports in the Foreign and Colonial Trade of the United Kingdom," *Journal of the Royal Statistical Society,* March 1877, pp. 19-34.

— "Progress on the External Trade of the United Kingdom in Recent Years," *Journal of the Royal Statistical Society,* June 1893, pp. 185-207.

Bowen, Francis. *The Principles of Political Economy.* Boston: Little, Brown and Company, 1865.

The British Merchant, 3rd ed. vol. 1, Charles King (ed.). London: Printed for Thomas Osborne, 1748, pp. 155-161.

The British Merchant: A Collection of Papers Relating to the Trade of Commerce of Great Britain and Ireland. London: Charles King, 1743.

British Museum. *Additional Manuscripts,* 36785, folios 6,58.

British Museum, *Lansdowne, MSS,* Vol. 152, folios 176-178.

Bullock, Charles J. *Introduction to the Study of Economics,* 2nd ed., rev. New York: Silver, Burdett and Company, 1900.

Bullock, Charles J., Williams, John H., and Tucker, Rufus S. "The Balance of Trade of the United States," *The Review of Economic Statistics,* July 1919, pp. 215-254.

Cairnes, John Elliott. *Some Leading Principles of Political Economy Newly Expounded.* New York: Harper and Brothers, 1874.

Cary, John. *An Essay on the Coyn and Credit of England as they stand with respect to its Trade.* Bristol: Privately printed, 1696.

— *An Essay on the State of England in Relation to its Trade, its Poor, and its Taxes for Carrying on the present war against France.* Bristol: Printed by W. Bonny for the author, 1695.

Chamberlain, Hugh. *A Collection of some Papers writ upon Several Occasions, Concerning Clipt and Counterfeit Money, and Trade, so far as it relates to the Exportation of Bullion.* London: Printed for Benjamin Tooke, 1696.

Clapham, Sir John. *A Concise Economic History of Britain from the Earliest Times to 1750.* Cambridge: University Press, 1949.

Clark, G. N. *Guide to English Commercial Statistics 1696-1782.* London: Office of the Royal Historical Society, 1938.

Child, Sir Josiah. *A New Discourse of Trade,* 4th ed. London: Printed for J. Hodges, 1698.

Clough, Shepard. *The Economic Development of Western Civilization.* New York: McGraw Hill Book Company, Inc., 1959.

Coke, Roger. *A Discourse of Trade.* London: N. Brome, 1670.

The Commercial and Financial Chronicle. May 6, 1882, pp. 499-501.

Court, William Henry Bassano. *A Concise Economic History of Britain from 1750 to Recent Times.* Cambridge: University Press, 1954.

Crammond, Edgar. "Discussion on Mr. George Paish's Paper," *Journal of the Royal Statistical Society,* September 1909, pp. 481-483.

Cunningham, William. *The Growth of English Industry and Commerce,* 5th ed. Cambridge: The University Press, 1915.

Dana, William B. "Why Do We Export Gold," *Commercial and Financial Chronicle,* March 30, 1895, pp. 542-544.

Devons, Ely. *An Introduction to British Economic Statistics.* Cambridge: University Press, 1956.

The Economist. November 24, 1877, pp. 1394-1396.

— December 8, 1877, pp. 1458-1459.

Fetter, Frank W. "The Term 'Favorable Balance of Trade'," *Quarterly Journal of Economics,* August 1935, pp. 621-645.

Fortrey, Samuel. "Englands Interest and Improvement," *A Reprint of Economic Tracts,* Jacob H. Hollander (ed.). Baltimore: John Hopkins Press, 1907.

Foster, John Leslie. *An Essay on the Principle of Commercial Exchanges.* London: Printed for J. Hatchard, 1804.

Fuchs, Karl Johannes. *The Trade Policy of Great Britain and her Colonies since 1860.* London: Macmillan and Co., Ltd., 1905.

Furnivall, Frederic J. (ed.). *William Stafford's Compendious or Briefe Examination of Certayne Ordinary Complaints.* London: N. Trubner and Co., 1876.

Gee, Josua. *The Trade and Navigation of Great Britain Considered,* 2nd ed. London: Sam Buckley, 1730.

Gibbins, Henry de Beltgens. *The Industrial History of England,* 3rd ed. London: Methuen and Co., 1894.

Giffen, Robert. "The Use of Import and Export Statistics," *Journal of the Royal Statistical Society,* June 1882, pp. 181-284.

Giuseppi, M. S. *A Guide to the Manuscripts Preserved in the Public Record Office.* London: His Majesty's Stationery Office, 1924.

Goschen, George Joachim. *The Theory of the Foreign Exchanges.* London:

Effingham Wilson, 1861.

Great Britain, *Board of Trade Journal.* "The Balance of Trade, An Estimate of Invisible Exports," January 15, 1920, pp. 71-73.

— "The Balance of Trade. The Years 1923, 1924 and 1925," January 21, 1926, pp. 68-71.

— "The Balance of Trade. The Years 1924, 1925, and 1926," January 27, 1927, pp. 92-93.

— "The Balance of Trade. The Years 1929, 1930, and 1931," February 18, 1932, pp. 216-220.

— "The Balance of Payments. The Years 1931, 1932 and 1933," February 22, 1934, pp. 277-281.

— "The Balance of Payments. The Years 1933, 1934 and 1935," February 20, 1936, pp. 259-263.

— "The Balance of Payments. The Years 1935, 1936 and 1937," February 17, 1938, pp. 230-234.

— "The Balance of Payments. The Years 1936, 1937 and 1938," February 23, 1939, pp. 284-289.

Great Britain, Customs Establishment, Statistical Office. *Annual Statements of Trade and Navigation of the United Kingdom with Foreign Countries and British Possessions.* Beginning in 1853.

— *Annual Statements of Trade of the United Kingdom with Foreign Countries and British Possessions.* Beginning in 1899.

Great Britain, Parliament, House of Commons. *Accounts and Papers,* Vol. LI, 1854-1855.

— *Accounts and Papers,* Vol. LXIII, 1871.

— *Journals of the House of Commons, December 3, 1697 to October 24, 1699,* Vol. XII. "Account of the State and Condition of the General Trade of England, 1670-1697," pp. 432-435.

— *Journal of the House of Commons 1711-1714,* Vol. XVII. "Scheme of Trade, as entered in the Custom-house Books in 1674," pp. 423-424.

— *Report from the Select Committee on the High Price of Gold Bullion.* Reprinted in *The Paper Pound 1797-1821.* London: King and Son, Ltd., 1919.

— *Reports 1796-1797,* No. 134, Vol. XIX.

Great Britain, Parliament, House of Lords. *The Manuscripts of the House of Lords 1695-1697.* Series 17 (new series), Vol. II. "An Account of trade of this Kingdom with all parts of the world by way of exportation and importations for 3 years, vizt., from Christmas 1692 until Christmas 1695." pp. 421-422.

— *The Manuscripts of the House of Lords 1697-1699,* Series 17 (new series), Vol. III. "Account of Trade with Ireland, Christmas 1692 to Christmas 1695," pp. 421-422.

— *The Manuscripts of the House of Lords, 1699-1702,* Series 17 (new series), Vol. IV. "An Abstract of the Inspector-General's Accounts of Imports and Exports, from Michaelmas 1696 to Christmas 1699," pp. 430-435.

Great Britain, Public Record Office. *Colonial Office,* 390/12.

— *Colonial Office,* 390/14.

— *Colonial Office Papers 1700-1701,* Series 388, Vol. 8, D.37. "An Abstract of the Estimates or Original Values of the Exports and Imports from

Michaelmas 1696 to Michaelmas 1697," prepared by Phillip Meadows.
— *Customs* 3/72.
— *Cusoms* 22, pp. 1, 192.
— 831 *Customs Accounts of the Kings Remembrancer's Department of the Exchequer,* E.122/241/1 and E.122/158/20, folios 1-3.

Great Britain, Treasury. *National Income and Expenditure of the United Kingdom, 1938 to 1946.* Cmd. 7009. London: His Majesty's Stationery Office, 1947.
— *United Kingdom Balance of Payments, 1946 and 1947.* Cmd. 7324. London: His Majesty's Stationery Office, 1948.
— *United Kingdom Balance of Payments, 1946 to 1949.* Cmd. 7928. London: His Majesty's Stationery Office, 1950.

Hall, Hubert. *A History of the Custom-Revenue in England,* Vol. II. London: Elliot Stock, 1885.

Harris, Joseph. *An Essay upon Money and Coins.* London: Printed by G. Hawkins, 1757.

Heckscher, Eli F. *Mercantilism.* London: George Allen and Unwin, Ltd., 1935.

Heidelbach, Alfred S. "Why Gold is Exported," *Forum,* February 1895, pp. 647-651.

Hobson, Charles K. *The Export of Capital.* London: Constable and Co., Ltd., 1914.
— "The Measurement of the Balance of Trade," *Economica,* May 1921, pp. 132-146.

Hull, Charles H. (ed.). "Political Arithmetick" (1690), *The Economic Writings of Sir William Petty,* Vol. I. Cambridge: University Press, 1899.

Hume, David. *Political Discourses,* 2nd ed. Edinburgh: Printed by R. Fleming, 1752.

Imlah, Albert H. "Real Value in British Foreign Trade, 1798-1853," *The Journal of Economic History,* November 1948, pp. 133-152.

"International Payments of the U.S. During the War," *Foreign Commerce Weekly,* March 10, 1945, pp. 6-7, 31.

"International Transactions of the United States During First Quarter 1946," *Survey of Current Business,* July 1946, pp. 16-21.

Jones, Richard. "Primitive Political Economy of England," *Edinburgh Review,* April 1847, pp. 426-452.

Kindersley, Robert. "British Overseas Investments in 1931," *The Economic Journal,* June 1933, pp. 187-204.

Krishna, Bal. *Commercial Relations between India and England.* London: George Routledge and Sons, Ltd., 1924.

Laughlin, J. Laurence. *Credit of the Nations.* New York: Charles Scribner's Sons, 1919.

League of Nations. *Memorandum on Balance of Payments and Foreign Trade Balances 1910-1923.* Geneva: 1924.
— *Memorandum on International Trade and Balance of Payments 1913-1927.* Geneva: 1928.
— *Memorandum on International Trade and Balances of Payments 1926-1928.* Geneva: 1929.

— *Memorandum on International Trade and Balances of Payments.* Geneva: 1930.

— *Memorandum on International Trade and Balances of payments 1927-1929.* Geneva: 1931.

Lewis, Cleona. *America's Stake in International Investments.* Washington: The Brookings Institute, 1938.

— *The International Accounts; A Constructive Criticism of Methods Used in Stating the Results of International Trade, Service and Financial Operations.* New York: The Macmillan Co., 1927.

Lipson, Ephriam. *The Economic History of England,* 2nd ed., Vols. I, II, and III. London: Adam and Charles Black, 1934.

The London Times, May 22, 1894, p. 9.

Lowndes, William. *A Report Containing an Essay for the Amendment of the Silver Coins.* London: Printed by Charles Bill, 1695.

Macpherson, David. *Annals of Commerce.* London: Nichols and Son, 1805.

Maizels, Alfred. "The Overseas Trade Statistics of the United Kingdom," *Journal of the Royal Statistical Society,* Part II, 1949, pp. 207-223.

Malynes, Gerald. *The Center of the Circle of Commerce.* London: Printed by William Jones, 1623.

— *England's View, in the unmasking of two Paradoxes; With a replication unto the answer of Maister J. Bodine.* London: 1603.

— *Lex Mercatoria, or, The Antient Law-Merchant.* London: Nicholas Bourne, 1629.

Marshall, John. *A Digest of all the Accounts Relating to the Population, Productions, Revenues, Financial Operations, Manufactures, Shipping, Colonies, Commerce, etc. of the United Kingdom of Great Britain and Ireland.* London: Printed by J. Haddon, 1833.

McCulloch, John Ramsey. *A Dictionary, Practical, Theoretical, and Historical, of Commerce and Commercial Navigation.* Philadelphia: A. Hart, 1852.

— *The Literature of Political Economy.* London: Longmans, Brown, Green and Longmans, 1845.

McCulloch, J. R. (ed.). *Early English Tracts on Commerce.* "Britannia Languens, or a Discourse of Trade" (1680). Cambridge: University Press, 1954.

Mears, Eliot G. "The Foreign Trade Statistics of the United States," *Journal of the American Statistical Association,* September 1935, pp. 501-516.

Mercator: or Commerce Retrieved. May 26, 1713, No. 2.

— October 22, 1713, No. 65.

Misselden, Edward. *The Circle of Commerce or the Ballance of Trade in the defense of Free Trade.* London: Printed for N. Bourne, 1623.

— *Free Trade; or, the Means to make trade florish.* London: John Legatt, 1622.

Moreau, Cesar. *State of the British Trade.* London: Treutell, Wurtz, Treuttel and Richter, 1824.

Mun, Thomas. *A Discourse of Trade: From England unto the East-Indies.* (1621). Reprinted, New York: The Facsimile Text Society, 1930.

— *England's Treasure by Forraign Trade.* London: 1664. Reprinted, New York: Macmillan and Co., 1895.

Newmarch, William. "On the Progress of the Foreign Trade of the United Kingdom since 1856, with Especial Reference to the Effects Produced upon it by the Protectionist Tariffs of other Countries," *Journal of the Royal Statistical Society*, June 1878, pp. 187-282.

Niles' National Register. July 21, 1838, p. 322.

North, Douglass C. "The United States Balance of Payments," *Studies in Income and Wealth*, Vol. XXIV. National Bureau of Economic Research, Princeton: University Press, 1960, pp. 573-627.

"Our International Balance Sheet," *The Commercial Year Book*, Vol. I. New York: 1896, pp. 225-231.

Paish, Sir George. "Great Britain's Capital Investments in Individual Colonial and Foreign Countries," *Journal of the Royal Statistical Society*, January 1911, pp. 167-187.

— "Great Britain's Capital Investments in Other Lands," *Journal of the Royal Statistical Society*, September 1909, pp. 465-480.

— *The Trade Balance of the United States*. United States National Monetary Commission. Washington: United States Government Printing Office, 1910.

Palgrave, R.H. Inglis, (ed.), *Dictionary of Political Economy*, Vol. II. London: Macmillan and Co., 1910, pp. 148-151.

Pitkin, Timothy. *A Statistical View of the Commerce of the United States of America*. Hartford: Printed by Charles Hosmer, 1816.

Pollexfen, John. *England and East-India Inconsistent in their Manufactures*. London: Privately Printed, 1697.

— *Of Trade, also of Coyn, Bullion, of Improving our Woolen Manufacture, To Prevent Exporting Wool. Of Ways and Means to Increase our Riches, etc.* London: John Baker, 1700.

Price, W. H. "The Origin of the Phrase 'Balance of Trade'," *Quarterly Journal of Economics*, November 1905, pp. 157-167.

Raguet, Condy. *A Treatise on Currency and Banking*. Philadelphia: Grigg and Elliott, 1840.

Ricardo, David. "Reply to Mr. Bosanquet's Practical Observations on the Report of the Bullion Committee." E. C. K. Gonner (ed.), *Economic Essays*. London: C. Bell and Sons, 1926.

Robinson, Henry. *Englands Safety, in Trades Encrease*. London: Nicholas Bourne, 1641.

Schlote, Werner. *British Overseas Trade from 1700 to the 1930's*. Translated by W. O. Henderson and W. H. Chalmer. Oxford: Basil Blackwell, 1952.

Schooling, John Holt. *The British Trade Book*, 3rd ed. London: John Murray, 1908.

Schumpeter, Elizabeth. *English Overseas Trade Statistics 1697-1808*. Introduction by T. S. Ashton. Oxford: Clarendon Press, 1960.

Schumpeter, Joseph A. *History of Economic Analysis*. New York: Oxford University Press, 1954.

Seaman, Ezra C. *Essays on the Progress of Nations*. New York: Baker and Scribner, 1846.

Seybert, Adam. *Statistical Annals*. Philadelphia: Thomas Dobson and Son, 1818.

Shaw-Lefevre, George J. (Baron Eversley). *The Balance of Trade*. London:

Cassell and Co., Ltd., 1903.

Simon, Mathew. "The United States Balance of Payments 1861-1900," National Bureau of Economic Research. *Studies in Income and Wealth,* Vol. XXIV. Princeton: University Press, 1960, pp. 629-715.

Speare, Charles F. "What America Pays Europe for Immigrant Labor," *North American Review,* January 1908, pp. 106-116.

Sterns, Worthy P. "The International Indebtedness of the United States in 1789," *Journal of Political Economy,* December 1897, pp. 27-53.

Steuart, James. *An Inquiry into the Principles of Political Economy,* Vol II. London: Printed for T. Cadell, 1767.

Stow, John. *A Survey of London.* Reprinted from the text of 1603 with an introduction by Charles L. Kingsford. Oxford: Clarendon Press, 1908.

Suviranta, Bruno. *The Theory of the Balance of Trade in England.* Helsingfors, 1923.

Taussig, Frank W. *International Trade.* New York: The Macmillan Co., 1927.

Tawney, R. H. and Powers, Eileen (eds.). *Tudor Economic Documents,* Vols. I and III. London: Longmans, Green and Co., 1924.

Taylor, Amos E. "Statistical Methods in Balance-of-Payments Estimates," *Journal of the American Statistical Association,* March 1937, pp. 65-74.

Thornton, Henry. *An Enquiry into the Nature and Effects of the Paper Credit of Great Britain,* F. A. von Hayek (ed.). New York: Farrar and Rinehart, Inc., 1939.

Tooke, Thomas. *A History of Prices and the State of Circulation in 1838 and 1839.* London: Longmans, Orme, Brown, Green and Longmans, 1840.

Tucker, Josiah. *The Elements of Commerce and Theory of Taxes,* (1755). *Josiah Tucker, A Selection from His Economic and Political Writings.* Edited by Robert L. Schuyler. New York: Columbia University Press, 1931.

United Nations. *Balance of Payments 1939-1945.* Geneva, 1948.

— *Studies and Reports on Statistical Methods.* Subcommittee on Balance of Payments Statistics of League of Nations Committee of Statistical Experts. Geneva, 1947.

U.S. Bureau of the Census. *Historical Statistics of the United States, Colonial Times to 1957.* Washington, D.C.: United States Government Printing Office, 1960.

U.S. Department of Commerce, Bureau of Foreign and Domestic Commerce. *Economic Series No. 1.* "American Direct Investments in Foreign Countries-1936," prepared by Paul D. Dickens. Washington, D. C.: United States Government Printing Office, 1938.

— *Economic Series No. 3.* "The Balance of International Payments of the United States in 1937." Washington, D. C.: United States Government Printing Office, 1938.

— *Economic Series No. 4.* "Overseas Travel and Travel Expenditures in the Balance of International Payments of the United States 1919-1938," prepared by August Maffry. Washington, D. C.: United States Government Printing Office, 1939.

— *Economic Series No. 23.* "The United States in the World Economy." Washington, D. C.: United States Government Printing Office, 1943.

— *Economic Series No. 65.* "International Transactions of the United States

During the War." Washington, D. C.: United States Government Printing Office, 1948.

— *Foreign Investments in the United States.* Washington, D. C.: United States Government Printing Office, 1937.

— *Trade Information Bulletin, No. 114.* "The Balance of International Payments of the United States in 1922." Washington, D. C.: United States Government Printing Office, 1923.

— *Trade Information Bulletin, No. 215.* "The Balance of International Payments of the United States in 1923." Washington, D. C.: United States Government Printing Office, 1924.

— *Trade Information Bulletin, No. 340.* "The Balance of International Payments of the United States in 1924." Washington, D. C.: United States Government Printing Office, 1925.

— *Trade Information Bulletin, No. 399.* "The Balance of International Payments of the United States in 1925." Washington, D. C.: United States Government Printing Office, 1926.

— *Trade Information Bulletin, No. 503.* "The Balance of International Payments of the United States in 1926." Washington, D. C.: United States Government Printing Office, 1927.

— *Trade Information Bulletin, No. 552.* "The Balance of International Payments of the United States in 1927." Washington, D. C.: United States Government Printing Office, 1928.

— *Trade Information Bulletin, No. 625.* "The Balance of International Payments of the United States in 1928." Washington, D. C.: United States Government Printing Office, 1929.

— *Trade Information Bulletin, No. 698.* "The Balance of International Payments of the United States in 1929." Washington, D. C.: United States Government Printing Office, 1930.

— *Trade Information Bulletin, No. 731.* "American Direct Investments in Foreign Countries," prepared by Paul D. Dickens. Washington, D. C.: United States Government Printing Office, 1930.

— *Trade Information Bulletin, No. 767.* "A New Estimate of American Investments Aboard," prepared by Paul D. Dickens. Washington, D. C.: United States Government Printing Office, 1931.

— *Trade Information Bulletin, No. 803.* "The Balance of International Payments of the United States in 1931." Washington, D. C.: United States Government Printing Office, 1932.

— *Trade Information Bulletin, No. 814.* "The Balance of International Payments of the United States in 1932." Washington, D. C.: United States Government Printing Office, 1933.

— *Trade Information Bulletin, No. 819.* "The Balance of International Payments of the United States in 1933." Washington, D. C.: United States Government Printing Office, 1934.

— *Trade Information Bulletin, No. 826.* "The Balance of International Payments of the United States in 1934." Washington, D. C.: United States Government Printing Office, 1935.

— *Trade Information Bulletin, No. 833.* "The Balance of International Payments of the United States in 1935." Washington, D. C.: United States Government Printing Office, 1936.

— *Trade Promotion Series, No. 104.* "Handbook on American Underwriting of Foreign Securities," prepared by Ralph Young. Washington, D. C.: United States Government Printing Office, 1930.

U. S., 33rd Congress, 1st Session. *Sen. Ex. Doc. 42, 1853-1854.*

U. S. *State Papers: Commerce and Navigation.* 1st Congress, 3rd Session, 1791, Doc. No. 6.

— *State Papers: Commerce and Navigation.* 2nd Congress, 1st Session, 1791, Doc. No. 7.

— *State Papers: Commerce and Navigation.* 16th Congress, 1st Session, 1819 Sen. Doc. No. 225.

U. S. Treasury Department. *Annual Report of the Director of the Bureau of Statistics, on the Commerce and Navigation of the United States, for the Fiscal Year Ended June 30, 1861.* Washington, D. C.: United States Government Printing Office, 1868.

Vanderlint, Frank A. and Williams, John H. "The Future of Our Foreign Trade," *The Review of Economic Statistics Supplement,* April 1920, pp. 1-28.

Vanderlint, Jacob. *Money Answers All Things,* 1734. *A Reprint of Economic Tracts,* Jacob H. Hollander, (ed.). Baltimore: Lord Baltimore Press, 1914.

Viner, Jacob. "Balance of Trade," *Encyclopaedia of Social Sciences,* Vol. II. New York: Macmillan Company, 1930, pp. 399-406.

— *Studies in the Theory of International Trade.* New York: Harper and Brothers, 1937.

Ware, Ray M. *The Development of the Concept of the Balance of Payments in the United Kingdom.* Unpublished doctoral dissertation, University of Kentucky, 1963.

Wells, David A. *Revenue of the United States.* London: Macmillan and Company, 1870.

Wheatley, John. *Remarks on Currency and Commerce.* London: Cadell and Davies, 1803.

Whitworth, Sir Charles, (ed.). *The Political and Commercial Works of that Celebrated Writer Charles D'Avenant,* Vol. I. London: Horsfield, 1771.

Whitworth, Sir Charles. *State of the Trade of Great Britain in its Imports and Exports, Progressively from the year 1697.* London: Printed for T. Cadell, 1776.

Williams, Faith M. "The Origin and Development of Modern Trade Statistics," *Journal of the American Statistical Association,* June 1921, pp. 732-742.

Williams, John H. "The Balance of International Payments of the United States for the Year 1920," *The Review of Economic Statistics Supplement,* June 1921, pp. 170-199.

— "The Balance of International Payments of the United States for the Year 1921, with an Estimate of the Unfunded Foreign Balance on January 1, 1922," *The Review of Economic Statistics,* July 1922, pp. 201-214.

Wood, William. *A Survey of Trade.* London: W. Hinchlieffe, 1718.

Yarranton, Andrew. *England's Improvement by Sea and Land.* London: 1677. Reprinted in Dove, Patrick. "Account of Andrew Yarranton,"

The Elements of Political Science. London: Johnson and Hunter, 1854.
Young, Arthur. *Political Essays Concerning the Present State of the British Empire.* London: T. Cadell, 1772.

Section II: Theory and Methodology

Aftalion, Albert. *Monnaie, Prix et Change.* Paris: Receuil Sirey, 1927.
Aliber, Robert Z. "The Management of the Dollar in International Finance," *Princeton Studies in International Finance,* No. 13. Princeton: International Finance Section, Department of Economics, Princeton University, 1964.
Altman, Oscar L. "Foreign Market for Dollars, Sterling and Other Currencies," *Staff Papers.* International Monetary Fund, Vol. VIII, No. 1 (December 1961), pp. 313-352.
— "Recent Developments in Foreign Markets for Dollars and Other Currencies," *Staff Papers.* International Monetary Fund, Vol. X, No. 1 (March 1963), pp. 48-96.
— "Quelques Aspects du Problème de l'Or," *Cahiers de l'Institut de Science Economique Appliquée,* Series R, No. 7 (October 1962), Paris.
— "The Management of International Liquidity," *Staff Papers.* International Monetary Fund, Vol. XI, No. 2 (July 1964), pp. 216-245.
Angell, James W. "The Reorganization of the International Monetary System: An Alternative Proposal," *The Economic Journal,* Vol. LXXI (December 1961), pp. 691-708.
— *The Theory of International Prices.* Cambridge, Mass.: Harvard University Press, 1926.
Annual Report of the International Monetary Fund, 1963-1964. Washington, D. C.: International Monetary Fund, 1964.
Badger, Donald C. "The Balance of Payments: A Tool of Economic Analysis," *Staff Papers.* International Monetary Fund, Vol. II, No. 1 (September 1951), pp. 86-197.
Bagehot, Walter. *Lombard Street: A Description of the Money Market,* with a New Introduction by Frank C. Genovese. Homewood, Illinois: Richard D. Irwin, Inc., 1962.
Balance of Payments Manual, (3rd ed.). Washington, D. C.: International Monetary Fund, 1961.
The Balance of Payments of the United States: 1949-1951. A Supplement to the *Survey of Current Business.* United States Department of Commerce, Washington, D. C.: United States Government Printing Office, 1952.
Balance of Payments Yearbooks. International Monetary Fund. Washington, D. C.: International Monetary Fund, (published annually).
Bell, Philip W. "Private Capital Movements and the U. S. Balance of Payments Position" in *Factors Affecting the United States Balance of Payments.* Compilation of Studies Prepared for the Subcommittee on International Exchange and Payments of the Joint Economic Committee, Congress of the United States. Washington, D. C.: United States Government Printing Office, 1962, pp. 395-481.

Bernstein, Edward M. "The Adequacy of United States Gold Reserves," *American Economic Review, Papers and Proceedings*, Vol. LI (1961), pp. 439-446.

— *International Effects of U. S. Economic Policy*. Joint Economic Committee, United States Congress, 86th Congress, 2nd Session, Study Paper No. 16. Washington, D. C.: United States Government Printing Office, 1960.

— "The Problems of International Monetary Reserves," *International Payments Imbalances and Need for Strengthening International Financial Arrangements*. Joint Economic Committee of the Congress of the United States. Hearings Before the Subcommittee on International Exchange and Payments. Washington, D. C.: United States Government Printing Office, 1961, pp. 107-137.

Bloch-Lainé, Fr. and Others. "La Balance des Payements de la Zone Franc," *Statistiques et Etudes Financières, Annuaire 1930-1959*, Part IX (December 1960).

Cassel, Gustav. *Money and Foreign Exchange After 1914*. New York: The Macmillan Co., 1922.

Census of American-Owned Assets in Foreign Countries. United States Treasury Department. Washington, D. C.: United States Government Printing Office, 1947.

Census of Foreign-Owned Assets in the United States. United States Treasury Department. Washington, D. C.: United States Government Printing Office, 1945.

Coombs, Charles A. "Treasury and Federal Reserve Foreign Exchange Operations," *Monthly Review* of the Federal Reserve Bank of New York. Vol. 42, No. 9 (September 1962), pp. 1138-1153.

— "Treasury and Federal Reserve Foreign Exchange Operations," *Monthly Review* of the Federal Reserve Bank of New York, Vol. 45, No. 9 (September 1963), pp. 162-172.

— "Treasury and Federal Reserve Foreign Exchange Operations and the Gold Pool," *Federal Reserve Bulletin*, Vol. 50, No. 3 (March 1964), pp. 294-307.

— Iklé, M., Ranali, E., and Tüngeler, J. "Conversations on International Finance," *Monthly Review* of the Federal Reserve Bank of New York, Vol. 45, No. 8 (August 1963), p. 120.

Crump, Norman. *The ABC of the Foreign Exchanges* (12th ed.). London: Macmillan and Co., Ltd., 1958.

Day, A. C. L. "Memorandum of Evidence," Committee on the Working of the Monetary System (Radcliffe Committee), *Principal Memoranda of Evidence*. London: H. M. Stationery Office, 1960, Vol. 3.

Economic Policies and Practices: A Description and Analysis of Certain European Capital Markets (paper No. 3). Materials prepared for the Joint Economic Committee, Congress of the United States, 88th Congress, 2nd Session, Joint Committee Print. Washington, D. C.: United States Government Printing Office, 1964.

Einzig, Paul A. *A Dynamic Theory of Forward Exchange*. London: Macmillan and Co., Ltd., 1961.

— *The Euro-Dollar System: Practice and Theory of International Interest Rates.* New York: St. Martin's Press, Inc., 1964.
— *The History of Foreign Exchange.* London: Macmillan and Co., Ltd., 1962.
Friedman, Milton. "The Case for Flexible Exchange Rates," *Essays in Positive Economics.* Chicago: The University of Chicago Press, 1953, pp. 157-203.
Fleming, Marcus. "The Fund and International Liquidity," *Staff Papers.* International Monetary Fund, Vol. XI, No. 2 (July 1964), pp. 177-215.
Foreign Business Investments in the United States. A Supplement to the *Survey of Current Business.* United States Department of Commerce, Washington, D. C.: United States Government Printing Office, 1962.
Foreign Investments in the United States. A Supplement to the *Survey of Current Business.* United States Department of Commerce, Washington, D. C.: United States Government Printing Office, 1953.
Gardner, Walter R. "An Exchange Market Analysis of the U. S. Balance of Payments," *Staff Papers,* International Monetary Fund, Vol. VIII, No. 2 (May 1961), pp. 195-211.
Gordon, Wendell. "The Criterion for an Adverse Balance of Payments," *American Economic Review,* Vol. LIII, No. 1, Part 1 (March 1963), pp. 139-141.
— "The Criterion for an Adverse Balance of Payments: Reply," *American Economic Review,* Vol. LIII, No. 5 (December 1963), pp. 1101-1103.
Haberler, Gottfried. "A Survey of International Trade Theory," *Special Papers on International Economics,* No. 1 (September 1955). Princeton: International Finance Section, Department of Economics and Sociology, Princeton University, 1955.
Hall, Ray Ovid. *International Payments: A Science.* Washington: Privately published by the author and out of print, 1946.
— "Some Neglected Relationships in the Balance of Payments," *American Economic Review,* Vol. XXXI, No. 2 (March 1941), pp. 81-86.
Harrod, Sir Roy F. "Europe and the Money Muddle." *Economic Journal,* Vol. LXVIII (September 1958).
— "Imbalance of International Payments," *Staff Papers.* International Monetary Fund, Vol. III, No. 2 (April 1953), pp. 1-46.
— "Plan for Restoration of Full Convertibility of the Dollar Together with a Revision of the Gold Content of the Dollar," *Gold Reserve Act Amendments.* Hearings before a Subcommittee of the Committee on Banking and Currency, March 30, 1954. Washington, D. C.: United States Government Printing Office, 1954, pp. 129-138.
Heilperin, Michael. "Monetary Reform in an Atlantic Setting," *International Payments Imbalances and Need for Strengthening International Payments Arrangements.* Hearings before the Subcommittee on International Exchange and Payments, Joint Economic Committee, United States Congress, 87th Congress, 1st Session. Washington, D. C.: United States Government Printing Office, pp. 331-340.
Holmes, Alan R. *The New York Foreign Exchange Market.* New York: Federal Reserve Bank of New York, 1959.

— and Klopstock, Fred H. "The Market for Dollar Deposits in Europe," *Monthly Review* of the Federal Reserve Bank of New York, Vol. 42, No. 11 (November 1960), pp. 197-202.

Horsefield, J. Keith. "International Liquidity," *Finance and Development* (The Fund and Bank Review), Vol. I, No. 3 (December 1964), pp. 170-177.

Høst-Madsen, Poul. "Asymmetries Between Balance of Payments Surpluses and Deficits," *Staff Papers*. International Monetary Fund, (July 1962), pp. 182-201.

Hume, David. "Of the Balance of Trade" in his *Political Discourses* (1752), as quoted in Monroe, A. E. *Early Economic Thought*. Cambridge, Mass.: Harvard University Press, 1924, pp. 325 ff.

"International Monetary Arrangements: The Problem of Choice," *Report on the Deliberations of an International Study Group of 32 Economists*. Princeton: International Finance Section, Department of Economics, Princeton University, August 10, 1964.

International Reserves and Liquidity. Washington, D. C.: International Monetary Fund, 1958.

"Introduction to the Fund," *Finance and Development* (The Fund and Bank Review), Vol. I, No. 1 (June 1964), pp. 3-14.

Jacobsson, Per, quoted in "Fund Report at ECOSAC," *International Financial News Survey*. Washington, D. C.: International Monetary Fund, Vol. XIII, No. 16 (April 28, 1961), pp. 124-126.

— *Summary Proceedings of the Sixteenth Annual Meeting of the Board of Governors of the International Monetary Fund, 1961*. Washington, D. C.: International Monetary Fund, 1961, pp. 27-29, 157-158.

Janssen, Richard F. "Figure Feud: While U. S. Wrestles with Payments Deficit, Economists Fuss Over How to Figure It," *Wall Street Journal*, October 31, 1963.

Johnson, Norris O. *Eurodollars in the New International Money Market*. New York: First National City Bank, (no date).

Kenen, Peter B. "Reserve-Asset Preferences of Central Banks and Stability of the Gold Exchange Standard," *Princeton Studies in International Finance*, No. 10. Princeton: International Finance Section, Department of Economics, Princeton University, 1963.

Klopstock, Fred H. "The International Status of the Dollar," *Essays in International Finance*, No. 28. Princeton: International Finance Section, Department of Economics and Sociology, Princeton University, 1957.

Lary, Hal. B. *Problems of the United States as World Trader and Banker*. New York: National Bureau of Economic Research, Inc., 1963.

de Lattre, André, *Les Finances Extérieures de la France*. Paris: Presses Universitaires de France, 1959.

Law, John. *Premier Mémoire sur les Banques, Présenté a son Altesse Royale Monseigneur le Duc d'Orléans, Régent de France*. Paris (circa 1776). Reproduced by Eugène Daire in *Economistes Financiers du Dix-Huitième Siècle*. Paris. Chez Guillaumin et Cie., Libraires, 1851.

Lederer, Walther. "The Balance of Payments in 1963," *Survey of Current*

Business, Vol. 44, No. 3 (March 1964), pp. 14-23.

— "The Balance on Foreign Transactions: Problems of Definition and Measurement," *Special Papers in International Economics*, No. 5. Princeton: International Finance Section, Department of Economics, Princeton University, 1963.

"The London Gold Market," *Quarterly Bulletin* of the Bank of England (March 1964). Reprinted in part as a special supplement to the *Monthly Review* of the Federal Reserve Bank of New York, Vol. 50, No. 3 (March 1964).

La Balance des Payements: Etude Methodologique. Paris: Institut de la Statistique et des Etudes Economiques, 1957.

MacDougall, Sir Donald. "The Dollar Problem: A Reappraisal," *Essays in International Finance*, No. 35. Princeton: International Finance Section, Department of Economics, Princeton University, 1960.

Machlup, Fritz. *International Trade and the National Income Multiplier*. Philadelphia: The Blakiston Co., 1943. Reprinted by Augustus M. Kelley, New York, 1961.

— *International Payments, Debts and Gold* (collected essays). New York: Charles Scribner's Sons, 1964.

— "Plans for the Reform of the International Monetary System," *Special Papers in International Economics*, No. 3. Princeton: International Finance Section, Department of Economics, Princeton University, August 1962.

— Three Concepts of the Balance of Payments and the So-Called Dollar Shortage," *Economic Journal* (March 1960), pp. 46-48.

Meade, James. *The Balance of Payments*. Oxford: Oxford University Press, 1951.

— "The Case for Variable Exchange Rates," *Three Banks Review*, No. 27 (September 1955), pp. 3-27.

— "The Future of International Trade and Payments," *Three Banks Review*, No. 5 (June 1961), pp. 15-38.

Merwin, Charles L. "The Road to Bretton Woods," *Finance and Development (The Fund and Bank Review)*, Vol. I. No. 2 (September 1964), pp. 59-64.

Metzler, Lloyd A. "The Transfer Problem Reconsidered," *Journal of Political Economy*, Vol. 50, 1942, pp. 397 ff.

Ministère des Finances, Direction des Finances Extérieures, *Balance des Payements de l' Année 1960 entre la Zone Franc et les Pays Etrangers*. Paris: Imprimerie Nationale (no date).

Ministerial Statement of the Group of Ten and Annex Prepared by Deputies. (No place or publisher), August 10, 1964.

Mints, Lloyd W. *Monetary Policy for a Competitive Society*. New York: Macmillan and Co., 1950.

Morgenstern, Oskar. *On the Accuracy of Economic Observations*. Princeton: Princeton University Press, 1963.

Note on Balance of Payments Statistics. Report of the Subcommittee on Balance of Payments Statistics of the League of Nations Committee of Statistical Experts. Studies and Reports on Statistical Methods No. 9. Geneva, 1947.

Nurkse, Ragnar. "Conditions of International Monetary Equilibrium," *Essays in International Finance,* No. 4. Princeton: International Finance Section, Department of Economics, Princeton University, Spring 1945. Reprinted in Howard S. Ellis and Lloyd A. Metzler, *Readings in the Theory of International Trade.* Philadelphia: The Blakiston Company, 1950, pp. 3-34.

Petruzzelli, Nicholas Michael. "Some Technical Aspects of Foreign Trade Statistics with Special Reference to Valuation" in *The Catholic University of America Studies in Economics,* Vol. 17. Washington: The Catholic University of America Press, 1946.

Powelson, John P. *Economic Accounting.* New York: McGraw Hill Book Company, Inc., 1955.

Prindl, Andreas. *The West African Currency Board: An Analysis of a Colonial Monetary System.* Unpublished dissertation for the doctorate in international economics, University of Kentucky, 1964.

Report of the Review Committee for Balance of Payments Statistics to the Bureau of the Budget. *The Balance of Payments of the United States: A Review and Appraisal.* Washington, D.C.: United States Government Printing Office, 1965.

Ricardo, David. *Principles of Political Economy and Taxation.* E. C. K. Gonner, ed. London: George Bell and Sons, 1891.

Roosa, Robert V. *The Beginning of a New Policy.* Reprinted in *Factors Affecting the United States Balance of Payments.* Compilation of Studies Prepared for the Subcommittee on International Exchange and Payments of the Joint Economic Committee. Washington, D. C.: United States Government Printing Office, 1962, pp. 327-332.

— *Banking and the Balance of Payments. Ibid.,* pp. 333-340.

— *Federal Reserve Operations in the Money and Government Securities Markets.* New York: Federal Reserve Bank of New York, 1956.

Rueff, Jacques. "The West is Risking a Credit Collapse," *Fortune,* Vol. LXIV (July 1961), pp. 126-127, 262, 267-268.

Salant, Walter S., Despres, Emile, Krause, Lawrence B., Rivlin, Alice M., Salant, William A., and Tarshis, Lorie. *The United States Balance of Payments in 1968.* Washington, D. C.: The Brookings Institution, 1963.

Stamp, Maxwell. "The Fund and the Future," *Lloyds Bank Review,* 1958, pp. 1-20.

— "Changes in the World's Payment System," *Moorgate and Wall Street,* Spring 1961.

Szymczak, M. S. *Monetary Policy in a Free Economy.* An address at the School of Banking, University of Wisconsin, Madison, August 29, 1950. Reprinted in part under the title "The Constructive Role of Monetary Policy" in Samuelson, Paul A., Bishop, Robert L., and Coleman, John R. *Readings in Economics.* New York: McGraw-Hill Book Company, Inc., 1955, pp. 118-128.

Thornton, Henry. *Inquiry into the Nature and Effects of the Paper Credit of Great Britain.* London: 1802. Reprinted, Philadelphia: by James Humphreys for Mathew Carey, 1807.

Triffin, Robert. "The Evolution of the International Payments System: Historical Reappraisal and Future Perspectives," *Princeton Studies in International Finance*, No. 12. Princeton: International Finance Section, Department of Economics, Princeton University, 1964.

— *Gold and Dollar Crisis*. New Haven: Yale University Press, 1960.

— "The Presentation of the U. S. Balance of Payments Statistics, General Comments," *1961 Proceedings of the Business and Economic Statistics Section*. Washington, D. C.: American Statistical Association, 1962, pp. 51-52.

Turot, Paul. "Le Marché des Capitaux à Court Terme en Europe et l'Euro-Dollar," *Banque*, Paris (April 1961), pp. 215 ff.

U. S. Business Investment in Foreign Countries. A Supplement to the *Survey of Current Business*. United States Department of Commerce, Washington, D. C.: United States Government Printing Office, 1960.

Wasserman, Lawrence Bernard. "An Essay on Balance of Payments Construction and Interpretation." Unpublished M.A. thesis, University of Kentucky, 1962.

Wasserman, Max J. "The Compression of French Wholesale Prices During Inflation, 1919-1926," *The American Economic Review*, Vol. XXVI, No. 1 (March 1936), pp. 66-73.

Wasserman, Max J., Hultman, Charles W. and Zsoldas, Laslo. *International Finance*. New York: Simmons-Boardman Publishing Corp., 1963.

Wasserman, Max J. and Hultman, Charles W. *Modern International Economics: A Balance of Payments Approach*. New York: Simmons-Boardman Publishing Corp., 1962.

Williams, John Burr. *International Trade Under Flexible Exchange Rates*. Amsterdam: North-Holland Publishing Company, 1954.

Young, John Parke. *The International Economy*, (4th ed.). New York: The Ronald Press Company, 1963.

Zolotas, Xenophon. *Summary Proceedings of the Thirteenth Annual Meeting of the Board of Governors of the International Monetary Fund, 1958*. Washington, D. C.: International Monetary Fund, 1958, p. 91.

— *Summary Proceedings of the Twelfth Annual Meeting of Board of Governors of the International Monetary Fund, 1957*. Washington, D. C.: International Monetary Fund, 1957, p. 42.

APPENDIX A

APPENDIX A.1

SUBSIDIARY DOCUMENTS TO THE BALANCE OF
TRADE, TWENTY-EIGHTH YEAR OF EDWARD III

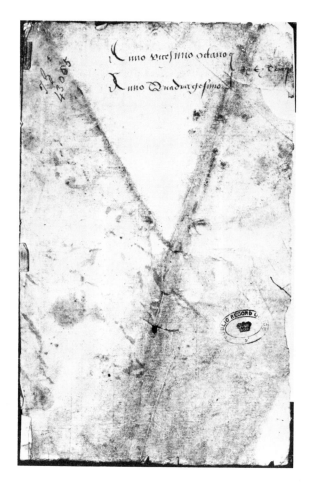

British Crown copyright; reproduced by permission of the Controller of
H.M. Stationery Office.
Source: Great Britain, Public Record Office, 831, *Customs Accounts of the
King's Remembrancer's Department of the Exchequer*, E.122/158/
20 folios 1-3.

APPENDIX A.1 (Cont'd.)

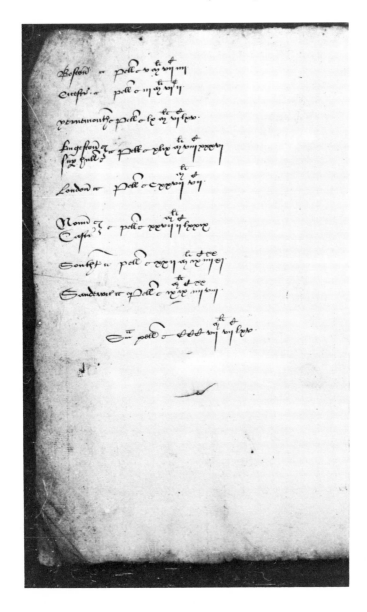

APPENDIX A.1 (Cont'd.)

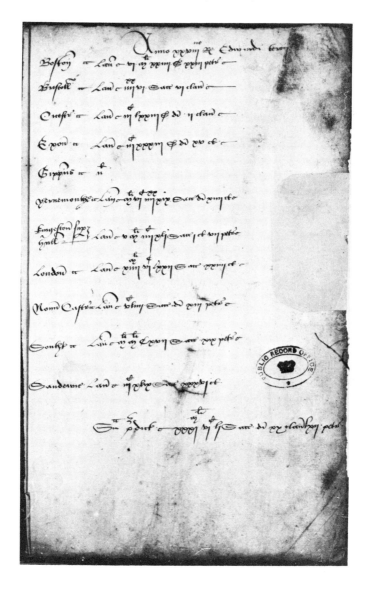

APPENDIX A.1 (Cont'd.)

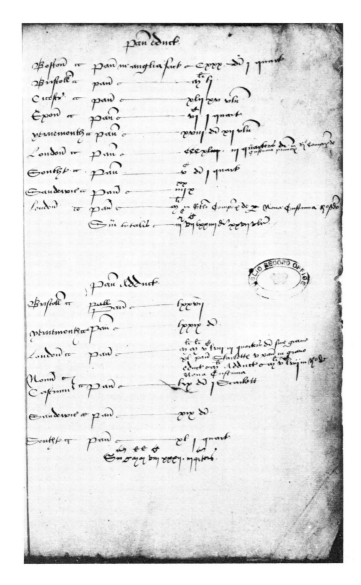

APPENDIX A.1 (Cont'd.)

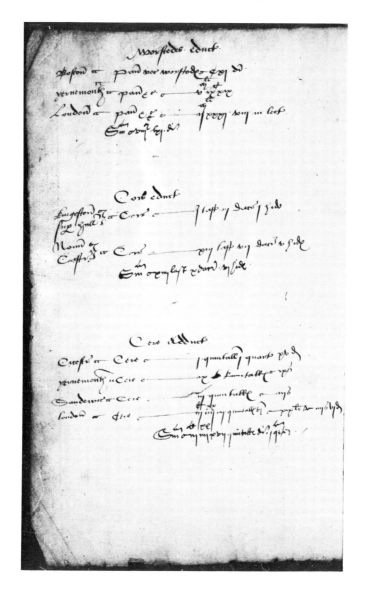

APPENDIX A.1 (Cont'd.)

APPENDIX A.1 (Cont'd.)

British Crown copyright; reproduced by permission of the Controller of H.M. Stationery Office.

Source: Great Britain, Public Record Office 831, *Customs Accounts of the King's Remembrancer's Department of the Exchequer*, E.122/248/1.

APPENDIX A.1 (Cont'd.)

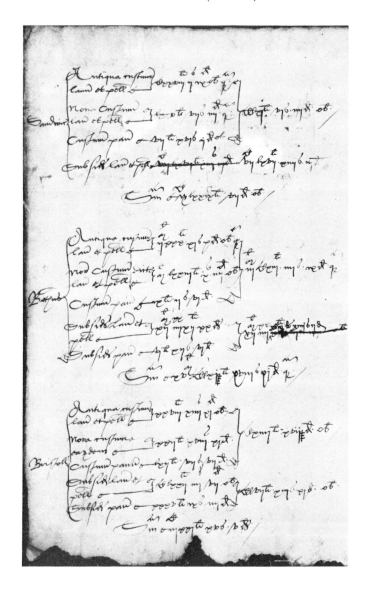

APPENDIX A.1 (Cont'd.)

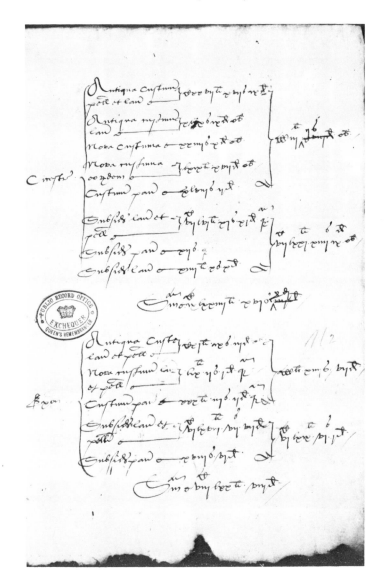

APPENDIX A.1 (Cont'd.)

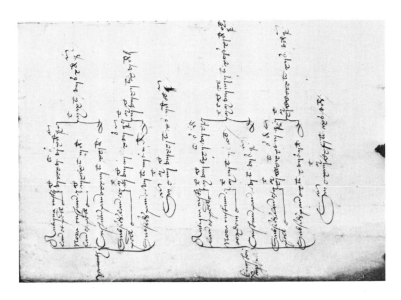

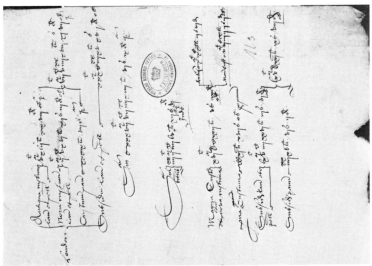

APPENDIX A.2
A Scheme of Trade with France, 1668-1669

156   *The* British *Merchant.*

LONDON, 29 *Nov.* 1674.

A SCHEME of the Trade, as it is at present carried on between *England* and *France*, in the Commodities of the Native Product and Manufacture of each Country; Calculated as exactly as possible, in Obedience to the Command of the Right Honourable the Lords Commissioners for the Treaty of Commerce with *France*: And humbly tender'd to their Lordships.

Quantities.	Commodities exported *from England into* France.		*l. s. d.*	Amount of Particulars. *l. s. d.*	Total Amount of Exports. *l. s. d.*
	Woollen and Silk Manufactures.				
354	Pieces of *Norwich* Stuffs,	at	2 00 0 *per* Pc.	708 0 0	
5564	Pieces of Serges and Perpetuanas,		2 10 0	13910 0 0	
2288	Pieces of single Bays,		2 10 0	5764 0 0	
166	Small Minikin Bays,		6 00 0	996 0 0	
466	Small double Bays,		4 00 0	1864 0 0	
2140	Dozen Mens Worsted Hose,		2 00 0	4280 0 0	
832	Dozen Mens Worsted Hose,		1 05 0	1040 0 0	
1170	Dozen of Childrens Hose,		0 08 0	468 0 0	

Source: Charles King, (ed.), *The British Merchant,* 3rd ed., London: Printed for Thomas Osborne, 1748, I, 156-161.

APPENDIX A.2 (Cont'd.)

The Trade of England *in general.*   157

Quantity & Item	Unit price		Total		
400 Yards of Flannel,	0 01 0 0		20	0	0
1200 C. Goads of Cotton,	9 00 0 0		10800	0	0
112 Long Cloths,	10 00 0 *per* Cl.		1120	0	0
42 Short Cloths,	8 00 0 0		336	0	0
829 *Spaniſh* Cloths,	15 00 0 0		12435	0	0
97 Double *Northern* Dozens,	5 00 0 0		485	0	0
69 Single *Northern* Dozens,	5 00 0 0		138	0	0
13 *Devon* Dozens,	2 00 0 0		26	0	0
173 Cloth Raſhes,	5 00 0 0		865	0	0
6 Pennyſtones,	3 00 0 0		18	0	0
3585 Kerſies,	1 15 0 0		6273	0	3
960 lb *Engliſh* wrought Silk,	2 00 0 0		1920	0	0
			63466	0	0

This is the full of what was Exported, according to the Cuſtom-Houſe Books in the Port of *London,* from *Michaelmas* 1668, to *Michaelmas* 1669. And for all *England* we calculate one third part more. Amounts in all to   84621 06 8

Since 1669, the Exports as we conceive are diminiſhed, and not increaſ'd.

2500 Fodder of Lead, at	12 0 0 *per* Fod.		30000	0	0
6000 Hundred of Tin, at	4 0 0 *per* C.		24000	0	0

100 Tuns

APPENDIX A.2 (Cont'd.)

158   *The* British *Merchant.*

100 Tuns of Allom, at	24 0 0 *per* Ton.	2400 00 0	
Calves Skin and Leather		10000 00 0	
Several Sorts of Skins, Glew, Lanthorn Leaves, Butter, Copperas, Old Shoes, Sea Coal, Tobacco Pipes, Gloves, Red Lead, Linfeed, Candles, Iron Ware, Haberdashery Ware, and other trivial Commodities, which may amount *per annum* to		20000 00 0	
			86400 00 0
Balance gain'd by the *French* from us yearly, besides the Toys, Gloves, Laces, &c.			171021 06 8
			965128 17 4
			1136150 04 0

Commodities imported into England from France.

Linen and Silk Manufactures.

Quantities.		Amount of Particulars.	Total Amount of Imports.
	l. s. d.	*l. s. d.*	*l. s. d.*
6000 Pieces of Lockram and Dowlas, at	6 0 0 *per* Pc.	360000 00 0	
17000 Hund. of Vitry and Noyals Canvas	6 0 0 *per* Hun.	102000 00 0	
5000 Hund. of *Normandy* Canvas,	7 0 0	35000 00 0	

APPENDIX A.2 (Cont'd.)

The Trade of England *in general.*   159

2500 Pieces of Quintins,	0 10 0 *per* Pc.	1250 00 0
1500 Pieces of dyed Linen,	1 00 0	1500 00 0
7604 Yards of Diaper Tabling,	0 02 0	760 08 0
33896 Yards of Diaper Napkining,	0 01 0	1694 16 0
1376 Dozens of Buckrams,	2 10 0	3440 00 0
1200 Bolts of Poldavies,	0 15 0	900 00 0
2820 Pair of old Sheets,	0 05 0	705 00 0
105000 Pound of wrought Silk,	2 00 0	300000 00 0
		——— 807250 04 0

Note, That this Year 1674, there hath been received at the Port of *Dover* only, as we are inform'd, 15000 *l.* for Custom of wrought Silk : So that considering what may be convey'd away privately, and that greatQuantities are worth from 3 *l.* to 4 *l.* the Pound, we believe the wrought Silk may amount to much more in value than what is above.

11000 Tuns of French Wine one Year with another cost	12 10 0 *per*Tun.	137500 00 0
4000 Tuns of Brandy one Year with another, at	20 00 0	80000 00 0
		——— 217500 00 0
160000 Reams of Paper,	at 0 05 0 *per* Ream	40000 00 0
		1500 Pcs

APPENDIX A.2 (Cont'd.)

160   *The* British *Merchant.*

1500 Pcs of Pruens,	4 00		6000 00 0
400 Hundred of Feathers,	5 00 0 *per* Hund.		2000 00 0
5000 Hundred of Kidskins,	3 00 0		15000 00 0
3000 Weight of Salt,	2 00 0 *per* Weig.		6000 00 0
6000 Hundred of Rozin,	0 08 0 *per* Hund.		2400 00 0

Vinegar, Rape, Cyder, Wadd, Cork, Oakam, Soap,
Turpentine, Capers, Olives, Brignoles, Parchment,
Window-Glass, Teasels, Corn-Fans, Basket-Rods,
Box-Wood, and Cremor Tartar, which may amount
per Annum at least to   4000 00 0
                              ——————
                              111400 00 0

1136150 04 0

Besides all manner of Toys for Women and Children Fans, Jessamin Gloves, Laces, Point Laces, rich embroider'd Garments, and rich embroidered Beds, and other Vestments, which are of an incredible *Value.*

By the Account above your Lordships may perceive, that the Linen and Silk Manufactures only, Imported from *France,* amount to upwards of Eight Hundred Thousand Pounds, and the Manufactures of Wool and Silk Exported from *England* thither, do not amount to Eighty Five Thousand Pounds. As also all other Commodities of the Product and Manufacture of *England* Exported into *France,* do

APPENDIX A.2 (Cont'd.)

The Trade of England *in general.*　　161

do not amount to Ninety Thoufand Pounds more. Whereas the Wines, Brandies, and other Commodities of the Product and Manufacture of *France* Imported into *England*, amount to upwards of Three Hundred and Twenty Thoufand Pounds ; befides an incredible Value of Toys, rich Apparel, Point-Lace, &c. So that it is apparent that the Exports of our Native Commodities and Manufactures to *France*, are lefs in Value by at leaft one Million, of Pounds Sterling, than the Native Commodities and Manufactures of *France*, which we receive from thence. And if it pleafe your Lordfhips to reflect thereupon, your Lordfhips will eafily difcern the great Prejudice the *Englifh* Nation hath fuftained, and the great Advantage the *French* have, and do daily make, by holding this Treaty in fufpence ; this Nation being upon the Matter excluded Trade thither, while in the mean time the *French* enjoy all and as great Advantages as they can reafonably expect by any Treaty.

Patience Ward,
Thomas Papillon,
James Houblon,
William Bellamy,
Michael Godfrey,

George Toriano,
John Houblon,
John Houghe,
John Mervin,
Peter Paravicine,

John Dubois,
Benj. Godfrey,
Edm. Harrifon,
Benj. Delaune.

APPENDIX A.3

EXTRACTS FROM THE BOOK OF TABLES:
EXPORTS AND IMPORTS INTO THE CITY OF LONDON
1662-1663 AND 1668-1669
ENGLAND'S EXPORTS BY COUNTRY OF
DESTINATION, 1662-1663

Reproduced by permission of the Trustees of the British Museum.
Source: British Museum, *Additional Manuscripts*, 36785, fols. 6 and 58.

APPENDIX A.3 (Cont'd.)

SUMMARY OF ENGLAND'S EXPORTS AND IMPORTS
1662-1663

The Totall Value of all Goods Imported into ye City of London from ye severall Kingdomes & Countries for one year from Michas 1662 to Michas 1663

Country	Value
Turkey	375656 01 00
Germany	581913 88 00
Flanders	242405 02 00
Holland	490926 11 0
France	647206 16 00
Spaine	584437 05 00
Italie	284372 12 00
Portugall	80691 08 00
Eastland	259992 17 00
Russia	17785 14 00
East India	384071 18 00
Barbary	158096 13 00
Scotland	20012 04 00
Ireland	46461 17 00
Plantations	484671 02 00
Summ Totall	4016319 18 00

The Totall Value of all Goods Exported from ye City of London to ye severall Kingdoms and Countries for one year from Michas 1662 to Michas 1663

Country	Value
Turkey	167601 07
Germany	1925 93 04
Flanders	1086321 8
Holland	10521 07
France	376005 06
Spaine	425280 01
Italie	170478 19
Portugall	146061 17
Sweden	6219 17
Denmark	387691 10
Poland	27805 17
Russia	28024 19
East India	24051 02
Africa	69765 15
Scotland	221003 10
Ireland	23190 00
Plantations	1059729 18
Summ Totall	2022812 04

APPENDIX A.4

LEDGERS OF THE INSPECTOR-GENERAL OF EXPORTS
AND IMPORTS, 1696-1697.
ENGLAND'S EXPORTS BY COUNTRY OF DESTINATION
1696-1697

British Crown copyright; reproduced by permission of the Controller of H.M.
Stationery Office.

Source: Great Britain, Public Records Office, *Customs 22*, pp. 1 and 192.

APPENDIX A.4 (Cont'd.)

SUMMARY OF ENGLAND'S EXPORTS BY COUNTRY OF DESTINATION, 1696-1697

192.

Abstract

The Amount of the severall Estimates of the Goods Exported From the Port of London From Mich: 1696 to Mich: 1697. viz.

Page		English Manufact. £ s d	Forr. Goods In time £ s d	Forr. Goods Out of time £ s d	Totall £ s d
3	Barbary	247 18 2	. . .	. . .	247 18 2
3	Canaries	36963 17 10	11,753 0 6	811 4 7¾	49528 2 11¾
6	Den. & Norway	12001 5 1	2961 15 3½	115 16 0	15078 16 4½
9	E. Country	91196 18 5½	20,990 0 7	905 4 7¾	116,392 3 8¼
11	E. Indies	53984 12 10	11,982 2 2½	1,070 4 3¾	67036 19 4¼
18	Flanders	127,697 12 3	32895 0 7	11,645 3 2½	172,237 16 0½
23	Germany	234,188 15 1¼	84653 6 6¼	6,169 13 11½	325,311 15 10½
31	Guinea	7879 7 10	2,188 4 3½	2709 8 8	13,077 0 9½
35	Holland	361512 5 5½	448,013 11 10¼	80,972 13 8	891,128 10 11¾
18	Ireland &c.	4135 19 6½	7170 11 11¾	3255 2 0	14,561 13 6¼
34	Italy	15975 7 1¾	5565 6 1¼	1,092 13 10	22,631 7 1
56	Maderas	2,420 1 3¼	3672 14 0½	668 0 3	6760 15 6¾
59	Newfoundld.	16347 2 7¾	1790 4 2½	396 1 6	18,533 8 4¼
62	Portugall	102357 11 9½	5303 17 5¾	2361 9 6	110,025 18 9¼
67	Scotland	9771 3 10	2,051 10 2½	2688 2 11¼	14,510 16 11¾
73	Spaine	44,761 7 8½	16335 8 6¼	2020 9 9	63102 15 11¾
7[illegible]	Streights	72518 13 3	13,193 1 1½	1873 13 3	87,585 7 7½
8[illegible]	Sweden	7700 0 10½	8550 3 4½	222 8 1	16472 12 4
84	Turkey	14760 15 0	972 9 6	18 18 0	15752 3 0
85	Venice	2956 4 11	428 13 1½	18 16 4½	3403 15 2
87	Isle of Jersey	1472 4 5	124 7 9	75 11 6½	1,672 3 7½
88	Antegoa (English Plantations)	4403 19 1½	1494 1 3½	352 3 2¼	6250 4 5¾
92	Barbados	39167 2 7	22,490 16 1¼	7,184 7 9½	68,842 7 3¾
101	Bermudes	347 9 4¼	28 13 4	48 11 5	424 14 1¼
103	Carolina &c.	6761 6 8¼	1,269 3 7½	964 7 11	8,994 18 3¾
107	Huds. Bay	1,168 12 1½	24 13 1½	98 13 7	1,291 19 8
109	Jamaica &c.	24,654 4 5¾	19,468 7 11	4,109 12 4½	48,232 4 9
117	New York	2930 2 4	571 7 1	739 0 6½	4,240 9 11½
121	Mounts.	1,399 0 4½	995 1 6	153 8 3	2547 10 1½
123	New Eng.	43,163 11 4¼	16,862 11 2¾	2979 14 0½	63,005 16 7½
131	New Province	1,078 11 5	304 15 2	39 8 9½	1,422 15 4½
132	Virg. & Mary.	19,645 7 2	6,605 3 9¼	2,117 6 9½	28,367 17 8¾
	Totalls	1,399,182 4 10½	751,610 5 0¼	137,880 10 9	2,288,673 0 7¾

APPENDIX B

Selected United States Balance of Payments Tables Proposed by the Review Committee for Balance of Payments Statistics

The Review Committee for Balance of Payments Statistics, established by the Bureau of the Budget in 1963 to examine various aspects of United States balance of payments methods, proposed new tabular presentations for these compilations. The summary table, to replace the standard one in current use, was shown and discussed in Chapter 8. This Appendix presents eleven of the detailed and supporting tables as well as the condensed table proposed by the Committee.

The detailed and supporting tables have been prepared to present breakdowns and additional aspects of the principal accounts shown on the summary table. By so doing, they supply additional information useful to a more complete understanding of the United States balance of payments position. Although not indicated on these Appendix tables, the proposed detailed and supporting tables are keyed into the new summary table to provide easy cross reference.

Many of the proposed tables present quarterly, in addition to annual, data. These quarterly figures are also given in seasonally adjusted form where appropriate. Geographical breakdowns have also been envisaged for a number of the tables. The recommended regions and countries to be included in these breakdowns are: Canada, Latin American Republics, United Kingdom, other Western Europe, Eastern Europe, Australia, New Zealand and South Africa, other countries, international institutions and unallocated.

The condensed table is designed to display the essential features of the summary table in a reduced form and is shown on Table B.1. Tables B.2 and B.3 present merchandise exports and imports by end-use category, a classification significant for certain analytical purposes. An important feature of this table is that the balance of payments merchandise data are reconciled with the Census Bureau foreign trade statistics.

The table showing services, investment income and remittances, B.4, includes data which is now published by Commerce, but on an irregular basis. This table provides for its periodic release. In addition, travel and transport are combined; direct investment fees and royalties are included with other income and memorandum accounts are provided for reinvested earnings.

Figures showing military transactions have been presented irregularly by Commerce and Table B.5 puts them on a regular publication basis. Table B.6, showing government non-military grants and long-term credits, is designed to accomplish four objectives: (a) it reconciles balance of payments data with figures published by Commerce in *Foreign Grants and Credits;* (b) it explains the item "foreign currency balances and short-term claims;" (c) it identifies foreign currency grants and loans and (d) it presents United States grants and credits transactions without introducing an analytical bias.

The movements of foreign official capital, except claims of monetary institutions, are shown on Table B.7, which is designed to indicate the official claims on the United States more clearly than the present Commerce tables do. Long-term private capital, presented on Table B.8, is new and embodies features important for analytical purposes. It provides, among other things, additional information concerning investment in securities.

The suggested Table B.9, Short-Term Private Capital, gives greater detail concerning the movement of United States and foreign short-term capital than the present balance of payments tabulations and excludes official claims. Table B.10, presenting United States reserves, IMF position and liabilities to foreign official monetary institutions, is designed to facilitate the analysis of surpluses and deficits. It indicates concisely the United States position with the IMF, distinguishing between the gold and the credit tranches. In addition, it gives a breakdown of United States liabilities to foreign official monetary institutions.

The international investment position of the United States has not been usually included among the Commerce balance of payments presentations but has formed part of separate statistical series. Proposed Table B.11 incorporates this investment position in the balance of payments tables. It affords background for the analysis of the balance of payments long- and short-term capital accounts. Table B.12, International Transactions in the United States National Income and Product Accounts, implements the Review Committee's recommendation that balance of payments transactions be more closely integrated with these accounts.

The source for all of the tables presented in this Appendix is: Report of the Review Committee for Balance of Payments Statistics to the Bureau of the Budget, *The Balance of Payments Statistics of the United States: A Review and Appraisal*. Washington, D. C.: U. S. Government Printing Office, 1965.

TABLE B.1
CONDENSED U. S BALANCE OF PAYMENTS

Type of transaction

Goods, services and remittances [net receipts (+)] ....
  Merchandise exports ....
  Merchandise imports ....
  Services, except military, and remittances (net) ....
  Military payments less military receipts ....
U.S. Government grants and capital (net) ....
Foreign official capital, except claims of monetary insti-
  tutions (net) ....
Long-term private capital (net) ....
Short-term private capital, except claims of foreign
  commercial banks (net) ....
Short-term claims of foreign commercial banks (net).....
Net errors and omissions ....
Balance settled by official transactions ....

TABLE B.2

Merchandise Exports by End-Use Categories

Merchandise exports, adjusted
  plus Exports deducted from Census data (other than military grant-aid shipments)[1]
  less Exports added to Census data[2]
  plus Valuation changes and other adjustments[3]

Merchandise exports, Census basis, excluding military grant-aid shipments
  Re-exports of foreign merchandise
  Exports of domestic merchandise
    Food and beverages
      Grains and preparations
      Other food and beverages
    Agricultural materials used in industry
      Cotton, unmanufactured
      Tobacco and other agricultural materials
    Fuels
      Coal and related fuels
      Petroleum and petroleum products
    Other nonagricultural materials used in industry
      Iron and steelmaking raw materials
      Steel mill products, castings and forgings
      Nonferrous and other primary metals, unmanufactured
      Finished metal parts, supplies and components
      Wood and paper industrial supplies
      Chemicals and pharmaceuticals
      Industrial textile yarns and fabrics
      Rubber, glass and other materials
    Materials used in agriculture
    Capital equipment
      Electrical machinery
      Construction machinery and tractors
      Other machinery and related items
      Trucks, busses, automotive parts, truck tires
      Aircraft, vessels and railway equipment
    Special category military equipment
    Consumer goods, except food
      Passenger cars
      Appliances and other durable goods
      Textiles and other nondurable goods
    Other and unclassified

Memoranda:
  Merchandise exports of current year or quarter financed by current disbursements of Government grants and credits (included in "merchandise exports, adjusted").
  Merchandise exports of other years or quarters financed by current disbursements of Government grants and credits (included in "merchandise exports, adjusted" for other years or quarters).
  Total merchandise exports financed by current disbursements of Government grants and capital (equals "Grants and credits spent in the United States on U.S. merchandise exports").

---

[1] Sales of military equipment under contracts arranged by the Department of Defense to the extent that Census data include them; exports of domestically owned goods sent abroad for storage (such as grain to Canada); exports to Panama Canal Zone; exports of exposed motion picture film for rental.
[2] Exports of nonmonetary gold and silver and of electrical energy; noncommercial exports (mail parcels, mainly gifts, valued under $50).
[3] Detail major items.

TABLE B.3

MERCHANDISE IMPORTS BY END-USE CATEGORIES

Merchandise imports, adjusted
　plus Imports deducted from Census data[1]
　less Imports added to Census data[2]
　plus Valuation changes and other adjustments[3]

Merchandise imports, Census basis
　Food and beverages
　　Coffee, raw or green
　　Other food and beverages
　Petroleum and petroleum products
　Paper and paper base products
　　Paper base stocks
　　Newsprint and other paper products
　Other materials used in nondurable goods manufacturing
　　Textile materials, crude and semifinished
　　Fabrics and other finished textile materials
　　Other unfinished materials
　　Other finished materials
　Selected building materials, except metals
　　Lumber and other unfinished materials
　　Finished materials
　Other materials used in durable goods manufacturing
　　Metals, crude and semifinished
　　Finished metal products
　　Other unfinished materials
　　Other finished materials
　Materials used in agriculture
　　Feedstuffs
　　Crude and semimanufactured materials
　　Manufactured materials
　Capital equipment
　Consumer goods, except food
　　Passenger cars, parts and tires
　　Other durable goods
　　Textile manufacturers
　　Other nondurable goods
　　Unmanufactured consumer goods

Noncommercial and unclassified

---

[1] Defense Department imports which are carried in the military expenditures account of the balance of payments; imports of domestically owned goods returned from storage abroad (e.g., grain from Canadian storage); imports from Panama Canal Zone.
[2] Imports of nonmonetary gold and silver and of electrical energy.
[3] Detail major items.

TABLE B.4

SERVICE, INVESTMENT INCOME, AND REMITTANCES

Transport and travel receipts
    Receipts of U.S. carriers, ocean and air freight
    Receipts of U.S. carriers, ocean and air passenger fares
    Port expenditure of foreign carriers in the U.S.
    Other transport receipts
    Expenditure by foreign residents in the U.S.
Transport and travel payments
    Payments to foreign carriers, ocean and air freight
    Payments to foreign carriers, ocean and air passenger fares
    Port expenditure of U.S. carriers abroad
    Other transport payments
    Expenditure by U.S. residents abroad
Investment income and related receipts
    Income on U.S. direct investment abroad
        Interest, profits and dividends
            Mining and petroleum
            Manufacturing
            Trade and other
        Fees and royalties
    Income on other U.S. private investments abroad
        Foreign dollar bonds held by U.S. residents
        Other U.S. long-term claims
        U.S. short-term claims
    Income on U.S. government credits and investments
        Dollar receipts
        Foreign-currency receipts
Investment income and related payments
    Income on foreign direct investments in the U.S.
        Interest, profits, and dividends
            Manufacturing
            Financial and Insurance
            Other
        Fees and royalties
    Income on other U.S. private obligations to foreigners
        Dividends
        Other
    Income on U.S. government obligations to foreigners
        Marketable securities
        Other obligations
Miscellaneous service receipts
    Government, except military
    Private, except from direct-investment affiliates
        Fees and royalties
        Engineers and contractors services
        Film rentals
        Expenditure by foreign official establishments
        Other
Miscellaneous service payments
    Government, except military
    Private, except to direct-investment affiliates
        Fees and royalties
        Insurance
        Other
Remittances and pensions
    Private remittances (net)
        Individual
        Institutional
    Government pensions and transfers

Memoranda:
    The following amounts are not included in direct-investment income:
        U.S. share in reinvested earnings of foreign subsidiaries of U.S. firms
            Mining and petroleum
            Manufacturing
            Trade and other
        Foreign share in reinvested earnings of U.S. subsidiaries of foreign firms
            Manufacturing
            Financial and Insurance
            Other

TABLE B.5

MILITARY RECEIPTS AND PAYMENTS

Military receipts

Military payments[1]
    Expenditure by troops, civilian personnel, post exchanges, etc.
    Construction expenditure
    Contractual services
    Contribution to NATO multilateral construction programs
    Offshore procurement under the Military Assistance Program
    Procurement of major equipment
    Purchases of other equipment, supplies and materials, except imports of fissionable materials
    Imports of fissionable materials under AEC contracts

---

[1] Except capital transactions such as net prepayments, and interest receipts.

TABLE B.6

GOVERNMENT GRANTS AND CAPITAL

Nonmilitary grants and long-term credits (sum of "nonmilitary grants, balance of payments basis" sum of "long-term credits, balance of payments basis")
    Net nonmilitary ("other") grants, as in *Foreign Grants and Credits* and
        Major foreign-assistance programs[1]
        Other
    less Transfers to other categories and adjustments, net[2]
    Nonmilitary grants, balance of payments basis
    Long-term credits, as in *Foreign Grants and Credits*
        Major foreign-assistance programs[1]
        Export-Import Bank Act credits
        Other
    plus Investments in international institutions, except IMF
    plus Other long-term credits and investments
    less Transfers to other categories and adjustments, net[2]
    Long-term credits, balance of payments basis

Scheduled repayments of long-term credits
    Principal collections, as in *Foreign Grants and Credits*
        Major foreign-assistance programs[1]
        Export-Import Bank Act credits and British loan
        Other
    plus Other repayments and returns
    less Advance repayments
    less Other transfers to other categories and adjustments, net[2]

Foreign-currency balances and short-term claims
    Other assistance net, as in *Foreign Grants and Credits*
        Increase (+) in foreign-currency balances, net
            Currencies received from farm product sales[3]
            plus Currencies received in repayment of long-term credits (included in principal collections, above)
            plus Other foreign-currency acquisitions
            less Currencies disbursed as grants and loans (included in nonmilitary grants and long-term credits, above)
            less Other foreign-currency disbursements
        Increase(+) in short-term claims, net
    less Transfers to other categories and adjustments, net[2]

Memoranda:
    The disposition of new grants and credits is estimated as follows:
        Grants and credits spent or held in the U.S.
            Spent on U.S. merchandise exports
            Spent on U.S. services (including interest)
            Used to repay recipients' debts
                To U.S. Government lending agencies
                To U.S. commercial banks and others
            Held in the U.S. pending final use[4]
                Held in restricted accounts[5]
                Undisbursed subscriptions and contributions to international nonmonetary institutions[6]
        Grants and credits resulting in direct dollar payments to foreign countries and international institutions[7]

---

[1] Mutual Security (and related) Acts, and Agricultural Trade Development and Assistance Act (PL-480, as amended).
[2] Detail major items.
[3] Net of proceeds used by U.S. Government agencies for purchases of goods and services from recipient countries.
[4] Net of withdrawals and disbursements; negative items represent net withdrawals and disbursements.
[5] Will be spent in the United States.
[6] Final use not always known.
[7] Sum of "nonmilitary grants and long-term credits" and "foreign-currency balances and short-term claims" *less* grants and credits spent or held in the United States.

TABLE B.7

FOREIGN OFFICIAL CAPITAL, EXCEPT CLAIMS OF MONETARY INSTITUTIONS

Investments and claims of foreign governments, except monetary institutions
    Advance payments for U.S. military exports
    Investments in nonmarketable nonconvertible U.S. securities
    Miscellaneous claims on the U.S. Government[1]
Investments and claims of international nonmonetary institutions[2]
    Demand deposits
    Time deposits[3]
    Bankers' acceptances, commercial paper, etc.[3]
    U.S. Government obligations
        Treasury bills and certificates
        Marketable bonds and notes
        Other[4]

[1] Includes some claims related to military procurement.
[2] International institutions other than International Monetary Fund, Bank for International Settlements, and European Fund.
[3] Negotiable time certificates of deposits are excluded from "time deposits" and included in "bankers' acceptances, commercial paper, etc."
[4] Including special U.S. Government obligations issued in connection with U.S capital subscriptions and contributions to international institutions.
Changes are adjusted to reflect variations in coverage and may not necessarily correspond to changes computed from successive amounts outstanding.

TABLE B.8

LONG-TERM PRIVATE CAPITAL

U.S. direct investments abroad, net
    Long-term claims on foreign affiliates, net
    Short-term claims on foreign affiliates, net
    Mining and petroleum
    Manufacturing
    Trade and other
Foreign direct investments in the U.S., net
    Long-term claims on U.S. affiliates, net
    Short-term claims on U.S. affiliates, net
    Manufacturing
    Financial and insurance
    Other
Transactions in foreign securities, net
    U.S. purchases of new foreign issues
        International and regional institutions
        Other governmental issues
        Private issues
    Redemptions (—) of foreign securities held by U.S. residents
    Net U.S. purchases (+) of outstanding securities
        Foreign bonds
        Foreign stocks
Transactions in domestic securities, net
    Net foreign purchases (+) of U.S. Government bonds and notes
    Net foreign purchases (+) of other domestic bonds
    Net foreign purchases (+) of domestic stocks
Other U.S. investments abroad, net
    Long-term bank loans to foreigners, net
    Other U.S. long-term claims and investments, net

Other foreign investments in the U.S., net

Memoranda:
    Supplementary data on gross issues of foreign securities
        Gross amounts offered
            Public offerings
            Private placements
        less Discounts and commissions
        less Estimated foreign purchases at time of issue
        U.S. purchases of new foreign securities

TABLE B.9
SHORT-TERM PRIVATE CAPITAL[1]

U.S. claims on foreigners reported by U.S. banks[2]
    Dollar claims
        Claims on major finincial centers[3]
        Claims on others
        By type:
            Bank loans to official monetary institutions
            Bank loans to others
            Acceptances
            Items in process of collection
            Other dollar claims
    Foreign-currency claims
        Claims on major financial centers[3]
        Claims on others

Other U.S. claims on foreigners
    Dollar claims reported by U.S. nonfinancial concerns[4]
        Claims on major financial centers[3]
        Claims on others
    Foreign-currency claims reported by U.S. nonfinancial concerns[4]
        Claims on major financial centers[3]
        Claims on others

Foreign claims on the U.S. except dollar claims of foreign commercial banks reported by U.S. banks
    Reported by U.S. banks
        Claims of major financial centers[3]
        Claims of others
        By type:
            Demand and time deposits[5]
            Bankers' acceptances, commercial paper, etc.[5]
            U.S. Treasury bills and certificates
            Other claims, including foreign-currency claims[6]
    Reported by U.S. nonfinancial concerns[4] [7]
        Claims of major financial centers[3]
        Claims of others

Short-term dollar assets of foreign commercial banks reported by U.S. banks[8]
    Claims on major financial centers[3]
    Claims of others
    By types:
        Demand deposits
        Time deposits[5]
        Bankers' acceptances, commercial paper, etc.[5]
        U.S. Treasury bills and certificates

---

[1] Based on data in the *Treasury Bulletin* and *Federal Reserve Bulletin* (which provide additional regional detail on amounts outstanding): excludes short-term capital movements between parent firms and their affiliates (see direct investments).

[2] Includes claims of U.S. banks on their foreign branches and claims of foreign branch banks and agencies in the U.S. on their head offices abroad: includes claims of customers held by or reported by U.S. commercial banks. Also includes Federal Reserve loans to foreign official institutions, secured by gold.

[3] United Kingdom, European Economic Community, Switzerland and Canada.

[4] Data for most recent quarter estimated from partial preliminary returns.

[5] Negotiable time certificates of deposits are excluded from "time deposits" and included in "bankers' acceptances, commercial paper, etc."

[6] Includes foreign-currency claims of foreign commercial banks.

[7] Includes claims of foreign banks on U.S. nonfinancial concerns.

[8] Includes claims of foreign banks on their branches and agencies in the U.S. and claims of foreign branches of U.S. banks on their head offices.

Changes are adjusted to reflect variations in coverage and may not necessarily correspond to changes computed from successive amounts outstanding.

TABLE B.10
RESERVES, IMF POSITIONS, AND U.S.
LIABILITIES TO FOREIGN OFFICIAL MONETARY INSTITUTIONS

U.S. holdings of gold, convertible currencies, and other reserve assets [net increase (+)]
    Gold stock[1]
    Treasury and Federal Reserve holdings of convertible foreign currencies
    Other reserve assets

IMF position [net increase in drawing rights (+)][2]
    Gold tranche position
    Drawings on credit tranche position

U.S. liabilities to foreign official monetary institutions [net increase (−)][3]
    Demand deposits at U.S. banks
    Time deposits at U.S. banks[4]
    Bankers acceptances, commercial paper, etc.[4]
    U.S. government obligations
        Marketable:
            Treasury bills and certificates
            Bonds and notes
        Nonmarketable:
            Convertible[5]
            Nonconvertible[6]
    Other U.S. liabilities

---

[1] Includes Exchange Stabilization Fund holdings. Changes include the following domestic sales to (+) and purchases from (−) the monetary gold stock.

[2] The United States quota in the IMF stands at $4,125 million. Under appropriate circumstances, the United States may draw sums from the IMF equal to twice the total quota *less* IMF holdings of U.S. dollars (other than dollar investments described in note 3 below). At (latest date), IMF holdings of U.S. dollars totaled —— million; hence, total U.S. drawing rights were —— million.

[3] Includes IMF holdings of U.S. dollars bought with gold which the IMF may reacquire, and invested in U.S. Treasury securities: these amount to —— million on (latest date). They do not figure in the computation of the IMF position above.
Includes liabilities incurred by drawings on bilateral credit arrangements with foreign central banks and other monetary institutions. At (latest date), these arrangements totaled —— million in currencies.

[4] Negotiable time certificates of deposit are excluded from "time deposits" and included in "bankers acceptances, commercial paper, etc."

[5] At (latest date), amount outstanding included —— million of dollar securities and —— million of foreign-currency securities.

[6] At (latest date), amount outstanding included —— million of dollar securities and —— million of foreign-currency securities.

Changes are adjusted to exclude changes in coverage and may not necessarily correspond to changes computed from successive amounts outstanding.

TABLE B.11

THE INTERNATIONAL INVESTMENT POSITION OF THE UNITED STATES

U.S. investments and claims on foreigners, total[1] [2]
  Private investments and claims
    Direct investments
      Mining
      Petroleum
      Manufacturing
      Trade
      Other[3]
    Foreign dollar bonds
    Other long-term foreign securities[4]
    Long-term bank loans
    Other long-term claims
    Short-term investments and claims
      Claims reported by U.S. banks[5]
      Other short-term investments and claims[6]
  U.S. government investments and claims
    Long-term credits and claims
      Major foreign assistance programs
      Export-Import Bank Act credits
      Subscriptions to international institutions[7]
      British loan and other postwar credits[8]
      Other[9]
    Foreign-currency balances and short-term claims[10]
    Reserves and IMF gold-tranche position[11]

Foreign investments and claims on the U.S., total[1]
  Private investments and claims
    Direct investments
      Manufacturing
      Financial and insurance
      Other
    U.S. government bonds and notes
    Corporate, state, and municipal bonds
    Corporate stocks
    Other long-term claims
    Short-term investments and claims
      Claims of foreign commercial banks[5]
      Other short-term investments and claims[5]
  Official investments and claims
    Investments and claims of international institutions[12]
    Investments and claims of foreign governments, except monetary institutions[13]
    U.S. liabilities to foreign official monetary institutions and drawings on IMF
      credit-tranche position[11]

---

[1] Excludes U.S. holdings of foreign currency (notes and coin) and foreign holdings of U.S. currency (notes and coin).
[2] Includes the U.S. gold stock.
[3] Unallocated amounts include investments in shipping companies registered in Panama and Liberia.
[4] Primarily securities payable in foreign currencies, but some dollar assets, including participation in loans made by the International Bank for Reconstruction and Development.
[5] For detail, see Table —.
[6] Mutual Security (and related) Acts, and Agricultural Trade Development and Assistance Act (Public Law 480, as amended); includes loans repayable in foreign currency.
[7] Except IMF.
[8] RFC, Lend-lease, surplus property, and grant settlements.
[9] Includes loans repayable in foreign currency.
[10] Except for Treasury and Federal Reserve holdings of convertible foreign currencies included with reserves.
[11] For detail, see Table —.
[12] For detail, see Table —.
[13] U.S. Government liabilities arising from foreign prepayments against U.S., military exports, and miscellaneous Government liabilities.

TABLE B.12

INTERNATIONAL TRANSACTIONS IN THE
U. S. NATIONAL INCOME AND PRODUCT ACCOUNTS

Exports of goods and services, except transfers under military grants[1]
    Merchandise exports, adjusted
    Service receipts

Imports of goods and services[2]
    Merchandise imports, adjusted
    Service payments

Balance on goods and services[3]
Net unilateral transfers to foreign countries, except transfers under military grants[4]
    U.S. Government nonmilitary grants
    Remittances and pension payments (net)

---

[1] Equals "Exports of goods and services" in the national income accounts.
[2] Equals "Imports of goods and services" in the national income accounts.
[3] Equals "Net exports of goods and services" in the national income accounts.
[4] Equals "Net transfer payments to foreigners" in the national income accounts.
[5] Equals "Net foreign investment" in the national income accounts.

APPENDIX C

Regional and country breakdowns of a nation's balance of payments find their counterpart in the consolidated balances of payments where two or more nations combine to prepare a single statement for the countries as a group. The Sterling, Franc and Escudo Monetary Areas prepare these consolidated statements for the Area as a whole. The Escudo Area does not construct a balance of payments for metropolitan Portugal alone, although the Sterling and Franc Areas develop balances of payments for the United Kingdom and France separately.

It is comparatively simple for a monetary area to prepare consolidated balances of payments because these institutions generally apply common regulations, have a central monetary reserve fund and uniform balance of payments accounting systems, based in part on exchange records. Since the area constitutes, in certain respects, an international monetary unit, consolidated balances of payments are appropriate. One such statement, that for the Franc Area, is presented on Table C.1.

The recent growth in importance of customs unions, free trade areas, common markets and the Organization for Economic Cooperation and Development (OECD), has raised the question of whether or not it would be advisable for them to likewise prepare consolidated balances of payments. The closer the economic integration of these groups, such as that in the European Common Market (EEC), the greater the utility of, and interest in, such consolidations. None of these organizations has, as yet, published such compilations.

The Bank for International Settlements has, however, prepared consolidated balances of payments for the Common Market, the European Free Trade Association and the entire European membership of the OECD considered as a unit. Table C.2 presents this tabulation.

Since the balance of payments records have not as yet been combined in these organizations, the construction of consolidated statements presents certain difficulties, similar to those encountered in the elaboration of consolidated balance sheets and income statements. The international economic transactions among the members themselves must be eliminated and those of the members with the rest of the world combined. Numerous technical and accounting difficulties arise in the process of consolidation.

Finance and Development (the Fund and Bank Review), a quarterly publication of the IMF and IBRD, Vol. 1, No. 2 (September 1964), p. 122, has published statements of the over-all balances for some twenty countries and the combined over-all surpluses and deficits for the following groups of countries: countries exporting mainly manufactured products; countries exporting mainly primary products; the EEC; Latin American Republics; the United States and Canada; Continental Europe. In addition, the excess of surpluses over deficits due to an increase in monetary gold and to errors and omissions has been computed. Table C.3 presents these statements of the over-all balances.

If the movement toward economic integration continues to grow, if it becomes more complete and, finally, should economic lead to political integration, the utility of these consolidated statements will undoubtedly increase.

TABLE C.1

BASIC GLOBAL DATA, FRENCH FRANC AREA BALANCE OF PAYMENTS, 1961
(*In millions of U.S. dollars*)

	1957 Credit	1957 Debit	1958 Credit	1958 Debit	1959 Credit	1959 Debit	1960 Credit	1960 Debit	1961 Credit	1961 Debit
A. Goods and Services	5,117.4	6,509.9	5,219.8	5,505.4	5,940.7	5,240.6	7,033.5	6,476.8	7,983.7	7,128.8
1. Merchandise f.o.b.	3,751.7	4,885.5	3,651.7	4,079.1	4,262.5	3,849.3	4,962.2	4,982.2	5,757.7	5,386.9
2. Nonmonetary gold	....	....	216.0	—	—	8.0	....¹	....¹	....¹	....¹
3, 4. Transportation and insurance	208.4	617.8	203.3	380.3	239.5	318.1	268.9	315.8	306.1	344.4
5. Travel	138.2	228.6	167.1	109.9	325.6	140.2	511.2	277.0	577.2	368.8
6. Investment income	218.9	178.2	171.9	177.1	180.5	196.7	219.1	182.2	228.2	200.3
7. Government, n.i.e.	410.3	86.9	400.8	181.6	388.2	197.2	398.8	210.1	440.5	243.0
8. Other services	389.9	512.9	409.0	577.4	535.4	531.1	673.3	509.5	674.0	576.4
Net goods and services	—	1,392.5	—	285.6	700.1	—	556.7	—	854.9	—
B. Transfer Payments	96.1	28.4	152.6	40.8	116.5	104.4	122.4	105.1	261.9	113.9
9. Private	5.9	20.5	21.2	26.7	47.5	15.4	75.0	20.2	129.7	25.1
10. Central government	90.2	7.9	131.4	14.1	69.0	89.0	47.4	84.9	132.2	88.8
Net transfer payments	67.7	—	111.8	—	12.1	—	17.3	—	148.0	—
Net total (1 through 9)	—	1,407.1	—	291.1	732.2	—	611.5	—	959.5	—
Net total (1 through 10)	—	1,324.8	—	173.8	712.2	—	574.0	—	1,002.9	—
C. Capital and Monetary Gold	1,346.7	—	190.2	—	—	824.1	—	582.1	—	1,056.7
Nonmonetary sectors ²	142.4	—	119.2	—	347.7	—	119.5	—	213.2	—
11. Direct investment ³	....	....	....	....	....	....	82.0	—	101.6	—
11.1. In franc area	....	....	....	....	....	....	155.8	—	199.3	—
11.2. Abroad	....	....	....	....	....	....	—	53.8	—	97.7
12. Other private long-term ³,⁴	205.5	—	220.1	—	644.3	—	264.1	—	326.4	—
12.1. Liabilities	199.0	—	170.5	—	507.6	—	223.5	—	283.6	—
12.2. Assets	6.5	—	49.8	—	136.7	—	40.6	—	42.8	—
13. Other private short-term ³,⁴	58.6	—	—	4.5	—	163.9	—	41.8¹	—	105.0¹
13.1. Liabilities	....	....	....	....	....	....	43.6	—	27.0	—
13.2. Assets	58.6	—	—	4.5	—	163.9	—	85.4	—	132.0
14. Local government	....	....	....	....	....	....	....	....	....	....
15. Central government ³	—	121.7	—	96.4	—	132.7	—	184.8	—	109.8
15.1. Long-term loans received	0.2	122.0	55.0	107.5	64.9	157.7	0.5	135.9	11.2	88.4
15.2. Long-term loans extended	0.7	—	0.8	12.7	1.3	6.4	0.5	9.2	0.9	22.2
15.3. Other long-term capital	—	0.6	—	50.0	—	34.8	—	42.5	—	11.5
Monetary sectors ⁵	1,204.3	—	71.0	—	—	1,171.8	—	701.6	—	1,269.9
16. Commercial banks: liabilities ⁵,⁶	35.0	—	—	10.0	264.0	—	172.3	—	308.0	—
16.1. In foreign exchange	55.0	—	—	14.4	195.2	—	105.4	—	265.1	—
16.2. In francs ⁷	....	....	4.4	—	68.8	—	66.9	—	42.9	—
17. Commercial banks: assets ⁵,⁶	160.7	—	—	119.5	121.6	—	—	186.4	—	185.8
18. Central institutions: liabilities ⁶	473.7	—	594.4	—	—	558.8	—	326.3	—	497.8
18.1. To IMF	262.5	—	131.5	—	31.5	—	—	184.5	—	250.5
18.2. EPU debit balance	175.4	—	241.4	—	8.8	—	—	—	—	—
18.3. Repayments on post-EPU debts	—	—	—	—	—	139.5	—	—	—	320.5
18.4. Foreign holdings of francs ⁵	41.7	—	24.8	—	28.5	—	41.1	—	53.2	—
18.5. Other	—	5.9	196.9	—	—	—	—	—	—	0.2
19. Central institutions: assets ⁶	534.9	—	—	393.9	—	998.6	—	361.2	—	894.3
19.1. IMF subscriptions	....	....	—	1.6	—	313.8	—	2.1	—	2.1
19.2. Convertible currencies	212.0	—	—	206.8	—	185.0	—	24.4	—	488.7
19.3. Other claims	....	19.3	—	16.6	—	19.6	16.7	—	16.5	—
19.4. Monetary gold	342.2	—	—	168.9	—	540.2	—	351.4	—	480.0
Net errors and omissions	—	21.9	—	16.4	111.9	—	8.1	—	53.8	—

¹ The table covers the transactions of the French franc area with the rest of the world.
² Purchases and sales of gold by the Bank of France in the Paris market are included in item 13.
³ Commercial bank long-term capital is included in nonmonetary sectors' capital.
⁴ For 1957–59, direct investment transactions are included in items 12 and 13.
⁵ For 1957–59, some private short-term capital is included in item 12. For 1957, some commercial bank short-term liabilities are included in items 12, 17, and 18.4 (see footnote 7).
⁶ Central government short-term capital is included in items 18 and 19.
⁷ For 1957, commercial bank liabilities in francs are included in item 18.4 (see also footnote 5).

¹ The table covers the transactions of the French franc area with the rest of the world.

Source: IMF, *Balance of Payments Yearbook*, Vol. 14 (May 1963).

Second

TABLE C.2

Consolidated Balances of Payments for
European OECD Countries, 1962.[1]
(In millions of U.S. Dollars)

	EEC	EFTA	Total European OECD
Balance of trade	+300	−2,705	−3,865
Net invisible items	+545	+2,000	+3,720
Balance on current account	+845	− 705	− 145
Capital movements, long- and short-term[2]	−475	+1,765	+1,770
Over-all balance	+370	+1,060	+1,625

[1] OECD includes: EEC (Belgium, Luxembourg, France, West Germany, Italy, the Netherlands); EFTA (Austria, Denmark, Norway, Portugal, Sweden, Switzerland, United Kingdom); others (Greece, Ireland, Spain, Turkey). The United States and Canada are not included in the *European* OECD.

[2] Long- and short-term capital are not shown separately.

Source: Adapted from Bank for International Settlements, Basle, Switzerland, *Thirty-third Annual Report*, April 1, 1962-March 31, 1963, issued June 10, 1963, p. 99.

TABLE C.3

Over-all Balances of International Payments,[1]
First and Second Half, 1963
(In millions of U.S. dollars)

	First half 1963	Second half 1963
A. Countries exporting mainly manufactured products		
United States	−1,469	−864
United Kingdom	−124	−334
Common Market countries	1,043	606
Belgium-Luxembourg	136	51
France	717	398
Germany, Federal Republic of	243	477
Italy	−143	−456
Netherlands	90	136
Austria	25	122
Switzerland	−164	367
Denmark, Norway, Sweden	101	104
Japan	283	22
Total, Group A	−305	−21

[1] For most countries, over-all balances have been measured by changes

TABLE C.3 (Continued)

B. Countries exporting mainly primary products		
Australia	115	378
Canada	155	−18
Finland	−9	44
New Zealand	65	−91
Portugal	−24	59
South Africa	79	40
Spain	−22	109
Subtotal, more industrialized countries	359	521
Latin American Republics	54	303
Argentina	35	101
Other	19	202
Miscellaneous sterling countries	141	16
Other Europe	−45	23
Other countries	421	148
Subtotal, less industrialized countries	571	490
Total, Group B	930	1,011
C. Excess of surpluses	625	990
1. Owing to increase in world monetary gold	285	560
2. Owing to errors and omissions	340	430
D. Memorandum items		
United States and Canada	−1,314	−882
Continental Europe in Group A	1,005	1,199
Group B, excluding Canada	775	1,029

in official gold and foreign exchange assets, in payments agreement credit and debit balances, in net IMF positions, and in (other) liabilities to foreign monetary authorities (the latter being entered in fact only for the United States, the United Kingdom, and Canada). For some countries, however, balances so measured have been adjusted for certain advance debt repayments between governments and, in the case of Japan, for drawings and repayments on short-term credits negotiated by Japanese authorities in connection with the 1961-62 balance of payments difficulties.

Source: *Finance and Development* (The Fund and Bank Review). A quarterly publication of the IMF and IBRD, Washington. Vol. 1, No. 2 (September 1964), p. 122.

APPENDIX D

Notes on the Interpretation of the Balance of Payments

There are no discrete accounts on the balance of payments; they are all more or less closely related. This renders it difficult, if not impossible, to apply the laboratory technique of holding some of the accounts stationary as constants, while selected others are allowed to vary and then observing the results. Assume that the feedback ratio of tied foreign grants is 80 per cent and that the amount of foreign grants is $5 billion. One cannot infer from these data that the amount of exports resulting from the grants would amount to $4 billion, and that this sum could be deducted from total exports to arrive at a figure representing net commercial exports.

The grants may have released funds owned by the recipients which were used to import goods from third countries. These third countries, in turn, might use these funds to pay for purchases in the United States. Some of the exports to the recipient country might have been made in the absence of grants. The grants may not be related to the donor's exports in the same period, but may have been used earlier or carried forward for use in future periods.

Alone, the balance of payments does not justify inferences showing the causes of a surplus or deficit or the movement of any of the accounts. It reveals the changes in receipts and payments but does not indicate the factors which occasioned them. The mere fact that one or a group of accounts has changed does not warrant the conclusion that these changes *caused* a surplus or deficit. The analyst cannot reason, for instance, that the reduction or termination of United States aid or capital outflows would automatically restore balance of payments equilibrium. They might aid in the solution of the deficit problem, but the impact of their reduction on the other accounts, notably exports, must also be determined.

Balance of payments debits and credits are very closely related. The small size of surpluses and deficits relative to the magnitude of other accounts bears witness to this fact. In addition, the payments of any nation tend to flow back in the form of receipts and vice versa.

Certain factors which act over time are important in interpreting the balance of payments. These are cyclical movements, seasonal variations and random fluctuations. Cyclical movements have an important impact on the merchandise and services trade. During the downswing, they tend to lower imports in countries where this phase of the cycle prevails and consequently to reduce the exports of their trading partners. Upswings have the opposite effects. A cyclical downswing generally tends to reduce a nation's deficit or to increase its surplus provided it is not accompanied by similar downswings in its trading partners. An upswing will tend to exaggerate deficits or reduce surpluses unless it is accompanied by similar cyclical movements abroad. From the exclusive point of view of surpluses and deficits, the ideal situation for a country is to experience a downswing while its trading partners are going through the opposite movement.

Private direct foreign investment is also subject to the effect of the cycle. The recent rapid economic expansion of the Common Market countries, partly a cyclical phenomenon, served to stimulate United States direct investment in these areas. Likewise, recessions at home have served to check private United States investment abroad. Cyclical swings also affect domestic and foreign rates of interest and consequently the movement of long- and short-term portfolio capital.

The impact of the cycle on balances of payments must be detected and isolated when attempting to discern longer term trends. Balance of payments surpluses and deficits ascribable to the cycle are likely to be of a temporary or short-run character and do not necessarily indicate a condition of fundamental disequilibrium.

Quarterly balance of payments data are often subject to seasonal variation and for some short-run analytical purposes, the quarterly data must be adjusted to eliminate it. This is especially important when using quarterly data to project annual balance of payments figures. Different methods of eliminating this variation are employed for the several accounts and frequently special techniques are employed for this purpose. All balance of payments accounts do not, however, display a seasonal characteristic and, in addition, this variation may carry opposite signs (+ or −) in the several accounts. The effects of seasonal variation on surplus and deficit measurement are likely to be very pronounced.[1]

Seasonal variation characterizes United States services to a greater extent than trade transactions. This is due principally to the concentration in the third quarter of each year of payments on the travel account and the heavy receipts in the fourth quarter of income on investments. In the United States, there is a larger than average outflow of capital in the second and fourth quarters and a smaller in the first and third. The volatility and lumping of certain transactions, notably capital movements, often renders seasonal adjustments difficult.[2]

Balance of payments interpretation is hampered by the appearance from time to time of unusual and often large shifts in the individual accounts. These random and volatile changes may distort the balance of payments for a quarter, a year or even longer periods. When quarterly figures are multiplied to obtain an annual rate, these random changes can distort the results. Additionally, they render the comparison of changes in surpluses and deficits difficult.

A number of cases in recent United States balance of payments history illustrates these effects. The Suez crisis of 1956-1957 served to increase United States exports as did also wheat sales to the Soviet Union in 1964. The dock strike of 1963 affected both merchandise exports and imports for several months and the announcement of the interest equalization tax proposal served to check foreign investment in this country. Since these random

---

[1] See Tables 11.1 and 11.2 in Chapter 11 of: Report of the Review Committee for Balance of Payments Statistics to the Bureau of the Budget, *The Balance of Payments of the United States: A Review and Appraisal.* Washington, D. C.: U. S. Government Printing Office, 1965, pp. 149-150.

[2] *Ibid.*, pp. 149-151.

changes affect international economic relations, they cannot be ignored, but their significance for purposes of analysis must be carefully weighed.

A study of the balances of payments of the major industrial countries over an extended period of time reveals that they reflect, like other economic statistical series, the growth element. Although the effects of growth are likely to be manifest in most of the accounts, they will be more distinctly marked in some than in others. Thus if a hitherto agricultural economy starts a period of growth marked by internally-financed industrial expansion, the merchandise accounts are likely to mirror this fact to a greater extent than income on investment.

The relative growth rate of a reserve center such as the United States is a matter of some importance. Since the reserve-accumulating nations will doubtless require increasing amounts of dollar reserves as their trade expands, the United States may be condemned to running balance of payments deficits to supply the additional funds. Such a situation is likely to prevail unless another international payments system is adopted, the velocity of the international circulation of the dollar increased or the present payments mechanism made more effective. These deficits "in perpetuity" will only be dangerous if the growth rate of the United States falls below those of other nations by substantial amounts over a protracted period of time.[3]

Shifts in the terms of trade are likewise reflected on the

---

[3] An interesting use of growth rates was made in conjunction with the preparation of a projection of the United States balance of payments for a period of years ending in 1968. See: Walter S. Salant, Emile Despres, Lawrence B. Krause, Alice M. Rivlin, William A. Salant and Lorie Tarshis, *The United States Balance of Payments in 1968.* Washington: The Brookings Institution, 1963. The balance of payments effects of projected rates of growth were also computed by a working party of the European Economic Community (Common Market). See: Communauté Economique Européenne (Commission), "Les Perspective de Développement Economique dans la CEE de 1960 à 1970." (Mimeographed). Brussels: Services des Publications des Communautés Européennes, 1962. A summary in English of this report has been prepared: European Economic Community (Commission), "Report by the Working Party on Problems of Economic Structure and Long-term Development on Economic Development Prospects in EEC from 1960 to 1970." (Mimeographed). No place or date.

balance of payments and their movement, cyclical or other, constitutes an important element in the interpretation of these tabulations. Changes in the terms of trade are usually mirrored to a greater extent by the merchandise accounts than the others although their impact is likely to be noticed on all of them.

Alterations in the terms of trade are especially important for countries which tend to live internationally on the export earnings of relatively few agricultural and mineral commodities and which import manufactured goods. They are also significant for those nations which require considerable amounts of external capital and rely upon their merchandise exports to service these loans.[4] For highly industrialized nations, which export a wide variety of manufactured products, the movement of the terms of trade is less important from a balance of payments point of view.

Since the balance of payments is cast in value magnitudes, it reflects price changes and the effects of these movements are of primary significance in the analysis of these compilations. Rising prices contribute toward deficits or the reduction of surpluses and falling prices have the opposite effects (see Chapter 11). Although many statistical time series are presented in terms of constant currency units, it is not customary to prepare balances of payments adjusted for changes in price. Although such adjustments present many difficulties, especially for services transactions, direct and portfolio investments, they are not impossible. The field of price-adjusted statements offers a promising area for the balance of payments analyst.

Forming the basis for policy determination, the measurement and analysis of balance of payments surpluses and deficits probably constitutes the most important aspect of the interpretation of this statement. This topic was treated in Chapter 9 where it was pointed out that there is little agreement concerning either the surplus and deficit concept or its measurement.

---

[4] See Table 9.5, Chapter 9, for the balance of payments of Brazil which reflects the dominating influence exerted by coffee exports.

The balance of payments tabular presentation as proposed by the Review Committee for Balance of Payments Statistics marks a step forward in the solution of this analytical problem. The proposed classification of accounts (see Chapter 8 and Appendix B) facilitates surplus and deficit analysis by separating the key accounts, providing the balance on each and presenting detail on which to base inferences and conclusions.

The movement of surpluses and deficits is reflected in the reserve accounts which were treated in Chapter 10. Certain facilities for the defense of the rate of exchange, which is an important function of reserves, are not shown on balances of payments. These are the forward market transactions, swaps, reciprocal credit arrangements and medium-term, non-marketable bonds denominated in dollars and foreign currencies. Alone, the balance of payments reserve accounts do not afford a complete guide to a nation's ability to defend its exchange rate.

From the point of view of the gold account, the territorial direction of United States surpluses and deficits assumes importance. Some nations endeavor to accumulate dollars rather than gold. Deficits with such nations do not usually threaten the United States gold stock. Others like to keep a certain proportion of their reserve assets in gold. Deficits with these countries often lead to gold outflows. However, non-gold reserve nations may use their dollar holdings to settle deficits with gold reserve holders and thus contribute indirectly to United States gold outflows.

The global balance of payments of any country is merely the counterpart of that of the rest of the world with the nation in question. Were all countries to use the same concepts and methods, the surplus or deficit of any country would be matched by those of all the other nations. The fact that the United States is the world's major banking and reserve center serves to expose this country sharply to the balance of payments vicissitudes of other nations.

It should finally be noted that the balance of payments is but the starting point for the analysis of a country's international economic relations and position. Much other information is usually required to arrive at useful inferences as well as to determine policy. The balance of payments is the point at which a very large number of forces come into focus. Taken alone, it has a story to tell, but the rationale of this story must be sought elsewhere.

Author Index

Subject Index

THE TEXT OF THIS BOOK HAS BEEN
SET IN 10 POINT CALEDONIA TYPE
BY THE H. P. JOHNSON CO., INC., FREEPORT, N. Y.
IT HAS BEEN PRINTED ON HAMILTON LOUVAIN PAPER
BY EDWARDS BROS., ANN ARBOR, MICHIGAN, AND BOUND
IN COLUMBIA MILLS TITLE LINEN CLOTH BY
THE NATIONAL PUBLISHING COMPANY, OF PHILADELPHIA.